FORD
PARTS INTERCHANGE
MANUAL

Paul A. Herd

MBI Publishing Company

First published in 1995 by MBI Publishing Company, PO Box 1, 729 Prospect Avenue, Osceola, WI 54020-0001 USA

Manager at Motorbooks International Wholesalers & Distributors, 729 Prospect Avenue, PO Box 1, Osceola, WI 54020-0001 USA

All drawings and illustrations are reproduced with permission from the Ford Motor Company.

Library of Congress Cataloging-in-Publication Data
Herd, Paul A.
    Ford parts interchange manual 1959–1970/Paul Herd.
        p. cm.
    Includes index.
    ISBN 0-7603-0077-1 (pbk.)
    1. Ford automobile—Parts—Catalogs. I. Title.
TL215.F7H47   1995
629.28'722—dc20   95-36601

On the front cover: The ever-popular 1964 1/2 Mustang. *Dan Lyons*

On the back cover: **Top:** A 1968 390ci engine used in GT models. **Bottom:** Alternators have an identification number stamped on the housing.

Printed in the United States of America

Contents

Acknowledgments

This book would not have been possible without the assistance of the following people: T.R. Spencer of the Ford Motor Company, who graciously allowed me to use factory information and illustrations; Lisa K. Finch and the others at Special Events; the members of the Greater Ozarks Mustang Club; the staff of R and R Auto Salvage; and a special thanks to all of the Ford and Mercury owners who allowed me to photograph their vehicles.

Preface

Ford and Mercury are as different as left and right. Ford has always had the image of a tougher, working man's car, while the Mercury models have always had the more elegant sophisticated image. Yet they are both siblings from the same family—The Ford Motor Company—and they share many parts. These parts are interchangeable. Thus, you can find some parts on a full-size Mercury that will fit your Mustang.

Interchange is what this manual is all about. It is designed to help you locate parts at the salvage yard or at a swap meet. It can also save you money, by showing you that a part that was used on your Mach I Mustang can also be found on the full-size Galaxie models, of which there were more built.

Information from this guide was mostly drawn from the Ford and Lincoln Mercury master parts catalogs for the years 1960–64 and 1965–72. These catalogs are extensive in both size and detail. They are also laid out in a manner that can be hard to decipher for the average enthusiast. So the purpose of this book is to give you the interchange information, but put it in a simple, easy-to-understand format.

Interchange is based on part numbers and/or casting numbers. The format of this book should not be cross referenced with any parts catalog. The code is my own design that was developed for this series.

Every effort was made to ensure that information used this manual is correct. Therefore, no responsibility can be taken if any inaccuracy exists.

Introduction

How to Use This Book

This book is divided into eleven different sections which are further divided into individual subdivisions that make up the entire section. For example chapter 1 is divided by components such as cylinder block, short block, crankshaft, connecting rods, and so on.

At the beginning of each of these subdivisions is an interchange listing of the models, along with other necessary data to allow you to find the part you're looking for. It will look similar to this:

Hinges, Hood

Model Identification

Mustang	Interchange Number
1964-1/2–66	4
1967–70	7

Fairlane/Torino	Interchange Number
1960	1
1961	2
1962	3
1963–65	4
1966–69	5
1970	6

By finding your model and model year in the chart you will be able to find the Interchange Number that will list the models that the particular part can be found on. Then trace through the interchange to find the interchange number you are looking for. The interchange is listed in numerical order. For example, if you were trying to find hood hinges for your 1968 Torino you would look for Interchange Number 5, where you will find a section like this:

Interchange Number: 5

Part Number(s): C6OZ16796B (right), C6OZ1697B (left)
Usage: 1966–67 Fairlane, 1966–67 Comet, 1966–70 Falcon, 1968–69 Torino, and 1968–69 Montego—all models and body styles

Part numbers—if listed—are either the original or original replacement numbers. Usage lists the models that part was used on. Notes list things to watch for during your interchange, such as body-style restrictions or modifications that can be done to make other parts fit. It may also give a cross reference to another interchange that will also fit.

Decoding VIN Tag and Certification Plate

1959–70

Technically speaking, there is no VIN plate used on pre-1968 models; instead, the VIN (Vehicle Identification Number) was part of the patent plate, also called a warranty plate or certification sticker. The overall design of the plates changed many times, but it was always located on the left front door's latch face. It is listed as the serial number, warranty number, or VIN, according to model year.

Beginning in 1968, the VIN number appeared on a separate plate that is attached to the instrument panel and is readable through the windshield on either the passenger's or driver's side.

While the location may have changed, the pattern of the VIN did not. It begins with the last digit of the model year (9 for 1959, 0 for 1960, 1 for 1961, 2 for 1962, 3 for 1963, 4 for 1964, 5 for 1965, 6 for 1966, 7 for 1967, 8 for 1968, 9 for 1969, and 0 for 1970). This is followed by a single letter for the assembly plant.

The following plant location and codes were used: A for Atlanta, B for Oakville, D for Dallas, E for Mahwah, F for Dearborn, G for Chicago, H for Lorain, J for Los Angeles, K for Kansas City, L for Long Beach, N for Norfolk, P for Twin Cities, R for San Jose, S for Allen Park, T for Metuchen, U for Louisville, W for Wayne, X for St. Thomas, Y for Wixom, and Z for St. Louis. Note: Long Beach was used only from 1960–65.

Next is a series of two digits that represents the model code. This is an extensive list, so refer to the accompanying charts on page 224 for the codes. You will note that many different models and body styles may use the same codes in different model years.

The original engine is coded in the fifth character in the VIN by a single letter. Refer to the accompanying charts for code breakdown.

Also on the warranty or certification label or plate is information on the transmission, rear axle, build date, and district code (what part of the country the car was ordered in), along with exterior and interior trim colors. Of all the information on the plate, the build date may be the most important in interchanging due to changes that occurred in the line at certain build dates. However, be aware of the fact that doors are fairly easily changed, and the original unit may be replaced with a used door. For 1968 models, cross-reference the VIN numbers on the plate on the door and that one on the instrument panel before accessing any parts that are used accordingly to build date. Use the accompanying charts to help you decode your door label or plate.

FORD CAR PARTS

1965 WARRANTY PLATE - TYPICAL

(U. S. built vehicles)

Located on the latch face of the left Front Door.

The Warranty Plate Includes:

1. Miscellaneous vehicle data (first line) consisting of codes which identify Body Type, Color of Exterior Paint, Trim, Production Date, District (and D.S.O. number where applicable), Rear Axle Ratio and Transmission.
2. Vehicle Warranty Number (second line) consisting of Codes which identify Model Year, Assembly Plant, Series, Engine and Numerical Sequence of Assembly.

The page number(s) on which the Codes are listed is shown in parenthesis.

MISCELLANEOUS VEHICLE DATA (54A EM 22 17 K 26 1 3) FIRST LINE

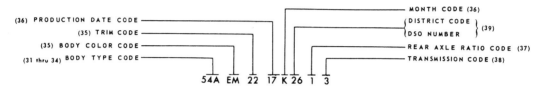

```
(36) PRODUCTION DATE CODE ─────────────┐                    ┌───── MONTH CODE (36)
            (35) TRIM CODE ──────────┐  │              ┌─── DISTRICT CODE   } (39)
      (35) BODY COLOR CODE ───────┐  │  │              │    DSO NUMBER
(31 thru 34) BODY TYPE CODE ───┐  │  │  │   ┌───────────── REAR AXLE RATIO CODE (37)
                               │  │  │  │   │  ┌────────── TRANSMISSION CODE (38)
                             54A EM 22 17 K 26 1 3
```

"54A"---- Galaxie 500 4 Door Sedan

"RM"---- Ivy Green lower body, Wimbledon White upper body
(For two tone vehicles first digit indicates lower body color and second digit indicates upper body color.)
Numerals following the color Code are for Company information.

"58"---- Ivy Gold cloth and vinyl
Refer to 1965 Soft Trim Section for complete instructions and Trim Code listing.

"17"---- Seventeenth Day of Month

"K"---- October

"26" ---- Washington District (and DSO number when applicable)
Refer to Page 34 for complete explanation

"1" ---- Rear Axle Ratio of 3.00 to 1

"4" ---- (FX) Dual Range Transmission

Black Background Plate Identifies a Unit Painted with M30J (Non-Acrylic) Enamel. (Solid Color Unit or the Lower Body Color when Unit is Two-Tone.)

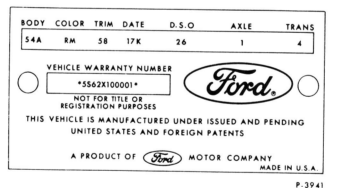

BODY	COLOR	TRIM	DATE	D.S.O	AXLE	TRANS
54A	RM	58	17K	26	1	4

VEHICLE WARRANTY NUMBER
5S62X100001
NOT FOR TITLE OR REGISTRATION PURPOSES

Ford

THIS VEHICLE IS MANUFACTURED UNDER ISSUED AND PENDING UNITED STATES AND FOREIGN PATENTS

A PRODUCT OF Ford MOTOR COMPANY
MADE IN U.S.A.

P-3941

Grey Background Plate Identifies a Unit Painted with M32J (Acrylic) Enamel. (Solid Color Unit or the Lower Body Color when Unit is Two-Tone.)

VEHICLE WARRANTY NUMBER (*5S62X100001*) SECOND LINE

```
                    5 S 62 X 100001
(24) MODEL YEAR CODE ────┘ │  │ │      └──── NUMERICAL SEQUENCE (30)
(24) ASSEMBLY PLANT CODE ──┘  │ │                OF ASSEMBLY
(25 thru 28) SERIES CODE ─────┘ └──────── ENGINE CODE (29,30)
```

"*"---- Asterisks precede and follow the vehicle Warranty Number to prevent unauthorized addition of numbers or symbols.

"5" ---- 1965 Model

"S" ---- Assembled at Pilot Plant

"62"---- 4 Door Sedan

"X"---- 8 cyl. Engine--352 C.I.D.--4 Venturi carburetor

"100001"---- First Ford Series vehicle assembled at Pilot Plant during Model Year

1965 Ford warranty plate used in cars built in America.

1966/69 WARRANTY PLATE - TYPICAL

Located on the latch face of the left Front Door

The Warranty Plate includes:

1. Warranty Number (first line) consisting of codes which identify Model Year, Assembly Plant, Series, Engine and Numerical Sequence of assembly.

2. Miscellaneous Vehicle Data (second line) consisting of codes which identify Body Type, Color of Exterior Paint, Trim, Production Date, District (and DSO number where applicable), Rear Axle Ratio and Transmission.

The page number(s) on which the Codes are listed is shown in parenthesis.

(FIRST LINE) VEHICLE WARRANTY NUMBER (6-E-44-Y-500001)

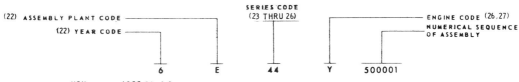

"6"	---	1966 Model
"E"	---	Assembled at Mahwah Plant
"44"	---	4 Door Sedan
"Y"	---	8 cyl. engine - 390 C.I.D. - 2 Venturi carburetor
"500001"	---	First Mercury unit assembled at Mahwah Plant during model year

Black Background Plate Identifies a Unit Painted with M30J (Non-acrylic) Enamel. (Solid Color Unit or the Lower Body Color when Unit is Two-Tone)
(Not used on Lincoln)

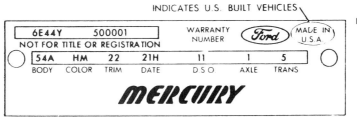

INDICATES U.S. BUILT VEHICLES

INDICATES CANADIAN BUILT VEHICLES

Grey Background Plate Identifies a Unit Painted with M32J (Acrylic) Enamel. (Solid Color Unit or the Lower Body Color when Unit is Two-Tone and all Lincolns)

P-8023

(SECOND LINE) MISCELLANEOUS VEHICLE DATA (54A-HM-22-21H-11-1-5)

"54A"	---	Monterey 4 Door Sedan
"HM"	---	Sandstone lower body, Polar White upper body (For two-tone vehicles first digit indicates lower body color and second digit indicates upper body color)
"22"	---	Blue all vinyl Refer to appropriate Soft Trim Section for complete instructions and Trim Code listing.
"21"	---	Twenty first day of month
"H"	---	August
"11"	---	Boston district (and DSO number when applicable) Refer to page 12 for complete explanation.
"1"	---	Rear axle ratio of 3.00 to 1
"S"	---	4 speed manual transmission

Typical 1966–69 warranty plate.

FORD CAR PARTS

1970/ SAFETY STANDARDS CERTIFICATION LABEL - TYPICAL

(REPLACES METAL WARRANTY PLATE)

(ALL EXCEPT BRONCO - REFER TO PAGES 40 THRU 44 FOR BRONCO WARRANTY PLATE CODES)

(NOT USED ON 1970 MAVERICK BEFORE 8/11/69)

Located on the latch face of the left Front Door.

The Certification Label includes.

1. Built date (e.g. 9/69) in upper left hand corner which indicates the month and year in which the unit was built.

2. Vehicle Identification Number (left half of first line) consisting of Codes which identify Model Year, Assembly Plant, Series, Engine and Numerical Sequence of Assembly (also shown in upper right hand corner).

3. Miscellaneous Vehicle Data (right half of first line plus second line) consisting of Codes which identify Body Type, Color of Exterior Paint, Trim, Rear Axle Ratio, Transmission and District (and D.S.O. number where applicable).

The page number(s) on which the Codes are listed is shown in parenthesis.

VEHICLE IDENTIFICATION NUMBER (0S54H100001) FIRST LINE

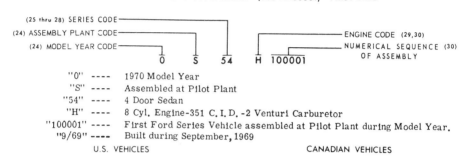

"0" ----	1970 Model Year	
"S" ----	Assembled at Pilot Plant	
"54" ----	4 Door Sedan	
"H" ----	8 Cyl. Engine-351 C.I.D.-2 Venturi Carburetor	
"100001" ----	First Ford Series Vehicle assembled at Pilot Plant during Model Year.	
"9/69" ----	Built during September, 1969	

U.S. VEHICLES   CANADIAN VEHICLES

MANUFACTURED BY FORD MOTOR COMPANY	500001

9/69 THIS VEHICLE CONFORMS TO ALL APPLICABLE U.S. FEDERAL MOTOR VEHICLE SAFETY STANDARDS IN EFFECT ON DATE OF MANUFACTURE SHOWN ABOVE

VEH IDENT NO	BODY	COL
0S54H100001	54A	B

TRIM	AXLE	TRNS	DSO
5A	6	X	33

NOT FOR TITLE OR REGISTRATION

MADE IN U.S.A.

MANUFACTURED BY FORD MOTOR COMPANY	500001

9/69 THIS VEHICLE CONFORMS TO ALL APPLICABLE FEDERAL MOTOR VEHICLE SAFETY STANDARDS IN EFFECT ON DATE OF MANUFACTURE SHOWN ABOVE

VEH IDENT NO	BODY	COL
0S54H100001	54A	B

TRIM	AXLE	TRNS	DSO
5A	6	X	33

NOT FOR TITLE OR REGISTRATION

MADE IN CANADA

MISCELLANEOUS VEHICLE DATA (54A B 5A 6 X 33) SECOND LINE

P-7184

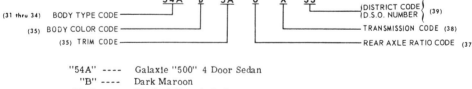

"54A" ----	Galaxie "500" 4 Door Sedan
"B" ----	Dark Maroon
"5A" ----	Black cloth and vinyl
Solid colors ----	1970/71 Single digit code
----	1972 Two digit code
Two tones ----	1970/71 Two digit code
----	1972 Four digit code
	Refer to appropriate Soft Trim Section for complete instructions and Trim Code listing.
"6" ----	Rear Axle Ratio of 3.00 to 1
"X" ----	FMX - Cruise-O-Matic Transmission
"33" ----	Detroit District (and D.S.O. number when applicable)

Refer to Page 13 for complete explanation

1970 safety standards certification label.

Chapter 1

Engine

Engine

There is no code stamped on the block itself that can be used to identify the cubic-inch displacement of the block. Casting numbers can be helpful, and they are given when known. But be warned that some blocks used several different casting numbers and in some cases one casting is not interchangeable with the other.

Engines are identified by a tag attached to the engine. This tag is used on all late-1964–70 models, and the tag is located under the coil attaching bolt. On this tag is the displacement, assembly plant, model year, change level, engine code (useful in identifying high-performance engines), and date of production. Be warned, though, that this tag is easily lost or replaced with a fake tag, so you should not rely solely on this tag for identification.

Engine type was also coded into the VIN plate. It is the fifth symbol in the series of characters.

Cylinder Blocks

Model Identification

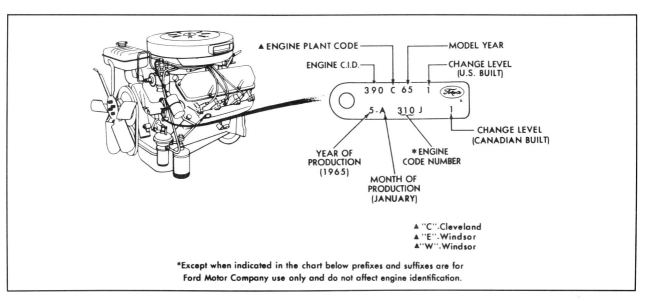

Engine identification tag.

Interchange

Interchange Number: 1
Part Number(s): C4AZ6010-B
Casting Number: C5AE6015E
Usage: 1963–early-1964 Fairlane, Comet, full-size Ford, and early-1964-1/2 Mustang (except with K-code 271hp)
Note(s): Used until build date August 20, 1964. Has five mounting holes for flywheel.

Interchange Number: 2
Part Number(s): C40Z610C
Casting Number: C40E or C30E
Usage: 1963–early-1964 Fairlane, Comet, full-size Ford, and early-1964 Mustang with 289ci K-code 271hp
Note(s): Used until build date August 20, 1964. Has five mounting holes for flywheel.

Interchange Number: 3
Part Number(s): D1TZ6010-B
Casting Number: C50E, C80E-A, or C5AE6015E
Usage: Late-1964–67 Fairlane, Mustang, and Comet; 1967 Cougar; 1968 Torino; 1968 Montego; and 1968–70 Falcon. With 289ci engine (except 271hp K-code version); 1968–73 Mustang; 1968–74 Torino; 1968–70 full-size Ford; 1968–74 Cougar; 1968–74 Montego; 1968–70 Falcon; 1972–74 Maverick; 1972–74 Comet (compact). All 1968–74 models with 302ci engine except Boss.
Note(s): Used after build date August 20, 1964. Has six mounting holes for flywheel. Not interchangeable with earlier models, unless fly-wheel is also changed.

Interchange Number: 4
Part Number(s): C50Z6010C
Usage: Late-1964–67 Mustang, Fairlane, and Comet; and 1967 Cougar. All models with 289ci 271hp K-code in VIN.
Note(s): Used after build date August 20, 1964. Has six mounting holes for fly-wheel.

The 289ci engine was a very popular choice, from its introduction in 1962 to the last one built in 1968.

In 1968, the 289ci engine was phased out and replaced with the 302ci, which was available in a variety of power outputs ranging from a mildly tuned two-barrel mill to a stout four-barrel plant (shown) to the mighty Boss.

Interchange Number: 5
Part Number(s): D1ZZ6010B (Boss)
Usage: 1969–71 special high-performance application in Mustang and Cougar only
Note(s): No interchange. Four-bolt mains. The 302ci Boss is listed as being available as a model as well as an over-the-counter package. However, I have never seen an original 1971 Boss 302ci Mustang. If they exist they would be extremely rare—less than twenty, I would guess.

Interchange Number: 6
Part Number(s): D1AZ6010-B (Windsor type)
Usage: All 1969–74 models with 351ci Windsor block and two-bolt mains
Note(s): All two-barrel blocks in 1969 were Windsor.

Interchange Number: 7
Part Number(s): D0AZ6010C (Cleveland type)
Casting Number: DOAZ-D
Usage: 1970–74 all models with 351ci Cleveland block and two-bolt mains (for two-barrel only in 1970 models and for both two- and four-barrel models 1971–up); 1971 Mustang and Cougar with Cobra Jet engines
Note(s): Used in all models, but found mostly in Torino, Montego, Mustang, and Cougar.

Interchange Number: 8
Part Number(s): DOAZ6010D (Cleveland type) 1970 four-barrel
Casting Number: D0AE-J or D0AE-G
Usage: 1969–70 Cleveland block with four-barrel only (four-bolt mains)
Note(s): All four-barrel blocks in 1970 were Cleveland.

Interchange Number: 9
Part Number(s): B9AE6010B
Casting Number: EDG015 or 5751091
Usage: 1959–60 Ford full-size, 1959–60 Edsel, and 1958–60 Thunderbird—all with 352ci engine
Note(s): Both the 302ci and 352ci powerplants in the Edsel are interchangeable: the bare block is the same. The special high-performance 352ci V–8 in the 1960 Ford is not interchangeable.

The 351ci Windsor appeared in 1969 and the 351ci Cleveland (shown) in 1970. While the two motors are the same size, very few parts will interchange.

Interchange Number: 10
Part Number(s): C3AZ610AB
Casting Number: C2AE
Usage: Late 1960–62 full-size Ford and Mercury models with 352ci V–8 only

Interchange Number: 11
Part Number(s): C8AZ6010C
Usage: 1961–63 full-size Ford (except 1961–62 Galaxie models with triple carburetion) and Mercury; 1961–63 Thunderbird with 390ci engine (all outputs)

Interchange Number: 12
Part Number(s): C3AZ6010Y
Usage: 1961–62 Galaxie special 390ci with four-barrel and triple two-barrel carburetion and a mechanical camshaft
Note(s): Thunderbirds with triple carbs used the block in Interchange Number 11.

Interchange Number: 13
Part Number(s): C3AZ6010S
Usage: 1961–64 Galaxie police sedan
Note(s): Used in police cars only, but a great performance block if you can find it.

Interchange Number: 14
Part Number(s): C8AZ6010C
Casting Number: Some cast C5AE-A
Usage: 1966–67 Fairlane, 1966–67 Comet, 1968–70 Torino, 1968–70 Montego, 1966–70 Mustang, 1965–69 full-size Ford, 1965–69 full-size Mercury, and 1967–70 Cougar—all outputs including GT models
Note(s): A 410ci V–8 in 1965–67 is the same block and will interchange as a bare unit.

Interchange Number: 15
Part Number(s): C4AZ610-B
Casting Number: 5AE-D
Usage: 1963–67 Ford and Mercury full-size with 427ci engine
Note(s): A powerful engine that was available with a single four-barrel and twin four-barrels. Not the SOHC engine.

Interchange Number: 16
Part Number(s): C8AZ6010-G
Casting Number: CAE-C
Usage: 1968 Mustang, Cougar, Torino, and Montego
Note(s): Four-barrel application used in selected models before the 428ci V–8 took its place.

Interchange Number: 17
Part Number(s): C6AZ6010-F
Casting Number: 6AE-A
Usage: 1966–70 full-size Ford and Mercury, 1968–70 Fairlane GT, 1968–70 Cyclone, 1968–70 Mustang, and 1968–70 Cougar (also used in police cars)
Note(s): This block was also used with Cobra Jet and Super Cobra Jet appellations. Interchange above is for bare block only.

Interchange Number: 18
Part Number(s): D1VZ6010A
Casting Number: C8VE-F or C8VY-A (1968); C9VE-B (1969); DOSZ-A or DOSZ-D (1970); D1VZ, D1VE, or D1ZE-AZ (1971)
Usage: 1968–71 full-size Ford, 1968–71 Thunderbird, 1969–70 Torino, 1968–71 Mustang, 1968–71 Cougar, and 1968–71 full-size Mercury—all with 429ci engine except Cobra Jet, Super Cobra Jet or Boss 429ci; 1968–75 Lincoln, 1971–75 Thunderbird, and 1972–75 full-size Mercury—all with 460ci engine
Note(s): Interchange is limited to bare blocks only.

Interchange Number: 19
Part Number(s): D1OZ6010A
Casting Number: DOOE-B
Usage: 1969–71 Torino GT, Cyclone, Mustang, and Cougar—all with Super Cobra Jet; 1969–71 full-size Ford police car

Interchange Number: 20
Part Number(s): C9AZ6010B
Usage: 1969–70 Mustang Boss 429ci and Cougar Eliminator 429ci
Note(s): Special high-performance race block. Limited production. No interchange.

Short Block

Model Identification

289ci	Interchange Number
1963 195hp two-barrel	1

The 390ci engine first appeared in 1961 and was available with high-performance options such as three two-barrels. The 390ci continued into 1970 and is a very desirable high-performance powerplant.

Interchange

Interchange Number: 1
Part Number(s): C3AZ6009J
VIN Code: C
Engine: 195hp 289ci two-barrel
Usage: 1963 full-size Ford, 1963 Fairlane, and 1963 Comet
Note(s): Uses a front cover with oil fill hole.

Interchange Number: 2
Part Number(s): C3OZ6009-D
VIN Code: D
Engine: 271hp 289ci four-barrel
Usage: 1963 full-size Ford, 1963 Fairlane, and 1963 Comet
Note(s): Uses a front cover with oil fill hole.

Interchange Number: 3
Part Number(s): C4AZ6009B
VIN Code: C (two-barrel) or D (four-barrel)
Engine: 195hp 289ci two-barrel and 210hp four-barrel
Engine Tag Code: 557, 558, or 561 (two-barrel); 550B or 551B (four-barrel)
Usage: 1964 two-barrel and 1965 four-barrel in full-size Ford, 1964 Fairlane, and 1964 Comet
Note(s): This powerplant was used with two-barrel carburetion in 1964 only and with four-barrel with regular fuel in 1965.

Interchange Number: 4
Part Number(s): C4OZ6009E
VIN Code: K
Engine: 271hp 289ci four-barrel
Engine Tag Code: 563 or 564
Usage: 1964-early 1965 Mustang, Fairlane, Comet, and full-size Ford.
Note(s): Uses a five-bolt flywheel.

Interchange Number: 5
Part Number(s): C5OZ6009B
VIN Code: K
Engine: 271hp 289ci four-barrel
Engine Tag Code: 245, 246, or 55
Usage: Late-1964–67 Mustang, Fairlane, and Comet; 1967 Cougar
Note(s): Uses a six-bolt flywheel.

Interchange Number: 6
Part Number(s): D1TZ6009-E
VIN Code: see notes below
Engine: 210hp 302ci two-barrel or 235hp 302ci four-barrel
Engine Tag Code: 271, 272, 273, 274, 275, 276, 277, 279, 280, 281, 282, 285, 287, or 288 (F-codes); 283 or 284 (J-codes)
Usage: 1968–72 Mustang, Cougar, Torino, Montego, full-size Ford, and full-size Mercury—all with 302ci, except 1969–71 Boss 302ci; also used on 1966–67 289ci short block except 271hp version
Note(s): J-code for two-barrel; F-code for four-barrel, which was available in 1968 only.

Interchange Number: 7
Part Number(s): D1TZ6009-C
VIN Code: D
Engine: 210hp 302ci two-barrel
Engine Tag Code: 276, 277, 278, or 286
Usage: 1969–72 Torino and Montego police cars
Note(s): Same output as the regular 302ci two-barrel, but built for long-mileage duty. Could make good performance block.

Interchange Number: 8
Part Number(s): D1ZZ6009C
VIN Code: G
Engine: 290hp 302ci four-barrel
Engine Tag Code: 299 or 300
Usage: 1968–71 Boss 302ci Mustang and 1969–70 Cougar Eliminator
Note(s): Four-bolt mains; no interchange.

Interchange Number: 9
Part Number(s): D1AZ6009E
VIN Code: H
Engine: 250hp 351ci Windsor two-barrel
Engine Tag Code: 200, 201, 202, 203, 205, 206, or 207
Usage: 1969–73 Mustang, Torino, Montego, full-size Ford, full-size Mercury, and Cougar
Note(s): Windsor engine is most commonly found in full-size Ford and Mercury cars.

Interchange Number: 10
Part Number(s): C9OZ6009B
VIN Code: M
Engine: 290hp 351ci Windsor four-barrel
Engine Tag Code: 208, 209, 210, 211, 212, or 213
Usage: 1969 Torino, Mustang, Cougar, full-size Ford, and full-size Mercury
Note(s): Windsor engine. Used this year only.

Interchange Number: 11

Part Number(s): DOZ6009D
VIN Code: H
Engine: 250hp 351ci Cleveland two-barrel
Engine Tag Code: 600, 601, 602, 604, 606, 610, 611, 614, 615, or 632
Usage: 1970–73 Mustang, Torino, Montego, full-size Ford, and full-size Mercury
Note(s): Cleveland engine. Better for restoration or high-performance than the Windsor. VIN code is the same as for the Windsor two-barrel.

Interchange Number: 12

Part Number(s): DOAZ6009C
VIN Code: M
Engine: 250hp 351ci Cleveland four-barrel
Engine Tag Code: 608, 609, 613, 616, 617, or 630
Usage: 1970–73 Mustang, Torino, Montego, full-size Ford, and full-size Mercury
Note(s): Cleveland engine. Great building block for high-performance engine. Later Cobra Jet engines were built on this block as a base.

Interchange Number: 13

Part Number(s): C0AE6009A
VIN Code: X
Engine: 352ci two-barrel
Usage: 1958–60 full-size Ford and full-size Mercury

Interchange Number: 14

Part Number(s): C1AE6009R
VIN Code: Y
Engine: 300hp or 360hp 352ci four-barrel
Usage: 1958–60 full-size Ford and full-size Mercury (see notes)
Note(s): Two output levels were available. Standard was 300hp, but a special performance option with 360hp was available in Thunderbird and Galaxie 500 XLs.

Interchange Number: 15

Part Number(s): C3AZ6009AE
VIN Code: X
Engine: 200hp 352ci two-barrel
Engine Tag Code: 287, 289ci 1964–68 only
Years Used: 1961–68 full-size Ford and full-size Mercury

Interchange Number: 16

Part Number(s): C2AZ6009D
VIN Code: Z
Engine: 390ci (see notes)
Usage: 1961–62 full-size Ford and full-size Mercury
Note(s): Same short block was used with three different outputs. All used the Z code. Used from 1960–62 was a single four-barrel rated at 300hp; next was a high-output version with a single four-barrel rated at 375hp that was used in 1961 only, as was the 400hp version with triple two-barrel carbs.

Interchange Number: 17

Part Number(s): C6AZ6009U
VIN Code: M
Engine: 390ci six-barrel
Usage: 1961–63 full-size Ford and full-size Mercury
Note(s): Used mainly in Thunderbird, but will swap into a full-size model or 1966-up Torino or Mustang without any problems.

Interchange Number: 18

Part Number(s): C6AZ6009T
VIN Code: Y or H
Engine: 265hp 390ci two-barrel
Usage: 1966–70 full-size Ford and full-size Mercury, 1966–67 Fairlane, 1968–70 Torino, 1968–70 Montego, and 1966–67 Comet
Note(s): Original Mercury and Montego used a special engine that ran on premium fuel. It was listed as part number C6AZ6009T and was coded "H" in the VIN.

Interchange Number: 19

Part Number(s): C6OZ6009A
VIN Code: S
Engine: 335hp 390ci four-barrel
Engine Tag Code: 318, 319, 321, 322, or 324
Usage: 1966 Fairlane GT, 1966 Cyclone GT, and 1966 Mustang GT
Note(s): Used only on these models.

Interchange Number: 20

Part Number(s): C7OZ6009E
VIN Code: S (GT) or Z (non-GT)
Engine: 335hp (GT) or 320hp (non-GT) 390ci four-barrel
Engine Tag Code: 318, 319, 321, 322, or 324 (GT); 313, 315, 341, 343, or 351ci (non-GT)
Usage: 1967 Fairlane GT, 1967 Cyclone GT, 1967 Mustang GT, 1967 Cougar GT, 1968 full-size Ford and full-size Mercury, 1968 Torino (non-GT), 1968 Montego (non-GT), 1968 Mustang (non-GT), and 1968 Cougar (non-GT)
Note(s): The 390ci four-barrel in 1968 is the same as that used in the 1967 GT models. This interchange applies only to the short block. However, the engine used in 1968 390ci GT models does not interchange.

Interchange Number: 21

Part Number(s): C6AZ6009U
VIN Code: S
Engine: 390ci four-barrel 335hp
Engine Tag Code: 318, 319, 321, 322, or 324
Usage: 1968–69 Torino GT, 1968–69 Cyclone GT, 1968–69 Mustang GT, and 1968–69 Cougar GT

Interchange Number: 22

Part Number(s): C6AZ6009AG
VIN Code: See notes
Engine: 427ci production-line engine
Engine Tag Code: W-359, -361, -350, -359, -360, or -364; R-361, -353, or -362

In 1968, the 428ci engine became available with the Cobra Jet package when installed in Mustang, Cougar Torino, or Montego GT models.

Years Used: 1963–mid-1968—all models

Note(s): Not to be confused with SOHC. Code Q used in 1963–65 single four-barrel engines rated at 410hp. Code W used from 1966 to 1968 with engines rated at 410hp (1966–67) and 390hp (1968). Code R was used with two four-barrels and the engine was rated at 425hp all years. The 427ci was phased out of production in 1968 and replaced with 428ci V-8. Powerplant is rare.

Interchange Number: 23
Part Number(s): C6AE6007-363S
VIN Code: not used
Engine: 420hp 427ci SOHC type
Engine Tag Code: 363
Years Used: 1962–67
Models Usage: None. Over-the-counter engine; not installed in production models

Interchange Number: 24
Part Number(s): C6AE6007-359J
Engine: Nonrated 427ci eight-barrel SOHC type
Engine Tag Code: 359
Years Used: 1962–67—all models
Usage: None. Over-the-counter engine; not installed in production models

Interchange Number: 25
Part Number(s): C6AZS6009J
VIN Code: Q
Engine: 345hp 428ci four-barrel
Engine Tag Code: 400, 401, or 410
Usage: 1968 full-size Ford and 1968 full-size Mercury, except with Cobra Jet applications

Interchange Number: 26
Part Number(s): C7AZ6009E
VIN Code: P
Engine: 360hp 428ci four-barrel
Engine Tag Code: 404 or 405
Years Used: 1966–70 Ford and Mercury police cars
Note(s): Tough high-performance engine. Makes a good base for high-performance application.

Interchange Number: 27
Part Number(s): C9ZZ6009E
VIN Code: R
Engine: 335hp 428ci four-barrel Cobra Jet
Engine Tag Code: 407, 408, 418, 419, 420, or 421
Usage: 1968–70 Torino, Montego, Mustang, and Cougar
Note(s): Excellent performance or restoration engine.

Interchange Number: 28
Part Number(s): C9ZZ6009F
VIN Code: R
Engine: 428ci four-barrel Super Cobra Jet
Engine Tag Code: 422, 423, 424, 425, or 426
Usage: 1969–70 Torino, Montego, Mustang, and Cougar

Interchange Number: 29
Part Number(s): D0SZ6009A
VIN Code: N
Engine: 360hp 429ci four-barrel
Engine Tag Code: 811, 812, 813, 814, 815, 816, 817, 818, or 819
Usage: 1969–71 full-size Ford and full-size Mercury and 1969–71 Thunderbird
Note(s): Two-barrel versions are the same short block and will interchange.

Interchange Number: 30
Part Number(s): D0OZ6009E
VIN Code: C
Engine: 370hp 429ci four-barrel Cobra Jet
Engine Tag Code: 824, 826, 833, or 834
Years Used: 1970–71 Torino, Montego, Mustang, and Cougar; also in Ford and Mercury police cars

Interchange Number: 31
Part Number(s): D1ZZ6009B
VIN Code: C
Engine: 375hp 429ci four-barrel Super Cobra Jet
Engine Tag Code: 829, 830, 831, 832, 835, 836, 837, or 838
Usage: 1970–71 Torino, Mustang, Cougar, and Montego

Interchange Number: 32
Part Number(s): C9AZ6009C
VIN Code: Z
Engine: 385hp 429ci Boss four-barrel
Engine Tag Code: 820 or 828
Usage: 1969–70 Mustang Boss 429ci

Crankshafts

Model Identification

289ci	Interchange Number
1962–68, except 271hp	1
1962–68 271hp	2

302ci	Interchange Number
1968–70, except Boss	3
1968–70 Boss	4

351ci	Interchange Number
1969–70 Windsor	5
1969–70 Cleveland	6

352ci	Interchange Number
1959–61, all	7

390ci	Interchange Number
1961–62, all except high-performance	8, 9
1961–62 high-performance	10
1966–70, all	11

427ci	Interchange Number
1962–63	12, 13
1964–67	14, 15
1968, all	16

428ci	Interchange Number
1968–70, except Super Cobra Jet	14, 18
1968–70 Super Cobra Jet	19, 20

429ci	Interchange Number
1970, except Boss	22
1970 Boss	23, 24

Interchange

Interchange Number: 1
Part Number(s): C3AZ6303F
Type: Iron
Casting Numbers: C3A2 or C303-F
Usage: 1962–68 289ci (except 271hp version) and 1962–66 260ci and 221ci engines
Note(s): Interchange Number 2 will fit and is better for performance.

Interchange Number: 2
Part Number(s): C3OZ6303B
Type: Steel
Casting Numbers: C3AE-D, C3AF-F, or C3AE-N C308E-B
Usage: 1963–67 289ci, 271hp engine
Note(s): Can be used in lesser-power engines, but castings C3A2 or C303-F (iron cranks) should *never* be used in place of a steel crank.

Interchange Number: 3
Part Number(s): D2OZ6303-B
Type: Iron
Casting Number: 2M
Usage: 1968–73 302ci engines, except Boss
Note(s): Replacement crankshaft marked 2MA on one of the counterweights. Do not use in 302ci Boss.

Interchange Number: 4
  Part Number(s): D0Z26303A
  Type: Steel
  Usage: 1969–71 302ci Boss engine

Interchange Number: 5
  Part Number(s): C9OZ6303A
  Type: Iron
  Casting Number: 3M
  Usage: 1969–73 351ci Windsor engine
  Note(s): Will not fit Cleveland engines. Not suitable for high-per-
    formance applications.

Interchange Number: 6
  Part Number(s): C9OZ6303A
  Type: Iron
  Casting Number: 4M
  Usage: 1970–73 351ci Cleveland engine
  Note(s): Will not fit Windsor engines. Good general-performance
    crankshaft.

Interchange Number: 7
  Part Number(s): C4AZ6303E
  Type: Iron
  Casting Numbers: EDD or EDT (1959), C0AE-B (1960–61), or
    C3AE-A (1963)
  Usage: 1959–63 352ci engine

Interchange Number: 8
  Part Number(s): C3AZ6303B
  Type: Iron
  Casting Numbers: C1AE or C3E-B
  Usage: 390ci Ford engines from 1961 through build date
    November 1, 1962, and 390ci Mercury engines from 1961
    through build date October 15, 1962
  Note(s): Interchange Numbers 9 and 10 will fit if timing chain and
    rods are swapped.

Interchange Number: 9
  Part Number(s): C4AZ6303G
  Type: Iron
  Casting Numbers: C3AE-E, C4AE-B, or C4AE-D
  Usage: 390ci Ford engines from November 1, 1962, build dates
    through 1965, and 390ci Mercury engines from October 15,
    1962, build dates through 1965
  Note(s): Interchange Number 10 will fit if timing chain and rods
    are swapped.

Interchange Number: 10
  Part Number(s): C3AZ6303C
  Type: Steel
  Casting Numbers: C2AE-D or C3AE-C
  Usage: 1961–63 390ci engine with high-performance packages
    and 1961–62 406ci engine

Interchange Number: 11
  Part Number(s): C6AZ6303A
  Type: Iron
  Casting Number: 2U
  Usage: 1966–69 390ci engine, all outputs

Interchange Number: 12
  Part Number(s): C4AZ6303H
  Type: Iron
  Casting Number: C3AE-U
  Usage: 1962–63 427ci, except race car
  Note(s): Street version of high-performance crankshaft.

Interchange Number: 13
  Part Number(s): C5AZ6303C
  Type: Steel
  Usage: 1962–65 off-road use
  Note(s): Racing version of standard crankshaft.

Interchange Number: 14
  Part Number(s): C9ZZ6303B
  Type: Iron
  Casting Number: 1UB on number 7 counterweight
  Usage: 1966–70 428ci Cobra Jet up to casting date December 26,
    1968. 1966–67 410ci engine; 1962–67 427ci engine; and
    1961–62 406ci engine

Interchange Number: 15
  Part Number(s): C5AZ6303C
  Type: Steel
  Usage: 1966–67 427ci engine with four-barrel
  Note(s): Street usage.

Interchange Number: 16
  Part Number(s): C8AZ6303B
  Type: Iron
  Usage: 1968 427ci engine with four-barrel
  Note(s): Street version.

Interchange Number: 17
  Part Number(s): C5AZ6303C
  Type: Steel
  Usage: 1967–68 427ci engine with eight-barrel

Interchange Number: 18
  Part Number(s): C9ZZ6303E
  Type: Steel
  Casting Number: A
  Usage: 1969 428ci engines, after casting date December 26,
    1968, through 1970, with Cobra Jet package

Interchange Number: 19
  Part Number(s): C9ZZ6303D
  Type: Steel
  Casting Number: B
  Usage: 1969 428ci engines, after casting date December 26,
    1968, through 1970, with Super Cobra Jet package

Interchange Number: 20
  Part Number(s): C9ZZ6303A
  Type: Steel
  Casting Number: H on number 1 counterweight
  Usage: 1969 428ci engines before casting date December 26,
    1968, with Super Cobra Jet package
  Note(s): Interchange Number 19 will fit if pistons are swapped.

Interchange Number: 21
  Part Number(s): D0OZ6303A
  Type: Iron
  Casting Number: H on number 1 counterweight
  Usage: 1968–71 429ci engines (except Boss)

Interchange Number: 22
  Part Number(s): C9AZ6303A
  Type: Steel
  Casting Number: C9AE-A
  Usage: 1969 429ci Boss with tag 820S

Interchange Number: 23
  Part Number(s): C9AZ6303C
  Type: Steel
  Usage: 1969 429ci Boss with tag code 820T, and all 1970 429ci
    Boss

Crankshaft Damper

Model Identification

289ci	Interchange Number
1963–68 two-barrel, regular fuel	1
1963–68 two- or four-barrel, except 271hp, regular fuel	4
1963–64 four-barrel, 271hp	2
1965–67 four-barrel, 271hp	2

302ci

	Interchange Number
1968–69, except Boss	1
1970, except Boss	5
1969 Boss	6
1970 Boss	7

351ci

	Interchange Number
1969 Windsor	8
1970 Windsor	9
1970 Cleveland	10

390ci

	Interchange Number
1968–70, all	11

Interchange

Interchange Number: 1
Part Number(s): C3AZ6316B
Usage: 1963–68 289ci two-barrel (regular fuel only) and 1968–69 302ci (except Boss)
Note(s): Stamped C4AE6316C or D

Interchange Number: 2
Part Number(s): C5OZ6316A
Usage: 1963–64 289ci four-barrel (271hp)
Note(s): Identify by size—6.5in outside diameter by 3-31/64in.

Interchange Number: 3
Part Number(s): C5OZ6316C
Usage: 1965–67 289ci four-barrel (271hp)
Note(s): Identify by size—6.5in outside diameter by 3-37/64in.

Interchange Number: 4
Part Number(s): C5AZ6316B
Usage: 1965–68 289ci four-barrel (210hp) or two-barrel with premium fuel only
Note(s): Stamped C4AE6316C or C4AED. Will not fit 271hp versions.

Interchange Number: 5
Part Number(s): D2OZ6316A
Usage: 1970–73 302ci (except Boss)
Note(s): Identify by size—6.5in outside diameter by 4-1/8in.

Interchange Number: 6
Part Number(s): C9ZZ6316B
Usage: 1969 302ci Boss
Note(s): Identify by size and marks—6.5in outside diameter by 3-21/32in, with long timing marks.

Interchange Number: 7
Part Number(s): DOZZ6316A
Usage: 1970–71 302ci Boss
Note(s): Identify by size and marks—6.5in outside diameter with short timing marks.

Interchange Number: 8
Part Number(s): C9OZ6316 A
Usage: 1969 351ci Windsor
Note(s): Stamped C9OE6316. Size is 6-3/8in by 3-1/32in. Will not fit Cleveland engines.

Interchange Number: 9
Part Number(s): D2AZ6316A
Usage: 1970–74 351ci Windsor
Note(s): Identify by size—6-3/8in outside diameter by 4-1/8in. Not for use on Cleveland or other high-performance engines.

Interchange Number: 10
Part Number(s): D2AZ6316B
Usage: 1970–73 351ci Cleveland
Note(s): Identify by size—6.5in outside diameter by 3.5in. Will not fit Windsor.

Interchange Number: 11
Part Number(s): D2TZ6316A
Usage: 1968–70 390ci (all outputs)
Note(s): Earlier years, part of fan pulley.

Connecting Rods

Model Identification

289ci

	Interchange Number
1963–68, except 271hp	1
1963–64 271hp	2
1965–67 271hp	3

302ci

	Interchange Number
1968–70, except Boss	5
1968–70 Boss	3
1968–70, except Torino, Mustang, Cougar, or Montego	4
1968–70 race car	6

351ci

	Interchange Number
1969–70 Windsor	7
1969–70 Cleveland	8

352ci

	Interchange Number
1959–61, all	21

390ci

	Interchange Number
1963–65, except high-performance	9
1963–65 high-performance	10
1963–65 race car	11, 12
1966–70, except with Drag Pack	13
1966–70 Drag Pack	15

427ci

	Interchange Number
1965–68 stock	10
1965–68 race car	11, 12
1965–68 multiple carbs	12
1965–68 NASCAR	14

428ci

	Interchange Number
1968–70, except Cobra Jet, Super Cobra Jet, or police car	13
1968–70 Super Cobra Jet	15
1968–70 Cobra Jet	12
1968–70 police car	12

429ci

	Interchange Number
1970, except Cobra Jet, Super Cobra Jet, or Boss	17
1970 Cobra Jet, Super Cobra Jet, or police car	18
1970 Boss	19, 20

Interchange

Interchange Number: 1
Part Number(s): C3AZ6200D
Forging Number: C3AE-D
Usage: 1963–68 289ci, except 271hp versions
Note(s): Do not use in engines coded K in the VIN. Also used in 1964–up 260ci V-8s and will interchange.

Interchange Number: 2
Part Number(s): C3OZ6200C
Usage: 1963–64 289ci 271hp
Note(s): Used with engines coded K (D in 1963). Can be used in lower-powered version if 271hp crankshaft is used.

Interchange Number: 3
Part Number(s): C9ZZ6200B
Usage: 1965–67 289ci 271hp and 1969–71 Boss 302ci

Interchange Number: 4
Part Number(s): D3OZ6200A
Usage: 1968–73 full-size models and all 1971–73
Note(s): Not for use in 1968–70 Torino, Montego, Mustang, or Cougar with 302ci.

Interchange Number: 5
Part Number(s): C9OZ6200B
Usage: 1968–70 Torino, Mustang, Montego, and Cougar 302ci, except Boss
Note(s): Warning—those from a full-size model will not interchange.

Connecting rods can be identified by their forging numbers.

Interchange Number: 6
Part Number(s): DOZX6200A
Usage: 1970–71 302ci Boss race car
Note(s): Special heavy-duty rods. Excellent for street machines and those with blowers.

Interchange Number: 7
Part Number(s): C9OZ6200A
Usage: 1969–73 351ci Windsor

Interchange Number: 8
Part Number(s): C9ZZ6200B
Usage: 1970–73 351ci Cleveland and 1971 351ci Cobra Jet

Interchange Number: 9
Part Number(s): C3AZ6200B
Forging Number: C3AE6025A
Usage: 1963–65 390ci, except high-performance and police car

Interchange Number: 10
Part Number(s): C3AZ6200F
Forging Number: C3AE6025A
Usage: 1965 390ci police car, 1965 427ci, 1961–62 406ci, and 1963–65 390ci high-performance
Note(s): Stronger rod than most stock units.

Interchange Number: 11
Part Number(s): C9ZZ6200A
Usage: 1962–69 390ci over-the-counter, 1965–68 427ci, and 1968–70 428ci Super Cobra Jet
Note(s): Lemans-type, excellent high-performance rods. Will require the engine to be rebalanced on 427ci and 390ci.

Interchange Number: 12
Part Number(s): C6AZ6200C
Usage: 1962–70 390ci engine (racing package), 1962–66 427ci with multiple carbs, 1968–70 428ci Cobra Jet, and 1966–70 police car
Note(s): High-performance steel rods that require rebalancing on 390ci engines.

Interchange Number: 13
Part Number(s): C6AZ6200D
Usage: 1966–70 390ci without Drag Pack, 1966–68 428ci (except Cobra Jet, Super Cobra Jet, and police car), and 1966–67 Mercury 410ci

Interchange Number: 14
Part Number(s): C5AZ6200D
Usage: 1962–66 427ci Lemans-type
Note(s): Used a lot in NASCAR racing. Good for rebuilding a NASCAR replica

Interchange Number: 15
Part Number(s): C9ZZ6200A
Usage: 1968–70 428ci Super Cobra Jet
Note(s): Used in Drag Pack in 1968–70 390ci and 427ci. Will fit 1966–68 non-Super Cobra Jet 428ci. Will require rebalancing on 390ci, 427ci, and non-428ci Super Cobra Jets.

Interchange Number: 16
Part Number(s): C7OEZ6200A
Usage: 1962–68 427ci with medium- or high-riser intake manifold

Interchange Number: 17
Part Number(s): C8SZ6200A
Usage: 1968–73 429ci (except Cobra Jet, Super Cobra Jet, or Boss) and 1968–73 460ci
Note(s): Used in a variety of vehicles, including two-barrels.

Interchange Number: 18
Part Number(s): DOOZ6200A
Usage: 1970–71 429ci Cobra Jet, Super Cobra Jet, and police car

Interchange Number: 19
Part Number(s): C9AZ6200A
Usage: 1969 429ci Boss with tag number 820-S
Note(s): Be careful the proper rod is used with the proper crankshaft and pistons. Interchange Number 20 will fit if pistons and crankshaft are swapped also.

Interchange Number: 20
Part Number(s): C9AZ6200B
Usage: 1969 Boss with tag number 820-T and all 1970 Boss 429ci models
Note(s): Be careful the proper rod is used with the proper crankshaft and pistons. Interchange Number 19 will fit if pistons and crankshaft are swapped also.

Interchange Number: 21
Part Number(s): C1AZ6200C
Usage: 1959–66 352ci

Flywheel

Model Identification

289ci	Interchange Number
1963–64 manual, except 271hp	1
1963–64 automatic, except 271hp	19
1963–64 271hp manual	3, 4, 5
1965–68 manual	1, 2
1965–68 automatic	19
1965–68 271hp manual	3, 4

302ci	Interchange Number
1968–70 manual, except Boss	2
automatic, except Boss	19
Boss, all	6

351ci	Interchange Number
1969–70 Windsor manual	7
1969–70 Windsor automatic	20
1969–70 Cleveland manual	7
1969–70 Cleveland automatic	20

352ci	Interchange Number
1959–61 manual	8
1959–61 automatic	21

390ci	Interchange Number
1961–64 manual	8
1961–64 automatic	21
1965–70 manual, except 1966–67 GT models	9
1965–70 automatic, except 1966–67 GT models	22
1966–67 GT manual	10
1966–67 GT automatic	22

17

427ci	Interchange Number
1962–64 manual	11
1965 manual	12, 13
1966–67 manual	13
1968 manual	14
1968 automatic	22

428ci	Interchange Number
1966–70 manual, except Cobra Jet, Super Cobra Jet, and police car	14
1966–70 automatic, except Cobra Jet, Super Cobra Jet, and police car	23
1966–70 Cobra Jet and police car, manual	15
1966–70 Cobra Jet and police car, automatic	23
1966–70 Super Cobra Jet, manual	16
1966–70 Super Cobra Jet, automatic	23

429ci	Interchange Number
1969–71 manual, except Cobra Jet, Super Cobra Jet, police car, and Boss 429ci	17
1969–71 automatic, except Cobra Jet, Super Cobra Jet, police car, and Boss 429ci	24
1969–71 Super Cobra Jet, police car, and Boss 429ci, manual	18
1969–71 Super Cobra Jet, police car, and Boss 429ci, automatic	24

Interchange

Interchange Number: 1
Part Number(s): C3AZ6375J
Casting Number: C7ZE-A
Usage: 1963–64 full-size Ford, Fairlane, and Comet, 1964–67 Mustang, and 1967 Cougar 289ci with manual transmission, except 271hp
Note(s): Has 157 teeth.

Interchange Number: 2
Part Number(s): C5AZ6375S
Casting Number: C7AE-A
Usage: 1965–67 full-size Ford, Fairlane, and Comet; 1967–68 Falcon; 1967–68 Bronco (except 271hp); and 1968–73 302ci (except Boss)—all with manual
Note(s): Has 164 teeth with 10in or 10-1/2in clutch

Interchange Number: 3
Part Number(s): C3OZ6375-E
Casting Number: C7ZE-A
Usage: 1965–67 Mustang and Cougar 289ci K-code engine with manual transmission
Note(s): Has 157 teeth.

Interchange Number: 4
Part Number(s): C3OZ6375C
Usage: 1963–64 Fairlane and Cyclone and full-size models with 271hp 289ci

Interchange Number: 5
Part Number(s): C3OZ6375-B
Casting Number: C7OE-A
Usage: 1965 Fairlane and Cyclone with 271hp 289ci K-code engine and manual transmission
Note(s): Has 164 teeth.

Interchange Number: 6
Part Number(s): C9ZZ6375-B
Usage: 302ci Boss only
Note(s): Interchange Number 5 is reported to fit.

Interchange Number: 7
Part Number(s): C6TZ6375-C
Casting Number: C7TE-A
Usage: 1969–73 351ci Cleveland and Windsor and 1968 289ci with 11in clutch in Bronco
Note(s): Has 164 teeth.

Interchange Number: 8
Part Number(s): B8A6375A
Casting Number:
Usage: 1959–64 352ci, 1961–64 390ci, and 1961–62 406ci with manual transmission and 11in clutch
Note(s): Has 12.375in pressure-plate bolt circle and 153 teeth.

Interchange Number: 9
Part Number(s): C5AZ6375K
Casting Number: C5AE6375E
Usage: 1965–70 390ci engines with manual transmissions, except 1966–67 GT models
Note(s): Has a 12-3/8in pressure-plate bolt circle. Originally, early 1965 models used a 168-tooth flywheel until March 1, 1965. This unit was not available as a replacement part, but part number C5AZ6375K, with 184 teeth, will fit.

Interchange Number: 10
Part Number(s): C5AZ6375L
Casting Number:
Usage: 1966–67 Fairlane GT, 1966–67 Cyclone GT, 1966–67 Mustang GT, and 1967 Cougar GT—all with 390ci engine and manual transmission
Note(s): Has a 12-7/8in pressure-plate bolt circle and 184 teeth. Identify by the bolt-circle diameter to avoid confusion with wheel in Interchange Number 9.

Interchange Number: 11
Part Number(s): C3AZ6375E
Casting Number: C3AE6080C
Usage: 1962–64 427ci with manual
Note(s): Has 12-7/8in pressure-plate bolt circle, and crankshaft mounting holes are recessed. Diameter is 15-15/32in with 146 teeth.

Interchange Number: 12
Part Number(s): C5AZ6375E
Casting Number: C5AE6375G
Usage: 1965 427ci up to build date March 1, 1965, in Ford full-size and February 1, 1965, in full-size Mercury—both with manual

Interchange Number: 13
Part Number(s): C5AZ6375E
Casting Number: C5AE6375E
Usage: Late 1965–67 427ci with manual
Note(s): Build dates are after March 1, 1965, in Ford and February 1, 1965, in Mercury.

Interchange Number: 14
Part Number(s): C6AZ6375A
Usage: 1968 427ci engine and 1966–68 428ci (except Cobra Jet or Super Cobra Jet)—all with manual
Note(s): Replacement unit above has 184 teeth; original had 157 teeth. Both wheels have 12in pressure-plate bolt circle with a 14 -23/64in diameter.

Interchange Number: 15
Part Number(s): C8026375A
Casting Number: C8OEA
Usage: 1968–70 428ci Cobra Jet with manual
Note(s): Identify by 12-7/8in pressure-plate bolt circle.

Interchange Number: 16
Part Number(s): C9ZZ6375A
Casting Number:
Usage: 1969–70 models with 428ci Super Cobra Jet and manual
Note(s): Is 14-15/64in in diameter and has 184 teeth.

Interchange Number: 17
Part Number(s): C9AZ6375A
Casting Number: C9AE-A
Usage: 1969–71 429ci (except Cobra Jet, Super Cobra Jet, and Boss) with manual
Note(s): Is 15-3/8in in diameter with 176 teeth.

Interchange Number: 18
  Part Number(s): C9AZ6375C
  Usage: 1969–71 429ci Cobra Jet, Super Cobra Jet, and Boss with manual
  Note(s): Is 14-23/64in in diameter with 176 teeth.

Interchange Number: 19
  Part Number(s): C3AZ6375L
  Casting Number: C80P-C
  Usage: 1963–68 289ci (except 271hp) and 1968–74 302ci (except Boss) with automatic

Interchange Number: 20
  Part Number(s): C5AZ6375T
  Usage: 1969–71 351ci with automatic
  Note(s): Fits either Windsor or Cleveland, all types. Original unit has 168 teeth; replacement unit above has 164.

Interchange Number: 21
  Part Number(s): B8A6375B
  Usage: 1959–64 352ci, 1961–64 390ci, and 1958–60 430ci—all with Cruise-O-Matic
  Note(s): Has sixteen 7/16in bolt holes. Diameter is 14.96in with 153 teeth.

Interchange Number: 22
  Part Number(s): C5AZ6375D
  Usage: 1965–70 390ci (including GT models) and 1968 427ci with automatic
  Note(s): Has sixteen 7/64in bolt holes. Will not fit earlier models. Diameter is 14-1/2in with 184 teeth.

Interchange Number: 23
  Part Number(s): C6AZ6375B
  Casting Number: 6VP6380B or C7AP6375A
  Usage: 1966–73 428ci with automatic
  Note(s): Diameter is 15-17/32in. Two-barrel version will fit. Originally a two-piece design.

Interchange Number: 24
  Part Number(s): D1SZ6375A
  Usage: 1969–71 429ci and 1968–73 460ci with automatic
  Note(s): Diameter is 14-1/4in. Tip: Look for 460ci (in Lincoln); it is more common.

Flywheel Housing

Model Identification

289ci	Interchange Number
1963–early-1965, all	1
1965–68, all	2, 3

302ci	Interchange Number
1968–70, all, including Boss	2

351ci	Interchange Number
1969–70 Windsor	4
1970 Cleveland	5

352ci	Interchange Number
1959–62, all	6
1963–68, all	7

390ci	Interchange Number
1966–70, except full-size models	8
1966–70 full-size models	7

427ci	Interchange Number
1962–64, all	9
1965–68, except full-size models	11
1965–68 full-size models	10

428ci	Interchange Number
1966–68, except Cobra Jet and Super Cobra Jet	14
1966–68 Cobra Jet and Super Cobra Jet	12

429ci	Interchange Number
1969–70, all, including Boss	13

Interchange

Interchange Number: 1
  Part Number(s): C3OZ6392E
  Housing Number: C3AA6394-C
  Usage: 1963–early-1965 289ci and 260ci—all outputs with five flywheel bolts

Interchange Number: 2
  Part Number(s): C5AZ6392D
  Housing Number: C5AA6394B
  Usage: Late-1965–68 289ci (except 1965–67 Mustang and 1967 Cougar) and 1968–74 302ci (including Boss)
  Note(s): Has six-bolt flywheel. Will not fit earlier blocks.

Interchange Number: 3
  Part Number(s): D2OZ6392A
  Housing Number: C5DA6394A or C9OA6394A
  Usage: Late 1965–67 Mustang and 1965–67 Cougar 289ci with six-bolt flywheel

Interchange Number: 4
  Part Number(s): C9AZ6392A
  Housing Number: C9AA6394A
  Usage: 1970–71 Windsor block
  Note(s): Will not fit Cleveland.

Interchange Number: 5
  Part Number(s): C5TZ6392B
  Housing Number: C5TA6394A
  Usage: 1970–73 Cleveland, 1966–74 Bronco with V-8

Interchange Number: 6
  Part Number(s): B8A6366A
  Usage: 1959–62 352ci and 1961–62 390ci

Interchange Number: 7
  Part Number(s): C5AZ6392C
  Usage: 1963–68 352ci and 390ci full-size Ford and Mercury only

Interchange Number: 8
  Part Number(s): C6OZ6392C
  Usage: 1966–69 352ci and 390ci Fairlane, Cyclone, Mustang, and Cougar only

Interchange Number: 9
  Part Number(s): C3AZ6392A
  Housing Number: C3AA6394-A
  Usage: 1963–64 full-size 406ci and 1962–64 427ci

Interchange Number: 10
  Part Number(s): C5AZ6392C
  Usage: 1965–68 427ci full-size only
  Note(s): Do not use on mid-size or Mustang or Cougar.

Interchange Number: 11
  Part Number(s): C6OZ6392B
  Housing Number: C6OA6394B
  Usage: 1967–68 Fairlane GT and Cyclone GT427ci, 1967–68 Mustang, and 1967–68 Cougar
  Note(s): These models only; will not fit full-size models.

Interchange Number: 12
  Part Number(s): C6OZ6392C
  Usage: 1968–70 428ci Cobra Jet and Super Cobra Jet
  Note(s): Those from a full-size model will not interchange.

Interchange Number: 13
  Part Number(s): DOAZ6392A
  Housing Number: C9AA6394D
  Usage: 1969–71 429ci, including Super Cobra Jet and Boss

Interchange Number: 14
  Part Number(s): C5AZ6392C
  Housing Number: C8AA7515A
  Usage: 1968–70 428ci full-size models only

Pistons

Model Identification

289ci   Interchange Number
1963–68, all two-barrel 1
four-barrel, except 271hp 2, 3
four-barrel 271hp 4

302ci   Interchange Number
1968–70 two-barrel 1
1968–70 four-barrel, except Boss 2
1968–70 Boss 5

351ci   Interchange Number
1969–70 Windsor two-barrel 7
1969–70 Windsor four-barrel 6
1970 Cleveland two-barrel 8
1970 Cleveland four-barrel 8

352ci   Interchange Number
1959–66, except high-performance 9
1959–66 high-performance 10

390ci   Interchange Number
1961–62 special high-performance and multiple-carb 11
1966–70, except GT models 12
1966–68 GT models 13

427ci   Interchange Number
1962–65 four-barrel 14
1962–65 twin four-barrel 15
1966–67, all 16
1968, all 17

428ci   Interchange Number
1966–70, except Cobra Jet, Super Cobra Jet, and police 25
1968 Cobra Jet 18, 19
1969–70 Cobra Jet 19
1969–70 Super Cobra Jet 20
1966–68 police 18, 19

429ci   Interchange Number
1969–70, except Cobra Jet, Super Cobra Jet, Boss, and police 21
1969–70 Cobra Jet and Super Cobra Jet....................22
1969–70 Boss 429ci 23, 24

Interchange

Interchange Number: 1
Part Number(s): C8OZ6108N
Bore Size: 4in
Compression: 9.3:1
Usage: 1963–68 289ci two-barrel and 1968–72 302ci (except Boss)

Interchange Number: 2
Part Number(s): C8OZ6108R
Bore Size: 4in
Usage: 1965–67 289ci four-barrel 210hp for regular fuel and 1968 302ci four-barrel
Note(s): Used with engine code D in VIN.

Interchange Number: 3
Part Number(s): C5OZ6108
Bore Size: 4in
Compression: 9.8:1
Usage: 1965–67 289ci four-barrel for premium fuel
Note(s): The 225hp version is coded A in the VIN.

Interchange Number: 4
Part Number(s): C3OZ6108L
Bore Size: 4in
Compression: 10:1
Usage: 1964–67 289ci 271hp
Note(s): Coded K in the VIN.

Interchange Number: 5
Part Number(s): DOZZ6108A
Bore Size: 4in
Compression: 10:1
Usage: 1969–70 302ci Boss
Note(s): Forged pistons.

Interchange Number: 6
Part Number(s): C9OZ6108A
Bore Size: 4in
Compression: 10.7:1
Usage: 1969 351ci Windsor four-barrel only

Interchange Number: 7
Part Number(s): DAZ6108
Bore Size: 4in
Compression: 9.5:1
Usage: 1969–71 351ci Windsor two-barrel
Note(s): Do not use in Cleveland block.

Interchange Number: 8
Part Number(s): DOAZ6108A
Bore Size: 4in
Compression: 10.7:1 (1970); 11.4:1 (1971)
Usage: 1970–73, all 351ci Cleveland
Note(s): Pistons are cast-aluminum.

Interchange Number: 9
Part Number(s): COAZ6108A
Bore Size: 4in
Compression: 9.3:1
Usage: 1959–66 352ci four-barrel, except high-performance

Interchange Number: 10
Part Number(s): COAE6108AJ
Bore Size: 4in
Usage: 1960 high-performance
Note(s): Best original 352ci piston. They are for performance, but will fit other 352ci engines.

Interchange Number: 11
Part Number(s): C1AZ6108A
Bore Size: 4.05in
Usage: 1961–62 390ci special high-performance four-barrel, six-barrel, or eight-barrel

Interchange Number: 12
Part Number(s): C6AZ6108AG
Bore Size: 4.05in
Compression: 9.5:1
Usage: 1966–70 390ci two-barrel or four-barrel, except GT
Note(s): Interchange Number 13 will fit and provide better performance.

Interchange Number: 13
Part Number(s): C6AZ6108BG
Bore Size: 4.05in
Compression: 10.5:1
Usage: 1966–68 390ci GT

Interchange Number: 14
Part Number(s): C3AZ6108M
Bore Size: 4.236in
Usage: 1963–65 427ci four-barrel

Interchange Number: 15
Part Number(s): C3AZ6108W
Bore Size: 4.236in
Usage: 1963–65 427ci twin four-barrel

Interchange Number: 16
Part Number(s): C5AZ6108A
Bore Size: 4.236in
Compression: 11:1
Usage: 1966–67 427ci, all outputs
Note(s): Use with both single and multiple carburetors.

Interchange Number: 17
Part Number(s): C8AZ6108A
Bore Size: 4.236in
Compression: 10.9:1
Usage: 1968 427ci only
Note(s): Will not fit earlier models due to dome height.

Interchange Number: 18
Part Number(s): C80Z6108G
Bore Size: 4.130in
Compression: 10.6:1
Usage: 1968 428ci (until build date November 13, 1968) with Cobra Jet package and 1966–68 police car until above date
Note(s): Has a single valve pocket on the piston dome.

Interchange Number: 19
Part Number(s): C9ZZ6108Y
Bore Size: 4.130in
Compression: 10.6:1
Usage: 1968–70 428ci (after build date November 11, 1968) with Cobra Jet package and 1968–70 428ci police car
Note(s): Pistons have two valve pockets on piston dome.

Interchange Number: 20
Part Number(s): C9ZZ6108N
Bore Size: 4.130in
Compression: 10.5:1
Usage: 1968–70 428ci Super Cobra Jet

Interchange Number: 21
Part Number(s): DZAZ6108A
Bore Size: 4.360in
Compression: 10.5:1
Usage: 1968–73 429ci, except Cobra Jet, Super Cobra Jet, and Boss

Interchange Number: 22
Part Number(s): D1OZ6108B
Bore Size: 4.360in
Compression: 10.5:1
Usage: 1969–71 429ci Cobra Jet and Super Cobra Jet
Note(s): Replacement above is originally for Super Cobra Jet but is used by Ford for replacement in the Cobra Jet powerplants. They are better than the originals because they are forged.

Interchange Number: 23
Part Number(s): C9AZ6108A
Bore Size: 4.360in
Compression: 10.5:1
Usage: 1969 Boss 429ci with engine tag number 820S
Note(s): Due to the difference in weights of the pistons, the late style of Interchange Number 24 cannot be used unless the rods and crankshafts are also interchanged.

Interchange Number: 24
Part Number(s): C9AZ6108G
Bore Size: 4.360in
Compression: 10.5:1
Usage: 1969 Boss 429ci with engine tag number 820T and all 1970 Boss 429ci
Note(s): Due to the difference in weights of the pistons, the early style in Interchange Number 23 cannot be used unless the rods and crankshafts are also interchanged.

Interchange Number: 25
Part Number(s): C6AZ6108AN
Bore Size: 4.130in
Usage: 1966–70 428ci, except Cobra Jet, Super Cobra Jet, and police car

Camshaft

Model Identification

Interchange

Interchange Number: 1
Part Number(s): C3OZ625OV
Casting Number: UA
Type: Hydraulic
Usage: 1963–68 289ci (except 271hp) and 1968–70 302ci (except Boss)

Interchange Number: 2
Part Number(s): C3OZ625OC
Casting Number: Upside-down A followed by E
Type: Mechanical
Usage: 1963–67 289ci 271hp
Note(s): This cam will fit non-high-performance versions, but not vice versa.

Interchange Number: 3
Part Number(s): C9ZZ6250A
Casting Number: Upside-down A followed by EB
Type: Mechanical
Usage: 1969 Boss 302ci
Note(s): Interchange Number 4 will fit if the lifters are interchanged.

Interchange Number: 4
Part Number(s): DOZZ625OA
Casting Number: Upside-down A followed by ED
Type: Mechanical
Usage: 1970–71 302ci Boss only

Interchange Number: 5
Part Number(s): C9OZ625OA
Casting Number: 8F
Type: Hydraulic
Usage: 1969–72 351ci Windsor
Note(s): Do not use on Cleveland engines.

Interchange Number: 6
Part Number(s): DOAZ6250B
Casting Number: NB or 8N
Type: Hydraulic
Usage: 1970–71 351ci Cleveland two-barrel
Note(s): Good performance increase by swapping Interchange Number 7 along with lifters, pistons, and heads.

Interchange Number: 7
Part Number(s): DOAZ6250B
Casting Number: Backwards B followed by R
Type: Hydraulic
Usage: 1970–71 351ci Cleveland four-barrel

Interchange Number: 8
Part Number(s): C0AZ6250A
Casting Number: Y between last lobe and last journal
Type: Hydraulic
Usage: 352ci engines from 1959 to build date December 1, 1963
Note(s): Replacement camshaft was marked AA at the rear of cam.

Interchange Number: 9
Part Number(s): C6AZ6250A
Casting Number: Upside-down A followed by U, with white-painted 15-tooth distributor gear
Type: Hydraulic
Usage: 1966–69 390ci, except 1966–67 GT and 1967–71 two-barrel for regular fuel

Interchange Number: 10
Part Number(s): C6OZ6250B
Casting Number: Upside-down A followed by B
Type: Hydraulic
Usage: 1966–67 Fairlane GT, 1966–67 Cyclone GT, 1966–67 Mustang GT, 1967 Cougar GT, 1966–70 428ci police, and 1968–69 428ci Cobra Jet and Super Cobra Jet

Interchange Number: 11
Part Number(s): C7AZ6250A
Casting Number: Upside-down A followed by X or U with green paint on 15-tooth distributor gear
Type: Hydraulic
Usage: 1966–71 390ci two-barrel for regular fuel

Interchange Number: 12
Part Number(s): C3AZ6250D
Casting Number: Upside-down A followed by B or VB
Type: Mechanical
Usage: 1963–64 427ci up to May 1, 1963, with twin four-barrels
Note(s): Interchange Number 13 will fit if swapped with lifters.

Interchange Number: 13
Part Number(s): C3AZ6250AA
Casting Number: Upside-down A followed by B or BA
Type: Mechanical
Usage: 1965–67 427ci after May 1, 1963, with twin four-barrels or a single four-barrel

Interchange Number: 14
Part Number(s): C8AZ6250A
Casting Number: Upside-down A followed by BAB
Usage: 1968 427ci

Interchange Number: 15
Part Number(s): C6AZ6250A
Casting Number: Upside-down A followed by U
Type: Hydraulic
Usage: 1966–68 428ci (except Cobra Jet, Super Cobra Jet, or police car)

Interchange Number: 16
Part Number(s): C8SZ6250A
Casting Number: Backwards B followed by B
Type: Hydraulic
Usage: 1968-71 429ci (except Cobra Jet, Super Cobra Jet, Boss, or police car) and 1968–72 460ci engine

Interchange Number: 17
Part Number(s): C9AZ6250A
Type: Hydraulic
Usage: 1969–71 429ci Cobra Jet, Super Cobra Jet, and police; 1970–71 460ci police interceptor; and 1969 Boss 429ci

Interchange Number: 18
Part Number(s): DOAZ6250A
Type: Mechanical
Usage: 1969–70 429ci Super Cobra Jet and 1970 429ci Boss

Cylinder Heads

Interchange below is for the bare head unless otherwise indicated. Casting numbers listed are general numbers; sometimes they may change from year to year. For example, the code may be cast as C6ZZ-A in 1966 and as C8ZZ-A in 1968, even though they are the same cylinder head.

Special heads are required with emission controls from 1965–66 for the emission system to properly operate. Beginning in 1967, all heads have provisions for emission-control systems. Casting numbers are given when known. Usually, they are the same or nearly the same as the part number.

Model Identification

289ci	Interchange Number
1963–early-64, except 271hp	1
1963–early-64 271hp	5
Late-1964–66, except 271hp	2, 3
Late-1964–66 271hp	6
1967–68, except 271hp	4
1967–68 271hp	6, 7
1967–68 with emissions	8

302ci	Interchange Number
1968, all without emissions	9
1968 with emissions, except Boss	17
1969 non-Boss with manual	10
1969 non-Boss with automatic	11, 12
1969 Boss	15
1970 non-Boss with manual	13
1970 non-Boss with automatic	14
1970 Boss	16

351ci	Interchange Number
1969 Windsor	18
1970 Windsor	19
1970 Cleveland two-barrel	20
1970 Cleveland four-barrel	21

352ci	Interchange Number
1959–65	22, 23
1966–70	23

390ci	Interchange Number
1961–65	22, 23
1966–70	23

Engine displacement and the casting year are shown on the head.

Interchange

Interchange Number: 1
Part Number(s): C3AZ6049A
Casting Number: C3AE609OF
Usage: 1963–64 289ci through casting date February 24, 1964, except 271hp version

Interchange Number: 2
Part Number(s): C3OZ6049AE
Casting Number: C4AE or C4DE
Usage: 1964 to early-1966 289ci, all outputs except 271hp
Note(s): Used from casting date February 24, 1964, to change line level 9 on the engine tag.

Interchange Number: 3
Part Number(s): C5AZ6049AF
Casting Number: C5AE or C5DE
Usage: Late-1965 to early-1966 289ci, except 271hp
Note(s): Used from change level 9 to level 10 on the engine tag.

Interchange Number: 4
Part Number(s): C6OZ6049AF and C6AZ6049AG
Casting Number: C6AE or C6DE
Usage: Late-1966–68 289ci, except 271hp
Note(s): Used after change level 10 on the engine tag.

Interchange Number: 5
Part Number(s): C5OZ6049B
Usage: 271hp 289ci from 1963 up to build date August 20, 1964

Interchange Number: 6
Part Number(s): C7ZZ6049C
Usage: 271hp 289ci used from build dates August 20, 1964, to January 3, 1967

Interchange Number: 7
Part Number(s): C7ZZ6049B
Usage: Late-1967–68 289ci 271hp
Note(s): Usage begins at build date January 3, 1967.

Interchange Number: 8
Part Number(s): C60Z6049C (to change level 9), C60Z6049AE (to change level 10), C60Z6049H (to change level 12), C60Z6049A (to change level 13), or C60Z6049C (from change level 14)
Casting Numbers: Same as part numbers
Usage: 1966–68 289ci, except 271hp with emission controls (used mostly in California)
Note(s): Reports indicate that Interchange Number 17 will fit.

Interchange Number: 9
Part Number(s): C80Z6049A
Usage: 1968 302ci
Note(s): Reports indicate that Interchange Number 4 will fit.

Interchange Number: 10
Part Number(s): C9OZ6049C
Usage: 1969 302ci with manual transmission, except Boss
Note(s): Interchange Numbers 11 and 12 will fit.

Interchange Number: 11
Part Number(s): C9OZ6049D
Usage: 1969 302ci models with automatic built through March of 1969
Note(s): Interchange Number 12 will fit. See difference under Number 12.

Interchange Number: 12
Part Number(s): C9OZ6049G
Usage: 1969 models with automatic transmission built after March of 1969
Note(s): Early style has 3/8in-diameter rocker studs; later style has 5/16in-diameter rocker studs.

Interchange Number: 13
Part Number(s): C9OZ6049E
Usage: 1970 302ci with manual transmission, except Boss
Note(s): Interchange Number 14 will fit.

Interchange Number: 14
Part Number(s): D2OZ6049B
Usage: 1970–72 302ci with automatic transmission, except Boss.
Note(s): Used up to build date January 1, 1972.

Interchange Number: 15
Part Number(s): C9ZZ6049D (right side); DOZZ6049B (left side)
Usage: 1969 Boss Mustang or Cougar Eliminator with 302ci Boss only
Note(s): Each head is unique and fits only that side. Reports indicate that Interchange Number 16 will fit if swapped with all hardware.

Interchange Number: 16
Part Number(s): DOZZ6049A
Usage: 1970–71 302ci Boss
Note(s): Redesign of earlier 302ci Boss heads, so the two heads are interchangeable.

Interchange Number: 17
Part Number(s): C8AZ6049F (two-barrel) or C8OZ6049C (four-barrel)
Casting Number: C8OE609OK (two-barrel) or C08OE6090F(four-barrel)
Usage: 1968 302ci two-barrel with emission controls
Note(s): Used in California vehicles. Reports indicate that Interchange Number 8 will fit.

Interchange Number: 18
Part Number(s): D1OZ6049B
Casting Number: DOOE6090C
Usage: 1969 351ci Windsor

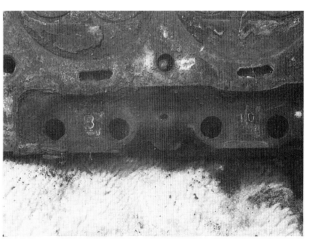

This piece was cast October 10, 1965, which meant it was installed in a 1966 model.

Interchange Number: 19
 Part Number(s): DOOZ6049A
 Casting Number: C90E6090B
 Usage: 1970–72 351ci Windsor
 Note(s): Has six valve-cover bolt holes.

Interchange Number: 20
 Part Number(s): D1AZ6049A
 Casting Number: DOOAE6090E or DOAE609J
 Usage: 1970–72 351ci Cleveland two-barrels

Interchange Number: 21
 Part Number(s): D1AZ6049B
 Casting Number: DOAE6090N or DOAE6090R
 Usage: All 1970–71 351ci Cleveland four-barrel

Interchange Number: 22
 Part Number(s): C2S266049B
 Casting Number: C2SE6090B
 Usage: 1959–65 352ci and 1961–65 390ci
 Note(s): Used up to build date December 1, 1965.

Interchange Number: 23
 Part Number(s): C8AZ6049M
 Casting Number: 6AE-A, 7AE-A, 8AE-A, or 9AE-A
 Usage: Late 1965–70 352ci and 390ci

Interchange Number: 24
 Part Number(s): C3AZ6049G
 Casting Number: C3AE6090D
 Usage: 427ci from 1962 to build date March 15, 1963

Interchange Number: 25
 Part Number(s): N/A
 Casting Number: C3AE6090G or C3AE6090J
 Usage: Late-1963–67 427ci
 Note(s): Begins at build date March 15, 1963.

Interchange Number: 26
 Part Number(s): C8AZ6049K
 Usage: 1968 427ci
 Note(s): Reports indicate that Interchange Number 27 will fit.

Interchange Number: 27
 Part Number(s): C8OZ6049K
 Usage: 1968–70 428ci Cobra Jet or Super Cobra Jet and 1966–70 428ci police car

Interchange Number: 28
 Part Number(s): C8AZ6049M
 Usage: 1966–70 428ci, except Cobra Jet, Super Cobra Jet, and police car.
 Note(s): *Not* used on Torino, Montego, Cougar, or Mustang.

Interchange Number: 29
 Part Number(s): C8AZ6049N
 Usage: 1968–70 428ci police car
 Note(s): Used in cars originally equipped with automatic transmissions but will fit cars with manual. Can be made to perform like Cobra Jet style.

Interchange Number: 30
 Part Number(s): DOOZ6049H
 Usage: 1970–71 429ci Cobra Jet, Super Cobra Jet, and 1969–71 police car

Interchange Number: 31
 Part Number(s): DOVZ6049D
 Usage: 1968–71 429ci (except Cobra Jet, Super Cobra Jet, Boss, and police cars) and 1968–71 460ci
 Note(s): Look for 460ci in Lincoln or 429ci in Thunderbird.

Interchange Number: 32
 Part Number(s): DOAZ6049C
 Usage: 1969–70 Boss 429ci

Valve Covers

Model Identification

289ci	Interchange Number
1963–65, except 1965 210hp or with emissions	1
1963–65 chrome	5
1965 210hp	3
1966–68, all with emissions	2, 4
1966–68 chrome	5, 6

302ci	Interchange Number
1968–70, except Boss or Mustang GT 350	4
1968–70 Boss	19
1968–70 GT 350	7
1968–70 chrome, except Boss	6

351ci Windsor	Interchange Number
1969–70	4
1969–70 chrome	6

351ci Cleveland	Interchange Number
1970, all	8

352ci	Interchange Number
1959–64, all	9
1959–64 chrome	10

390ci	Interchange Number
1961–64, all	9
1961–64 chrome	10
1965–70, all	11
1965–70 chrome	12, 13

427ci	Interchange Number
1962–64, all	9
1962–64 chrome	10
1965–68, all	18

428ci	Interchange Number
1966–70, except Cobra Jet, Super Cobra Jet, and police	11
1966–70 Cobra Jet, Super Cobra Jet, and police	13, 14

429ci	Interchange Number
1969–70, except Cobra Jet, Super Cobra Jet, police car, and Boss	15
1969–70 Cobra Jet, Super Cobra Jet, and police	17

Interchange

Interchange Number: 1
 Part Number(s): C6AZ6582G (either side)
 Color: Blue
 Usage: 1963–65 221ci, 260ci, or 289ci, all outputs (without emission controls, both sides); 1965–66 289ci driver's side *only*, except on 1965 289ci four-barrel 210hp

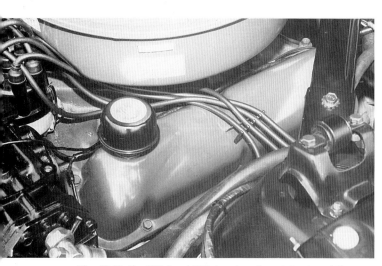

After 1967, the 289ci and 302ci engines (except Boss) used the same valve covers.

Interchange Number: 2
Part Number(s): C6AZ6582G (passenger's side) or C6AZ6582B (driver's side)
Color: Blue
Usage: 1965 to late-1966 289ci and 260ci, all outputs, with emission controls
Note(s): Used until build date May 2, 1966.

Interchange Number: 3
Part Number(s): CC5AE6582D (passenger's side) or C6AZ6582B (driver's side)
Color: Gold
Usage: 1965 289ci four-barrel 210hp
Note(s): Passenger-side is same as in Interchange Number 2.

Interchange Number: 4
Part Number(s): D2OZZ6582D (passenger's side) or D2OZ6582C (driver's side)
Color: Blue
Usage: Very-late-1966–68 289ci, 1968–73 302ci except Boss, 1968–70 Mustang GT 350, and 1969–72 351ci Windsor
Note(s): Late-built full-size cars in 1970 with 351ci Windsor used part number D2OZ6582C on both the driver's and passenger's sides. This change occurred on October 1, 1969.

Interchange Number: 5
Part Number(s): C6ZZ6582A (passenger's side) or C6ZZ6582B (driver's side)
Color: Chrome
Usage: 1963–66 289ci all outputs.
Note(s): Driver's side is the same as passenger's up to 1965 without emission controls. With emission controls from 1965–build date May 1, 1966, part number C6ZZ6582B was used. Part number C6ZZ6582A has no oil-fill hole.

Interchange Number: 6
Part Number(s): C6ZZ6582H (passenger's side) or C6ZZ6582J (driver's side)
Color: Chrome
Usage: Very-late-1966–68 289ci (all outputs), 1968–73 302ci (except Boss), or 1968 302ci in Mustang GT 350, and 1969–72 351ci Windsor
Note(s): Passenger's side has an oil-fill hole.

Interchange Number: 7
Part Number(s): S2MS6A582A (passenger's side)
S2MS6A582A (driver's side)
Color: Cast-aluminum
Usage: 1968–70 Mustang GT 350

Interchange Number: 8
Part Number(s): D2SZ6582GB (fits either side)
Color: Blue
Usage: 1970 351ci Cleveland, all outputs
Note(s): Also used on the driver's side only on 1971–72 351ci Cleveland and those with Cobra Jet.

Interchange Number: 9
Part Number(s): C3AZ6582L (passenger's side) or C3AZ6582J (driver's side)
Color: Painted
Usage: 1960–64 352ci or 390ci, 1962–63 406ci, and 1962–64 427ci, all outputs

Interchange Number: 10
Part Number(s): C3AZ6582F (passenger's side) or C3AZ6582G (driver's side)
Color: Chrome
Usage: 1960–64 352ci and 390ci, 1962–63 406ci, and 1962–64 427ci, all outputs

Interchange Number: 11
Part Number(s): C7AZ6582A (fits either side)
Color: Painted
Usage: 1965–70 390ci, 1965–67 352ci, and 1966–68 428ci (except Cobra Jet and Super Cobra Jet)

Interchange Number: 12
Part Number(s): C6OZ6582B (driver's side) or C6OZ6582A (passenger's side)
Color: Chrome
Usage: 1965–67 390ci, 1965–67 352ci, and 1966–67 428ci
Note(s): Driver's side is used on both sides on 1968–70 cars with 390ci or 428ci engines.

Interchange Number: 13
Part Number(s): C6OZ6582B (either side)
Color: Chrome
Usage: 1968–70 390ci and 1968–71 428ci (except Super Cobra Jet and Cobra Jet after build date February 14, 1969)
Note(s): Also used on the driver's side in 1965–68 models. Not used on Cobra Jet models after above date. Interchange Number 14 will fit.

Interchange Number: 14
Part Number(s): C9ZZ6582B (fits either side)
Color: Cast-aluminum
Usage: 1969–70 428ci Super Cobra Jet and 1969–70 428ci Cobra Jet after build date February 14, 1969
Note(s): Also used on driver's side on 429ci Cobra Jet and Super Cobra Jet.

Interchange Number: 15
Part Number(s): D1VZ6582A (passenger's side) or C8SV6582B (driver's side)
Color: Painted
Usage: 1968–71 429ci, except Cobra Jet, Super Cobra Jet, and police car

Interchange Number: 16
Part Number(s): D1OZ6582D (passenger's side) or DOOZ6582A (driver's side)
Color: Cast-aluminum
Usage: 1968–71 429ci Cobra Jet, Super Cobra Jet, and police car
Note(s): Also used on both sides on 1969–70 428ci Cobra Jet and Super Cobra Jet

Interchange Number: 17
Part Number(s): DOAZ6582B (fits either side)
Color: Cast-aluminum
Usage: 1969–70 429ci Boss

Interchange Number: 18
Part Number(s): C7AZ6582C (fits either side)
Color: Chrome
Usage: 1965–68 427ci

Interchange Number: 19
Part Number(s): C9ZZ6582C (fits either side)
Color: Cast-aluminum
Usage: 1969–71 302ci Boss

Chapter 2

Fuel Systems

Fuel Tanks

Model Identification

Cyclone	Interchange Number
1964–65, all	10
1966–69, all	1
1970, all	2

Cougar	Interchange Number
1967–68, all	6
1969, all	11
1970, all	7

Fairlane, Torino, Ranchero	Interchange Number
1959, all except Ranchero and with retractable hardtop	13
1959 Ranchero	14
1959 retractable hardtop	15
1960, all	16
1961, all	17
1962–65, all	3
1966–69, all except Ranchero	4
1966–69 Ranchero	5
1970, all except Ranchero	2
1970 Ranchero	12

Mustang	Interchange Number
1964-1/2–67, all	6
1969, all	11
1970, all	7

Interchange

Interchange Number: 1
> Part Number(s): C6GY9002C
> Capacity: 20gal
> Usage: 1966–69 Comet, Cyclone, and Montego—all body styles

Interchange Number: 2
> Part Number(s): DOOZ9002D or DOOZ9002E (California cars)
> Capacity: 22gal or 20gal (California cars)
> Usage: 1970 Ford Fairlane, Torino, and Montego (all body styles except station wagon)

Interchange Number: 3
> Part Number(s): C2OZ9002A
> Capacity: 16gal
> Usage: 1962–65 Fairlane and Mercury Meteor (all body styles except station wagon)

Interchange Number: 4
> Part Number(s): C8OZ9002F
> Capacity: 20gal
> Usage: 1966–69 Fairlane—all body styles except station wagon and pickup
> Note(s): Originally ,1966 models used a 16gal tank, except with 390ci, which used a 20gal unit. If replacing an original 16gal tank with a 20gal unit, swap fuel-level float and gauge from the 20gal unit.

Interchange Number: 5
> Part Number(s): DOOZ9002C
> Capacity: 20gal
> Usage: 1966–69 Ranchero, 1964–65 Comet station wagon, and 1965–70 Falcon station wagon

Interchange Number: 6
> Part Number(s): C5ZZ9002D
> Capacity: 16gal
> Usage: 1964-1/2–68 Mustang (all body styles) and 1967–68 Cougar (all body styles)

Interchange Number: 7
> Part Number(s): DOZZ9002A or DOZZ9002B (California cars)
> Capacity: 22gal
> Usage: 1970 Mustang and 1970 Cougar

Interchange Number: 10
> Part Number(s): C4GY9002A
> Capacity: 16gal
> Usage: 1964–65 Comet—all body styles except station wagon

Interchange Number: 11
> Part Number(s): C9ZZ9002A
> Capacity: 20gal
> Usage: 1969 Mustang and Cougar

Interchange Number: 12
> Part Number(s): DOOZ9002A or DOOZ9002B (California cars)
> Capacity: 22gal or 20gal (California cars)
> Usage: 1970 Ranchero only; no other interchange

Interchange Number: 13
> Part Number(s): B9AA9002A
> Capacity: 20gal
> Usage: 1959 full-size Ford—all body styles except Ranchero, station wagon, or retractable hardtop convertible

Interchange Number: 14
> Part Number(s): B9AA9002A
> Capacity: 20gal
> Usage: 1959 Ranchero and 1959 full-size Ford station wagon

Interchange Number: 15
    Part Number(s): B8AA9002B
    Capacity: 17.5gal
    Usage: 1958–59 full-size Ford retractable hardtop convertible (will
        not fit soft-top convertible)

Interchange Number: 16
    Part Number(s): COAA9002Z
    Capacity: 20gal
    Usage: 1960 full-size Ford—all body styles except station wagon

Interchange Number: 17
    Part Number(s): C1AA9002E
    Capacity: 20gal
    Usage: 1961 full-size Ford—all body styles except station wagon

Gas Caps

Model Identification

Cyclone	*Interchange Number*
1965–69 non-locking	5
1965–69 locking	19
1970 non-locking	4
1970 locking	20

Fairlane and Torino	*Interchange Number*
1959–61 non-locking	15
1962–65 non-locking	16
1962–65 locking	18
1966–69, except Ranchero, non-locking	2
1966–69, except Ranchero, locking	19
1966–69 Ranchero, non-locking	1
1966–69 Ranchero, locking	17
1970, except Ranchero, non-locking	4
1970, except Ranchero, locking	20
1970 Ranchero, non-locking	3

Mustang	*Interchange Number*
1964-1/2–66, except fastback and GT models	6
1964-1/2–66 GT models	7
1967–68, except fastback	6
1967–68 fastback, except GT models, GT 350, and GT 500	9
1967–68 GT models	7, 10
1967–68 GT 350 and GT 500	8
1968 GT/CS	9
1969, except GT, GT 350, GT 500, and Mach I models	6
1969 GT models	11
1969 Mach I without GT package	12
1969 GT 350 and GT 500, except GT/CS	5
1969 GT/CS	4
1970, except GT, GT 350, GT 500, and Mach I	6, 13

This cap was used on 1964-1/2–66 Mustang fastbacks or GT models.

This pop-off style cap was used on 1967–68 Mustang GT models.

1970 Mach I and GT models	14
1970 GT 350 and GT 500, except GT/CS	5
1970 GT/CS	4

Mustang Locking Caps	*Interchange Number*
1964-1/2–68, except GT, GT 350, GT 500, or with pop-up-type cap	17

This gas cap was used on 1969–70 Mach I without GT package.

Interchange

Interchange Number: 1
Part Number(s): CODZ9030D
Type: Vented, chrome finish
Usage: 1967–69 Ranchero,1960–63 Falcon, and 1963–69 Falcon station wagon

Interchange Number: 2
Part Number(s): C6OZ9030A
Type: Zinc-plated, 2.5in inside diameter
Usage: 1966–69 Fairlane (all except station wagon and pick-up), 1960–63 Galaxie except station wagon, and 1969–70 Mark III (without emissions in 1970)

Interchange Number: 3
Part Number(s): DOOZ9030A (non-vented, California models) or DOOZ9030B (vented, 49-state models)
Type: Vented (49-state models) or non-vented (California models)
Usage: 1970 Ranchero only; no interchange

Interchange Number: 4
Part Number(s): DOAZ9030A (vented, 49-state models) or DOAZ9030B (non-vented, California models)
Type: Vented (49-state models or California models)
Usage: 1970 Torino (all except station wagon and pickup), 1970 Galaxie (all body styles), 1970 Mustang GT 350 and 500 (non-vented, California models), 1970 Montego (all body styles), 1970 full-size Mercurys (all body styles), 1970 Mark III (non-vented, California models), and 1970 Cougar

Interchange Number: 5
Part Number(s): C7AZ9030A
Type: Vented, 2.47in diameter
Usage: 1965–67, Comet, 1968–69 Montego, 1965–70 full-size Mercury, 1970 Lincoln (without emissions), 1967–69 Cougar (except Eliminator), 1965–68 Meteor (all but station wagon), 1969–70 Meteor (all body styles), 1969–70 Mustang GT 350 and GT 500 (without emissions), 1965–68 Galaxie (except station wagon), and 1969–70 Galaxie (all body styles except 1970 California cars)

Interchange Number: 6
Part Number(s): C9ZZ9030A
Type: Special cap with Mustang emblem
Usage: 1964–70 Mustang except GT, GT 350, GT 500, and 1969–70 Mach I fastback

Interchange Number: 7
Part Number(s): C7ZZ9030C
Type: Special cap with GT emblem
Usage: 1966–67 Mustang GT only

Interchange Number: 8
Part Number(s): C82X9030A
Type: Special model usage
Usage: Used on Shelby 1967–68 GT 350 and GT 500

Interchange Number: 9
Part Number(s): C8ZZ9030C
Type: Pop-off cap with the Mustang emblem
Usage: 1967 Mustang fastback (except GT) and 1968 GT/CS

Interchange Number: 10
Part Number(s): C8ZZ9030D
Type: Pop-off cap with GT logo
Usage: 1967–68 Mustang GT only

Interchange Number: 11
Part Number(s): C9ZZ9030B
Type: Pop-off cap
Usage: 1969 Mustang GT models (except GT 350 and GT 500)

Interchange Number: 12
Part Number(s): C9ZZ9030C
Type: Pop-off cap
Usage: 1969 Mach I non-GT cars

Interchange Number: 13
Part Number(s): DOZZ9030A (vented, 49-state cars) or DOZZ9030B (non-vented, California cars)
Type: Vented (49-state cars) or non-vented (California cars)
Usage: 1970 Mustang (except Mach I), GT 350, and GT 500

Interchange Number: 14
Part Number(s): DOZZ9030D (non-vented, California cars) or DOZZ9030E (vented, 49-state cars)
Type: Pop-off cap, vented or non-vented
Usage: 1970 Mach I only (with or without GT package)

Interchange Number: 15
Part Number(s): B9AZ9030A
Type: Vented
Usage: 1959–61 full-size Ford

Interchange Number: 16
Part Number(s): C5AZ9030A
Type: Vented
Usage: 1962–65 Fairlane, 1965–68 full-size Ford, and 1965–66 Thunderbird

Interchange Number: 17
Part Number(s): C4RZ9030A
Type: Vented 3.75in-outside-diameter locking cap
Usage: 1964–68 Mustang (except pop-up type), 1970 Mustang (except fastback), 1967–69 Ranchero, 1965 Falcon, and 1967 Comet wagon

Interchange Number: 18
Part Number(s): C4RZ9030B
Type: Vented 2.25in-outside-diameter locking cap
Usage: 1965 Fairlane (except station wagon), 1966–70 Fairlane station wagon, 1965–68 Galaxie station wagon, 1965–66 Thunderbird, 1965–68 Meteor station wagon, 1965–69 Lincoln, and 1965–68 Mercury station wagon
Note(s): Will fit 1962–64 Fairlane.

Interchange Number: 19
Part Number(s): C4RZ9030C
Type: 2.25in-outside-diameter locking cap
Usage: 1965–69 Comet except station wagon, 1967–69 Cougar, 1967–70 Thunderbird, 1966–70 Falcon (up to build date January 1, 1970), 1967–68 full-size Mercury (except station wagon), 1969–70 full-size Mercury (all body styles), 1970 Mark III (without emissions), 1965–71 Meteor (except station wagon in 1965–68), and 1968–69 Torino (except Ranchero and station wagon)
Note(s): Will fit 1966–67 Fairlane. Interchange Number 20 will fit.

This gas cap was used on 1967–68 models without GT package.

Interchange Number: 20
    Part Number(s): DOOZ9030C
    Type: Locking cap
    Usage: 1970 Torino (except Ranchero) and 1970 Montego
        (except station wagon)

Fuel Pump

Model Identification

Interchange

Interchange Number: 1
    Part Number(s): C3AZ9350M
    ID number: 3734-S
    Manufacturer: Carter
    Usage: 1963–65 289ci, with oil pressure gauge
    Note(s): ID number on flange.

Interchange Number: 2
    Part Number(s): C3AZ9350B
    ID number: 3911-S
    Manufacturer: Carter
    Usage: 1965 289ci to build date February 25, 1965
    Note(s): ID number on flange.

Interchange Number: 4
    Part Number(s): C5AZ9350B
    ID number: 4193
    Manufacturer: Carter
    Usage: After February 25, 1965, through 1967 289ci V-8, except
        271hp and GT 350 Mustang
    Note(s): ID number on flange.

Interchange Number: 5
    Part Number(s): C6ZZ9350A
    ID number: 4201
    Manufacturer: Carter
    Usage: 1966–67 271hp 289ci—all models
    Note(s): ID number on flange.

Interchange Number: 6
    Part Number(s): S7MK9350
    Manufacturer: Carter
    Usage: 1967–68 GT 350 with Paxton supercharger
    Note(s): Pump is electric.

Interchange Number: 7
    Part Number(s): C8OZ9350A
    ID number: 4567
    Manufacturer: Carter
    Usage: 1968–69 289ci, 1968–69 302ci (except Boss), and 1969
        351ci Windsor (except full-size models)
    Note(s): ID number on flange.

Interchange Number: 8
    Part Number(s): C9ZZ9350A
    ID number: 4910-S
    Manufacturer: Carter
    Usage: 1969–71 302ci Boss engine
    Note(s): ID number on flange.

Interchange Number: 9
    Part Number(s): DOAZ9350B
    ID number: 4896-S or -SA
    Manufacturer: Carter
    Usage: 1970–72 302ci two-barrel—all models
    Note(s): ID number is on flange.

Interchange Number: 10
    Part Number(s): DOAZ9350A
    ID number: 4888-S
    Manufacturer: Carter
    Usage: 1970–72 351ci Windsor
    Note(s): ID number is on flange.

Interchange Number: 11
    Part Number(s): DOAZ9350A
    ID number: DOAE-E and 4861-S
    Manufacturer: Carter
    Usage: 1970–72 351ci Cleveland—all models
    Note(s): ID number on flange. Will also fit 1971 351ci Boss.

Interchange Number: 12
    Part Number(s): C3AZ9350R
    ID number: 3909-S
    Manufacturer: Carter
    Usage: 1966 Fairlane GT, 1966 Cyclone GT, 1965 full-size Ford,
        and 1965 full-size Mercury—all with 390ci four-barrel
    Note(s): Replaced with Part Number C3AZ9350U (ID Number
        4314-S).

Interchange Number: 13
    Part Number(s): C6AZ9350B
    ID number: 4194-S
    Manufacturer: Carter
    Usage: 1967 Fairlane GT, 1967 Cyclone GT, 1967 Mustang GT,
        1967 Cougar GT, 1968 Torino GT, 1968 Cyclone GT, 1966
        Fairlane with 390ci (except GT models), 1966 Comet with
        390ci (except Cyclone GT), 1966 Mustang with 390ci (except
        GT), and 1966 full-size Mercury with 410ci engine
    Note(s): ID number on flange.

Interchange Number: 14
Part Number(s): C7SZ9350A
ID number: 4385-S
Manufacturer: Carter
Usage: 1968 390ci, except GT models, and 1969 390ci four-barrel (except full-size models)
Note(s): ID number on flange.

Interchange Number: 15
Part Number(s): COAZ9350C
ID number: 0294
Manufacturer: Carter or Motorcraft
Usage: 427ci built from 1965 to February 1, 1967

Interchange Number: 16
Part Number(s): C7AZ9350B
ID number: 4442
Manufacturer: Carter
Usage: Late-1967 427ci V-8
Note(s): Begins at build date February 1, 1967

Interchange Number: 17
Part Number(s): C7AZ9350A
ID number: 4441-S
Manufacturer: Carter
Usage: 1968 427ci and 1968–70 428ci Cobra Jet
Note(s): ID number on flange.

Interchange Number: 18
Part Number(s): C9AZ9350A
ID number: 4842-S
Manufacturer: Carter
Usage: 1970 429ci Super Cobra Jet and 1970 429ci Boss
Note(s): ID number on flange.

Interchange Number: 19
Part Number(s): DOOZ9350A
ID number: 4907-S
Manufacturer: Carter
Usage: 1970–71 429ci Cobra Jet and 1969–71 429ci police car
Note(s): ID number on flange.

Interchange Number: 20
Part Number(s): DOVY9350A
ID number: DOVE-C
Manufacturer: Carter
Usage: 1969–72 429ci (except Cobra Jet, Super Cobra Jet, and 429ci Boss); also used in police cars.

Interchange Number: 21
Part Number(s): B55SZ9350C
ID number: C3RA-B
Manufacturer: Airtex
Usage: 1959–62 352ci (except high-performance and multiple carburetor), 1961–62 390ci (except high-performance and multiple carburetor), and 1958–62 292ci
Note(s): ID number on tag.

Interchange Number: 22
Part Number(s): COAZ9350E
ID number: 6974
Manufacturer: N/A
Usage: 1962–64 427ci, 1960–64 352ci high-performance and police car, and 1961–64 390ci high-performance
Note(s): Interchange Number 15 will fit.

Interchange Number: 23
Part Number(s): C6AZ9350B
ID number: 40425 or 4194-S
Manufacturer: Carter
Usage: 1966–70 428ci (except Cobra Jet, Super Cobra Jet, and police car) and 1966–69 390ci in full-size cars

Intake Manifolds
To conserve space, the two-barrel intakes are not covered here. Intakes are made of either cast-iron or cast-aluminum. The latter is

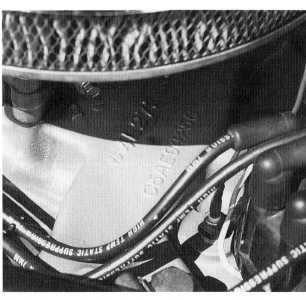

Manifolds can be identified by their casting number, which is very similar to the part number. This unit was for 1966–67 390ci engines.

more commonly found on special high-performance applications, but may fit lesser-powered engines of the same size.

A casting number can be found on the intake manifold. Note that the casting number may change slightly but the manifold will still fit. For example, the 1967 casting C7AE may change to C8AE in 1968, although it is still the same manifold.

Model Identification

289ci	Interchange Number
1963 four-barrel	1
1964 four-barrel	2, 3
1965–68, except GT 350	3
1965–68 GT 350	4

302ci	Interchange Number
1968 four-barrel	3
1969–70 Boss 302ci	5

351ci	Interchange Number
1969 Windsor four-barrel	6
1970 Cleveland four-barrel	7

352ci	Interchange Number
1959–61, except high-performance	8
1959–61 high-performance four-barrel	9
1965–66 four-barrel	10

390ci	Interchange Number
1960–61 four-barrel	9
1965 four-barrel	10
1966–67 four-barrel	11
1968 four-barrel, except GT models	22
1968 four-barrel GT models	18
1969–70 four-barrel, except GT models	23
1969–70 four-barrel GT models	18

427ci	Interchange Number
1962–65 four-barrel	12
1962–65 four-barrel SOHC	16
1962–65 twin four-barrel SOHC	17
1962–65 twin four-barrel	14
1962–65 twin four-barrel (drag race)	15
1966–67 four-barrel (street)	12
1966–67 twin four-barrel	13
1966–67 twin four-barrel (drag race)	15

428ci

429ci

Interchange

Interchange Number: 1
Part Number(s): C3OZ9424C
Type: Cast
Usage: 1963 289ci, all outputs

Interchange Number: 2
Part Number(s): C4OZ9424B
Type: Cast
Usage: 1964 289ci, all outputs (used until build date August 20, 1964, in Mustangs)

Interchange Number: 3
Part Number(s): C4OZ9424H
Type: Cast
Usage: 1964–68 289ci (except GT 350 models) and 1968 302ci four-barrel
Note(s): Will fit 1969–70 302ci, except Boss, without modification. Use in Mustangs beginning at build date August 20, 1964. Interchange Number 4 will fit with modification to gaskets. Interchange Number 6 is said to fit.

Interchange Number: 4
Part Number(s): C9OZ9424D
Type: Aluminum
Usage: 1965–68 GT 350 Mustang with either 289ci or 302ci

Interchange Number: 5
Part Number(s): C9ZZ9424C
Type: Aluminum
Usage: 1969–70 302ci Boss engine
Note(s): A racing manifold was available under Part Number DOZZ9424A.

Interchange Number: 6
Part Number(s): C9OZ9424B
Type: Cast
Usage: 1969 351ci Windsor four-barrel (used in 1969 only)
Note(s): Interchange Number 3 may fit. Cleveland intake will not fit.

Interchange Number: 7
Part Number(s): DOAZ9424C
Type: Cast
Usage: 1970–71 351ci Cleveland four-barrel
Note(s): 1971 351ci Boss or 351ci Cobra Jet intake will fit but is aluminum.

Interchange Number: 8
Part Number(s): C1AE9424B
Type: Cast
Usage: 1958–61 352ci and 1958–59 332ci (not for high-performance applications)

Interchange Number: 9
Part Number(s): C3AZ9424C
Type: Cast
Usage: 1960 352ci special high-performance, 1960–63 390ci high-performance, and 1961–62 406ci four-barrel

Interchange Number: 10
Part Number(s): C9ZZ9424A
Type: Cast
Usage: 1965–66 352ci four-barrel and 1965 390ci four-barrel

Interchange Number: 11
Part Number(s): C6AZ9424N
Type: Cast
Usage: 1966–67 390ci four-barrel

Interchange Number: 12
Part Number(s): C6AZ9424M
Type: Cast
Usage: 1965–68 427ci four-barrel

Interchange Number: 13
Part Number(s): C5AZ9424G
Type: Cast
Usage: 1966–67 street-use twin four-barrel (425hp)

Interchange Number: 14
Part Number(s): C8AX9424A
Type: Aluminum single plane
Usage: 1964–65 427ci twin four-barrel (street use)

Interchange Number: 15
Part Number(s): C8AX9424B
Type: Cast tunnel port
Usage: 1964–66 427ci twin four-barrel (drag strip use only)
Note(s): Will fit 1960–65 390ci.

Interchange Number: 16
Part Number(s): C4AE9424C
Type: Race use only
Usage: 1962–64 427ci SOHC with single four-barrel

Interchange Number: 17
Part Number(s): C4AE9424F
Type: Race use only
Usage: 1962–64 427ci SOHC with twin four-barrel

Interchange Number: 18
Part Number(s): C8OZ9424B
Type: Cast
Usage: 1968–69 428ci Cobra Jet, 1968 427ci four-barrel, 1968 428ci police car, and 1968–69 390ci GT
Note(s): Has 1.60in-diameter primary holes and 1.70in-diameter secondary holes. Interchange Number 24 will fit.

Interchange Number: 19
Part Number(s): DOVY9424A
Type: Cast
Usage: 1970 429ci, except Cobra Jet, Super Cobra Jet, and Boss

Interchange Number: 20
Part Number(s): DOOZ9424C
Type: Aluminum
Usage: 1970 429ci Cobra Jet and 1969–70 police car

Interchange Number: 21
Part Number(s): DOOZ9424B
Type: Aluminum
Usage: 1970 Super Cobra Jet and 1970 429ci Boss

Interchange Number: 22
Part Number(s): C8AZ9424C
Type: Cast-iron
Usage: 1968 390ci four-barrel and 1968 428ci (except Cobra Jet, Super Cobra Jet, and police car)

Interchange Number: 23
Part Number(s): C9ZZ9424A
Type: Cast-iron
Usage: 1969–70 390ci four-barrel (except GT models) and 1969–70 428ci (except Cobra Jet, Super Cobra Jet, and police car)
Note(s): Interchange Number 24 will fit.

Interchange Number: 24
Part Number(s): C6AZ9424H
Type: Aluminum
Usage: 1966–69 428ci police car and 1968–70 428ci Super Cobra Jet
Note(s): Will fit 390ci engines.

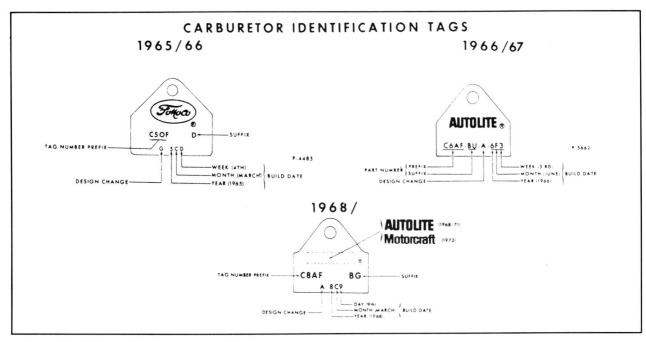

Carburetor identification tags.

Carburetors

Carburetors are identified by appearance and number of venturis. They are also identified by a stamping number on the body or on a tag attached to the carburetor. Most models used a Ford-built (Motorcraft) carburetor but a few Holley carbs were used. Holley carburetors will have the Holley part number stamped on the side of the air horn, but they will also have the Ford-installed ID tag.

The interchange is based on the original replacement part number. This is due to the fact that when carburetors got older they were deleted from use and grouped together. As was the case for the manifolds, the two-barrel carburetors are not covered.

Model Identification

289ci	Interchange Number
1963 four-barrel	1
1964–65, all except 271hp and GT 350	3
1964–65 271hp	2
1964–65 GT 350	6
1966–68, all except 271hp and GT 350	8
1966–68 271hp	2, 5
1966–68 GT 350	6, 7

302ci	Interchange Number
1968 four-barrel, except GT 350	8
1968 GT 350	9, 10
1969–70 Boss, street	11
1969–70 Boss, street machine	13
1969–70 Boss, drag racer	14

351ci	Interchange Number
1969 Windsor	8
1970 Cleveland	8

352ci	Interchange Number
1959–60, all except high-performance	15
1959–60 high-performance	16

390ci	Interchange Number
1960–64, all except high-performance	15, 17
1960–64 high-performance four-barrel	19
1960–64 triple two-barrel	34

	Interchange Number
1964–66, all except GT models	3, 20
1966 GT models	4
1967–68, all except GT models	8, 3
1967–68 GT models	21, 22
1969–70, all except GT models	20
1969–70 GT models	12

427ci	Interchange Number
1962–64 four-barrel	23
1962–64 twin four-barrel	35, 36
1962–64 racing four-barrel	26
1965–67 four-barrel	24
1965–67 twin four-barrel	
1965–67 racing four-barrel	26
1968 four-barrel	25
1968 racing four-barrel	26

428ci	Interchange Number
1966–70, all except Cobra Jet, Super Cobra Jet, and police	3, 12, 20
1968–69 Cobra Jet	26
1970 Cobra Jet	27
1967–70 GT 500	26
1966–70 Super Cobra Jet	26, 27
1966–70 police car	26
1966–70 twin four-barrel	37

429ci	Interchange Number
1969–70, all except Boss, Cobra Jet, Super Cobra Jet, and police car	12, 29, 30
1969 Boss	28
1970 Boss	33
1969–70 Cobra Jet	38
1969–70 Super Cobra Jet	31, 32
1969–70 police car	38

Interchange

Interchange Number: 1
    Part Number(s): C3OZ9510J (replacement)
    Carb ID Number(s): C3OF-AB or C3OF-AJ
    Type: Ford
    Usage: 1963 289ci V-8.

Interchange Number: 2

Part number C5ZZ9510L (replacement)
Carb ID Number(s): C4OF-AL, C4OF-AT, C4OF-BU, C4OF-BU, C4OF-BT, C4ZF-G, or C4ZF-H (1964); C5OF-J, C5OF-K, C5OF-L, C5OF-M, C5OF-T, or C5OF-U (1965)
Type: Ford
Usage: 1964–65 289ci 271hp
Note(s): Interchange Number 21 will fit.

Interchange Number: 3

Part Number(s): C9AZ9510AE (replacement stamped CA689A)
Carb ID Number(s): C5ZF-C, C5ZF-D, C5ZF-E, C5ZF-F, C5ZF-J, C5ZF-K, C5ZF-L, or C5ZF-M (1965); C6ZF-A, C6ZF-B, C6PF-H, C6ZF-E*, C6ZF-D#, C6AF-E#, C6OF-D, C6OF-E, C6OF-H#, or C6OF-J* (1966); C7AF-AG or C70F-G (1967)
Type: Ford
Usage: 1965–66 289ci four-barrel (except 271hp), 1965–67 390ci (except GT), and 1966 428ci (except police car)
Note(s): *With automatic transmission in California. #With manual transmission in California.

Interchange Number: 4

Part Number(s): C6OF9510K
Carb ID Number(s): C6OF-N or C6OF-M
Type: Holley
Usage: 1966 390ci GT models

Interchange Number: 5

Part Number(s): C4OZ9510G (replacement carb stamped CA351A)
Carb ID Number(s): DOPF-U, C7ZF-B#, or C7ZF-C*
Usage: 1967 289ci 271hp
Note(s): *With automatic transmission in California. #With manual transmission in California.

Interchange Number: 6

Carb ID Number(s): S2MS9510A
Type: Holley (715cfm)
Usage: 1965–67 GT 350 289ci

Interchange Number: 7

Carb ID Number(s): S8MS9510C
Type: Holley (600cfm)
Usage: 1968 GT 350 only

Interchange Number: 8

Part Number(s): D2AZ9510M (replacement stamped CA788A)
Carb ID Number(s): C7DF-A, C7DF-L, C7DF-AE, C7DF-C#, C7DF-AG#, C7CF-B^, C7DF-M^, C7DF-AF^, C7DF-D*, or C7DF-AH* (1967); C8AF-AS, C8PF-V, C8ZF-D*, or C8ZF-C# (1968); C9ZF-B#, C9ZF-D*, or C9ZF-D^ (1969); DOOF-C*, DOOF-Y*, DOOF-AC*, DOOF-D#, DOOF-Z#, DOOF-AB#, DOOF-C*, DOOF-Y*, DOOF-AC*, DOOF-G+, DOOF-H%, DOOF-AA%, DOOF-AD%, or C7AF-AC= (1970)
Type: Ford
Usage: 1967–68 289ci four-barrel (except 271hp), 1968 302ci four-barrel, 1969 351ci Windsor, 1970 351ci Cleveland four-barrel, and 1967–68 390ci four-barrel (except GT)
Note(s): #With manual transmission and emissions controls. *With automatic transmission and emissions controls. ^With automatic transmission but without emissions controls. +With manual transmission but with air conditioning. %With automatic transmission and air conditioning. =Originally 1967 390ci, except GT models.

Interchange Number: 9

Part Number(s): Same as ID number
Carb ID Number(s): S8MS9510A
Type: Holley 600cfm
Usage: 1968 302ci four-barrel with C4 or C6 automatic in GT 350 Mustang.

Interchange Number: 10

Part Number(s): Same as ID number
Carb ID Number(s): S8MS9510C
Type: Holley 600cfm
Usage: 1968 302ci four-barrel with manual transmission in Mustang GT 350

Interchange Number: 11

Part Number(s): DOZZ9510-Z (stamped CA782)
Carb ID Number(s): C9ZF-J, DOZF-Z, or D1ZF-VA
Type: Holley
Usage: 1969–71 302ci Boss (street version)

Interchange Number: 12

Part Number(s): D3PZ9510E
Carb ID Number(s): C9OF-E*, C9ZF-E#, C9ZF-F*, C7AF-AE#, C7MF-A#, C7AF-AF*, C7MF-B*, C7AF-AV*, C7AF-BA*, C7AF-AG#, C7AF-AD*, C7AF-BJ*, C7MF-E*, C8PF-V#, C8AF-A#, C8AF-AR#, C8AF-AS*, C8AF-B*, C8AF-C*, C9ZF-D*, DOAF-K*, DOAF-AG*, DOAF-AM*, DOAF-AN*, DOAF-L*, DOAF-AL*, DOPF-AF*, D1AF-MA*, D1OF-GA#, D2AF-AA*, D2AF-BA*, C8SF-G*, C8VF-J*, C8SF-H*, C9LF-A*, DOVF-A*, DOVF-C*, D1VF-AA*, D2VF-AA*, D2VF-BA*, D2PF-SA*, or D2VF-BB*
Type: Ford
Usage: 1969 390ci in GT models, 1966–70 428ci (except Cobra Jet, Super Cobra Jet, and police car), 1969–72 429ci (except Cobra Jet, Super Cobra Jet, Boss, and police car), 1968–72 460ci, and 1967 410ci
Note(s): #With manual transmission. *With automatic transmission.

Interchange Number: 13

Part Number/ID Number(s): DOZX9510A
Type: Ford 875cfm
Usage: Racing 302ci Boss
Note(s): Not tagged

Interchange Number: 14

Part Number/ID Number(s): DOZX9510B
Type: Ford 1425cfm
Usage: Ultra-high-rpm racing application 302ci Boss
Note(s): Not tagged

Interchange Number: 15

Part Number(s): C5SZ9510-A
Carb ID Number(s): COAE-K*, COAE-J#, C4A-R, C4A-N, C4AF-DF, C4AF-DG, C4AF-EH, C4AF-DF, C4AF-DG, C4AF-DZ, or C4AF-EA
Type: Ford
Usage: 1960–64 390ci with automatic transmission, except as noted below
Note(s): #1959–60 352ci with manual transmission. *1959–60 352ci with automatic transmission.

Interchange Number: 16

Part Number(s): COAE9510AA
Carb ID: COAE-AA
Type: Holley
Usage: 1960 352ci high-performance

Interchange Number: 17

Part Number(s): C3AZ9510AL
Carb ID Number(s): C1AE-AG or C1AE-AK (1961–62); C3AF-AV or C3AF-AT (1963)
Type: Ford
Usage: 1961–63 390ci with manual transmission

Interchange Number: 18

Part Number(s): CSF9510AB (replacement)
Carb ID Number(s): C1AE-AH, LSA1TA, LSA1TB, C1AE-AL, LSA1XA, or LSA1XB (1961); C2AF-U, C2AF-N, C2AF-S, C2AF-T, C2AF-Y, C2AF-Z, or C2AF-AK (1962); C3AF-BZ or C3AF-BV (1963); C4AF-DH, C4AF-DJ, C4AF-DV, or C4AF-DY (1964); C5SF-A or C5SF-B (1965)
Type: Ford
Usage: 1961–65 390ci with automatic transmission

Interchange Number: 19
Part Number(s): C3AZ9510G (replacement stamped CA280)
Carb ID Number(s): C1AE-AM
Type: Holley
Usage: 1961 390ci high-performance and 1961 406ci

Interchange Number: 20
Part Number(s): C9AZ9510AE
Carb ID Number(s): C4AF-DK, C4AF-DL, C4AF-EF, or C4AF-DU
(1964); C5AF-E or C5AF-Z (1965), C6PF-H, C60F-D, C60F-E,
C60F-J, C6SF-A, C6AF-AC, C6MF-E, C6MF-F, C6AF-AF, C6AF-
AG, or C6AF-E (1966), C7AF-AR, C7AF-F, C7AF-M, C8AF-AE,
or C8AF-BG (1967–68)
Type: Ford
Usage: 1964–69 390ci, 1966–67 410ci, and 1966–69 428ci
(except Cobra Jet, Super Cobra Jet, and police car)

Interchange Number: 21
Part Number(s): C9AZ9510-U (replacement stamped CA769)
Carb ID Number(s): C7OF-A#, C7OF-B*, C7OF-C^, or C8OF-C^
Type: Holley
Usage: 1967 390ci GT and 1968 390ci GT with manual transmission
Note(s): #With manual transmission but without emissions controls. *With automatic transmission but without emissions controls. ^With manual transmission and with emissions controls.

Interchange Number: 22
Part Number(s): C8OZ9510D (replacement stamped CA583)
Carb ID: C7OF-D or C8OF-D
Type: Holley
Usage: 1967–68 390ci GT with automatic transmission and emissions controls

Interchange Number: 23
Part Number(s): C3AE9510B
Carb ID Number(s): C3AE-B (Holley number 2668)
Type: Holley
Usage: 1963–64 427ci with single four-barrel

Interchange Number: 24
Part Number(s): C5AF9510BV
Carb ID Number(s): C5AF-BV
Type: Holley
Usage: 1965–67 427ci with single four-barrel

Interchange Number: 25
Part Number(s): C9OZ9510N
Carb ID Number(s): C8AF-AD
Type: Holley
Usage: 1968 427ci with single four-barrel

Interchange Number: 26
Part Number(s): C9AZ9510U
Carb ID Number(s): C8OF-AA, C8OF-AB, C9AF-U, C9AF-M,
C9AF-ED, C9AF-N, or C9AF-XX
Type: Holley
Usage: 1962–68 427ci with racing medium-high-riser intake and automatic transmission, 1967–68 Mustang GT 500, 1968 428ci Cobra Jet with automatic transmission, 1968 428ci police car, and 1968–69 Super Cobra Jet

Interchange Number: 27
Part Number(s): DOZZ9510H
Carb ID Number(s): DOZF-G, DOZF-H, DOZF-U, DOZF-T, DOZF-AA, DOZF-AB, DOZF-AC, DOZF-AD, or DOZF-XZ
Type: Holley
Usage: 1970 428ci Cobra Jet and Super Cobra Jet
Note(s): Will fit 1969–70 GT 500 Mustangs.

Interchange Number: 28
Part Number(s): C9AZ9510S
Carb ID Number(s): C9AF-S
Type: Holley
Usage: 1969 429ci Boss

Interchange Number: 29
Part Number(s): D2AZ9510D
Carb ID Number(s): DOAF-K, DOAF-AG, DOAF-AM, or DOAF-AN
Type: Ford
Usage: 1970–71 429ci (except Cobra Jet, Super Cobra Jet, or Boss) with automatic transmission

Interchange Number: 30
Part Number(s): D3PZ9510E
Carb ID Number(s): DOAF-L#, DOAF-AL#, DOPF-AF, DOAF-K,
DOAF-AG, DOAF-AM, DOAF-AN, D1MF-GA, D1AF-MA,
D1OF-GA, D2AF-AA, D2AF-BA, C9LF-A, C8SF-G, C8SF-H,
C9LF-A, C8SF-G, DOVF-A, DOVF-C, D1VF-AA, DOPF-AF,
D1VF-CA, D1VF-DA, D2VF-AA, D2VF-BA, D2PF-SA, or D2VF-BB
Type: Ford
Usage: 1970–72 429ci (except Cobra Jet, Super Cobra Jet, and Boss) and 1968–72 460ci
Note(s): #Originally with four-speed manual transmission. All others originally with automatic transmission but will fit 1970 cars with manual transmission.

Interchange Number: 31
Part Number(s): DOOF9510N
Carb ID Number(s): DOOF-A, DOOF-B, or DOOF-N
Type: Holley
Usage: 1970 429ci Super Cobra Jet with manual transmission

Interchange Number: 32
Part Number(s): DOOZ9510N
Carb ID Number(s): DOOF-R
Type: Holley
Usage: 1970 429ci Super Cobra Jet with automatic

Interchange Number: 33
Part Number(s): DOZZ9510H
Carb ID Number(s): DOOF-S, DOZF-G, DOZF-H, DOZF-U, DOZF-T, DOZF-AA, DOZF-AB, DOZF-AC, or DOZF-AD
Type: Holley
Usage: 1970 429ci Boss

Interchange Number: 34
Part Number(s): center carbs C1AE9510AV (Holley number 2436A); outboard carbs C1AE9510AU (Holley number 2437A)
Carb ID Number(s): center carbs C1AE-AV (Holley number 2436A); outboard carbs C1AE-AU (Holley number 2437A)
Type: Holley
Usage: 1961–63 390ci and 406ci with triple two-barrel carburetion
Note(s): These are for the full-sized Ford and Mercury. Thunderbirds used C2SEA (center) and C2SE-E (outboard) and will interchange.

Interchange Number: 35
Part Number(s): C2AE9510-CB
Carb ID Number(s): C2AE-CB
Type: Holley
Usage: 1962 406ci 427ci with twin four-barrels

Interchange Number: 36
Part Number(s): C3AE9510-C
Carb ID Number(s): C3AE-C
Type: Holley
Usage: 1963–65 406ci and 427ci twin four-barrels

Interchange Number: 37
Part Number(s): C5AF9510BD
Carb ID Number(s): C5AF-BC or C5AF-BD
Type: Holley
Usage: 1966-70 427ci and 428ci with twin four-barrels

Interchange Number: 38
Part Number(s): DOOZ9510B
Carb ID Number(s): DOOF-E (automatic transmission) or DOOF-F (manual transmission)
Type: Rochester
Usage: 1969–70 429ci Cobra Jet and 1969–70 429ci police car

Air Cleaners

Air cleaners are identified by their basic shape and design. There are two basic designs: those used with ram air systems and those without. Those with ram air used a system of seals or air duct assemblies to draw cold air into the carburetors.

An identification number (the location of which varies but is usually on the base) is used on the air cleaner. The number may be stamped or applied as a decal.

Model Identification

289ci	Interchange Number
1964–68, all except 271hp	31
1964–68 271hp, all except California	2
1964–68 271hp California	1

302ci	Interchange Number
1968 Cyclone without ram air	35
1968 Cyclone with ram air	n/a
1968 Cougar without ram air	35
1968 Cougar with ram air	n/a
1969 Cougar Eliminator without ram air	36
1969 Cougar Eliminator with ram air	n/a
1970 Cougar Eliminator without ram air	3
1970 Cougar Eliminator with ram air	n/a
1968 Torino without ram air	35
1968 Torino with ram air	n/a
1968 Mustang, all except GT 350	12
1968 Mustang GT 350	n/a
1969 Mustang (except Boss) without ram air	12
1969 Mustang (except Boss) with ram air	23
1969 Mustang GT 350	32
1969 Mustang Boss without ram air	12
1969 Mustang Boss with ram air	23
1970 Mustang (except Boss) without ram air	n/a
1970 Mustang (except Boss) with ram air	21
1970 Mustang GT 350	32
1970 Mustang Boss without ram air	3
1970 Mustang Boss with ram air	20

351ci Windsor	Interchange Number
1969 Cyclone without ram air	37
1969 Cyclone with ram air	33
1970 Cyclone with ram air	21
1969 Cougar without ram air	37
1969 Torino without ram air	37
1969 Mustang without ram air	37
1969 Mustang with ram air	33

Many different high-performance engines used this open-element air cleaner.

351ci Cleveland	Interchange Number
1970 Cyclone without ram air	34
1970 Cyclone with ram air	22
1970 Cougar without ram air	34
1970 Torino without ram air	34
1970 Torino with ram air	38, 28
1970 Mustang without ram air	34
1970 Mustang with ram air	22

352ci	Interchange Number
1959–67 four-barrel	6

390ci	Interchange Number
1961–65 four-barrel	6
1961–65 triple two-barrel	15
1966, all except GT models	6
1966 GT models	2
1967 Fairlane and Comet, all except GT models	6
1967 Mustang and Cougar, all except GT models	7
1967 Fairlane and Comet GT models	5
1967 Mustang and Cougar GT models	8
1968, all except GT models	9

The 1963–65 289ci used an air cleaner like this.

1970 302ci engine without Ram Air used this air cleaner.

1968 289ci 271hp used this type of air cleaner, which was also used in the 1969 302ci four-barrel engine, including Boss, without Ram Air.

1968 GT models	10
1969, all except GT models	11
1969 GT models	12, 36
1969 with ram air, except Mustang	26
1969 Mustang with ram air	23
1970, all without ram air	13
1970 Mustang with ram air	22

427ci	*Interchange Number*
1964–65 four-barrel	14
1964–65 twin four-barrel	16
1966–68 four-barrel	2
1966–68 twin four-barrel	16

428ci	*Interchange Number*
1966–68, all except Cobra Jet	2
1966–68 Cobra Jet	12, 17
1969 with ram air, all except Mustang	26, 27
1969 Mustang with ram air	22, 24, 25

429ci	*Interchange Number*
1969–70, all except Cobra Jet, Super Cobra Jet, Boss, and police	39
1969–70 Cobra Jet without ram air	4, 18, 19
1969–70 Cobra Jet with ram air	3
1969–70 Super Cobra Jet without ram air	19
1969–70 Super Cobra Jet with ram air	29, 30
1969–70 police car	4, 18, 19
1969–70 Boss	40

Interchange

Interchange Number: 1
Part Number(s): C4OF9600T
ID Number(s): C4OF9600T or C4OF9600R
Type: Closed emission single-snorkel
Dimensions: 14.05in diameter, 2.75in high
Color: Gold bronze
Usage: 1964 289ci 271hp in Fairlane and Comet in California. No other interchange.

Interchange Number: 2
Part Number(s): C5ZZ9600W
ID Number(s): C4DF9600H, C4DF9600L, C4OF9600N, or C4ZF9600Y (1964); C5OF9600C, C5MF9600N, or C5MF9600R (1965); C6AF9600AU, C6AF9600AV, C6AF9600AY, or C6AF9600AZ (1967): C7AF9600J, C7AF9600K, C7ZF9600A, or C7ZF9600B (1966)
Type: Open-element
Dimensions: 14.05in diameter, 2.61in high
Color: Dark Ford Blue tray, chrome cover
Usage: 1964–67 289ci 271hp in all models (except 1964 California cars), 1961–62 390ci police car, 1966–68 428ci in Galaxie 7.0 liter, 1966 Fairlane 390ci GT, 1966 Cyclone GT 390ci, and 1962–68 427ci

Interchange Number: 3
Part Number(s): DOOZ9600C
ID Number(s): DOOF9600C, DOZF9600C, or DOZF9600R
Type: Special snorkel-type air cleaner
Dimensions: 16.79in diameter, 3.66in high
Color: Dark Ford Blue, chrome cover
Usage: 1970 302ci Boss without ram air, 1970 429ci Cobra Jet with ram air in Torino GT and Cyclone GT, and 1970 Cougar Eliminator 302ci without ram air

Twin four-barrel engines used this type of air cleaner.

1970 351ci Cleveland used the same air cleaner regardless of carburetor size.

Interchange Number: 4
Part Number(s): DOZZ9600A
ID Number(s): DOGF96OOC or DOOF9600E
Type: Special snorkel-type air cleaner
Dimensions: 16.79in diameter, 3.66in high
Color: Dark Ford Blue
Usage: 1970 429ci Cobra Jet without ram air and 1971 Boss 302ci
Note(s): 1970 460ci base is the same; just replace chrome lid.

Interchange Number: 5
Part Number(s): C7OZ9600B
ID Number(s): C7OF9600A or C7OF9600B
Type: Unsilenced
Dimensions: 17.25in diameter, 4.22in high
Color: Dark Ford Blue, chrome cover
Usage: 1967 390ci in Fairlane GT or Cyclone GT

Interchange Number: 6
Part Number(s): C3AZ9600P
ID Number(s): C5AF9600T, C5AF9600U, or C5AF9600 (1965);
C6AF9600D, C6AF9600E, C6AF9600F, C6AF9600G,
C6AF9600AN, C6AF9600AR, C6AF9600AS, C6AF9600AT,
C6GF9600A, or C6GF9600L (1966); C7AF9600L,
C7AF9600M, C7AF9600N, C7AF9600R, C7AF9600S, or
C7AF9600T (1967)
Type: Single-snorkel cake-pan-style tray
Dimensions: 17.25in diameter, 4.22in high
Color: Dark Ford Blue
Usage: 1966–67 Fairlane and Comet 390ci (except GT), 1959–67
full-size with 390ci or 352ci

Interchange Number: 7
Part Number(s): C7SZ9600A
ID Number(s): C7SF9600A, C7ZF9600J, C7ZF9600K, or
C7ZF9600XA
Type: Single-snorkel
Dimensions: 16.79in diameter, 3.66in high
Color: Dark Ford Blue, chrome cover
Usage: 1967 390ci in Mustang and Cougar, except GT

Interchange Number: 8
Part Number(s): C7ZZ9600F
ID Number(s): C7ZF9600E or C7ZF9600F
Type: Unsilenced closed tray
Dimensions: 16.79in diameter, 3.66in high
Color: Dark Ford Blue, chrome cover
Usage: 1967 Mustang GT 390ci, 1967 Cougar 390ci GT only, and
1968 Mustang GT (Canada only)

Interchange Number: 9
Part Number(s): C8OZ9600A
ID Number(s): C8OF9600A
Type: Single-snorkel
Dimensions: 17in diameter, 4.20in high
Color: Ford Blue
Usage: 1968 Torino 390ci, 1968 Montego 390ci, 1968 Cougar
390ci, and 1968 Mustang 390ci—all except GT

Interchange Number: 10
Part Number(s): C8OZ9600B
ID Number(s): C8OF9600B
Type: Unsilenced closed tray
Dimensions: 17in diameter, 4.20in high
Color: Ford Blue tray, chrome cover
Usage: 1968 Torino GT 390ci, Cyclone GT 390ci, 1968 Mustang
GT 390ci, and 1968 Cougar GT 390ci

Interchange Number: 11
Part Number(s): C9OZ9600E
ID Number(s): C9OF9600E or C9OF9600L
Type: Single-snorkel
Dimensions: 16.79in diameter, 3.66in high
Color: Ford Blue
Usage: 1969 Torino 390ci, 1969 Montego 390ci, 1969 Mustang
390ci, and 1969 Cougar 390ci—all except GT

Interchange Number: 12
Part Number(s): C8OZ9600C
ID Number(s): C8OF9600C or C8OF9600E
Type: Unsilenced closed tray
Dimensions: 16.79in diameter, 3.66in high
Color: Ford Blue, chrome cover
Usage: 1969 Torino GT 390ci, Mustang GT 390ci, Cougar GT
390ci, Cyclone GT 390ci, 1969 428ci Cobra Jet (until build
date February 19, 1969), and 1969 Boss Mustang 302ci—all
without ram air

Interchange Number: 13
Part Number(s): DOAZ9600C
ID Number(s): DOAF9600D or DOAF9600C
Type: Single-snorkel
Dimensions: 16.79in diameter, 3.66in high
Color: Ford Blue, chrome cover
Usage: 1970 Mustang 390ci, 1970 Cougar 390ci, 1970 Torino
390ci, 1970 Montego 390ci, and 1970 428ci full-size Ford
and Mercury

Interchange Number: 14
Part Number(s): C5AZ9600R
ID Number(s): C4AF9600AY or C5AF9600R
Type: Open-element design
Dimensions: 14.05in diameter, 3.40in high
Color: Chrome top and tray
Usage: 1964–65 427ci and 1961–62 406ci with single four-barrel

Interchange Number: 15
Part Number(s): C2OZ9600A
ID Number(s): C2SZ9600A
Type: Open-element design
Dimensions: Oval in design
Color: Cast
Usage: 1961–63 390ci and 406ci with triple two-barrels

Interchange Number: 16
Part Number(s): C5MY9600B
ID Number(s): C5MF9600G, C5MF9600V, C5AF9600AR
C5AF9600AS, C5AF9600V, or C5AF9600Y
Type: Open-element design
Dimensions: Oval in design
Color: Chrome
Usage: 1962–67 406ci and 427ci with twin four-barrels

*Several different Mustang engines used this type of air cleaner in 1969
and 1970.*

Interchange Number: 17

Part Number(s): C9OZ9600H
ID Number(s): C9OF9600H or C9OF9600M
Type: Special single-snorkel design
Dimensions: 16.79in diameter, 3.66in high
Color: Blue tray, chrome cover
Usage: 1969 428ci Cobra Jet models after build date February 17, 1969
Note(s): Models before February 17, 1969, used Interchange Number 12.

Interchange Number: 18

Part Number(s): DOOZ9600A
ID Number(s): DOOF9600A or DOOF9600D
Type: Single-snorkel
Dimensions: 17.84in diameter, 4.20in high
Usage: 1970 429ci Cobra Jet without ram air

Interchange Number: 19

Part Number(s): DOOZ9600E
ID Number(s): DOGF9600C, DOOF9600E, DOOF9600H, or DOZF9600K
Type: Single-snorkel design
Dimensions: 16.79in diameter, 3.66in high
Color: Blue tray with chrome cover
Usage: 1970 429ci Super Cobra Jet without ram air

Interchange Number: 20

Part Number(s): DOZZ9600N
ID Number(s): DOZF9600N
Type: Used with Shaker-style ram air
Dimensions: 18.83in diameter
Ram-Air Accessories: Shaker scoop DOZZ9D646A (white) or DOZZ9D646 (black)
Usage: 1970 Boss 302ci Mustang with ram air

Interchange Number: 21

Part Number(s): DOZZ9600G
ID Number(s): DOZF9600G
Type: Single-snorkel design with plain intake tube for ram-air shaker scoop
Dimensions: 18.83in diameter, 6.14in high
Ram-Air Accessories: DOZZ9D646A (white) or DOZZ9D646 (black)
Usage: 1970 Mustang 351ci Windsor two-barrel

High-performance 352ci engines in 1960 used the Thunderbird air cleaner.

Interchange Number: 22

Part Number(s): DOZZ9600S
ID Number(s): DOZF9600S or DOZF9600AA
Type: Single-snorkel (has a vacuum cap on the tube) for use with Shaker-style ram-air scoop
Dimensions: 18.83in diameter, 6.25in high
Ram-Air Accessories: Shaker scoop C9ZZ9D646A
Usage: 1969 Mustang 351ci Windsor, 1969 Mustang 428ci Cobra Jet, 1970 Mustang 390ci four-barrel, and 1970 Mustang 351ci two- or four-barrel Cleveland—all with ram air

Interchange Number: 23

Part Number(s): C9ZZ9600J
ID Number(s): C9ZF9600J
Type: Single-snorkel with trap-door in air cleaner lid; seals to scoop on hood
Dimensions: 18.83in diameter, 5.82in high
Ram-Air Accessories: Rubber seal with motor operates trap-door
Usage: 1969 Mustang 302ci, 351ci, and 390ci with ram air

Interchange Number: 24

Part Number(s): DOZZ9600F
ID Number(s): DOZF9600F
Type: Single-snorkel trap-door in air cleaner lid
Dimensions: 18.83in diameter, 5.50in high
Usage: 1969 Mustang to February 17, 1969, with 428ci Cobra Jet

Interchange Number: 25

Part Number(s): C9ZZ9600F
ID Number(s): C9ZF9600F
Type: Single-snorkel, with provisions for air-cleaner-to-hood seal
Dimensions: 18.83in diameter, 5.50in high
Usage: 1969 428ci Cobra Jet models after February 17, 1969
Note(s): Marked Cobra Jet.

Interchange Number: 26

Part Number(s): CZZ9600B
ID Number(s): C9ZF9600B or C9ZF9600D
Type: Single-snorkel with trap-door in top
Dimensions: 18in diameter, 6.20in high
Usage: 1969 Torino GT and Cyclone GT until build date February 17, 1969, all engines

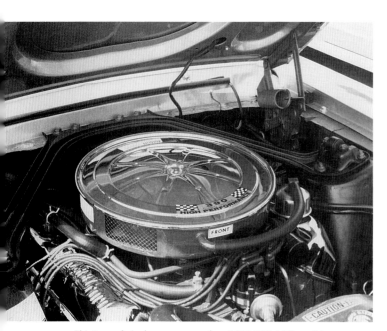

This type of air cleaner was used on 1968 390ci GT models.

Interchange Number: 27
Part Number(s): C9ZZ9600G
ID Number(s): C90Z9600G
Type: Single-snorkel, provision for hood-to-air-cleaner seal
Dimensions: 18in diameter, 6.20in high
Usage: Late-1969 Torino GT and Cyclone GT with 428ci Cobra Jet after build date February 17, 1969

Interchange Number: 28
Part Number(s): DOOZ9600E
ID Number(s): DOOF9600E, DOOF9600H, or DOZF9600K
Type: Single-snorkel with provisions for seals
Dimensions: 17in diameter, 7in high
Usage: 1970 Torino GT and Cyclone GT 351ci four-barrel only

Interchange Number: 29
Part Number(s): DOOZ9600C
ID Number(s): DOOF9600C
Type: Single-snorkel with provisions for seals
Dimensions: 18.83in diameter, 5.56in high
Usage: 1970 Torino GT 429ci Super Cobra Jet and 1970 Cyclone GT 429ci Cobra Jet

Interchange Number: 30
Part Number(s): DOZZ9600F
ID Number(s): DOOF9600F
Type: Single-snorkel with provisions for seals
Dimensions: 18.83in diameter, 5.34in high
Usage: 1970 Torino GT and Cyclone GT 429ci Super Cobra Jet

Interchange Number: 31
Part Number(s): C7AF9600F
ID Number(s): C7AF9600F
Type: Single-snorkel
Color: Blue
Dimensions: 14.62in diameter, 4.10in high
Usage: 1964–68 289ci four-barrel, except 271hp

Interchange Number: 32
Part Number(s): C9ZZ9600B
ID Number(s): C9ZF9600B
Type: Single-snorkel
Color: Chrome cover, blue tray
Dimensions: 18in diameter, 4.98in high
Usage: 1969–70 GT 350 and GT 500

Interchange Number: 33
Part Number(s): C9ZZ9600H
ID Number(s): C9ZF9600H
Type: Single-snorkel ram air
Dimensions: 18.83in diameter, 6.14in high
Usage: 1969 Mustang 351ci Windsor with ram air

Interchange Number: 34
Part Number(s): DOZZ9600M
ID Number(s): DOZF9600M or DOZF9600Z
Type: Single-snorkel.
Color: Blue
Dimensions: 17in diameter, 4.20in high
Usage: 1970 Mustang and Cougar 351ci Cleveland two-barrel or four-barrel without ram air

Interchange Number: 35
Part Number(s): C5ZZ9600D
ID number: C5ZF9600H, C7LF9600C, or C7LF9600D
Type: Single-snorkel
Color: Blue
Size: 17.25in diameter, 4.22in high
Usage: 1968 Montego, Torino, or Cougar 302ci four-barrel

Interchange Number: 36
Part Number(s): C9OZ9600G
ID number: C9OF9600G or C9WF9600A
Type: Single-snorkel
Color: Blue
Size: 18in diameter, 6.20in high
Usage: 1969 Cougar Eliminator 302ci four-barrel without ram air, 1969 Cyclone 428ci Cobra Jet without ram air, and 1969 Cyclone GT 390ci without ram air

Interchange Number: 37
Part Number(s): C8AZ9600D
ID number: C8AF9600D, CAF9600G, or CAF9600C
Type: Single-snorkel
Color: Blue
Size: 17.84in diameter, 4.20in high
Usage: 1969 351ci Windsor four-barrel; 1969 302ci two-barrel; and 1968 Montego, Torino, and Cougar 390ci two-barrel

Interchange Number: 38
Part Number(s): DOOZ9600E
ID number: DOOF9600E, DOOF600C, or DOOZ600H
Type: Single-snorkel with trap-door in top
Size: 17in diameter, 7in high
Usage: 1970 351ci Cleveland four-barrel with ram air

Interchange Number: 39
Part Number(s): DOOZ9600B
ID number: DOOF9600B, DOOF600C, or DOOZ600H
Type: Single-snorkel with trap-door in top
Size: 17.84in diameter, 4.20in high
Usage: 1969–70 429ci, except Cobra Jet, Super Cobra Jet, Boss, and police, and with ram air.

Interchange Number: 40
Part Number(s): C9ZZ9A600A
ID number: Not stamped
Type: Tray used a foam seal
Usage: 1969–70 429ci Boss Mustang

Chapter 3

Oiling and Cooling Systems

Oil Pans

Model Identification

289ci	Interchange Number
1963–66, all	1
1967–68, all	2

302ci	Interchange Number
1968–70, all except Boss	2
1968–70 Boss	3

351ci	Interchange Number
1969–70 Windsor, all	4
1969–70 Cleveland two-barrel	5
1969–70 Cleveland four-barrel	6

352ci	Interchange Number
1959, all	7
1960–65, all except special high-performance	8
1960–65 special high-performance	9

390ci	Interchange Number
1961–65, all except special high-performance	8
1961–65 special high-performance	9
1966–70, all	10

427ci	Interchange Number
1964–65, all	11
1966, all	12
1967, all	13

428ci	Interchange Number
1966–70, all except Cobra Jet, Super Cobra Jet	10
1966–70 Cobra Jet	14
1966–70 Super Cobra Jet	14
1966–70 police car	14

429ci	Interchange Number
1969–70, all except Boss	15
1969–70 Boss	16

Interchange

Interchange Number: 1
Part Number(s): C5AZ6675B
Usage: 1963–66 289ci—all models except Lincoln and full-size Mercury
Note(s): The 260ci V-8 uses the same pan and will interchange. Interchange Number 2 will fit.

Interchange Number: 2
Part Number(s): DOOZ6675C
Usage: 1967–68 289ci (all models except Lincoln) and 1968–74 302ci V-8 (all models except Boss Mustang and Cougar Eliminator)

Interchange Number: 3
Part Number(s): DOZZ6675A
Usage: 1969–71 302ci Boss Mustang and 1969–70 Cougar Eliminator; has deep sump and drain bolt on the side

Interchange Number: 4
Part Number(s): C9OZ6675A
Usage: 1969–74 351ci Windsor; not for use on Cleveland-built blocks

Interchange Number: 5
Part Number(s): DOAZ6675A
Usage: 1970–74 351ci two-barrel Cleveland and 1972–74 400ci Cleveland—all models

Interchange Number: 6
Part Number(s): D1ZZ6675
Usage: 1970–72 351ci Cleveland four-barrel, 1971–72 Boss 351ci, and 1971–72 351ci Cobra Jet

Interchange Number: 7
Part Number(s): B8A6675A
Usage: 1958-59 Ford 352ci or 332ci and 1958 Edsel Ranger

Interchange Number: 8
Part Number(s): C6AZ6675A
Usage: 1960–65 Ford full-size and 1961–66 Mercury 352ci and 390ci, except special high-performance

Interchange Number: 9
Part Number(s): C1AE6675F
Usage: 1960–62 352ci or 390ci with special high-performance or multiple carburetors (all models except Thunderbird)

Interchange Number: 10
Part Number(s): C6OZ6675A
Usage: 1966–70 390ci, 1966–70 428ci (except 1969–70 428ci Cobra or 428ci Super Cobra Jet), and 1968 427ci

Interchange Number: 11
Part Number(s): C1AE6675F
Usage: 1961–62 406ci and 1964–65 427ci (full-size models only)

Interchange Number: 12
Part Number(s): C1AZ6675G
Usage: 1966 427ci full-size Ford or Mercury
Note(s): Will fit Fairlane or Comet if 427ci is swapped in. May fit Mustang with 427ci swap.

Interchange Number: 13
Part Number(s): C7AZ6675A
Usage: 1967 427ci full-size Ford and Mercury and 1967 427ci Fairlane and Comet
Note(s): Will fit 1967 Mustang or 1967 Cougar if 427ci is installed.

Interchange Number: 14
Part Number(s): C9ZZ6675D
Usage: 1968–70 428ci; Cobra Jet, 1968–70 Super Cobra Jet, 1968–70 Torino police car, and 1968–70 Montego police car

Interchange Number: 15
    Part Number(s): DOOZ6675D
    Usage: 1970–73 429ci (except 1969–70 Boss) and 1970–73
        460ci (all except Lincoln Town Car)
    Note(s): Will fit 429ci Cobra Jet and Super Cobra Jet.

Interchange Number: 16
    Part Number(s): C9AZ6675A
    Usage: 1969–70 429ci Boss only; pan has a deep sump with six-
        quart capacity

Oil Pumps

Model Identification

289ci	Interchange Number
1963–68, all	1

302ci	Interchange Number
1968–70, all except Boss	1
1968–70 Boss	2

351ci	Interchange Number
1969–70 Windsor, all	3
1969–70 Cleveland, two-barrel or four-barrel	4

352ci	Interchange Number
1959–64, all except special high-performance or with multiple carbs	5
1959–64 special high-performance 1965–70, all	6

390ci	Interchange Number
1961–64, all except special high-performance	5
1961–64 special high-performance	8
1961–64 police car	7
1965–70, all	10

427ci	Interchange Number
1964–68, all	8

428ci	Interchange Number
1966–70, all except police car, Cobra Jet, and Super Cobra Jet	9
1966–70 Cobra Jet	10
1966–70 Super Cobra Jet	10
1966–70 police car	10

429ci	Interchange Number
1969–70, all except Cobra Jet, Super Cobra Jet, Boss, and police car	11
1969–70 Cobra Jet	12
1969–70 Super Cobra Jet	12
1969–70 Boss	12
1969–70 police car	12

Interchange

Interchange Number: 1
    Part Number(s): C2OZ6600A
    Usage: 1963–67 289ci (all outputs) and 1968–74 302ci (all out-
        puts except Boss)

Interchange Number: 2
    Part Number(s): C9ZZ6600B
    Usage: 1969–71 302ci Boss Mustang and 1969–70 Cougar
        Eliminator

Interchange Number: 3
    Part Number(s): C9OZ6600A
    Usage: 1969–74 351ci Windsor

Interchange Number: 4
    Part Number(s): DOAZ6600A
    Usage: 1970–74 351ci Cleveland, 1971–72 351ci Cobra Jet, and
        1971 351ci Boss

Interchange Number: 5
    Part Number(s): COAZ6600A
    Usage: 1959–64 352ci or 390ci, except high-performance, or
        with multiple carburetors
    Note(s): Interchange Number 6 will fit.

Interchange Number: 6
    Part Number(s): C8AZ6600A
    Usage: 1965–71 352ci and 1965–70 390ci (except police car)

Interchange Number: 7
    Part Number(s): COAE6600C
    Usage: 1960 352ci high-performance and 1961–65 390ci police
        car
    Note(s): Interchange Number 8 will fit.

Interchange Number: 8
    Part Number(s): C3AZ6600A
    Usage: 1961–62 390ci high-performance, 1962–63 406ci, and
        1963–68 427ci

Interchange Number: 9
    Part Number(s): C8AZ6600A
    Usage: 1966–68 428ci, except Cobra Jet, Super Cobra Jet, and
        police car

Interchange Number: 10
    Part Number(s): C9ZZ6600A
    Usage: 1968–70 428ci Cobra Jet and Super Cobra Jet and
        1966–70 police car

Interchange Number: 11
    Part Number(s): C8SZ6600B
    Usage: 1966–69 429ci, except Cobra Jet, Super Cobra Jet, and
        Boss
    Note(s): Interchange 12 will fit.

Interchange Number: 12
    Part Number(s): C9AZ6600A
    Usage: 1969–70 429ci Cobra Jet, 1970 429ci Super Cobra Jet,
        1969–70 429ci Boss, and 1969–70 police car
    Note(s): *Warning*—will fit Interchange Number 11, but not vice
        versa.

Radiator Core

The core is identified by an ID number that is stamped into the top of the core's tank or on the side mounting bracket. Factors that may have influence on the interchanging of cores are model, model year, and engine size.

Dimensions are given when known, but you should not rely on them for interchanging. However, these dimensions can be useful when looking for a larger core, such as might be needed in a high-powered street machine.

Model Identification

Cyclone	Interchange Number
1965–69 289ci, 302ci, and 351ci Windsor	8
1966 390ci, all	12
1967 390ci, all	13
1968–69 390ci without air conditioning, all except GT models	14
1968–69 390ci GT models without air conditioning	15
1968–69 390ci with air conditioning, all	15
1965–69 428ci, all	15
1970 302ci, all	10, 11
1970 351ci, all	11
1970 390ci, all	15
1970 429ci Cobra Jet without air conditioning	16, 17
1970 429ci Cobra Jet with air conditioning	18
1970 429ci Super Cobra Jet	18

Cougar	Interchange Number
1967–69 without air conditioning, all except 302ci Boss, 390ci, 428ci, and 289ci 271hp	20
1967–69 Boss 302ci without air conditioning	21
1967–69 289ci 271hp without air conditioning	21

Interchange

Interchange Number: 1
Identification Number: B9AA8005S
Type: Standard cooling
Dimensions: 24-1/8x18x1-5/8in
Usage: 1957–59 Ford passenger cars

Interchange Number: 2
Identification Number: B9AA8005M
Type: Heavy-duty cooling
Dimensions: 24-1/8x18x1-5/8in
Usage: 1957–59 Ford passenger cars with heavy-duty cooling option

Interchange Number: 3
Identification Number: C3AZ8005C
Type: Standard cooling
Dimensions: 22-1/2x17-1/2x1-1/4in
Usage: 1960–63 Ford with 352ci, 390ci, or 406ci (1961–62 only) with manual transmission

Interchange Number: 4
Identification Number: C3AZ8005B
Type: Standard and heavy-duty cooling; also with air conditioning
Dimensions: 22-1/2x17-1/4x2in
Usage: 1960–63 Ford full-size passenger car with 352ci, 390ci, or 406ci (1961–62 only) with automatic transmission or manual transmission with heavy-duty cooling or air conditioning.

Interchange Number: 5
Identification Number: C2OZ8005H
Type: Standard cooling
Dimensions: 20-1/4x17-3/8x1-1/4in
Usage: 1962–64 Ford Fairlane and Mercury Meteor with 260ci or 289ci (except 271hp) and 221ci with heavy-duty cooling

Interchange Number: 6
Identification Number: C2OZ8005E
Type: With air conditioning
Dimensions: 20-1/4x17-3/8x1-1/4in
Usage: 1962–64 Ford Fairlane and Mercury Meteor 289ci with hang-on (dealer-installed) air conditioning

Interchange Number: 7
Identification Number: C3OZ8005C
Type: Heavy-duty cooling
Dimensions: 20-1/4x17-3/8x2in
Usage: 1963–64 Ford Fairlane and Mercury Meteor with 289ci 271hp and 260ci with heavy-duty cooling

The radiator core can be identified by this number found stamped on top of the tank.

Interchange Number: 8

Identification Numbers: C5OE8005L (1965); C6DE8005D and C60E8005M (1966); C7OE8005E, C70E8005F, C7OE8005J, C7OE8005K, and C7OE8005N (1967); C8OE8005E (1968); C9OE8005G and C9OE8005H (1969)

Type: All

Dimensions: 20-1/4x17-3/8x1-1/4in

Usage: 1965–67 Fairlane, 1968–69 Torino, 1966–69 Comet, and 1968–69 Montego with 289ci (all except 1965 289ci 271hp); 1968–69 Torino; and 1968–69 Montego with 302ci or 351ci Windsor

Note(s): Replacement core. Original core was 17-1/4in wide.

Interchange Number: 10

Identification Number: C9AZ8005C, C9AE8005E, C9AE8005G, or C9AE8005H

Type: Varies with model

Dimensions: 26x17–7/8x2-1/4in

Usage: Late-1970 Torino or 1970 Montego with 302ci with manual transmission and air conditioning; 1969 full-size Ford police car with 390ci or 428ci; 1969 full-size Ford with 428ci or 390ci; and 1970 full-size Mercurys with 429ci without air conditioning

Note(s): Used after build date March 18, 1970.

Interchange Number: 11

Identification Number: DOAE8005A, DOAE8005B, DOAE8005E, DOAE8005F, DOOE8005C, DOOE8005D, or DOOE8005E

Type: Varies with model

Dimensions: 22-11/16x17-27/32x1-1/2in

Usage: Early-1970 Torino or Montego with 302ci manual transmission and air conditioning, 1970 Torino or Montego with six-cylinder, 1970 Torino or Montego with 351ci, and 1970 full-size Ford with 302ci or 351ci two-barrel with standard cooling and without air conditioning

Note(s): Used before build date March 18, 1970.

Interchange Number: 12

Identification Number: C6OE8005F, C6OE8005H, or C6OE8005AA

Type: Heavy-duty cool

Usage: 1966 Fairlane 390ci and 1966 Comet 390ci

Note(s): Will fit cars with 427ci engines.

Interchange Number: 13

Identification Number: C7OE8005C or C7OE8005D

Type: All

Dimensions: 23-1/4x17-3/8x1-1/4in Usage: 1967 390ci or 427ci Fairlane and 1967 390ci or 427ci Comet

Interchange Number: 14

Identification Number: C8OE8005A, C8OE8005B, C8OE8005D, or C8OE8005H

Type: Standard

Dimensions: 24-1/4x17-3/8x1-1/2in

Usage: 1968–69 390ci Torino (except GT) and 1968–69 390ci Montego (except GT models)—all without air conditioning

Interchange Number: 15

Identification Number: C8OE8005F

Type: Varies

Dimensions: 24-1/4x17-3/8x2-1/4

Usage: 1968–69 Torino GT 390ci, 1968–69 Cyclone GT 390ci, 1968–69 Torino 390ci with air conditioning, 1968–69 Montego 390ci with air conditioning (except GT models), 1968–69 Torino GT 428ci Cobra Jet, 1968–69 Cyclone GT 428ci Cobra Jet, and 1968 Montego or Torino with 427ci

Interchange Number: 16

Identification Number: DOAE8005C, DOAE8005D, DOOE8005A, DOOE8005B, DOOE8005B, DOOE8005F, DOOE8005G, or DOOE8005H

Type: Varies

Dimensions: 26x17-7/8x2-1/4

Usage: 1970 Torino or 1970 Montego with 302ci automatic and air conditioning from March 18, 1970; 1970 Torino or Montego with 351ci; 1970 Torino GT or Cyclone GT with 429ci Cobra Jet until build date July 28, 1968; 1970 429ci Torino, except Cobra Jet; 1970 full-size Ford with 351ci, two-barrel, 390ci two-barrel, or 429ci; and 1970 police car with 390ci or 428ci built before July 28, 1969.

Interchange Number: 17

Identification Number: C9AE8005E, C9AE8005G, or C9AE8005H

Type: Standard

Dimensions: 26x17-7/8x1-1/2in

Usage: 1970 Torino GT or 1970 Cyclone GT with 429ci Cobra Jet built after build date July 28, 1969; 1970 full-size Ford with 390ci or 429ci after date July 28, 1968; 1970 full-size Mercury with 390ci or 429ci

Interchange Number: 18

Identification Number: DOOE8005K

Type: Varies

Dimensions: 24-1/4x17-3/8x2-1/4

Usage: 1970 Torino GT or Cyclone GT with 429ci Super Cobra Jet without heavy-duty cooling or air conditioning, and 1970 Torino GT or Cyclone GT with 429ci Cobra Jet with air conditioning

Interchange Number: 19

Identification Number: C3DA8005H, C3DA8005K, C3DA8005L, C3DA8005M, C3DA8005N, C3DE8005HG, C3DE8005M, C3DE8005AT, C3DE8005AZ, C3DE8005BA, or C3DE8005BE (1963); C4DE8005D, C4DE8005S, C4ZE8005H, C4ZE8005M, or C4ZE8005N (1964–65)

Type: All

Dimensions: 17-1/4x17-1/2x1-1/4in

Usage: 1963–65 Falcon, 1963–65 Comet, and 1964-1/2–66 Mustang 260ci or 289ci, all outputs

Interchange Number: 20

Identification Number: C7ZE8005H, C7ZE8005J, C7ZE8005R, C7ZE8005S, C7ZE8005T, C7ZE8005U, or C7ZE8005AD (1967); C8ZE8005H (1968); C9ZE8005C, C9ZE8005D, C7ZE8005G, or C7ZE8005H (1969)

Type: Varies

Dimensions: 20-1/4x16–7/16x1-1/4in

Usage: 1967–69 Mustang and Cougar with 289ci, 302ci, or 351ci with these exceptions: 1968–69 with air conditioning, except for 1968 271hp version, and 302ci Boss

Interchange Number: 21

Identification Number: C8ZE8005E or CZE8005F (1968); CAE8005K (1969)

Type: Varies

Dimensions: 24-3/16x16x1-1/2in

Usage: 1968–69 289ci Mustang and Cougar with air conditioning or heavy-duty cooling options; 1968 Mustang and Cougar with 289ci 271hp (with or without air conditioning); 1968–69 302ci with air conditioning (except Boss); 1969 Boss 302ci Mustang and Cougar Eliminator; 1969 Mustang and Cougar with 351ci two-barrel with air conditioning

Interchange Number: 22

Identification Number: C9ZE8005M (1969); DOZE8005C, DOZE8005D, DOZE8005H, DOZE8005J, DOZE8005K, DOZE8005E, or DOZE8005S (1970)

Type: Varies

Dimensions: 20-1/4x16-7/16x1-1/4in

Usage: 1970 Mustang with six-cylinder or 302ci (all except Boss), 1970 Mustang 351ci two-barrel, 1970 Cougar 351ci without air conditioning or heavy-duty cooling

Note(s): Also found in late-build (after December 16, 1968) 1969 Mustangs with 250ci six-cylinder.

Interchange Number: 23
Identification Number: DOZE8005E
Type: Standard or heavy-duty cooling
Dimensions: 24-3/16x2-1/4in
Usage: 1970 Mustang 302ci Boss and 1970 Cougar 302ci Eliminator

Interchange Number: 24
Identification Number: DOWF8005B, DOZE8005A, DOZE8005B, or DOZE8005G
Type: Varies
Dimensions: 24-3/16x16x2-1/4in
Usage: 1970 Mustang and Cougar with 302ci with air conditioning (except Boss and Eliminator), 1970 Mustang 351ci with air conditioning, and 1970 351ci four-barrel with 3.5:1 axle and without air conditioning

Interchange Number: 25
Identification Number: C7ZE8005G, C7ZE8005V, C7ZE8005Y, or C7ZE8005Z
Type: Varies
Dimensions: 23-1/4x16x2in Usage: 1967 Mustang and Cougar with 390ci V-8 Note(s): Interchange Number 26 will fit, but shorter spacer may be needed.

Interchange Number: 26
Identification Number: C8AE8005A, C8AE8005B, C8AE8005C, C8AE8005K, C8AE8005L, C8AE8005M, C8AE8005S, or CSE8005A (1968); C9ZE8005AE (1969–70)
Type: Varies
Dimensions: 24-3/16x16x2-1/4in Usage: 1968–70 Cougar and 1969–70 Mustang with 390ci, 427ci, 428ci or 429ci (includes Boss and Cobra Jet) and with or without air conditioning

Fan Blade

Fan blades can be identified by their number of blades and diameter. But they can be more quickly identified by the ID number that is stamped on the rear of the face of one of the blades or the center hub. The ID number is given, as is the number of blades and the diameter, if known.

Model Identification

Fans have a number, stamped on the back side of one of the blades, that can be used for identification.

Interchange

Interchange Number: 1
ID Number(s): B9MM-E
Number of Blades: Four
Fan Diameter: 18-1/2in
Drive Type: Standard
Usage: 1959–62 full-size Ford, all engines without air conditioning, except 352ci

Interchange Number: 2
ID Number(s): B8AE-B
Number of Blades: Five
Fan Diameter: 18in
Drive Type: Standard
Usage: 1958–60 Ford full-size with 352ci engine; fan has blunt tips
Note: 1960 models use this fan and the fan in Interchange Number 3. They are not interchangeable.

Interchange Number: 3
ID Number(s): C0AE-D
Number of Blades: Five
Fan Diameter: 18in
Center Hole Diameter: 1in
Drive Type: Standard
Usage: 1960 Ford full-size with 352ci engine; fan has curved tips
Note: 1960 models use this fan and the fan in Interchange Number 2. They are not interchangeable.

Interchange Number: 4
ID Number(s): C0AE-B
Number of Blades: Five
Fan Diameter: 18in
Center Hole Diameter: 5/8in
Usage: 1960 Ford full-size with 352ci and air conditioning; 1960 Thunderbird built before May 13, 1960, with a 430ci engine; and 1961–62 full-size Ford with 292ci but without air conditioning

Interchange Number: 5
ID Number(s): C2AE-A
Number of Blades: Five
Fan Diameter: 18in
Drive Type: Standard
Usage: 1961–62 full-size Ford with 352ci or 390ci without air conditioning; 1962 full-size Ford with 352ci, 390ci, 406ci, or 427ci; and 1963–64 with 18in-diameter fan

Interchange Number: 6
ID Number(s): C1SE-A
Number of Blades: Five
Fan Diameter: 18in
Drive Type: Clutch
Usage: 1961 Ford 352ci and 390ci with air conditioning and 1962 292ci with air conditioning
Note(s): Blades are at rear of spider hub.

Interchange Number: 7
ID Number(s): C2OE-B; C30A-B, C4OE-B, or C5OE-B
Number of Blades: Four
Fan Diameter: 16in
Center Hole Diameter: 5/8in
Drive Type: Standard
Usage: 1962–65 Fairlane; 1963–65 Comet, Falcon, and full-size Ford; and 1964-1/2–65 Mustang with 289ci (except 271hp version)—all without air conditioning

Interchange Number: 8
ID Number(s): C3OE-C, C5OED, C6OE-D, C7AE-F, or C6OE-D
Number of Blades: Five
Fan Diameter: 17-1/4 in
Center Hole Diameter: 5/8in
Drive Type: Standard
Usage: 1963–65 Fairlane, Comet, and Mustang 289ci 271hp; 1966 289ci with emissions; 1966–67 full-size Fords with 289ci without air conditioning; 1967 Mustang 289ci 271hp; 1969 Cougar Eliminator 302ci without fan clutch; and 1971–72 Maverick with six-cylinder

Interchange Number: 9
ID Number(s): C6OE-E, C6OE-F C80E-B, or C5AE-A
Number of Blades: Seven
Fan Diameter: 18-1/4in
Center Hole Diameter: 2-3/8in
Drive Type: Power
Usage: 1966–67 Fairlane GT and Cyclone GT 390ci without air conditioning, 1966–67 Fairlane and Comet 390ci with integrated air conditioning, 1967 Mustang and Cougar with 390ci, 1967–69 Thunderbird with 390ci or 428ci, 1967 models with 427ci, and 1966 full-size Ford with 428ci

Interchange Number: 10
ID Number(s): C8OE-A
Number of Blades: Four
Fan Diameter: 19in
Center Hole Diameter: 5/8in
Drive Type: Standard
Usage: 1968–70 Torino GT and Cyclone GT 390ci without air conditioning; 1970–71 full-size Ford with six-cylinder

Interchange Number: 11
ID Number(s): C8OE-B
Number of Blades: Seven
Fan Diameter: 18-1/4in
Center Hole Diameter: 2-3/8in
Drive Type: Power
Usage: 1968–69 Torino and Montego with 390ci two-barrel or four-barrel with air conditioning; 1968–69 428ci Cobra Jet; 1968 427ci; and 1968–69 Mustang and Cougar with 390ci, 428ci Cobra Jet, or 427ci without air conditioning

Interchange Number: 12
ID Number(s): C6AE-E, C90E-A, C6OE-B, or C1VV-D
Number of Blades: Four
Fan Diameter: 17-1/2in
Center Hole Diameter: 5/8in
Drive Type: Standard
Usage: 1966–69 Mustang and 1967–69 Cougar 289ci or 302ci without air conditioning (except Boss or 271hp 289ci); 1968 Mustang 351ci without air conditioning; 1962–67 Fairlane, Comet, and Meteor 289ci without air conditioning (except 271hp version); 1968–71 Fairlane, Torino, and Montego 302ci or 351ci two-barrel without air conditioning; 1970–72 Mustang and Cougar six-cylinder or 302ci; 1970–72 full-size Ford 302ci or 351ci Windsor without air conditioning; 1966–68 Falcon 289ci without air conditioning; and 1972–74 Maverick six-cylinder

Interchange Number: 13
ID Number(s): C9OE-H
Number of Blades: Six
Fan Diameter: 18in
Center Hole Diameter: 5/8in
Drive Type: Standard
Usage: 1969–70 Torino GT, Cyclone GT, Mustang, and Cougar 428ci Super Cobra Jet without air conditioning; no other interchange

Interchange Number: 14
ID Number(s): C9ZE-E
Number of Blades: Seven
Fan Diameter: 18-1/4in
Center Hole Diameter: 2-5/8in
Drive Type: Power
Usage: 1969–70 428ci Cobra Jet with or without air conditioning (all 1969 models); and 1970 Mustang and Cougar 428ci Super Cobra Jet without air conditioning after August 1, 1969 (before this date, see ID code C9OE-H)

Interchange Number: 15
ID Number(s): C3DE-A
Number of Blades: Six
Fan Diameter: 15in
Center Hole Diameter: 5/8in
Drive Type: Standard
Usage: 1965 Mustang, Fairlane, Comet, and Meteor 289ci with hang-on air conditioning

Interchange Number: 17
ID Number(s): C5AE-B
Number of Blades: Five
Fan Diameter: 17in
Center Hole Diameter: 5/8in
Drive Type: Standard
Usage: 1965 Mustang and Comet 289ci with power steering, heavy-duty cooling, or emissions; 1967 Mustang and Cougar 289ci with manual transmission and without air conditioning; 1969–70 Mustang and Cougar six-cylinder with hang-on air conditioning; and 1965–67 Fairlane six-cylinder with heavy-duty cooling

Interchange Number: 18
ID Number(s): C6OE-C or C6OE-G
Number of Blades: Seven
Fan Diameter: 17-1/2in
Center Hole Diameter: 2-3/8in
Drive Type: Power
Usage: 1966–68 Mustang and Falcon 289ci with air conditioning; 1967–68 Cougar 289ci with air conditioning; 1966–67 Fairlane and Comet 289ci with integrated air conditioning; and 1967 Mustang and Shelby GT 350, all applications

Interchange Number: 19
ID Number(s): C6DE-A
Number of Blades: Five
Fan Diameter: 17-1/2in
Center Hole Diameter: 5/8in
Drive Type: Standard
Usage: 1966 Comet 289ci, 1967 mustang 289ci, and 1966–67 Fairlane 289ci—all with dealer-added hang-on air conditioning

Interchange Number: 20
ID Number(s): C8SE-B, C8SZ-B
Number of Blades: Five
Fan Diameter: 17-1/2in
Center Hole Diameter: 2-3/8in
Drive Type: Power
Usage: 1969 Boss 302ci Mustang and Cougar Eliminator with clutch, 1968–68 Thunderbird 429ci without air conditioning, 1968–70 302ci (except Boss with air conditioning), and 1969–70 351ci with air conditioning

Interchange Number: 21
ID Number(s): C9ZEF and C9ZE-D
Number of Blades: Seven
Fan Diameter: 18in
Center Hole Diameter: 3/4in
Drive Type: Standard
Usage: 1969 429ci Boss Mustang or Cougar; no other interchange

Interchange Number: 22
ID Number(s): C8SE-A
Number of Blades: Four
Fan Diameter: 17-9/16in
Center Hole Diameter: 5/8in
Drive Type: Standard
Usage: 1969–70 Mustang and Cougar 351ci without air conditioning, 1969 Torino and Montego 351ci with heavy-duty cooling, 1971–74 Maverick and Comet 302ci, and 1969–70 Falcon 302ci without air conditioning

Interchange Number: 23
ID Number(s): DOOE-A
Number of Blades: Seven
Fan Diameter: 19in
Center Hole Diameter: 5/8in
Drive Type: Standard
Usage: 1970–71 Mustang, Cougar, Torino, and Cyclone with 429ci Cobra Jet or Super Cobra Jet

Interchange Number: 24
ID Number(s): Unknown
Number of Blades: Five
Fan Diameter: 18in
Drive Type: Standard
Usage: 1959–60 Ford full-size 352ci

Interchange Number: 25
ID Number(s): DOZE-A
Number of Blades: Five
Fan Diameter: 18in
Center Hole Diameter: 1in
Drive Type: Standard
Usage: 1970 429ci Boss Mustang; no other interchange; rare find

Interchange Number: 26
ID Number(s): DOAE-A and D1AE-CA
Number of Blades: Five
Fan Diameter: 18-1/2in
Center Hole Diameter: 5/8in
Drive Type: Standard
Usage: 1971 Mustang and Cougar 302ci two-barrel or four-barrel (Boss); 351ci (including Boss and Cobra Jet) without air conditioning; 1972 Torino, Mustang, and Cougar 351ci Cleveland four-barrel with heavy-duty cooling; and 1970–72 full-size Fords with 351ci and air conditioning

Interchange Number: 27
ID Number(s): C7AE-A and C7AE-C
Number of Blades: Four
Fan Diameter: 19in
Center Hole Diameter: 5/8in
Drive Type: Standard
Usage: 1966–70 390ci without air conditioning (except GT models), 1967 428ci full-size Ford without air conditioning, and 1967 410ci without air conditioning

Interchange Number: 28
ID Number(s): DOSE-A
Number of Blades: Four
Fan Diameter: 19in
Center Hole Diameter: 2-3/8in
Drive Type: Power
Usage: 1969–70 429ci, except Cobra Jet, Super Cobra Jet, or Boss

Fan Drives

Model Identification

289ci	Interchange Number
1963–64 with hang-on air conditioning	2, 3
1965–68 with factory air conditioning	4
1965–68 without air conditioning	7

302ci	Interchange Number
1968–70 with factory air conditioning	4
1968–70 without air conditioning	7

390ci, 427ci, and 428ci	Interchange Number
1966–67 GT models	6

Example of a fan drive.

Interchange

Interchange Number: 1
Part Number(s): C2AZ8A616A
Usage: 1961–62 406ci and 427ci without air conditioning

Interchange Number: 2
Part Number(s): C2OZ8A616A
Dimensions: 3-5/8in deep, 2.56in diameter
Usage: 1962–64 (before October 23, 1963) 289ci with hang-on air conditioning

Interchange Number: 3
Part Number(s): C4AZ8A616A
ID Number(s): C4AA-C
Dimensions: 3-5/8in deep, 2.31in diameter
Usage: After October 23, 1963, to July 1, 1964, 289ci with hang-on air conditioning

Interchange Number: 4
Part Number(s): C6OZ8A616D
ID Number(s): C5OE-D, C6OE-D, or G6OE-G
ID Marks: Blue or yellow stripe
Dimensions: 3-5/8in deep
Usage: 1965–68 289ci with factory air conditioning and 1968 302ci with factory air conditioning

Interchange Number: 5
Part Number(s): C6ZZ8A616A
ID Number(s): C6ZE-A
ID Marks and Dimensions: 3-3/16in deep
Usage: Used with fan marked C6ZZ-A, typically 1966 Mustang before build date January 5, 1966 (after January 5, 1966, uses above unit) with hang-on air conditioning, and 1967 Mustang with hang-on air conditioning

Interchange Number: 6
Part Number(s): C7OZ8A616C
ID Number(s): C6OE-D or C6OE-F (1966); C7ZE-A or C7ZA-B (1967)
Dimensions: 2.91in deep
Usage: 1966–67 Cyclone and Fairlane 390ci with hang-on air conditioning, 1967 Fairlane and Cyclone 427ci without air conditioning, 1967 Mustang with factory air conditioning, and 1967 Mustang and Cougar 390ci with factory air conditioning

Interchange Number: 7
Part Number(s): C8OZ8A616B
ID Number(s): C8OE-B or C8OE-C
Usage: 1968–70 289ci, 302ci, 390ci, 427ci, and 428ci Cobra Jet without air conditioning; 1968 Torino GT and Cyclone GT 390ci, 427ci, and 428ci Cobra Jet without air conditioning

Interchange Number: 8
Part Number(s): C8OZ8A616A
ID Number(s): C8OE-A or C8OE-D
Usage: 1968–69 Torino, Montego, Cougar, or Mustang with 390ci two-barrel or four-barrel with factory air conditioning; also 1968 Mustang 390ci GT without air conditioning

Interchange Number: 9
Part Number(s): C9DZ8A616A
ID Number(s): C9ZE-B
Usage: 1969 Torino GT, Cyclone GT, Mustang, and Cougar with 428ci Super Cobra Jet; 1970 Torino GT, Cyclone GT, Mustang, and Cougar with 428ci Super Cobra Jet until build date August 1, 1969

Interchange Number: 10
Part Number(s): DOOZ8A616A
ID Number(s): DOOE-A
Usage: 1970–71 Torino GT, Cyclone GT, Mustang, and Cougar with 429ci (not used until build date August 1, 1969)

Water Pumps

A point to watch for in early models (those before 1966) is whether an alternator or generator is used. The water pump is grouped with this type of equipment. A water pump from a car with an alternator can fit a car with a generator, but not the other way around. Casting numbers are similar to part numbers (usually only a letter or letter is changed). For example, the part number C6AZ8510A may be cast as C6AE-A. Or it may be C6AE-A in 1966 and C7AE-A in 1967.

Model Identification

Interchange

Interchange Number: 1
Casting/ID Number(s): C2OE8501B or C2OE8501C
Usage: 1962–65 260ci and 289ci with generator, except 271hp
Note(s): This pump has a cast-steel body.

Interchange Number: 2
Casting/ID Number(s): C5AE8501B
Usage: 1962–65 260ci and 289ci with alternator, except 271hp
Note(s): This pump has an aluminum body and was used until change level number 8 on the engine tag. This change occurred around build date May 3, 1965.

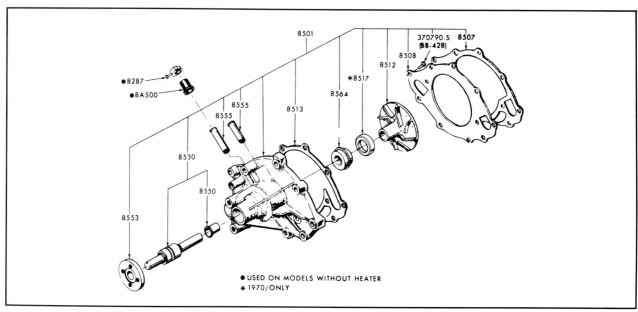

8287 •
8A500 •
8555
8555
8530
8550
8553
8501
8517 *
8564
8513
8512
8508
370790-S (BB-428)
8507

• USED ON MODELS WITHOUT HEATER
* 1970/ONLY

Water pump with cover for late 1965–68 289ci and 1968–70 302 and 351ci Windsor engines.

Interchange Number: 3
Part Number(s): C5AZ8501E
Usage: 1965–68 289ci (except 271hp), 1968–70 302ci (except Boss), and 1969 351ci
Note(s): After change level number 8 on 1965 models (build date approximately April 3, 1965). Interchange Number 4 will fit.

Interchange Number: 4
Part Number(s): D3U8501A
Usage: 1966–68 289ci with A.I.R. (except 271hp), 1968–73 302ci (except Boss), and 1969–73 351ci Windsor
Note(s): When using on a 289ci engine, the water bypass tube must be changed. This replacement part will fit 1962–65 models if the timing chain cover is also swapped.

Interchange Number: 5
Casting/ID Number(s): C3OE8501B
Usage: 1963–65 289ci 271hp; used only with a generator
Note(s): Interchange Number 6 will fit.

Interchange Number: 6
Part Number(s): C5OE-A
Usage: 1965–68 289ci 271hp with alternator
Note(s): Pump is cast-aluminum. It will fit Interchange Number 5 but not vice versa.

Interchange Number: 7
Part Number(s): C9ZZ8501A
Usage: 1969 302ci Boss Mustang or Cougar Eliminator

Interchange Number: 8
Part Number(s): DOZZ8501A
Usage: 1970–71 302ci Boss Mustang or Cougar Eliminator

Interchange Number: 9
Part Number(s): DOAZ8501E
Usage: 1970–72 351ci Cleveland (two-barrel and four-barrel), 1973–74 400ci Cleveland, and 1971 351ci Boss Mustang

Interchange Number: 10
Casting/ID Number(s): EDC8505B
Usage: 1958–60 352ci, except 1960 high-performance

Interchange Number: 11
Part/Casting Number: COAE8501A
Usage: 1960 352ci high-performance

Interchange Number: 12
Casting/ID Number(s): C1AE-A or C1SE-A
Usage: 1961 Ford full-size with 352ci or 390ci, all except 390ci high-performance or with multiple carbs

Interchange Number: 13
Casting/ID Number(s): C2AE8505A
Usage: 1962–65 352ci and 390ci except high-performance

Interchange Number: 14
Casting/ID Number(s): C2AE8505A, C3OE8505A, C4AE8501B, C5AE8501C, or C5AE8501D
Usage: 1961–63 390ci high-performance, 1962–63 406ci, and 1962–63 427ci
Note(s): Some are heavy-duty police types.

Interchange Number: 15
Casting/ID Number(s): C5AE8505A
Usage: 1966–67 Fairlane 390ci, 1966–67 Comet 390ci, 1967 Cougar and Mustang 390ci, and 1967–71 full-size Ford or Mercury 390ci and 428ci
Note(s): Interchange Number 16 will fit.

Interchange Number: 16
Casting/ID Number(s): DOAZ8501D (replacement)
Usage: 1968–70 Torino, Montego, Mustang, or Cougar with 390ci; 1967–68 427ci and 1968–70 428ci Cobra Jet

Interchange Number: 17
Part Number(s): D1VY8501B
Usage: 1970–71 429ci, all applications and all models except 429ci Boss Mustang; 1970 460ci in Lincoln through build date October 4, 1971

Interchange Number: 18
Part Number(s): C9VZ8501A
Usage: 1969–70 429ci Boss Mustang and Cougar Eliminator, 1969 429ci Galaxie, 1969 Mercury 429ci, 1968–69 Thunderbird 429ci, and 1968–69 460ci Lincoln

Chapter 4

Exhaust Systems

Exhaust Manifolds

Manifolds are largely interchangeable in the engine family. High-performance type manifolds can be adapted to non-high-performance heads for better performance.

Model Identification

Interchange

Interchange Number: 1
Part Number(s): C3AZ9430 (right); C3AZ9431B (left)
Usage: 1963 289ci or 260ci—all models
Note(s): The left unit was used on later models (see Interchange Number 2).

Interchange Number: 2
Part Number(s): C3AZ9430F (right); C3AZ9431B (left)
Usage: 1964–65 289ci or 260ci, all except 271hp.
Note(s): The left unit was used on earlier models (see Interchange Number 1).

Interchange Number: 3
Part Number(s): C3OZ9431B (left); C3OZ9430B or C3OZ9430C (right)
Usage: 1963–64 289ci 271hp
Note(s): C3OZ-B was used until build date March 31, 1964. Part Number C3OZ-C was used after this date.

Interchange Number: 4
Part Number(s): C3OZ9431A (left); C5ZZ9430A (right)
Usage: 1964-1/2–67 289ci 271hp
Note(s): Change was approximately March 21, 1964.

Interchange Number: 5
Part Number(s): DOOZ9431D (left); DOAZ9430C (right)
Usage: 1966–68 289ci except 271hp and GT 350; 1968–72 302ci except 302ci Boss.
Note(s): Right manifold used in all lines. Left unit not found in full-size models. 1974–76 302ci manifolds will fit but must be swapped with the hot-air duct and shroud.

Interchange Number: 6
Part Number(s): C9ZZ9430B (right); C9ZZ9431A (left)
Usage: 1969–71 Boss 302ci Mustang and 1969–70 302ci Cougar Eliminator
Note(s): Left manifold will fit both sides of GT 350 models if the Shelby flange is used and you improvise straight pipes from flange to muffler inlets.

Interchange Number: 7
Part Number(s): C9AZ9430A (right); C9OZ9431A (left)
Usage: 1969 351ci Windsor, all car lines and models; 1970 Torino, Montego Mustang, or Cougar two-barrel Windsor only
Note: Right manifold is used on 1970–71 full-size with 351ci Windsor.

Interchange Number: 8
Part Number(s): D2OZ9430B (right); DOAZ9431A (left)
Usage: 1970 Mustang or Cougar 351ci Cleveland two-barrel; 1970–71 Torino and Montego 351ci Cleveland two-barrel
Note(s): Right manifold unit used on 1971–72 full-size Ford with 351ci Cleveland two-barrel, but left manifold from full-size model will not interchange.

Interchange Number: 9
Part Number(s): DOAZ9430B (right); DOAZ9431B (left)
Usage: 1970 Mustang or Cougar 351ci Cleveland four-barrel, 1970–71 Torino and Montego 351ci four-barrel, 1971–72 Mustang and Cougar 351ci Cleveland Cobra Jet four-barrel (right manifold only), and 1972 Torino or Montego 351ci four-barrel (right manifold only)
Note(s): Left manifold on 1971 Mustang and Cougar or 1972 Torino and Montego manifold will not fit.

Interchange Number: 10
Part Number(s): C3SZ9430A (right); B8S9431A (left)
Usage: 1959 352ci in full-size Ford or Mercury and 1958–59 Edsel 361ci
Note(s): Not for use in high-performance applications. Right manifold can be found on later models (see Interchange Number 11).

Interchange Number: 11
Part Number(s): C3SZ9430A (right); C2AZ9431B (left)
Usage: 1960–62 full-size Ford or Mercury 352ci or 390ci, except for high-performance and police car

Interchange Number: 12
Part Number(s): C3AZ9430A (right); C3AZ9431A (left)
Usage: 1959–60 352ci high-performance and 1961 390ci high-performance, all in full-size Ford
Note(s): Will fit non-high-performance models also.

Interchange Number: 13
Part Number(s): C3AZ9430E (right); C3AZ9431E (left)
Usage: 1962 390ci high-performance, 1962–63 406ci (up to build date November 23, 1962), and 1962–64 Ford police car 390ci
Note(s): Will fit non-high-performance models also.

Interchange Number: 14
Part Number(s): C3AZ9430C (right); C3AZ9431F (left)
Usage: 1963 406ci (beginning at build date November 23, 1963) and 1963–64 427ci—both in full-size

Interchange Number: 15
Part Number(s): C3AZ9430A or C3AZ9430D (right); C3AZ9431D (left)
Usage: 1963–64 full-size 352ci or 390ci
Note(s): C3AZ-A was used until build date November 30, 1962; C3AZ-D was used beginning December 1, 1962.

Interchange Number: 16
Part Number(s): C5AZ9430C (right); C5AZ9431C (left)
Usage: 1965–67 full-size 427ci

Interchange Number: 17
Part Number(s): C6OZ9430A (right); C6OZ9431A (left)
Usage: 1966 Comet, Fairlane, and Mustang 390ci
Note(s): Manifolds from a full-size model will not interchange.

Interchange Number: 18
Part Number(s): C6OZ9430A or C9OZ9430B (right); C7OZ9431A (left)
Usage: 1967 Fairlane and Comet 390ci, 1967–70 Mustang and Cougar 390ci, and 1968–70 Torino and Montego 390ci
Note(s): C9OZ-B usage begins at build date February 15, 1968. Manifolds from a full-size model will not fit.

Interchange Number: 19
Part Number(s): C7OZ9430A (right); C7OZ9431C (left)
Usage: 1967 Comet and Fairlane 427ci, 1967–68 Mustang and Cougar 427ci, and 1968 Torino and Montego 427ci

Interchange Number: 20
Part Number(s): C6AZ9430A (right); C3AZ9431D (left)
Usage: 1966–67 full-size 428ci or 390ci, all except police car
Note(s): Left manifold on 1963–65 full-size 390ci or 352ci will fit.

Interchange Number: 21
Part Number(s): C8AZ9430A (right); C8AZ9431B (left)
Usage: 1968 full-size 428ci or 390ci (except police car) and 1969–70 Ford 428ci police car

Interchange Number: 22
Part Number(s): C8OZ9430C (right); C8OZ9431B (left)
Usage: 1968–70 Mustang, Cougar, Torino GT, and Cyclone GT 428ci Cobra Jet and Super Cobra Jet

Interchange Number: 23
Part Number(s): C9OZ9430C (right); C80Z9431B (left)
Usage: 1970 Mustang and Cougar 429ci Cobra Jet and Super Cobra Jet

Interchange Number: 24
Part Number(s): D2OZ9430C (right); DOOZ9431A (left)
Usage: 1970–71 Torino GT and Cyclone with 429ci Cobra Jet or 429ci Super Cobra Jet; 1971 Mustang and Cougar 429ci Cobra Jet (right manifold only)

Interchange Number: 25
Part Number(s): C9AZ9430B (right); C9AZ9431A (left)
Usage: 1969–70 Boss 429ci Mustang

Interchange Number: 26
Part Number(s): D3VY9430B (right); D4VY9431A (left)
Usage: 1970–71 Torino and Montego 429ci (except Cobra Jet, Super Cobra Jet, and police car); 1968–74 Lincoln, Mark III, and Mark IV 460ci

Interchange Number: 27
Part Number(s): S1MS9430A (right); S1MS9431A (left)
Usage: 1965–66 GT 350 Mustang 289ci
Note(s): Interchange Number 6 will fit with modification.

Mufflers

Model Identification
Muffler interchange is based on part number. A muffler can be used in many different applications, from a six-cylinder to a full-out high-performance powerplant like the 427ci. Some original mufflers were stamped with an ID number. Only dual exhaust mufflers are given.

Interchange

Interchange Number: 1
Part Number(s): C7AZ5230AH (either side)
Stamped: C5AA5230K, C5AA5230L, or C5AA5230AG
Usage: 1965–67 full-size Ford with six-cylinder, 289ci two-barrel with single exhaust (except 2-1/2in exhaust); 1965–66 full-size Ford with 352ci or 390ci with dual exhaust, 427ci with dual exhaust; 1965–66 Mercury full-size 390ci four-barrel with dual exhaust; and 427ci

Interchange Number: 2
Part Number(s): C5OZ5230C (left); C5OZ5230D (right)
Stamped: C5OA5230E (right), C5OA5230B (left)
Usage: 1962–65 Fairlane 289ci four-barrel, except 271hp

Interchange Number: 3
Part Number(s): C4OZ5230G (left); C4OZ5230F (right)
Stamped: C4OA5C257B (left); C4OA5C258B (right)
Usage: 1963–65 Fairlane 289ci 271hp

Interchange Number: 4
Part Number(s): C6ZZ5230F (left); C5ZZ5230E (right)
Stamped: C6ZA5C257B and D2ZJ5C258AA (left); C6ZA5C257B and D2ZJU5C257AA (right)
Usage: 1965 Mustang 289ci 271hp, 1965–66 GT 350, and 1966 Mustang with dual exhaust, all engines
Note(s): Used after build date October 15, 1964

Interchange Number: 5
Part Number(s): C5ZZ5230S (left); C5ZZ5230R (right)
Usage: 1964-1/2 Mustang, except 271hp
Note(s): Used before build date October 15, 1964

Interchange Number: 6
Part Number(s): C5ZZ5230C (transverse mounted)
Stamped: C4ZA5230N
Usage: 1964-1/2 Mustang 289ci 271hp and early and 1965 GT 350 Mustang
Note(s): Used after build date October 15, 1964

Interchange Number: 7
Part Number(s): C6OZ5230V (left); C6OZ5230U (right)
Stamped: C6OA5232D (left); C6OA5230BV (right)
Usage: 1966 Fairlane and Comet 390ci engine

Interchange Number: 8
Part Number(s): C5ZZ5230U (left or right)
Stamped: C4RA5230N
Usage: California 1966 Mustang 289ci four-barrel (except 271hp) and 1967–68 Mustang and Cougar 289ci with dealer-installed dual exhaust
Note(s): Mufflers are round in shape.

Interchange Number: 9
Part Number(s): C7AZ5230C (left); C7AZ5230AA (right)
Stamped: C7AA5232AL (left); C7AA5230DV (right)
Usage: 1967 full-size 427ci

Interchange Number: 10
Part Number(s): C7AZ5230Z (left); C7AZ5230S (right)
Stamped: C7AA5232AA (left); C7AA5230BU or C7AA5230BT (right)
Usage: 1967 full-size 428ci (7.0 liter model)

Interchange Number: 11
Part Number(s): C7OZ5230F (left); C7OZ5230E (right)
Stamped: C7OA5230A (left); C7OA5230F (right)
Usage: 1967 Fairlane and Comet 390ci engine

Interchange Number: 12
Part Number(s): C7OZ5230J (left); C7OZ5230H (right)
Stamped: C7OA5232C (left); C7OA5230G (right)
Usage: 1967 Fairlane and Comet 427ci

Interchange Number: 13
Part Number(s): C9ZZ5230E (transverse mounted)
Stamped: C8ZA5230C
Usage: 1967 Cougar with dual exhaust; 1967–68 Mustang 289ci and 390ci GT model; 1967–68 GT 350 and GT 500 models; 1968 Mustang 302ci four-barrel 289ci GT, 390ci, and 427ci; 1969 Mustang 351ci Windsor; and 1969 GT 350 Mustang

Interchange Number: 14
Part Number(s): C9ZZ5230C (transverse mounted)
Stamped: C9ZA5230C
Usage: 1967 Mustang 428ci (except GT 500 and GT 500 KR), 1968–70 Shelby GT 500, 1969 Boss 302ci, and 1969–70 Boss 429ci

Interchange Number: 15
Part Number(s): DOZZ5260R
Stamped: C7OA5230L, ED-C7OA5230L, C8OA5230V1, C8OA5230V2, C8OA5230AA, C8OA5230AB, C8OA5230AC, C8OA5230AD, C8OA5230AE, C8OA5230AE1, C8OA5230AE1, C8OA5230AE2, C8OA5230AF, C8OA5230AJ, C8OA5230AK, C8ZA5230D, C9OA5230H, C9OA5230K, C9OA5230L, C9OA5230M, C9OA5230S, C9OA5230T, C9OA5230U, C9OA5230V, C9OA5230Y, C9ZA5230M, C9ZA5230J, C9ZA5230E, DOAA5230AN, DOAA5230CB, DOOA5230S, DOOA5230V1, DOOA5230V2, DOOA5230Z, DOOA5230Z1, DOOA5230Z2, DOOA5230AA, DOOA5230AB, DOOA5230AC, DOOA5230AD, DOOA5230AE, DOOA5230AF, DOOA5230AL1, DOOA5230AL2, DOOA5230AM, DOZA5230A, DOZA5230G, DOZA5230H, DOZA5230L, DOZA5230M, or DOZJ5230B
Usage: Replacement units with many different applications—1968–71 Torino and Montego sedan and hardtop V-8 with single exhaust, 1968–71 Torino and Montego with dual exhaust, 1968–70 Cougar with single exhaust, 1968–69 Cougar 428ci, 1969–70 Cougar with dual exhaust, and 1968–70 Mustang with single exhaust (except 1968–69 six-cylinder)

Interchange Number: 16
Part Number(s): DOOZ5230N (replacement)
Usage: Replacement unit used in many different applications—1968 Cougar 302ci four-barrel and 390ci and 427ci with dual exhaust, 1968–69 Torino and Montego convertible and Ranchero with 289ci or 302ci two-barrel and single exhaust, 1970–71 Torino and Montego with single exhaust and two-barrel, and 1968–70 Falcon with 302ci and single exhaust

Interchange Number: 17
Part Number(s): DOOZ5230E (left); DOOZ5230F (right)
Stamped: DOZA5232B (left); DOZA5230D (right)
Usage: 1970 Mustang with 302ci Boss and 1969 Mustang 428ci, except with GT package and GT 500

Interchange Number: 18
Part Number(s): DOOZ5230G (left); DOOZ5230H (right)
Stamped: DOZA5235G (left); DOZA5230E (right)
Usage: 1970 Mustang 428ci with GT package only

Interchange Number: 19
Part Number(s): C0AZ5230A (replacement)
Dimensions: 29x6x6in
Usage: 1960–64 Ford full-size, all applications

Tailpipes

In some models the tailpipe includes a built-in resonator and was listed by Ford under the heading of resonator; the sub-part number of "5A289" will designate these. Some pipes are stamped with an ID number.

Model Identification

Cougar	Interchange Number
1967–68 390ci, all	7
1969–70 351ci, all	9

Interchange

Interchange Number: 1
Part Number(s): C5ZZ5A289A (left); C5ZZ5A289B (right)
Stamped: C5ZA5212C (left); C5ZA289B (right)
Dimensions: 51-5/8x2in
With Resonator: Yes
Usage: 1964-1/2 Mustang, except 271hp

Interchange Number: 2
Part Number(s): C5ZZ5255A
Stamped: C5ZA289B (right)
With Resonator: No
Usage: All 1964-1/2 289ci 271hp

Interchange Number: 3
Part Number(s): C7ZZ5255B (left); C7ZZ5255C (right)
Stamped: C7ZA5C207A (left); C7ZA5255A (right)
Dimensions: 18-5/16x2in
With Resonator: No
Usage: 1965–68 Mustang, with dual exhaust and factory-installed, transverse-mounted muffler

Interchange Number: 4
Part Number(s): C9ZZ5255A (left); C9ZZ5255B (right)
Stamped: C9ZA5C203A (left); C9Z5C262A (right)
Dimensions: 27–7/16x2in or 2-1/2in
With Resonator: No
Usage: 1969 Mustang GT with 428ci engine (except GT 500) and 1969–70 Boss 429ci with GT package

Interchange Number: 5
Part Number(s): C9ZZ5255N (left); C9ZZ5255M (right)
Dimensions: 26x2-1/4in
With Resonator: No
Usage: 1969–70 GT 500 Shelby Mustang; used with outer collector stamped S9MS5265A or S9MS5265B (Part Number C9ZZ5255K)

Interchange Number: 6
Part Number(s): C9ZZ5255D (left); C9ZZ5255E (right)
Stamped: C9ZA5C203B (left); C9ZA5C262C (right)
Dimensions: 22-5/8x2-1/4in or 2-1/8in
With Resonator: No
Usage: 1969–70 Mustang with 428ci without GT package and 1969–70 429ci Boss Mustang without GT package

Interchange Number: 7
Part Number(s): C7WY5255A (left); C7WY5255B (right)
Stamped: C7WY5C203A (left); C7WA5C262B (right)
Dimensions: 21x2in
With Resonator: No
Usage: 1967 Cougar with 390ci and dual exhaust

Interchange Number: 8
Part Number(s): DOWY5255ND (left); DOWY5255B (right)
Stamped: DOWJ55257B (left); DOWJ5255B (right)
Dimensions: 47-5/8x1-7/8in (left); 46-7/8x1-7/8in or 2in (right)
With Resonator: No
Usage: 1969–70 Cougar Eliminator 302ci and 1969 Cougar 428ci

Interchange Number: 9
Part Number(s): DOWY5255C (left); DOWY5255A (right)
Stamped: DOWJ55257A (left); DOWJ5255A (right)
Dimensions: 40-1/2x1-7/8in (left); 40x1-7/8in or 2in (right)
With Resonator: No
Usage: 1969–70 Cougar 351ci (two-barrel or four-barrel) and 390ci four-barrel with dual exhaust (with or without GT package)

Interchange Number: 10
Part Number(s): C5OZ5A289A (either side)
Stamped: C5OA5212A
Dimensions: 25-3/8x2in
With Resonator: Yes
Usage: 1962–65 Fairlane with 289ci four-barrel, except 271hp

Interchange Number: 11
Part Number(s): C6OZ5255A (left); C6OZ5255B (right)
Stamped: C6OA5C203B (left); C6OA5C262B (right)
Dimensions: 52-11/16x2in
With Resonator: No
Usage: 1966 Fairlane GT or Cyclone GT with 390ci and dual exhaust

Interchange Number: 12
Part Number(s): C7OZ5255J (left); C7OZ5255K (right)
Stamped: C7OA5C203H (left); C7OA5C262C EDC7 (right)
Dimensions: 34-11/16x2-1/4in
With Resonator: No
Usage: 1967 Fairlane GT or Cyclone GT 390ci and 427ci

Interchange Number: 13
Part Number(s): DOOZ5255C (left); DOOZ5255D (right)
Stamped: DOOJ55257A (left); DOOJ5255B (right)
Dimensions: 34-7/8x1-7/8in
With Resonator: No
Usage: 1968 Torino and Montego 390ci four-barrel, 428ci, or 427ci and factory-installed dual exhaust.

Interchange Number: 14
Part Number(s): DOOZ5255E (left); DOOZ5255F (right)
Stamped: DOOJ55257B (left); DOOJ5255C (right)
Dimensions: 37-1/2x1–7/8in With Resonator: No
Usage: 1968 Torino and Montego 390ci two-barrel; 1969 Torino and Montego 390ci four-barrel with dual exhaust, 428ci, and 427ci (quiet flow); 1970–71 Torino and Montego 351ci Cleveland four-barrel, 429ci "quiet style" except Cobra Jet or Super Cobra Jet.

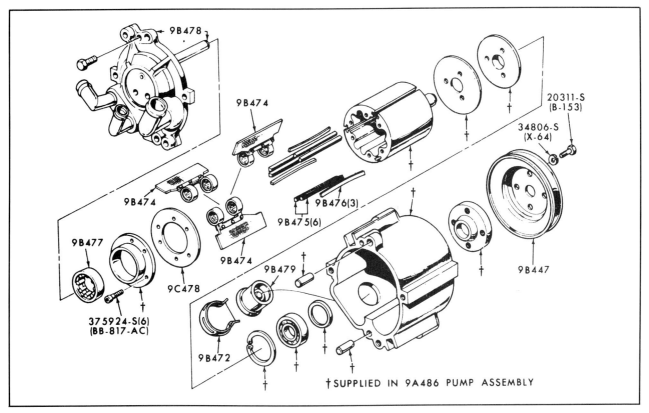

1966–67 style Termactor Emissions Control System Pump. 1968–70 is typical.

Interchange Number: 15
Part Number(s): DOOZ5255G (left); DOOZ5255H (right)
Stamped: DOOJ55257C (left); DOOJ5255J (right)
Dimensions: 49-1/4x1-7/8in or 2-1/4in
With Resonator: No
Usage: 1969 Torino and Montego with 428ci Cobra Jet (all body styles except Ranchero) and 1970–71 Torino or Montego 429ci Cobra Jet or 429ci Super Cobra Jet (all body styles except Ranchero)

Interchange Number: 16
Part Number(s): DODZ5255A (left); DODZ525B (right)
Stamped: DODJ55257A, C7OA5C203E, C7OA5C203F (left); DODJ5C207A (right)
Dimensions: 28-3/8x1-7/8in (left); 36x2in (right)
With Resonator: No
Usage: 1970–71 Ranchero 351ci Cleveland four-barrel and 429ci Cobra Jet with sporty or quiet duals and 1969 Ranchero with 428ci Cobra Jet

Thermactor Exhaust Air Pump

Model Identification

Interchange

Interchange Number: 1
Part Number(s): C6AZ9A486E
Usage: 1966 289ci and 1966–67 390ci, 410ci, and 428ci—all car lines including pickup
Note(s): Intake muffler-type pump with three hoses.

Interchange Number: 2
Part Number(s): C7AZ9A486B
Usage: 1967 289ci in Fairlane, Comet, Mustang, and Cougar
Note(s): Pump has two hoses.

Interchange Number: 3
Part Number(s): C8AZ9A486B
Usage: 1968–71 289ci and 302ci (including Boss), 1968–69 428ci, 1968 427ci; 1969–70 Boss 429ci, 1970 429ci (including Cobra Jet), and 1968–71 460ci—all car lines including pickups

Chapter 5

Transmissions

Four-Speed Manual

Three-speed manual transmissions are not covered here due to their lack of popularity and to conserve space. Two four-speed manual transmissions were used, one built by Warner and the other built by Ford. Certain transmissions are used with high-performance engines, and a non-high-performance transmission should *never* be placed behind a high-performance engine. However, a high-performance transmission can be used behind a non-high-performance engine.

To further identify the transmission, an ID code number is stamped on the case itself or, more commonly, on a metal tag riveted to the case. This information will give you the transmission model number, the build date, and its change level. The tag or stamp location varies, so see illustrations for locations.

Model Identification

Cougar	*Interchange Number*
1967 289ci, all except 271hp, Ford	29
1967 289ci 271hp, Ford	24
1967 390ci, Ford	30
1967 428ci, Ford	34
1968 289ci and 302ci, Ford	31
1968 390ci, 2.78:1 low gear	32
1968 390ci, 2.32: low gear	33
1968 428ci, Ford	34
1969 302ci, 2.32 low gear, all except Eliminator	35
1969 302ci, 2.78 low gear, all except Eliminator	36
1969 302ci Eliminator	24
1969 351ci, 2.32 low gear	35
1969 351ci, 2.78 low gear	36
1969 390ci, 2.32 low gear	37
1969 390ci, 2.78 low gear	38
1969 428ci, Ford	34
1970 302ci, all except Eliminator, 2.32 low gear	40
1970 302ci, all except Eliminator, 2.78 low gear	39
1970 302ci Eliminator	24
1970 351ci, 2.32 low gear	40
1970 351ci, 2.78 low gear	39
1970 428ci, all	41
1970 429ci, all	41

Cyclone	*Interchange Number*
1966–67 289ci, Ford	42
1966–67 390ci, all except GT models	43
1966–67 GT models	13
1968 289ci, all	14
1968 302ci, all	14
1969 351ci Windsor	14
1970 351ci Windsor, 2.32 ratio	19
1970 351ci Windsor, 2.78 ratio	18
1970 Cleveland, 2.32 ratio	16
1970 Cleveland, 2.78 ratio	17
1968–70 390ci, all except GT models	n/a
1968–70 390ci GT models	13
1968–70 427ci, all	15
1968–70 428ci, all	15
1968–70 429ci Cobra Jet	20
1968–70 429ci Super Cobra Jet	20

Fairlane and Torino	*Interchange Number*
1959–61 352ci, Warner	1
1959–61 390ci, Warner	1
1962–64 289ci, all except 271hp, Ford	9
1962–64 289ci 271hp, Warner	7
1962–64 289ci 271hp, Ford	8
1965 289ci, all except 271hp, Warner	11
1965 289ci, all except 271hp, Ford	8
1965 289ci 271hp, Warner	12
1965 289ci 271hp, Ford	10
1966–67 289ci, Ford	42
1966–67 390ci, all except GT models	43
1966–67 390ci GT models	13
1968 289ci, all	14
1968 302ci, all	14
1969 351ci Windsor	14
1970 351ci Windsor, 2.32 ratio	19
1970 351ci Windsor, 2.78 ratio	18
1970 351ci Cleveland, 2.32 ratio	16
1970 351ci Cleveland, 2.78 ratio	17
1968-70 390ci, all except GT models	n/a
1968-70 390ci GT models	13
1968-70 427ci, all	15
1968-70 428ci, all	15
1968-70 429ci Cobra Jet	20
1968-70 429ci Super Cobra Jet	20

Mustang	*Interchange Number*
1964-1/2 289ci, Ford	21
1965 289ci, all except 271hp, Ford	22, 23
1965 289ci, all except 271hp, Warner	25, 26
1965 289ci 271hp, Ford	24
1965 289ci 271hp, Warner	27
1966 289ci, all except 271hp, Warner	28
1966 289ci, all except 271hp, Ford	29
1966 289ci 271hp, Ford	24
1966 390ci, Ford	30
1967 289ci, all except 271hp, Ford	29
1967 289ci 271hp, Ford	24
1967 390ci, Ford	30
1967 428ci, Ford	34
1968 289ci and 302ci, Ford	31
1968 390ci, 2.78:1 low gear	32

Full-Size

Interchange Number

Interchange

Interchange Number: 1
Type: Warner T-10
Part Number(s): C2AZ7003F
ID Code: C2AA-D
Usage: 1959–62 full-size Ford and 1962 full-size Mercury with 352ci, 390ci, or 406ci

Interchange Number: 2
Type: Warner T-10
Part Number(s): C3AZ7003G
ID Code: C3AA-E
Usage: 1963 full-size Ford 352ci, 390ci, or 406ci, all except high-performance
Note(s): Interchange Number 4 will fit.

Interchange Number: 3
Type: Warner T-10
Part Number(s): C3AZ7003H
ID Code: C3AA-F
Usage: 1963 full-size Ford with 390ci high-performance or 406ci high-performance
Note(s): Interchange Number 4 will fit.

Interchange Number: 4
Type: Warner T-10
Part Number(s): C4AZ7003N
ID Code: C3AR-J, C3AR-K, C3AR-K, C4AR-S, C4AR-N, 4A3-N-1, 4A3-S-1 , or 4A3-R-1
Usage: 1963–64 full-size with 427ci, 1964 full-size Ford with 390ci

Interchange Number: 5
Type: Ford-built
Part Number(s): C4AZ7003F
ID Code: HEH-D
Usage: 1964 full-size Ford with 390ci

Interchange Number: 6
Type: Ford-built
Part Number(s): C6AZ7003B
ID Code: HEH-H, HEH-CG, HEH-R, HEH-CB, RUG-G, RUG-G1, RUG-G2, RUG-B, RUG-B1, or RUG-B2
Usage: 1964–67 427ci full-size and 1966–67 428ci full-size.

Interchange Number: 7
Type: Warner T-10
Part Number(s): C3OZ7003H
ID Code: C303G (1963); C303G-1 (1964)
Usage: 1963–64 Fairlane and 1963 Mercury Meteor 289ci 271hp

Interchange Number: 8
Type: Ford-built
Part Number(s): C5OZ7003C
ID Code: HEH-N
Usage: 1964–65 Fairlane 289ci 271hp

Interchange Number: 9
Type: Ford-built
Part Number(s): C5OZ7003F
ID Code: HEH-L or HEH-BN
Usage: 1965 Fairlane 289ci, except 271hp

Interchange Number: 10
Type: Ford-built
Part Number(s): C5OZ7003C
ID Code: HEH-N
Usage: 1965 Fairlane with 289ci 271hp

Interchange Number: 11
Type: Warner T-10
Part Number(s): C3OZ7003L
ID Code: HEK-J; HEK-S
Usage: 1965 Fairlane with 289ci, except 271hp

Interchange Number: 12
Type: Warner T-10
Part Number(s): C3OZ7003K
ID Code: HEK-K
Usage: 1965 Fairlane with 289ci 271hp

Four-speed shifter used in 1964-1/2–67 Mustangs (except T-5 models).

Interchange Number: 13
   Type: Ford-built
   Part Number(s): C6OZ7003H
   ID Code: HEH-CL (1966); RUG-J, RUG-J1, RUG-J2 (1967); or RUG-J2 (1968–69)
   Usage: 1966–67 Fairlane GT, 1966–67 Cyclone GT, 1968–70 Torino GT, and 1968–70 Cyclone GT
   Note(s): GT 390ci model version only. Non-GT 390ci transmissions will not withstand the horsepower of the GT engine.

Interchange Number: 14
   Type: Ford-built
   Part Number(s): C6OZ7003G
   ID Code: RUG-D2
   Usage: 1968 Torino 289ci and 302ci, 1969 Torino 351ci, 1968 Montego 289ci and 302ci, 1969 Montego 351ci, and 1967–68 Falcon 289ci and 302ci

Interchange Number: 15
   Type: Ford-built
   Part Number(s): C9OZ7003D
   ID Code: RUG-AJ
   Usage: 1968–69 Torino 428ci Cobra Jet and Super Cobra Jet and 1967–68 427ci

Interchange Number: 16
   Type: Ford-built
   Part Number(s): DOOZ7003F
   ID Code: RUG-AS or RUG-AS-1
   Usage: 1970–71 Torino, 1970–71 Montego 351ci Cleveland and 2.32:1 transmission low-gear ratio with 31-spline output shaft

Interchange Number: 17
   Type: Ford-built
   Part Number(s): DOOZ7003J
   ID Code: RUG-BA or RUG-B1A
   Usage: 1970 Torino and 1970 Montego with 351ci Cleveland and 2.78:1 transmission ratio

Interchange Number: 18
   Type: Ford-built
   Part Number(s): DOOZ7003D
   ID Code: RUG-AR or RUG-AR1
   Usage: 1970 Torino and 1970 Montego 351ci Windsor and 2.78:1 ratio.

Interchange Number: 19
   Type: Ford-built
   Part Number(s): DOOZ7003E
   ID Code: RUG-AT or RUG-AT1
   Usage: 1970 Torino and Montego 351ci Windsor with 2.32:1 ratio

Interchange Number: 20
   Type: Ford-built
   Part Number(s): DOOZ7003G
   ID Code: RUG-AU or RUG AU-1
   Usage: 1970 Torino and Montego 429ci Cobra Jet or Super Cobra Jet

Interchange Number: 21
   Type: Ford-built
   Part Number(s): C5ZZ7003A
   ID Code: HEG-G
   Usage: 1964-1/2 Mustang 289ci and 260ci
   Note(s): To build date August 20, 1964, with 302ci.

Interchange Number: 22
   Type: Ford-built
   Part Number(s): C5ZZ7003G
   ID Code: HEH-P
   Usage: 1965 Mustang 260ci and 289ci between build dates August 20, 1964, and December 30, 1964

Interchange Number: 23
   Type: Ford-built
   Part Number(s): C5ZZ700R
   ID Code: HEH-BT
   Usage: 1965 Mustang 289ci after build date February 1, 1965

Interchange Number: 24
   Type: Ford-built
   Part Number(s): C5ZZ7003YID
   ID Code: HEH-S, HEH-T, or HEH-BX
   Usage: 1965–67 Mustang 289ci 271hp and 1967 Cougar 289ci 271hp
   Note(s): Will fit 1969–70 Boss 302ci.

Interchange Number: 25
   Type: Warner-built
   Part Number(s): C5ZZ7003L
   ID Code: HEK-M
   Usage: 1965 Mustang 289ci before build date November 23, 1964.

Interchange Number: 26
   Type: Warner-built
   Part Number(s): C5ZZ7003T
   ID Code: HEK-V
   Usage: 1965 Mustang 289ci after build date November 23, 1964

Interchange Number: 27
   Type: Warner-built
   Part Number(s): C5ZZ7003N
   ID Code: HEK-R
   Usage: 1965 Mustang 289ci 271hp

Interchange Number: 28
   Type: Warner-built
   Part Number(s): C6ZZ7003C
   ID Code: HEK-AD
   Usage: 1966 Mustang 289ci, except 271hp

Interchange Number: 29
   Type: Warner-built
   Part Number(s): C6ZZ7003B
   ID Code: HEH-BW
   Usage: 1966–67 Mustang 289ci (except 271hp) and 1967 Cougar 289ci (except 271hp)

Interchange Number: 30
   Type: Ford-built
   Part Number(s): C7ZZ7003B
   ID Code: RUG-M, RUG-M1, or RUG-M2
   Usage: 1966–67 Mustang 390ci, 1967 Cougar 390ci.

Interchange Number: 31
   Type: Ford-built
   Part Number(s): C6ZZ7003E
   ID Code: RUG-E2
   Usage: 1968 Mustang 289ci or 302ci, 1968 Cougar 289ci or 302ci.

Interchange Number: 32
   Type: Ford-built
   Part Number(s): C7ZZ7003C
   ID Code: RUG-M2
   Usage: 1967 Mustang GT 390ci, 1967 Cougar GT 390ci. Both with 2.78:1 low gear ratio.

Interchange Number: 33
   Type: Ford-built
   Part Number(s): C8ZZ7003A
   ID Code: RUG-AD
   Usage: 1967 Mustang GT 390ci and Cougar GT 390ci—both with 2.32:1 low-gear ratio

Interchange Number: 34
   Type: Ford-built
   Part Number(s): C8ZZ7003D
   ID Code: RUG-S, RUG-AE, RUG-AE1, or RUG-AE2
   Usage: 1967–68 Mustang and Cougar 428ci, 1969 Boss 429ci, and 1967–69 GT 500 Mustang

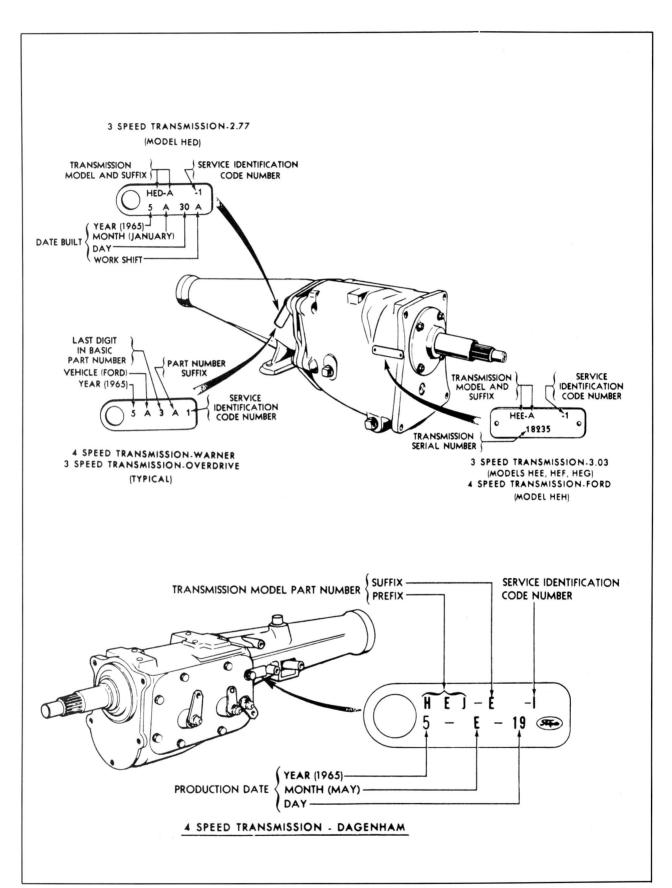

3 SPEED TRANSMISSION-2.77
(MODEL HED)

TRANSMISSION MODEL AND SUFFIX

SERVICE IDENTIFICATION CODE NUMBER

HED-A   -1

5 A 30 A

Date Built
YEAR (1965)
MONTH (JANUARY)
DAY
WORK SHIFT

LAST DIGIT IN BASIC PART NUMBER
VEHICLE (FORD)
YEAR (1965)

PART NUMBER SUFFIX

5 A 3 A 1

SERVICE IDENTIFICATION CODE NUMBER

4 SPEED TRANSMISSION-WARNER
3 SPEED TRANSMISSION-OVERDRIVE
(TYPICAL)

TRANSMISSION MODEL AND SUFFIX

SERVICE IDENTIFICATION CODE NUMBER

HEE-A   -1

18235

TRANSMISSION SERIAL NUMBER

3 SPEED TRANSMISSION-3.03
(MODELS HEE, HEF, HEG)
4 SPEED TRANSMISSION-FORD
(MODEL HEH)

TRANSMISSION MODEL PART NUMBER
SUFFIX
PREFIX

SERVICE IDENTIFICATION CODE NUMBER

H E J - E - I

5 - E - 19

PRODUCTION DATE
YEAR (1965)
MONTH (MAY)
DAY

4 SPEED TRANSMISSION - DAGENHAM

Manual transmission identification tag locations.

Interchange Number: 35
Type: Ford-built
Part Number(s): C9ZZ7003A
ID Code: RUG-AG
Usage: 1969 Mustang 302ci and 351ci with 2.32: 1 low-gear ratio, except Boss 302ci

Interchange Number: 36
Type: Ford-built
Part Number(s): C6ZZ7003F
ID Code: RUG-E3
Usage: 1969 Mustang 302ci and 351ci; 1969 Cougar 302ci and 351ci engine with 2.78:1 low-gear ratio

Interchange Number: 37
Type: Ford-built
Part Number(s): C8ZZ7003C
ID Code: RUG-AD1
Usage: 1969–70 Mustang 390ci and 1969–70 Cougar 390ci—both with 2.32 low-gear ratio

Interchange Number: 38
Type: Ford-built
Part Number(s): C7ZZ7003E
ID Code: RUG-M3
Usage: 1969 Mustang and Cougar 390ci and 2.78 low-gear ratio

Interchange Number: 39
Type: Ford-built
Part Number(s): DOOZ7003D
ID Code: RUG-AV or RUG-AV1
Usage: 1970 Mustang, 1970 Cougar 302ci and 351ci with 2.78:1 low-gear ratio, and 1971–73 Mustang and Cougar 351ci Cleveland and 351ci Boss

Interchange Number: 40
Type: Ford-built
Part Number(s): DOOZ7003E
ID Code: RUG-AW or RUG AW1
Usage: 1970 Mustang and Cougar 302ci and 351ci with 2.32 low-gear ratio

Interchange Number: 41
Type: Ford-built
Part Number(s): DOOZ7003H
ID Code: RUG-AZ or RUGAZ1
Usage: 1970 Mustang GT 500, Boss 429ci, 429ci Cobra Jet, and 429ci Super Cobra Jet; and 1970 Cougar 429ci Cobra Jet and Super Cobra Jet

Interchange Number: 42
Type: Ford-built
Part Number(s): C6OZ7003D
ID Code: RUG-D, RUGD1, or RUGD2
Usage: 1966–67 Fairlane and Comet 289ci

Interchange Number: 43
Type: Ford-built
Part Number(s): C6OZ7003F
ID Code: RUG-C, RUG-C1, or RUG-C2
Usage: 1966–67 Fairlane and Comet 390ci (except GT)

Automatic Transmission

Type and model of transmission can be determined by a visual inspection. There are five different models of automatic transmissions used in the Ford models covered in this guide: FM2, FX and FMX (Cruise-O-Matic), C4, and the mighty C6—all of which can be identified by sight if you know what to look for.

A good way of quickly identifying the type of automatic transmission is the number of pan bolts.

The two-speed FM2, which was used in early models, used 14 bolts on the pan. However, the Cruise-O-Matic (FX and FMX) also used 14 bolts, but the FM2 housing is a one-piece unit, where the Cruise-O-Matic has separate converter, case, and extension housings.

The C4 transmission is the most common of the automatics and it can be identified by an 11-bolt pan. It can also be distinguished by oval pads on both the right and left sides of the case.

Performance automatic transmission is the C6 unit. It can be most readily identified by its one-piece case with prominent ribs on top of the converter housing.

Note that in some models there is a difference between those with a console shift and those with a column shift. These are noted as not interchangeable in this guide but can be made to fit, if the valve control assembly is changed. This is a simple procedure and can be accomplished by the average enthusiast with ordinary tools.

Transmissions can also be identified by a code number that is on a metal tag, or a pad on the transmission. Locations vary according to type; see illustrations for details.

Model Identification

Cougar	Interchange Number
1967 289ci, all except 271hp	33
1967 289ci 271hp	34
1967 390ci, all	35
1967 428ci GT 500	38
1968 289ci, all	33
1968 302ci, all	36
1968 390ci two-barrel	37
1968 390ci four-barrel	35
1968 427ci, all	38
1968 428ci, all	38
1969 302ci, all except Eliminator	39
1969 351ci two-barrel	40
1969 351ci four-barrel	41
1969 390ci, all	42
1969 427ci, all	43
1969 428ci, all	43
1970 302ci, all except Eliminator	44
1970 351ci two-barrel	45
1970 351ci four-barrel	46
1970 390ci, all	42
1970 429ci, all	47

Cyclone	Interchange Number
1966 289ci, column	54
1966 289ci, console	55
1966 390ci, all except GT models	61, 62, 63, 64
1966 390ci GT, console	13
1967 289ci, column	56
1967 289ci, console	21, 57
1967 390ci two-barrel, column, all except GT models	50
1967 390ci two-barrel, console, all except GT models	51
1967 390ci four-barrel, column, all except GT models	52
1967 390ci four-barrel, console, all except GT models	53
1967 390ci GT, column	14
1967 390ci GT, console	15
1968–69 289ci and 302ci, column	20
1968–69 289ci and 302ci, console	21
1968–69 351ci two-barrel, column	48
1968–69 351ci two-barrel, console	49
1968–69 351ci four-barrel, column	22
1968–69 351ci four-barrel, console	23
1968–69 390ci two-barrel, column, all except GT models	50
1968–69 390ci two-barrel, console, all except GT models	51
1968–69 390ci GT four-barrel, column	16
1968–69 390ci GT four-barrel, console	17
1968–69 427ci, column	18
1968–69 427ci, console	19
1968–69 428ci, column	18
1968–69 428ci, console	19
1970 302ci 351ci two-barrel, column	57
1970 302ci 351ci two-barrel, console	58
1970 302ci 351ci four-barrel, column	24
1970 302ci 351ci four-barrel, console	25
1970 390ci GT, column	16
1970 390ci GT, console	17
1970 429ci, column, all except Cobra Jet and Super Cobra Jet	26

Interchange

Interchange Number: 1
Type: MX
Part Number(s): COAP7000C
ID Code: PBL-AG
Usage: 1959–60 full-size Ford with 352ci four-barrel

Interchange Number: 2
Type: FM2
Part Number(s): COAP7000G
ID Code: PBS-C or PBS-D
Usage: 1959–60 full-size Ford with 352ci four-barrel

Interchange Number: 3
Type: FX
Part Number(s): C1AP7000C
ID Code: PCD-A, PCD-C, or PCD-D PCD-D1
Usage: 1961–62 full-size Ford 352ci with column shift

Interchange Number: 4
Type: FX
Part Number(s): C2AP7000B
ID Code: PCD-F or PCD-F1
Usage: 1961–62 full-size Ford 352ci with console shift

Interchange Number: 5
Type: MX
Part Number(s): C2AP7000C
ID Code: PCE-S
Usage: 1961–62 full-size Ford 390ci with column shift

Interchange Number: 6
Type: MX
Part Number(s): C1AP7000Z
ID Code: PCE-G
Usage: 1961–62 full-size Ford 390ci with console shift

Interchange Number: 7
Type: C4
Part Number(s): C4OP7000G
ID Code: PCW-W or PCW-W1
Usage: 1964 Fairlane 289ci, except 271hp

Interchange Number: 8
Type: C4
Part Number(s): C4OP7000H
ID Code: PCW-AB
Usage: 1964 Fairlane 289ci 271hp four-barrel

Interchange Number: 9
Type: C4
Part Number(s): C5OP7000F
ID Code: PCW-AD
Usage: 1965 Fairlane 289ci, except 271hp with console shift

Interchange Number: 10
Type: C4
Part Number(s): C5OP7000B
ID Code: PCW-M
Usage: 1965 Fairlane 289ci four-barrel except 271hp with column shift

Interchange Number: 11
　　Type: C4
　　Part Number(s): C5OP7000D
　　ID Code: PCW-AC
　　Usage: 1965 Fairlane 289ci 271hp four-barrel with column shift

Interchange Number: 12
　　Type: C4
　　Part Number(s): C5OP7000H
　　ID Code: PCW-AF
　　Usage: 1965 Fairlane 289ci 271hp with console shift

Interchange Number: 13
　　Type: C6
　　Part Number(s): C6OP7000H
　　ID Code: PDD-V
　　Usage: 1966 Fairlane and Cyclone GT 390ci with console shift
　　Note(s): Non-GT models used a different transmission and will not interchange. GT unit is heavy-duty; the non-GT transmission is lighter-duty. Both are C6.

Interchange Number: 14
　　Type: C6
　　Part Number(s): C7OP7000M
　　ID Code: PGA-R or PGA-R-1
　　Usage: 1967 Fairlane and Cyclone GT 390ci with column shift
　　Note(s): Non-GT models used a different transmission and will not interchange. GT unit is heavy-duty; the other is lighter-duty. Both are C6.

Interchange Number: 15
　　Type: C6
　　Part Number(s): C8OP7000J
　　ID Code: PGA-M or PGA-M1
　　Usage: 1967 Fairlane and Cyclone GT 390ci with console shift
　　Note(s): Non-GT models used a different transmission and will not interchange. GT unit is heavy-duty; the other is lighter-duty. Both are C6.

Interchange Number: 16
　　Type: C6
　　Part Number(s): C9OP7000H
　　ID Code: PGA-R2 (1968); PGA-V or PGA-AC (1969)
　　Usage: 1968–69 Torino GT 390ci and 1969 Cyclone GT 390ci, both with column shift
　　Note(s): Non-GT models used a different transmission and will not interchange. GT unit is heavy-duty; the other is lighter-duty. Both are C6.

Interchange Number: 17
　　Type: C6
　　Part Number(s): C9OP7000G
　　ID Code: PGA-M2 (1968); PGA-W or PGA-AD (1969)
　　Usage: 1968–69 Torino and Cyclone GT 390ci with console shift
　　Note(s): Non-GT models used a different transmission and will not interchange. GT unit is heavy-duty; the other is lighter-duty. Both are C6.

Interchange Number: 18
　　Type: C6
　　Part Number(s): C8OP7000AJ
　　ID Code: PGB-Y or PGB-AG
　　Usage: 1968 Torino and Montego 428ci, 428ci Cobra Jet, and 428ci Super Cobra Jet—all with column shift

Interchange Number: 19
　　Type: C6
　　Part Number(s): C8OP7000AK
　　ID Code: PGB-Z; PGB-AH
　　Usage: 1968 Torino and Montego 428ci, 428ci Cobra Jet, and 428ci Super Cobra Jet—all with column shift

Interchange Number: 20
　　Type: C4
　　Part Number(s): C8OP7000G
　　ID Code: PEE-V or PEE-B
　　Usage: 1968–69 Torino and Montego 289ci and 302ci—all models with column shift

Interchange Number: 21
　　Type: C4
　　Part Number(s): C8OP7000H
　　ID Code: PEE-M
　　Usage: 1967 Fairlane and Comet 289ci and 1968–69 Torino and Montego 289ci and 302ci—all models with console shift

Interchange Number: 22
　　Type: FMX
　　Part Number(s): C9OP7000C
　　ID Code: PHB-F
　　Usage: 1969 Torino and Montego 351ci four-barrel with column shift

Interchange Number: 23
　　Type: FMX
　　Part Number(s): C9OP7000D
　　ID Code: PHB-G
　　Usage: 1969 Torino and Montego 351ci four-barrel with console shift

Interchange Number: 24
　　Type: FMX
　　Part Number(s): DOOP7000T
　　ID Code: PHB-R
　　Usage: 1970 Torino and Montego 351ci Cleveland four-barrel with column shift

Interchange Number: 25
　　Type: FMX
　　Part Number(s): DOOP7000U
　　ID Code: PHB-S
　　Usage: 1970 Torino and Montego 351ci Cleveland four-barrel with console shift

Interchange Number: 26
　　Type: C6
　　Part Number(s): DOOP7000G
　　ID Code: PJB-A, PJC-E, or PJB-J
　　Usage: 1970 Torino 429ci (except Cobra Jet and Super Cobra Jet) and 1970 Montego 429ci (except Cobra Jet and Super Cobra Jet with column shift)

Interchange Number: 27
　　Type: C6
　　Part Number(s): DOOP7000H
　　ID Code: PJB-B, PJC-F
　　Usage: 1970 Torino 429ci (except Cobra Jet and Super Cobra Jet) and 1970 Montego 429ci (except Cobra Jet and Super Cobra Jet with column shift)

Interchange Number: 28
　　Type: C6
　　Part Number(s): D1OP7000GA
　　ID Code: PJC-A
　　Usage: 1970–71 Torino GT 429ci Cobra Jet and Super Cobra Jet and 1970–71 Montego 429ci Cobra Jet and Super Cobra Jet with column shift
　　Note(s): Special heavy-duty application; do not use non-Cobra Jet transmission.

Interchange Number: 29
　　Type: C6
　　Part Number(s): DOOP7000HA
　　ID Code: PJB-A or PJC-E
　　Usage: 1970–71 Torino GT and Cyclone GT 429ci Cobra Jet and Super Cobra Jet with console shift
　　Note(s): Special heavy-duty application; do not use non-Cobra Jet transmission.

Interchange Number: 30
　　Type: C4
　　Part Number(s): C4ZP7000B
　　ID Code: PCW-H
　　Usage: 1964-1/2–65 Mustang 289ci, all except 271hp

Interchange Number: 31
Type: C4
Part Number(s): C6ZP7000B
ID Code: PCW-AS
Usage: 1965–66 Mustang 289ci four-barrel engine, all except 271hp

Interchange Number: 32
Type: C4
Part Number(s): C6ZP7000C
ID Code: PCW-BA
Usage: 1964-1/2–66 Mustang 289ci 271hp

Interchange Number: 33
Type: C4
Part Number(s): C8ZP7000H
ID Code: PEE-C or PEE-C1
Usage: 1967–68 Mustang and Cougar 289ci, except 271hp

Interchange Number: 34
Type: C4
Part Number(s): C7ZP7000E
ID Code: PEE-K
Usage: 1967 Mustang and Cougar 289ci 271hp
Note(s): Will fit 1968 models.

Interchange Number: 35
Type: C4
Part Number(s): C8ZP7000A
ID Code: PGA-P, PGA-P1, or PGA-P2
Usage: 1966–68 Mustang and 1967–68 Cougar 390ci four-barrel

Interchange Number: 36
Type: C4
Part Number(s): C8ZP7000B
ID Code: PEE-S
Usage: 1968 Mustang and Cougar 302ci

Interchange Number: 37
Type: C6
Part Number(s): C8WP7000A
ID Code: PGA-S
Usage: 1968 Mustang and Cougar 390ci two-barrel
Note(s): Interchange Number 35 is a heavy-duty unit and will fit, but not vice versa.

Interchange Number: 38
Type: C6
Part Number(s): C8ZP7000M
ID Code: PGA-AF
Usage: 1968 Mustang and Cougar 427ci, 428ci Cobra Jet, and 428ci Super Cobra Jet; and 1968 GT 500 Mustang

Interchange Number: 39
Type: C4
Part Number(s): C9ZP7000C
ID Code: PEE-AC
Usage: 1969 Mustang and Cougar 302ci, except Boss and Eliminator

Interchange Number: 40
Type: FMX
Part Number(s): C9ZP7000A
ID Code: PHB-E
Usage: 1969 Mustang and Cougar 351ci Windsor two-barrel
Note(s): Interchange Number 41 will fit but not vice versa.

Interchange Number: 41
Type: FMX
Part Number(s): C9ZP7000B
ID Code: PHB-H
Usage: 1969 Mustang and Cougar 351ci Windsor four-barrel
Note(s): Warning—do not use two-barrel version behind this engine.

Interchange Number: 42
Type: C6
Part Number(s): C9ZP7000J
ID Code: PGA-Y, PGA-AE
Usage: 1969–70 Mustang and Cougar 390ci

Interchange Number: 43
Type: C6
Part Number(s): C9ZP7000H
ID Code: PGA-AF1
Usage: 1969 Mustang and Cougar 427ci and 428ci Cobra Jet and Super Cobra Jet; 1969–70 GT 500 Mustang

Interchange Number: 44
Type: C4
Part Number(s): D2ZP7000DA
ID Code: PEE-AC1
Usage: 1970–71 Mustang and Cougar 302ci, except Boss and Eliminator
Note(s): 1972–73 Mustang and Cougar 302ci unit will fit, but it has a seatbelt warning lead that must be taped off.

Interchange Number: 45
Type: FMX
Part Number(s): DOZP7000A
ID Code: PHB-E1
Usage: 1970 Mustang and Cougar 351ci two-barrel

Interchange Number: 46
Type: FMX
Part Number(s): DOZP7000B
ID Code: PHB-P
Usage: 1970 Mustang and Cougar 351ci four-barrel Cleveland
Note(s): Do not use two-barrel version; it will not fit.

Interchange Number: 47
Type: C6
Part Number(s): DOZP7000J
ID Code: PGB-AF2
Usage: 1970–71 Mustang and Cougar 429ci Cobra Jet

Interchange Number: 48
Type: FMX
Part Number(s): C9OP7000A
ID Code: PHB-C
Usage: 1969 Torino and Montego 351ci two-barrel with column shift

Interchange Number: 49
Type: FMX
Part Number(s): C9OP7000B
ID Code: PHB-D
Usage: 1969 Torino and Montego 351ci two-barrel with console shift

Interchange Number: 50
Type: C6
Part Number(s): C7OP7000E
ID Code: PGA-B, PGA-B1, or PGA-B2
Usage: 1967 Fairlane and Comet 390ci two-barrel with column shift

Interchange Number: 51
Type: C6
Part Number(s): C8OP7000B
ID Code: PGA-C, PGA-C1, or PGA-C2
Usage: 1967–68 Fairlane and Comet 390ci two-barrel with console shift

Interchange Number: 52
Type: C6
Part Number(s): C7OP7000G
ID Code: PGA-F
Usage: 1967 Fairlane and Comet 390ci four-barrel (except GT) with column shift

Interchange Number: 53
    Type: C6
    Part Number(s): C7OP7000H
    ID Code: PGA-G
    Usage: 1967 Fairlane and Comet 390ci four-barrel (except GT) with console shift

Interchange Number: 54
    Type: C4
    Part Number(s): C6DP7000D
    ID Code: PCW-AN or PCW-AY
    Usage: 1966 Fairlane and Comet 289ci and 1966 Fairlane and Comet 200ci six-cylinder taxi—all with column shift
    Note(s): A heavy-duty transmission code, PCW-AZ was used in 1966 Fairlane and Comet 289ci taxi and police cars and will fit.

Interchange Number: 55
    Type: C4
    Part Number(s): C6OP7000E
    ID Code: PCW-AZ
    Usage: 1966 Fairlane and 1966 Comet 289ci with console shift

Interchange Number: 56
    Type: C4
    Part Number(s): C7OP7000AH
    ID Code: PEE-J or PEE-J1
    Usage: 1967 Fairlane and Comet 289ci with column shift
    Note(s): Heavy-duty unit codes PEE-E and PEE-E1 were used in 1967 Fairlane and Comet 289ci taxi

Interchange Number: 57
    Type: C4
    Part Number(s): DOOP700R
    ID Code: PEF-D, PEF-D1, or PEF-D2
    Usage: 1970 Torino and Montego 351ci two-barrel with column shift

Interchange Number: 58
    Type: C4
    Part Number(s): DOOP700S
    ID Code: PEF-E, PEF-E1, or PEF-E2
    Usage: 1970–71 Torino and Montego 351ci two-barrel with console shift

Interchange Number: 59
    Type: C4
    Part Number(s): DOOP7000D
    ID Code: PEE-V1, PEE-V2, or PEE-V3
    Usage: 1970–71 Torino and Montego 302ci two-barrel with column shift

Interchange Number: 60
    Type: C4
    Part Number(s): DOOP7000C
    ID Code: PEE-M1, PEE-M2, or PEE-M3
    Usage: 1970–71 Torino and Montego 302ci two-barrel with console shift

Interchange Number: 61
    Type: C6
    Part Number(s): C6OP7000B
    ID Code: PDD-J
    Usage: 1966 Fairlane and Comet 390ci two-barrel with column shift

Interchange Number: 62
    Type: C6
    Part Number(s): C6OP7000C
    ID Code: PDD-P
    Usage: 1966 Fairlane and Comet 390ci two-barrel with console shift

1967 Mustang T-5 models used a Hurst shifter.

Interchange Number: 63
    Type: C6
    Part Number(s): C6OP7000A
    ID Code: PDD-E
    Usage: 1966 Fairlane and Comet 390ci four-barrel (except GT) with column shift

Interchange Number: 64
    Type: C6
    Part Number(s): C6OP7000D
    ID Code: PDD-R
    Usage: 1966 Fairlane and Comet 390ci four-barrel (except GT) with console shift

Gear Shift Lever, Manual

Model Identification

Cougar	Interchange Number
1967, all	10
1968, all	11, 12
1969, all	13
1970, all	14

Cyclone	Interchange Number
1966–67, all	6
1968, all	7
1969, all	8
1970, all	9

Fairlane and Torino	Interchange Number
1959–61 without console	1
1959–61 with console	2
1963–65 without console	4
1963–65 with console	5
1966–67, all	6
1968, all	7

Interchange

Interchange Number: 1
Part Number(s): C3AZ7210G
Usage: 1959–63 full-size Ford without console shift, all engines

Interchange Number: 2
Part Number(s): C4AZ7210F
Usage: 1962–64 full-size Ford with console shift, all engines

Interchange Number: 3
Part Number(s): C4AZ7210E
Usage: 1963–64 full-size Ford with console shift, all engines

Interchange Number: 4
Part Number(s): C4OZ7210C
Usage: 1963–65 Fairlane and 1963 Mercury Meteor without console shift, all engines

Interchange Number: 5
Part Number(s): C4OZ7210D
Usage: 1963–65 Fairlane and 1963 Mercury Meteor with console shift, all engines

Interchange Number: 6
Part Number(s): C6OZ7210L
Usage: 1966–67 Fairlane and Comet, all engines and with or without console shift

Interchange Number: 7
Part Number(s): C8OZ7210D
Usage: 1968 Torino and Montego, all engines and with or without console shift

Interchange Number: 8
Part Number(s): C9OZ7210C
Usage: 1969 Torino and Montego, all engines and with or without console shift

Interchange Number: 9
Part Number(s): DOOZ7210A
Usage: 1970 Torino and Montego, all engines and with or without console shift
Note(s): Hurst shifter. Mustang will not interchange, due to linkage.

Interchange Number: 10
Part Number(s): C5ZZ7210M
Usage: 1964-1/2–67 Mustang and 1967 Cougar, all engines and with or without console shift

Interchange Number: 11
Part Number(s): C8ZZ7210A
Usage: 1968 Mustang and Cougar until build date January 2, 1968, all engines and with or without console shift

Interchange Number: 12
Part Number(s): C8ZZ7210B
Usage: 1968 Mustang and Cougar after build date January 2, 1968, all engines and with or without console shift

Interchange Number: 13
Part Number(s): C9ZZ7210B
Usage: 1969 Mustang and Cougar, all engines with or without console shift

Interchange Number: 14
Part Number(s): DOZZ7210B
Usage: 1970 Mustang and Cougar, all engines and with or without console shift
Note(s): Hurst shifter. Torino and Montego unit will not fit due to linkage.

Gear Shift Lever, Automatic

Model Identification

1964-1/2–66 Mustang automatic floor shifter.

63

1967–68 Mustang/Cougar automatic floor shifter without console.

351ci Interchange

Interchange Number: 1
    Part Number(s): B6A7210D
    Shifter Location: Column
    Usage: 1956–62 full-size Ford

Interchange Number: 2
    Part Number(s): C2OZ7210AP
    Shifter Location: Column
    Usage: 1962 Fairlane and Meteor

Interchange Number: 3
    Part Number(s): C3OZ7210A
    Shifter Location: Column
    Usage: 1963–65 Fairlane

Interchange Number: 4
    Part Number(s): C6OZ7210B
    Shifter Location: Column
    Usage: 1966 Fairlane, Comet, and Falcon

Interchange Number: 5
    Part Number(s): C7OZ7210C
    Shifter Location: Column
    Usage: 1967 Fairlane, Comet, and Falcon

352ci Interchange Number: 6
    Part Number(s): C9AZ7210G
    Shifter Location: Column
    Usage: 1968–69 Torino and Montego, 1968–70 Falcon, and
        1968–69 full-size Ford and Mercury (without tilt steering)

Interchange Number: 7
    Part Number(s): DOZ7210A
    Shifter Location: Column
    Usage: 1970–72 Torino and Montego, 1970–72 full-size Ford and
        Mercury, and 1970–73 Thunderbird—all without lock column
        and without tilt wheel in full-size models and Thunderbird.
    Note(s): A few 1970 models (early-built) had the 1969 non-lock-
        ing column and used the 1969 lever.

Interchange Number: 8
    Part Number(s): C2AZ7210L
    Shifter Location: Floor
    Usage: 1962–64 full-size Ford and 1965 Fairlane
    Note(s): Will fit 1962–64 Fairlane, although the shifter is not stock.

Interchange Number: 9
    Part Number C6OZ7210H
    Shifter Location: Floor
    Usage: 1966–67 Fairlane and Comet and 1966 Falcon

Interchange Number: 10
    Part Number(s): C8OZ7210B
    Shifter Location: Floor
    Usage: 1968–71 Torino and Montego

Interchange Number: 11
    Part Number(s): C5ZZ7210H
    Shifter Location: Floor
    Usage: 1964-1/2–66 Mustang

Interchange Number: 12
    Part Number(s): C7ZZ7210A
    Shifter Location: Floor
    Usage: 1967–68 Mustang and Cougar with console

Interchange Number: 13
    Part Number(s): C7ZZ7210C
    Shifter Location: Floor
    Usage: 1967–68 Mustang and Cougar without console

Interchange Number: 14
    Part Number(s): C9ZZ7210C
    Shifter Location: Floor
    Usage: 1969–72 Mustang and Cougar

Knob, Shift Lever

Model Identification

Cougar	Interchange Number
1967 four-speed	4
1967 automatic, floor	6
1968–69 four-speed	3
1968–69 automatic, floor	8
1970 four-speed	5
1970 automatic, floor	9

Cyclone	Interchange Number
1966–67 column	2
1966–67 automatic, floor	6
1966–67 four-speed	4
1968–69 column	2
1968–69 automatic, floor	8
1968–69 four-speed	3
1970 column	2
1970 automatic, floor	9
1970 four-speed	5

Fairlane and Torino	Interchange Number
1959–61 column	1
1959–61, floor without console	10
1959–61, floor with console	11
1962–64 column	2
1962–64 automatic, floor	7
1962–64 four-speed	11
1965 column	2
1965 automatic, floor	7

Interchange

Interchange Number: 1
Part Number(s): COAZ7213A
Type/Location: Automatic on column.
Usage: 1960–62 full-size Ford

Interchange Number: 2
Part Number(s): D3OZ7213A
Type/Location: Automatic on column
Usage: 1965–67 Fairlane, 1966–67 Comet, 1968–72 Torino, 1968–72 Montego, 1967–72 Thunderbird, 1970–72 Maverick, 1971–72 Comet, 1966–70 Falcon, 1967–72 full-size Ford, and 1968–72 full-size Mercury

Interchange Number: 3
Part Number(s): C8OZ7213F
Type/Location: Four-speed on floor
Usage: 1965 Fairlane and Falcon; 1968–69 Torino, Montego, Mustang, Cougar, and full-size Ford; and 1968–70 Falcon
Note(s): Walnut grain.

Interchange Number: 4
Part Number(s): C8WY7213D
Type/Location: Four-speed on floor
Usage: 1964-1/2–67 Mustang; 1967 Cougar; and 1966–67 Fairlane, Comet, and Falcon

Interchange Number: 5
Part Number(s): D1OZ7213A
Type/Location: Four-speed on floor
Usage: 1970–71 Torino, Montego, Mustang, and Cougar—all with Hurst shifter
Note(s): Torino/Montego and Cougar/Mustang shift levers will not interchange, but tee-bar handle will.

Interchange Number: 6
Part Number(s): C5ZZ7213M
Type/Location: Automatic on floor
Usage: 1965–67 Mustang and Cougar; 1965–67 full-size Ford; 1966–67 Falcon, Fairlane, and Comet; 1972 Mustang, Torino, and Montego; and 1967–68 full-size Mercury
Note(s): Chrome handle.

Interchange Number: 7
Part Number(s): C2AZ7213F
Type/Location: Automatic on floor
Usage: 1962–65 Fairlane, 1962–64 full-size Ford, and 1962–65 full-size Mercury
Note(s): Knob-type black.

Interchange Number: 8
Part Number(s): C8OZ7213*
Type/Location: Automatic on floor
Usage: 1968–69 Mustang, Torino, Montego, and Cougar (except X-R7G)
Note(s): *Last part of part number varies according to color. Knobs matched interior trim.

Interchange Number: 9
Part Number(s): DOOZ7213*
Type/Location: Automatic on floor
Usage: 1970 Mustang and Cougar and 1970–71 Torino and Montego
Note(s): * Last part of part number is color. Various colors were used in 1970 and matched the interior. Early-1971 Torinos and Montegos used a black knob only. Use on those models up to build date November 8, 1971. Paint to match your trim color.

Interchange Number: 10
Part Number(s): C2AZ7213B
Type/Location: Four-speed on floor
Usage: 1959–64 full-size Ford without console
Note(s): Black knob. Used with both Warner and Ford-built transmissions.

Interchange Number: 11
Part Number(s): C2AZ7213E
Type/Location: Four-speed on floor
Usage: 1959–64 full-size Ford with console and 1964 Fairlane, Falcon, and Comet
Note(s): Walnut-grain knob. Used with both Warner- and Ford-built transmissions.

Shift Dial, Automatic

Model Identification

Interchange

Interchange Number: 1
Part Number(s): COAF15805A
Usage: 1959–60 full-size Ford with two-speed (FM) automatic on the column

Interchange Number: 2
Part Number(s): COAF15805B
Usage: 1960 full-size Ford with three-speed (MX) automatic on the column

Interchange Number: 3
Part Number(s): C4OZ7B033B
Usage: 1962–65 Fairlane, 1962–63 Meteor, and 1965 Falcon—all with C4 automatic on the column

Interchange Number: 4
Part Number(s): C6OZ7A213A
Usage: 1966 Fairlane and 1966 Falcon with C4 or C6 automatic on the column

Interchange Number: 5
Part Number(s): C7OZ7A213A
Usage: 1967 Fairlane and 1967 Falcon with automatic on the column

Interchange Number: 6
Part Number(s): C8OZ7E055A
Usage: 1968–69 Torino, Montego, and Falcon with automatic on the column
Note(s): Paint to match.

Interchange Number: 7
Part Number(s): DOOZ7E055*
Usage: 1970 Torino and Montego with automatic on the column
Note(s): *Last part of number color code originally matched interior trim. Paint to match.

Interchange Number: 8
Part Number(s): C4AZ7A213C
Usage: 1964–65 Fairlane and 1962–64 full-size Ford with automatic on the floor
Note(s): Lettering P-R-N-D1-D2-L.

Interchange Number: 9
Part Number(s): C6OZ7A213D
Usage: 1966–67 Fairlane and Comet with automatic on the floor
Note(s): Lettering P-R-N-D1-D2-L.

Interchange Number: 10
Part Number(s): C8OZ7A213A
Usage: 1968–71 Torino and Montego with automatic on the floor
Note(s): Lettering P-R-N-D1-D2-L.

Interchange Number: 11
Part Number(s): C5ZZ7A213C
Usage: 1964-1/2–66 Mustang with automatic on the floor, without console

Interchange Number: 12
Part Number(s): C5ZZ7A213D
Usage: 1964-1/2–66 Mustang with automatic on the floor, with console

Interchange Number: 13
Part Number(s): C7ZZ7A213A
Usage: 1967–68 Mustang and Cougar with automatic on the floor, without console

Interchange Number: 14
Part Number(s): C7ZZ7A213C
Usage: 1967–68 Mustang and Cougar XR7G with automatic on the floor, with console

Interchange Number: 15
Part Number(s): C9ZZ7A213A
Usage: 1969–70 Mustang and Cougar, 1970–72 Maverick, and 1971–72 Comet (compact)—all with automatic on the floor

Interchange Number: 16
Part Number(s): C4GY7A213A
Usage: 1964–65 Comet with C4 automatic on the column

Interchange Number: 17
Part Number(s): C6GY7A213A
Usage: 1966–67 Comet with C4 or C6 automatic on the column

Interchange Number: 18
Part Number(s): C6OZ7A213C
Usage: 1966 Fairlane and Comet with automatic on the floor
Note(s): Lettering P-R-N-D-L.

Interchange Number: 19
Part Number(s): C7WY7D443A
Usage: 1967–68 Cougar (except XR7G) with automatic on floor, without console
Note(s): Part of bezel.

Interchange Number: 20
Part Number(s): C7WY7D443B
Usage: 1967–68 Cougar (except XR7G) with automatic on floor, with console
Note(s): Part of bezel.

Boot, Shift Manual

Model Identification

Cougar	Interchange Number
1967–68, all	8
1969, all	9
1970 four-speed	7

Cyclone	Interchange Number
1966–68, all	5
1969, all	6
1970, all	7

Fairlane and Torino	Interchange Number
1959–61, all	1
1962–63 without console	3
1962–63 with console	2, 4
1964–65 without console	3

1967–68 Mustang/Cougar automatic floor shifter with console.

Interchange

Interchange Number: 1
    Part Number(s): COAZ7277A
    Usage: 1959–61 full-size Ford

Interchange Number: 2
    Part Number(s): C2AZ7277D
    Usage: 1962–63 Fairlane and full-size Ford with console—both up
        to build date December 13, 1962
    Note(s): 3-3/4x4in, 11/16x3, 5/16x4-15/16 bolt pattern.

Interchange Number: 3
    Part Number(s): C2AZ7277G
    Usage: 1962–65 Fairlane and 1962–64 full-size Ford without con-
        sole
    Note(s): Round base pattern.

Interchange Number: 4
    Part Number(s): C4AZ7277B
    Usage: 1963–65 Fairlane, 1963–64 full-size Ford—both after build
        date December 13, 1962, and with console
    Note(s): 3-13/16x5-11/16x3-1/4x5-5/16 bolt pattern.

Interchange Number: 5
    Part Number(s): C6OZ7277A
    Usage: 1966–67 Fairlane, 1968 Torino, 1966–67 Comet, 1968
        Montego, and 1966–68 Falcon
    Note(s): 4-1/16x4-5/8x1-11/16.

Interchange Number: 6
    Part Number(s): C9OZ7277A
    Usage: 1969 Torino and Montego
    Note(s): 6x4-1/8x1-13/16 high.

Interchange Number: 7
    Part Number(s): DOZZ7277B
    Usage: 1970–71 Torino and Montego and 1970 Mustang and
        Cougar four-speed
    Note(s): Boot stamped DOZB7B118A or DOZB7B118E.

Interchange Number: 8
    Part Number(s): C5ZZ7277B
    Usage: 1964-1/2–68 Mustang and 1967–68 Cougar

Interchange Number: 9
    Part Number(s): C9ZZ7277A
    Usage: 1969 Mustang and Cougar (four-speed) and 1970 Must-
        ang and Cougar (four-speed only)

Disc, Clutch

    Clutch discs are identified by the disc's diameter and the number, size, and color of springs. The letters used below (S—small and L—large) refer to the size of the springs on the disc.

Model Identification

Interchange

Interchange Number: 1
    Part Number (Disc): C6OZ7550G
    Diameter: 10in
    Number of Springs: 6L, 6S
    Color: L-pink, S-orange
    Usage: 1963–67 Fairlane 289ci, 1966–67 Comet 289ci, 1968–71
        Torino and Montego 302ci, 1964-1/2–65 Mustang 260ci,
        1968–72 Mustang 302ci (except Boss), 1971 Maverick 302ci,
        and 1965 and 1967–70 Falcon 289ci and 302ci
    Note(s): Not for 271hp 289ci. Three-speed only in 1965 models.

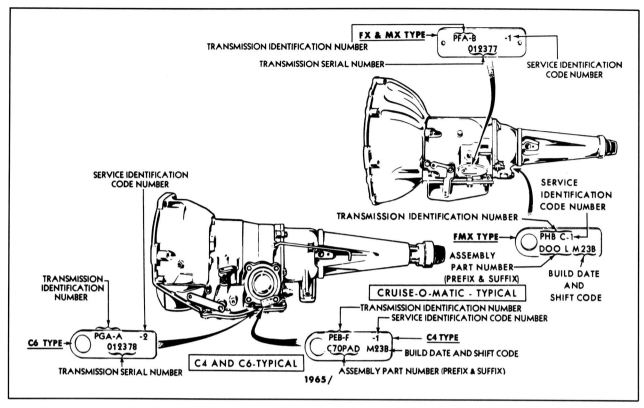

FX & MX TYPE→ PFA-B -1
TRANSMISSION IDENTIFICATION NUMBER 012377
TRANSMISSION SERIAL NUMBER
SERVICE IDENTIFICATION CODE NUMBER

SERVICE IDENTIFICATION CODE NUMBER

TRANSMISSION IDENTIFICATION NUMBER

SERVICE IDENTIFICATION CODE NUMBER

FMX TYPE→ PHB C-1
ASSEMBLY DOO L M 23B
PART NUMBER
(PREFIX & SUFFIX) BUILD DATE AND SHIFT CODE

CRUISE-O-MATIC - TYPICAL

TRANSMISSION IDENTIFICATION NUMBER
SERVICE IDENTIFICATION CODE NUMBER

TRANSMISSION IDENTIFICATION NUMBER

PEB-F -1 ←C4 TYPE
C7PAD M23B BUILD DATE AND SHIFT CODE
ASSEMBLY PART NUMBER (PREFIX & SUFFIX)

C6 TYPE→ PGA-A -2
012378
TRANSMISSION SERIAL NUMBER

C4 AND C6-TYPICAL

1965/

Automatic transmission identification tag locations.

Interchange Number: 2
Part Number (Disc): C5AZ7550F
Diameter: 10-1/2in
Number of Springs: 6L, 4S
Usage: 1963–65 Fairlane 289ci four-barrel (except 271hp), 1966–67 Fairlane six-cylinder with heavy-duty clutch, and 1964-1/2–65 Mustang 289ci (except 271hp)—all with four-speed; 1965–66 full-size Ford 289ci with three-speed

Interchange Number: 3
Part Number (Disc): C7ZZ7550B
Diameter: 10-1/2in
Number of Springs: 8
Color: Gray
Usage: 1963–65 Fairlane 289ci 271hp, 1965–67 Mustang 289ci 271hp, 1969–70 Boss 302ci Mustang, 1969–70 Cougar Eliminator, and 1967 Cougar 289ci 271hp

Interchange Number: 4
Part Number (Disc): C7OZ7550B
Diameter: 11-1/2in
Number of Springs: 8L
Color: Not painted
Usage: 1966–67 Fairlane GT, 1966–67 Cyclone GT, 1966–67 Mustang GT, 1967 Cougar GT—all with 390ci
Note(s): Do not use smaller-diameter disc that was used on non-GT cars.

Interchange Number: 5
Part Number (Disc): C5AZ7550D
Diameter: 11-1/2in
Number of Springs: 5L, 5S
Color: Aluminum
Usage: 1967–68 Fairlane and Comet 427ci, 1970 Torino and Montego with 429ci Cobra Jet and Super Cobra Jet, 1971 Mustang and Cougar 429ci, 1965–67 full-size Ford and Mercury 427ci, 1967–68 Mustang 427ci, 1967–68 Cougar 427ci, and 1969–70 Boss 429ci Mustang

Interchange Number: 6
Part Number (Disc): D1OZ7550A
Diameter: 11in
Number of Springs: 6L, 3S
Color: L—orange, S—green
Usage: 1968–71 Torino, Montego, Mustang, and Cougar, all 390ci in 1968 or 351ci and 390ci in 1969–71

Interchange Number: 7
Part Number (Disc): C6AZ7550D
Diameter: 11in
Number of Springs: 5L, 5S
Color: Aluminum
Usage: 1968–69 Torino 428ci Cobra Jet and Super Cobra Jet, 1969 Montego 428ci Cobra Jet and Super Cobra Jet, 1968–70 Mustang 428ci Cobra Jet and Super Cobra Jet, 1969–70 Cougar 428ci Cobra Jet and Super Cobra Jet, 1967–70 GT 500 Mustang, 1966–69 full-size Ford 428ci, and 1970 Torino 429ci (except Cobra Jet and Super Cobra Jet)

Interchange Number: 8
Part Number (Disc): C6DZ7550C
Diameter: 10in
Number of Springs: 6L, 6S
Color: N/A
Usage: 1966–67 Mustang and 1967 Cougar 289ci, except 271hp.

Interchange Number: 9
Part Number (Disc): C5AZ7550C
Diameter: 11in
Number of Springs: 8L
Color: Aluminum
Usage: 1966–67 Fairlane and Comet 390ci (except GT) and 1965 full-size Ford and Mercury 390ci
Note(s): Do not use in GT models.

Converter

Converters are grouped according to the type of automatic transmission or the performance range. High-performance converters usually have a higher stall speed. They should not be used in a lower performance version unless the high-performance transmission is also swapped. Some converters are marked with an identification number, and this can be used to identify the unit.

Model Identification

Cougar, Cyclone, Fairlane, Torino, and Mustang	*Interchange Number*
1959–61 352ci, all	1, 2
1962–65 289ci, all except C4	4
1962–65 289ci with C4	10
1966–67 289ci, all except C4	
1966–67 289ci with C4	6
1966–67 390ci, all	5
1966–67 427ci, all	5
1968–69 302ci, all except C4	3
1968–69 C4	6
1968–69 351ci Windsor, all except C4	3
1968–69 351ci Windsor with C4	6
1968–69 351ci Cleveland with C4	8
1968–69 351ci Cleveland with C6	9
1968–69 390ci, all	5
1968–69 428ci, all	5
1968–69 429ci, all	5

Interchange

Interchange Number: 1
Part Number(s): C2AZ7902D
Usage: 1959–62 full-size Ford 352ci

Interchange Number: 2
Part Number(s): C3AZ7902M
Stamped: 20, 24, 32, or 35
Usage: 1963 full-size Ford 352ci and 390ci

Interchange Number: 3
Part Number(s): C9ZZ7902A
Stamped: 49, 54, or 56
Usage: 1968–74 Torino, 1968–74 Montego, 1968–74 Mustang, 1968–74 Cougar, and 1970–74 full-size Ford—all with six-cylinder, 302ci, or 351ci Windsor engines and FMX Cruise-O-Matic

Interchange Number: 4
Part Number(s): C4AZ7902D
Stamped: AB or N
Usage: 1964–65 Fairlane, 1965 Falcon, 1965 Comet, and 1964 full-size Ford, all 289ci and Cruise-O-Matic

Interchange Number: 5
Part Number(s): C8AZ7902A
Stamped: 26, 31, 37, 43, 44, 45, 46, 53, 55, 58, 59, 62, 63, or 66
Usage: 1966–71 Ford and Mercury cars with 390ci, 427ci, 428ci, 429ci, or 460ci engine with C6 (except 1966–67 full-size Ford and Thunderbird with 428ci)
Note(s): Later-model 1968–up converters will fit earlier 1966–67 cars, but earlier-model converters may not fit later 1968–up cars

Interchange Number: 6
Part Number(s): C6AZ7902M
Stamped: AJ, AY, or BC
Usage: 1966–67 Fairlane and Comet, 1968–69 Torino and Montego, 1966–69 Mustang, 1967–69 Cougar, and 1966–70 Falcon—all with 289ci, 302ci, or 351ci engines and C4

Interchange Number: 7
Part Number(s): DOOZ7902A
Stamped: BP or BV
Usage: 1970–72 Torino, Montego, Mustang, and Cougar with six-cylinder or 302ci engines and C4 transmission

Interchange Number: 8
Part Number(s): DOOZ7902B
Usage: 1970–73 Torino, Montego, Mustang, and Cougar with 351ci Cleveland

Interchange Number: 9
Part Number(s): DC2OZ7902A
Stamped: 64, 65, 69, or 70
Usage: 1970–72 351ci Cleveland four-barrel with C6

Interchange Number: 10
Part Number(s): C5AZ7902E
Stamped: N or AB
Usage: 1964 Fairlane, all engines with C4

Pedal, Clutch

Model Identification

Cougar	*Interchange Number*
1967, all	7
1968, all	8
1969, all	9
1970, all	10

Cyclone	*Interchange Number*
1966–67, all	3
1968–69, all	4
1970, all	5

Fairlane and Torino	*Interchange Number*
1959–61, all	1
1962–65, all	2
1966–67, all	3
1968–69, all	4
1970, all	5

Mustang	*Interchange Number*
1964-1/2–66, all	6
1967, all	7
1968, all	8
1969, all	9
1970, all	10

Interchange

Interchange Number: 1
Part Number(s): C2AZ7519A
Usage: 1962–64 full-size Ford with four-speed only
Note(s): Three-speed on column will not fit.

Interchange Number: 2
Part Number(s): C3OZ7519A
Usage: 1962–65 Fairlane and 1962–63 Mercury Meteor

Interchange Number: 3
Part Number(s): C9OZ7519A
Usage: 1966–67 Fairlane, Comet, and Falcon

Interchange Number: 4
Part Number(s): C9OZ7519A
Usage: 1968–69 Torino and Montego and 1968–70 Falcon

Interchange Number: 5
Part Number(s): DOOZ7519A
Usage: 1970–71 Torino and Montego

Drive Shaft

Each drive shaft is identified by its length and diameter. Length is measured from center of eye to center of eye. Interchange is with yoke and universal joints installed. Note that there may be more interchanges if the shaft by itself is used. As a rule of thumb, try swapping by matching dimensions.

Each yoke is also identified by its dimensions. Overall length is from end of stem to center of eye. Diameter is the height of the eye-span that attaches to the u-joint that connects the front yoke to the shaft. Like the shaft, the yoke itself can have interchanges other than those listed.

Model Identification

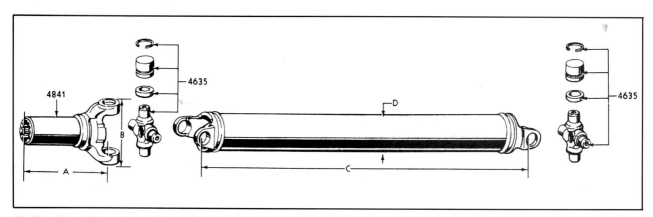

Identify a driveshaft by its length (C) and diameter (D), and the yoke by length (A) and span (B).

Mustang

Interchange

Interchange Number: 1
Part Number(s): C3OZ4602H
Dimensions: Shaft 53-39/64x3in, yoke 8-3/32x3-1/2in
Usage: 1962–64 Fairlane, except station wagon with manual transmission

Interchange Number: 2
Part Number(s): C3OZ4602J
Dimensions: Shaft 53-3/64x3in, yoke 8-3/32x3-1/2in
Usage: 1963–64 Fairlane—all except station wagon with Cruise-O-Matic automatic or with overdrive four-speed manual

Interchange Number: 3
Part Number(s): C4OZ4602A
Dimensions: Shaft 58-13/64x3in, yoke 8-3/32x3-1/2in
Usage: 1964 Fairlane with V-8 and C4 automatic, all except station wagon.

Interchange Number: 4
Part Number(s): C4OZ4602B
Dimensions: Shaft 56-5/8x3in, yoke 8-3/32x3-1/2in
Usage: 1964 Fairlane 289ci two-barrel

Interchange Number: 5
Part Number(s): C4OZ4602C
Dimensions: Shaft 58-1/2x3in, yoke 7-5/8x3-15/32
Usage: 1964 Fairlane station wagon with six-cylinder or 289ci two-barrel with four-speed manual or automatic and 1965 Fairlane, except station wagon

Interchange Number: 6
Part Number(s): C4OZ4602G
Dimensions: Shaft 57-35/64x3in, yoke 8-3/32x3-1/2in
Usage: 1963–65 Fairlane 289ci 271hp, except station wagon

Interchange Number: 7
Part Number(s): C6OZ4602D
Dimensions: Shaft 54-1/32x3in, yoke 8-3/32x3-1/2in
Usage: 1966–67 Fairlane and Comet and 1968–69 Torino and Montego—all body styles (except Ranchero and station wagon) with 390ci engine and manual

Interchange Number: 8
Part Number(s): C6OZ4602B
Dimensions: Shaft 54-1/32x3in, yoke 8-5/32x3-29/32in
Usage: 1966–67 Fairlane and Comet and 1968–69 Torino and Montego—all body styles (except Ranchero and station wagon) with 390ci engine with C6 automatic

Interchange Number: 9
Part Number(s): C6OZ4602E
Dimensions: Shaft 54-15/32x3in, yoke 8-7/32x3-7/8in
Usage: 1966–69 Ranchero, 1966–69 Fairlane station wagon, 1966–69 Comet station wagon—all 390ci and manual

Interchange Number: 10
Part Number(s): C6OZ4602A
Dimensions: Shaft 51-1/64x3in, yoke 8-5/32x3-29/32in
Usage: 1966–67 Fairlane station wagon, 1966–69 Ranchero, 1966–67 Comet station wagon, 1968–69 Torino station wagon, and 1968–69 Montego station wagon—all 390ci and C6

Interchange Number: 11
Part Number(s): C7OZ4602A
Dimensions: Shaft 51-7/16x3in, yoke 8-5/32x3-29/32in
Usage: 1967 Fairlane and Comet 427ci with four-speed, 1968–69 Torino GT with 428ci Cobra Jet or Super Cobra Jet engine and four-speed transmission, except Ranchero; 1968 Torino and Montego 427ci.

Interchange Number: 12
Part Number(s): C6OZ4602V
Dimensions: Shaft 58-43/64x3in, yoke 8-7/32x3-1/2in
Usage: 1966–67 Fairlane and Comet 289ci two-barrel and 1968–69 Torino and Montego 302ci—all with manual or C4 automatic

Interchange Number: 13
Part Number(s): C6OZ4602U
Dimensions: Shaft 55-41/64x3in, yoke 8-7/32x3-1/2in
Usage: 1966–69 Ranchero, 1966–67 Fairlane station wagon, 1966–67 Comet station wagon—all with 289ci or 302ci and manual

Interchange Number: 14
Part Number(s): C8OZ4602B
Dimensions: Shaft 54-1/32x3-1/2in, yoke 8-5/32x3-29/32in
Usage: 1968–69 Torino and Cyclone 428ci Cobra Jet and Super Cobra Jet automatic and 1968 Torino and Montego 427ci automatic—all body styles except Ranchero and station wagon

Interchange Number: 15
Part Number(s): C9OZ4602G
Dimensions: Shaft 54-15/32x3in, yoke 8-5/32x3-29/32in
Usage: 1969 Ranchero 428ci and four-speed

Interchange Number: 16
Part Number(s): C9OZ4602H
Dimensions: Shaft 51x3in, yoke 8-5/32x3-29/32in
Usage: 1969 Ranchero 428ci automatic

Interchange Number: 17
Part Number(s): C5ZZ4602J
Dimensions: Shaft 52-25/32x2-3/4in, yoke 8-1/4x3-3/16in* or 8-3/32x3-3/16in+
Usage: 1964-1/2–66 Mustang 289ci (except 289ci 271hp) manual
Note(s): *Until build date December 15, 1964. +After build date December 15, 1964. Drive shaft is the same for all years, but the yoke must be changed accordingly.

Interchange Number: 18
Part Number(s): C5ZZ4602H
Dimensions: Shaft 51-1/16x2-3/4in, yoke 8-3/32x3-3/16in
Usage: 1964-1/2–66 Mustang 289ci (except 289ci 271hp) with C4 automatic

Interchange Number: 19
Part Number(s): C5ZZ4602E
Dimensions: Shaft 49-23/32x2-3/4in, yoke 8-3/32x3-3/16in
Usage: 1964-1/2–66 Mustang 289ci 271hp with manual

Interchange Number: 20
Part Number(s): C7ZZ4602F
Dimensions: Shaft 50-31/32x3in, yoke 8-3/32x3-1/2in
Usage: 1967–68 Mustang (except 1968 GT) 289ci and 302ci, 1969–70 Mustang with six-cylinder and 302ci two-barrel with 7-1/4in rear axle
Note(s): Not for Boss. Cougar drive shaft will not interchange.

Interchange Number: 21
Part Number(s): C7ZZ4602C
Dimensions: Shaft 51-1/64x3in, yoke 8-3/32x3-7/8in
Usage: 1967–69 Mustang 390ci, 1969–70 Boss 302ci Mustang, 1970 Mustang 351ci, and Cleveland four-barrel with manual transmission; 1967 Mustang 289ci 271hp; 1967 Mustang GT 350 and GT 500*; and 1970 Mustang 429ci Cobra Jet and Super Cobra Jet with four-speed
Note(s): Cougar drive shaft will not interchange. *Shelby Mustangs used the same drive shaft assembly, but the yoke must be changed. The Shelby GT yoke is the same as that used with the automatic 390ci Mustang with C6 transmission, even though the GT 350 and 500 used a four-speed transmission.

Interchange Number: 22
Part Number(s): C8ZZ4602C
Dimensions: Shaft 46-19/32x3-1/2in, yoke 8-7/32x3-1/2in
Usage: 1967–69 Mustang 390ci, 1968–70 Mustang 427ci and 428ci, 1970 Mustang 429ci Cobra Jet and Super Cobra Jet—all with C6 automatic

Interchange Number: 23
Part Number(s): C8ZZ4602A
Dimensions: Shaft 50-7/32x3in, yoke 8-7/32x3-1/2in
Usage: 1968 Mustang GT 289ci or 302ci two-barrel, 1969–70 Mustang with six-cylinder or 302ci or 351ci Windsor with 8-3/4in with manual or C4 automatic transmissions.
Note(s): Cougar drive shaft will not interchange.

Interchange Number: 24
Part Number(s): C9ZZ4602C
Dimensions: Shaft 50-7/8x3in, yoke 8-7/32x3-1/2in
Usage: 1969–70 Mustang 429ci Boss and Cobra Jet four-speed

Interchange Number: 25
Part Number(s): DOZZ4602A
Dimensions: Shaft 50-5/8x3-1/2in, yoke 8-5/32x3-29/32in
Usage: 1970 Mustang with 351ci four-barrel and FMX automatic
Note(s): Use with 31-spline axle shaft. Cougar drive shaft will not interchange.

Interchange Number: 26
Part Number(s): C7WY4602E
Dimensions: Shaft 54-3/16x2-3/4in, yoke 9-7/16x3-1/2in
Usage: 1967–68 Cougar 289ci
Note(s): Mustang shaft will not interchange.

Interchange Number: 27
Part Number(s): C8WY4602B
Dimensions: Shaft 49-41/64x3in, yoke 8-1/4x3-1/2in
Usage: 1967–68 Cougar 390ci and 427ci with C6 automatic and 1968–69 Cougar 428ci engine with C6
Note(s): Mustang shaft will not interchange.

Interchange Number: 28
Part Number(s): C7WY4602B
Dimensions: Shaft 53-1/2x3in, yoke 8-7/32x3-7/8in
Usage: 1967–69 Cougar 390ci with manual transmission, 1969 Cougar Eliminator 302ci, 1967–68 289ci 271hp manual, 1970 Cougar 351ci Cleveland with manual, 1967–68 427ci Cougar four-speed, and 1968–69 428ci four-speed
Note(s): Mustang shaft will not interchange.

Interchange Number: 29
Part Number(s): C9WY4602A
Dimensions: Shaft 53-9/32x3in, yoke 8-7/32x3-1/2in
Usage: 1969–70 Cougar with 351ci Windsor and FMX automatic
Note(s): Mustang shaft will not interchange.

Interchange Number: 30
Part Number(s): C9WY4602B
Dimensions: Shaft 53-1/4x3-1/4in, yoke 8-7/32x3-1/2in
Usage: 1969–70 Cougar 351ci Windsor with manual
Note(s): Mustang shaft will not interchange.

Interchange Number: 31
Part Number(s): DOWY4602A
Dimensions: Shaft 53-9/16x3in, yoke 8-7/32x3-1/2in
Usage: 1970 Cougar 351ci Cleveland two-barrel with FMX automatic
Note(s): Mustang shaft will not interchange.

Interchange Number: 32
Part Number(s): COAA4602D
Dimensions: Shaft 56-17/32x2-3/4in, yoke n/a
Usage: 1959–60 full-size Ford 352ci with Cruise-O-Matic, three-speed overdrive, or manual

Interchange Number: 33
Part Number(s): C2AZ4602F
Dimensions: Shaft 56-1/2x2-3/4in, yoke n/a
Usage: 1961 full-size Ford 352ci with Cruise-O-Matic, 1961 full-size Ford police car with manual, 1961–62 full-size Ford 390ci high-performance with manual, and 1961–62 full-size Ford 292ci and 352ci

Interchange Number: 34
Part Number(s): C1AA4602L
Dimensions: Shaft 56-35/64x3in, yoke n/a
Usage: 1961 full-size Ford 390ci high-performance with manual

Interchange Number: 35
Part Number(s): DOOZ4602E
Dimensions: Shaft 59-13/16x3in, yoke n/a
Usage: 1970–71 Torino and Montego 302ci with manual or C4 automatic—all body styles except Ranchero and station wagon

Interchange Number: 36
Part Number(s): DOOZ4602F
Dimensions: Shaft 56-13/16x3in, yoke n/a
Usage: 1970–71 302ci Ranchero, Torino, and Montego station wagon—all with manual or C4

Interchange Number: 37
Part Number(s): DOOZ4602J
Dimensions: Shaft 58-5/8x3-1/2in, yoke n/a
Usage: 1970–71 Torino and Montego 351ci two-barrel with manual or C4—all body styles except Ranchero and station wagon

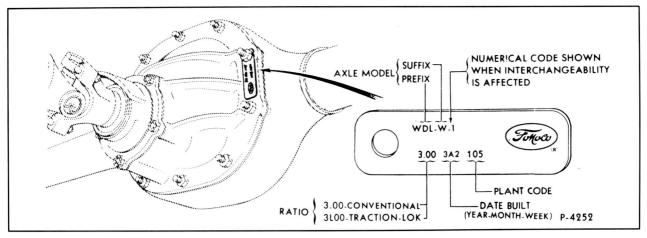

Location of rear axle identification tag.

Interchange Number: 38
Part Number(s): DOOZ4602L
Dimensions: Shaft 55-11/16x3-1/2in, yoke n/a
Usage: 1970–71 Ranchero and 1970–71 Montego and Torino station wagon—all 351ci two-barrel with manual or C4 automatic

Interchange Number: 39
Part Number(s): DOOZ4602A
Dimensions: Shaft 55-9/32x3-1/2in, yoke n/a
Usage: 1970–71 Torino and Montego 351ci four-barrel with four-speed and 1970–71 Torino and Montego 429ci four-speed or C6 automatic—all body styles except Ranchero and station wagon

Interchange Number: 40
Part Number(s): DOOZ4602B
Dimensions: Shaft 52-5/16x3-1/2in, yoke n/a
Usage: 1970–71 Ranchero 351ci four-barrel with four-speed and 1970–71 Ranchero or Torino and Montego station wagon with 429ci four-barrel or C6 automatic

Interchange Number: 41
Part Number(s): DOOZ4602G
Dimensions: Shaft 59-7/32x3in, yoke n/a
Usage: 1970 Torino and Montego 351ci four-barrel with FMX automatic—all body styles except Ranchero and station wagon
Note(s): Interchange Number 42 will fit when FMX transmission is replaced with a C6 automatic.

Interchange Number: 42
Part Number(s): D1OZ4602A
Dimensions: Shaft 55-1/4x3-1/2in, yoke n/a
Usage: 1971 Torino and Montego 351ci four-barrel with C6 automatic—all body styles except Ranchero and station wagon

Interchange Number: 43
Part Number(s): DOOZ4602N
Dimensions: Shaft 56-1/4x3in, yoke n/a
Usage: 1970 Ranchero or Torino and Montego station wagon with 351ci four-barrel with FMX automatic
Note(s): 1971 Ranchero or 1971 Torino and Montego station wagon with 351ci four-barrel will fit when the FMX is replaced with the C6 transmission.

Interchange Number: 44
Part Number(s): C9ZZ4602B
Dimensions: Shaft 50-5/8x3in, yoke 8-7/32x3-1/2in
Usage: 1969–70 Mustang with 351ci two-barrel and FMX automatic
Note(s): Cougar drive shaft will not interchange.

Interchange Number: 45
Part Number: C60Z4602W
Dimensions: Shaft 55-41/64x3in, yoke 8-7/32x3-1/2
Usage: 1966–69 Ranchero, 1966–67 Fairlane station wagon, and 1966–67 Comet station wagon—all with 289ci or 302ci and automatic transmission

Rear Axle

Identification

Effective with 1963 models, all axles came with an identification tag that was attached to the front carrier of the axle approximately at the one o'clock position. On this tag is a coded message that identifies the axle type.

Below this code is the ratio, followed by the build date and assembly plant code. If the traction-lock option is used, then the letter L is added to the ratio code (3.25 for standard or 3L25 with traction lock). The build date looks something like this—5C3, which breaks down as follows: 5 for 1965, the letter code C for build month March (A for January to L for December), and 3 for the third week of that month.

Housing, Rear Axle:

This is the bare axle assembly without ring gears and pinion. The ID code is the first three letters of the axle identification code explained above.

Model Identification

Cougar	Interchange Number
1967–69 8in	14
1967–69 9in	16, 17
1970 8in	15
1970 9in	17, 18, 19

Cyclone	Interchange Number
1966–67 8in	20
1966–67 9in	3
1968–69 8in	6
1968–69 9in	4
1970 8in	8
1970 9in	10

Fairlane and Torino	Interchange Number
1959–61 8-3/4	21
1962–65 8in	1
1962–65 9in	2
1966–67 8in, all except Ranchero	20
1966–67 9in, all except Ranchero	3
1966–67 Ranchero 8in	5

73

Interchange

Interchange Number: 1
Part Number(s): C4OZ4010B
Ring Gear Size: 8in
Base Code: WCL
Usage: 1962–64 Fairlane and 1962–63 Meteor 289ci, except 271hp

Interchange Number: 2
Part Number(s): C3OZ4010B
Ring Gear Size: 9in
Base Code: WCL, WDK, or WCU
Usage: 1963–65 Fairlane 289ci 271hp engine

Interchange Number: 3
Part Number(s): C7OZ4010D
Ring Gear Size: 9in
Base Code: WEB or WED
Usage: 1966–67 Fairlane and Comet 390ci and 427ci engine—all body styles except station wagon and Ranchero

Interchange Number: 4
Part Number(s): C9OZ4010C
Ring Gear Size: 9in
Base Code: WDW-K2, WEB, WED, WFC, WFA-A, or WFA-E
Usage: 1968–69 Torino and Montego 390ci, 427ci, and 428ci
Note(s): 44-1/2in spring seat to spring seat (center line).

Interchange Number: 5
Part Number(s): C9OZ4010A
Ring Gear Size: 8in
Base Code: WDY or WEA
Usage: 1966–69 Ranchero, 1966–67 Fairlane station wagon, 1966–67 Comet station wagon, 1968–69 Torino station wagon, and 1968–69 Montego station wagon—all with 289ci or 302ci
Note(s): 41-1/4in spring seat center.

Interchange Number: 6
Part Number(s): C9OZ4010D
Ring Gear Size: 8in
Base Code: WDW (except WDW-K2) or WDZ
Usage: 1968–69 Torino and Montego 302ci, except Ranchero and station wagon
Note(s): 41-1/2in spring seat center.

Interchange Number: 7
Part Number(s): C9OZ4010B
Ring Gear Size: 9in
Base Code: WEC, WEE, WFA-A, WFA-B, or WFA-C
Usage: 1966–69 Ranchero, 1966–67 Fairlane station wagon, 1966–69 Comet station wagon, and 1968–69 Torino station wagon—all 390ci or 428ci
Note(s): 41-3/16 in spring seat center.

Interchange Number: 8
Part Number(s): DOOZ4010B
Ring Gear Size: 8in
Base Code: WDW or WFJ
Usage: 1970–71 Torino, and Montego, except Ranchero and station wagon
Note(s): 44-7/16in spring seat center.

Interchange Number: 9
Part Number(s): DOOZ4010A
Ring Gear Size: 8in
Base Code: WDY, WEK
Usage: 1970–71 Ranchero and 1970–71 Torino and Montego station wagon
Note(s): 41-3/16in spring seat center.

Interchange Number: 10
Part Number(s): DOOZ4010C
Ring Gear Size: 9in
Base Code: WEB, WFA-E, WFA-G, WFC-B, WFC-C, WFC-G, WFC-N, or WFU-D
Usage: 1970–71 Torino and Montego, except Ranchero and station wagon
Note(s): 44-7/16in spring seat center

Interchange Number: 11
Part Number(s): DOOZ4010D
Ring Gear Size: 9in
Base Code: WEC, WEA-D, WEA-H, WEA-H, WEA-J, WFC-F, WFC-J, or WFC-R
Usage: 1970–71 Ranchero; 1970–71 Torino and Montego station wagon
Note(s): 41-3/16in spring seat center.

Interchange Number: 12
Part Number(s): C4DZ4010G
Ring Gear Size: 7-1/4in
Base code: WCY
Usage: 1964-1/2–66 Mustang, 1964 Comet, and 1964–65 Falcon
Note(s): Integral carrier. Not a good performance axle.

Interchange Number: 13
Part Number(s): C4DZ4010F
Ring Gear Size: 8in
Base Code: WCZ or WDJ
Usage: 1964-1/2–66 Mustang and 1964–65 Falcon 289ci

Interchange Number: 14
Part Number(s): C7ZZ4010E
Ring Gear Size: 8in
Base Code: WCZ or WDJ
Usage: 1967–69 Mustang Cougar

Interchange Number: 15
Part Number(s): DOZZ4010A
Ring Gear Size: 8in
Base Code: WCZ or WFL
Usage: 1970 Mustang and Cougar

Interchange Number: 16
Part Number(s): C9ZZ4010B
Ring Gear Size: 9in
Base Code: WES or WFD
Usage: 1967–68 Mustang and 1967–68 Cougar up to build date April 1, 1968
Note(s): High-performance axle.

Interchange Number: 17
Part Number(s): DOZZ4010C
Ring Gear Size: 9in
Base Code: WES, WFB, WFD, or WFU
Usage: 1968–70 Mustang and Cougar beginning at build date April 1, 1968, to June 1, 1970
Note(s): High-performance axle.

Interchange Number: 18

Part Number(s): DOZZ4010D
Ring Gear Size: 9in
Base Code: WES, WFB, WFD, or WFU
Usage: 1970 Mustang and Cougar beginning at build date June 1, 1970, to build date September 25, 1970.
Note(s): High-performance axle.

Interchange Number: 19

Part Number(s): DOZZ4010E
Ring Gear Size: 9in
Base Code: WES, WFB, WFD, or WFU
Usage: 1970 Mustang and Cougar beginning at build date June 1, 1970
Note(s): High-performance axle.

Interchange Number: 20

Part Number(s): C6OZ4010J
Ring Gear Size: 8in
Base Code: WDW or WDZ
Usage: 1966–67 Fairlane and Comet 289ci—all except station wagon and Ranchero

Interchange Number: 21

Part Number(s): C3AZ4010D
Ring Gear Size: 8in
Base Code: WBS
Usage: 1959–64 full-size Ford
Note(s): Standard-duty axle. Not used with 427ci, 406ci, or 390ci engines.

Interchange Number: 22

Part Number(s): C3AZ4010G
Ring Gear Size: 9in
Base Code: WBT, WBV, or WCN
Usage: 1959–64 full-size Ford 427ci, 406ci, and 390ci
Note(s): Heavy-duty axle.

Shafts, Rear Axle

Axle shafts are greatly interchangeable between mid-sized cars (1966–67 Fairlane, 1966–67 Comet, 1968–70 Torino, and 1968–70 Montego) and the Mustang and Cougar line. But note that the early Mustangs (1964-1/2–66) with the small 7-1/4in ring gear axle did not use the Fairlane and Comet axles. Instead, these axles can be found in Falcons and early-1964–65 Comets with the 7-1/4in axles. Note though that Falcons with a V-8 used the larger 8in-diameter ring gear that was used on the majority of models covered in this manual.

Model Identification

Cougar	Interchange Number
1967–68 8in or 9in	8, 3
1969–70 8in	8, 3
1969–70 9in	5

Cyclone	Interchange Number
1966–69 8in or 9in (28 splines)	3
1966–69 9in (31 splines)	4
1970 8in or 9in (28 splines)	6
1970 9in (31 splines)	5

Fairlane and Torino	Interchange Number
1959–61 8-3/4in	9
1959–61 9in	10
1962–65 8in (28 splines)	1
1962–65 9in (28 splines)	2
1966–69 8in or 9in (28 splines)	3
1966–69 9in (31 splines)	4
1970 8in or 9in (28 splines)	6
1970 9in (31 splines)	5

Mustang	Interchange Number
1964-1/2–66 7-1/4in	7
1964-1/2–66 8in	1
1964-1/2–66 9in	2
1967–68 8in or 9in	8, 3
1969–70 8in	8, 3
1969–70 9in	5

Interchange

Interchange Number: 1

Part Number(s): C2OZ4234A (right), C2OZ4235A (left)
Length(s): 30-1/8in (right), 26-5/64in (left; 28 splines)
Usage 1962–65 Fairlane, 1965–66 Mustang, and 1964–65 Falcon and Comet with V-8—all with 8in ring gear axle

Interchange Number: 2

Part Number(s): C5OZ4234B (right), C5OZ4235A (left)
Length(s): 30-1/8in (right), 26-5/64in (left; 28 splines)
Usage: 1962–65 Fairlane 1965–66 Mustang with 9in ring gear axle

Interchange Number: 3

Part Number(s): C9OZ4234A (right), C9OZ4235B (left)
Length(s): 30-1/8in (right), 27-1/16 (left; 28 splines)
Usage: 1966–67 Fairlane, 1968–69 Torino, 1966–67 Comet, 1968–69 Montego, 1969–70 Mustang (after March 15, 1969), 1969–70 Cougar, 1969–70 Falcon (after March 15, 1969)—all with 8in or 9in ring gear axle
Note(s): Falcons built before the above dates used a different set of axles and will not interchange.

Interchange Number: 4

Part Number(s): C2OZ4234C (right), C2OZ4235D (left)
Length(s): 30-1/8in (right), 27-1/16in (left; 31 Splines)
Usage: 1967 Fairlane, 1968–69 Torino, 1967 Comet, 1968–69 Montego, 1967–70 Mustang, and 1967–70 Cougar—all 427ci, 428ci, 429ci, or 351ci four-barrel Cleveland
Note(s): Tough axles. Used in special high-performance applications with 9in axle only. Also used in Boss Mustang and Cougar Eliminator.

Interchange Number: 5

Part Number(s): DOOZ4234A (right), DOOZ4235B (left)
Length(s): 31-7/8in (right), 27-13/16in (left; 31 splines)
Usage: 1970–71 Torino and Montego
Note(s): Excellent racing axle shaft. Use with 9in axle. Special high-performance version used in the Cobra GT with 429ci and Cyclone and Spoiler with 429ci or 351ci Cleveland four-barrel.

Interchange Number: 6

Part Number(s): DOOZ4234C (right), DOOZ4235D (left)
Length(s): 31-7/8in (right), 27-13/16in (left; 28 splines)
Usage: 1970–71 Torino and Montego
Note(s): With 8in or 9in axle. Good general axle.

Interchange Number: 7

Part Number(s): C4DZ4234A (right), C4DZ4235B (left)
Length(s): 29-15/16in (right), 26-7/16in (left; 24 splines)
Usage: 1964-1/2–66 Mustang and 1964–65 Falcon—all with 7-1/4in axle built in USA only.
Note(s): Not a good performance axle. Used mainly on 289ci two-barrel or six-cylinder. Canadian built cars used a different left axle.

Interchange Number: 8

Part Number(s): C6OZ4234F (right), C6OZ4235B (left)
Length(s): 31-1/8in (right), 27-1/16in (left; 28 splines)
Usage: 1967–69 Mustang, 1966–67 Falcon, and 1967–69 Cougar with 8in or 9in axle
Note(s): Used before build date March 15, 1969. After that date use Interchange Number 3.

Interchange Number: 9

Part Number(s): COAZ4234A (right), COAZ4235A (left)
Length(s): 32-13/64in (right), 27-27/32in (left; 28 splines)
Usage: 1959–60 full-size Ford, except with heavy-duty 9in axle

Interchange Number: 10

Part Number(s): COAW4234D (right), COAW4235C (left)
Length(s): 32-29/64 (right), 28-3/32 (left; 28 splines)
Usage: 1959–60 full-size Ford heavy-duty 9in axle

Chapter 6

Suspension and Steering Systems

Control Arms, Front

Model Identification

Cougar	*Interchange Number*
1967–70 upper	4
1967 lower	9
1968–70 lower	10

Cyclone	*Interchange Number*
1965 upper	5
1965 lower	8
1966–70 upper	4
1966–67 lower	9
1968–70 lower	10

Fairlane and Torino	*Interchange Number*
1959–61 upper	12
1959 lower	13
1960–61 lower	14
1962–65 upper	3
1962–65 lower	8
1966–70 upper	4
1966–67 lower	9
1968–70 lower	10

Mustang	*Interchange Number*
1964-1/2–66 upper	5
1964-1/2–66 lower	8
1967–70 upper	4
1967 lower	9
1968–70 lower	10

Interchange

Interchange Number: 1

Part Number(s): B7AA3082A (fits either side)
Location: Upper
Usage: 1959–64 full-size Ford, 1959–64 full-size Mercury, and 1958–60 Edsel

Interchange Number: 2

Part Number(s): D2AZ3082A (fits either side)
Location: Upper
Usage: 1965–72 full-size Ford, 1972 Torino and Montego, 1965–72 full-size Mercury, and 1965–72 Thunderbird

Interchange Number: 3

Part Number(s): C3OZ3082A (right), C3OZ3083A (left)
Location: Upper
Usage: 1962–65 Fairlane and 1962–63 Mercury Meteor

Interchange Number: 4

Part Number(s): DOOZ3082A (fits either side)
Location: Upper
Usage: 1966–67 Fairlane, 1968–71 Torino, 1966–67 Comet, 1968–71 Montego, 1967–73 Mustang (except Boss 429ci), 1967–73 Cougar, 1970–73 Maverick, 1971–73 Comet (compact), and 1966–70 Falcon

Interchange Number: 5

Part Number(s): C4DZ3082B
Location: Upper
Usage: 1964-1/2–66 Mustang, 1964–65 Falcon, and 1964–65 Comet

Interchange Number: 6

Part Number(s): C9ZZ3082A
Location: Upper
Usage: 1969 Boss 429ci Mustang only

Interchange Number: 7

Part Number(s): C2AZ3078B (right), C2AZ3079A (left)
Location: Lower
Usage: 1959–62 full-size Ford, 1959–60 Thunderbird, 1961–62 full-size Mercury, and 1958–60 Edsel
Note(s): Those with larger engines or heavy-duty suspension used stronger arms. This should be kept in mind when interchanging. When replacing also, find a car equipped like yours, or go up. For example, if your car has a 289ci engine, find a car with a 352ci or 390ci engine. These arms will be stronger. Always replace arms in pairs when you do this. Tip: Station wagons usually have stronger arms.

Interchange Number: 8

Part Number(s): C4OZ3078A (right), C4OZ3079A (left)
Location: Lower
Usage: 1962–65 Fairlane and 1964–65 Comet

Interchange Number: 9

Part Number(s): C7OZ3078B (fits either side)
Location: Lower
Usage: 1966–67 Fairlane, 1966–67 Comet, 1966–67 Falcon, 1967 Mustang, and 1967 Cougar

Interchange Number: 10

Part Number(s): D1OZ3078A (fits either side)
Location: Lower
Usage: 1968–71 Torino, 1968–71 Montego, 1968–73 Mustang, 1968–73 Cougar, 1970–73 Maverick, 1971–73 Comet (compact), and 1968–70 Falcon

Interchange Number: 11

Part Number(s): C4DZ3078A (fits either side)
Location: Lower
Usage: 1964-1/2–66 Mustang, 1964–65 Falcon, and 1962–63 Comet

Interchange Number: 12
Part Number(s): C3AZ3082A (right), C3AZ3083A (left)
Location: Upper
Usage: 1959–64 full-size Ford, 1961–64 full-size Mercury, and 1959–60 Edsel
Note(s): Interchange without shaft or ball joint.

Interchange Number: 13
Part Number(s): B9AZ3078A (right), B9AZ3079A (left)
Location: Lower
Usage: 1957–59 full-size Ford and Mercury and 1959 Thunderbird.
Note(s): Interchange Number 14 will fit if front bushings are swapped.

Interchange Number: 14
Part Number(s): C2AZ3078B (right), C2AZ3079B (left)
Location: Lower
Usage: 1960–62 full-size and Mercury and 1960 Thunderbird
Note(s): Models with 406ci or 427ci use heavy-duty arms. Heavy-duty arms used in station wagon with 390ci.

Coil Springs, Front
All Ford and Mercury models covered in this guide are fitted with coil springs. The interchange below is a guide to alert you to what models and makes used the same coil springs. However, there are different tensions available that were used with certain options and models. When interchanging coil springs look for springs from a car that has the same or larger engine as your car. The ride may be harsher if you use springs from a car that had a larger engine, but handling will be greatly improved. Always replace springs in pairs, preferably from the same car. Mismatched springs or springs with a lower rating could cause a dangerous handling condition.

Either dabs of paint or colored stripes are used to identify the usage and rating of the springs. Use the interchanges and charts below to identify the springs.

Interchange

Interchange Number: 1
Part Number(s): Varies according to tension
Usage: 1957–59 full-size Ford, 1957–59 full-size Mercury, and 1957–60 Thunderbird
Note(s): Cars with a V-8 use higher spring rates than those with a six-cylinder. Convertibles use higher spring rates than sedans or coupes. Station wagons and Rancheros use same rates as convertibles. Springs from station wagons with the 352ci engine and air conditioning are heavy-duty and excellent for a coupe.

Interchange Number: 2
Part Number(s): Varies according to tension
Usage: 1960–64 full-size Ford, 1961–64 full-size Mercury, and 1960 Edsel
Note(s): Bigger engines use stiffer springs. Cars with 390ci high-performance, 406ci or 427ci used springs stamped C2AA in 1962.

Interchange Number: 3
Part Number(s): Varies according to tension
Usage: 1962–65 Fairlane, 1962–63 Mercury Meteor
Note(s): Cars with a V-8 use higher spring rates than those with a six-cylinder. Convertibles use higher spring rates than sedans or coupes. Tip: Heavy-duty units are color-coded with either a pink or white stripe.

Interchange Number: 4
Part Number(s): Varies according to tension
Usage: 1966–67 Fairlane and Comet, 1968–71 Torino and Montego, 1966–67 Ranchero (except 1966 Ranchero with 200ci six-cylinder), and 1966–70 Falcon
Note(s): Cars with V-8s use higher spring rates than those with six-cylinders. Convertibles use higher spring rates than sedans or coupes. Some springs have larger-diameter wire and were used with handling packages.

Interchange Number: 5
Part Number(s): Varies according to tension
Usage: 1964-1/2–73 Mustang and 1967–73 Cougar
Note(s): Boss 302ci springs can be found commonly in 1971–73 302ci fastbacks with the competition handling package.

Springs, Rear
All models covered in this guide used rear leaf springs. Leaf springs are identified by either color code marks or a stamping number on one of the leaves. Unlike coil springs, leaf springs do not need to be replaced in pairs. But beware that unlike coil springs some leaf springs may vary in rating from one side to the other. For example: the driver's side might be rated at 1,230lb and the passenger's side may be rated at 1,260lb. This helps counteract engine torque to avoid wheel hopping on takeoff. So be sure of the position of the springs when swapping.

The interchange below is based on the proper rating and physical fit. Remember, you can go up in ratings but never down. Tip: Rear leaf springs have the added benefit that leaves can be added or removed to make the desired number of leaves and rating.

Model Identification

Cougar	Interchange Number
1967	
all except GT models	34
GT models	35
1968	
without handling package	
hardtop	34
convertible	34
with handling package	
hardtop	35
convertible	35
1969	
302ci, 351ci, or 390ci	
hardtop	
all except Eliminator and GT package	37
Eliminator	39
GT package	38
convertible	
without GT package	40
with GT package	41
428ci	
hardtop	39
convertible	39
1970	
302ci or 351ci	
hardtop	42
convertible	43
Eliminator	39
428ci	
hardtop	39
convertible	44

Cyclone	Interchange Number
1966	
289ci	
hardtop	13
convertible	15
390ci	
hardtop	14, 15
convertible	20
1967 390ci	
hardtop	16
convertible	15, 20
1968	
302ci hardtop	21
390ci	
GT fastback	23
GT hardtop	26
except GT hardtop	22

Interchange

Interchange Number: 1
Part Number(s): C4DZ5560J (either side)
Number of Leaves: 4
Rating: 650lb
ID Number(s): C4ZA5556B, C4ZA5556D, C4ZA5556F, C4ZA5556N C4ZA5556U, C4ZA5556K, C4ZA5556L, C4ZA5556S, C4ZA5556Y, C4ZA5556U, C7ZA5556M, C7ZA5556Z, C7ZA5556Y, C7ZA5556J, C7ZA5556AB, or C4DA5556U
Usage: 1964–67 Mustang fastback and convertible with six-cylinder or 289ci engine and 1964 Falcon with six-cylinder or 260ci eight (except station wagon)
Note(s): Without GT package in 1967.

Interchange Number: 2
Part Number(s): C5ZZ5560C (either side)
Number of Leaves: 4
Rating: 610lb
ID Number(s): C4ZA5556C, C4ZA5556E, C4ZA5556M, or C4ZA5556T
Usage: 1964-1/2–66 Mustang hardtop with 289ci or six-cylinder

Interchange Number: 3
Part Number(s): C7ZZ5560M (either side)
Number of Leaves: 4
Rating: 665lb
ID Number(s): C7ZA5556N, C7ZA5556AD, C7ZA5556AS, C7ZA5556AT, C7ZA5556AU, C7ZA5556AV, C7ZA5556AG, C7ZA5556AL, C7ZA5556AM, C9ZA5556K, or C9ZA5556M
Usage: 1967–69 Mustang fastback and convertible 390ci and 1967–68 Mustang fastback and convertible 289ci, GT handling package, 1967–68 GT 350 and GT 500, 1969 Mustang fastback and convertible 302ci or 351ci with GT handling package (all body styles), and 1968 Mustang hardtop 302ci 289ci or 390ci without GT package
Note(s): On 1969 models built after September 10, 1968, only, Interchange 5 will fit.

Interchange Number: 4
Part Number(s): C7ZZ5560U (either side)
Number of Leaves: 4
Rating: 625lb
ID Number(s): C7ZA5556AG, C7AZ5556AJ, C7AZ5556AN, C7AZ5556S, C7AZ5556AF, D0ZA5556A, or D0ZA5556B
Usage: 1967–69 Mustang hardtop 390ci, 1967–69 Mustang hardtop 289ci, 302ci, or 351ci with GT handling package, 1970 Mustang hardtop 302ci or 351ci, 1971 Mustang fastback 302ci or 351ci without GT handling package—except Boss models or Cleveland four-barrel

Interchange Number: 5
Part Number(s): C9ZZ5560A (either side)
Number of Leaves: 4
Rating: 700lb
ID Number(s): C9ZA5556B or CODZ5556Z
Usage: 1969 Mustang fastback 302ci, except Boss 302ci and GT 350; 1969–72 Mustang convertible 302ci, 351ci, or 390ci four-barrel, except GT 350; and 1969 Mustang Mach I with 351ci or 390ci
Note(s): All built before September 10, 1968. Interchange Numbers 1 and 6 will fit but are some what lower-rated.

Interchange Number: 6
Part Number(s): C9ZZ5560H (either side)
Number of Leaves: 4
Rating: 595lb
ID Number(s): C9ZA5556R, DOZA5556E, or DOZA5556F
Usage: 1969–70 Mustang fastback 302ci except Boss 302ci and GT 350 models; 1969–70 Mach I 302ci, 351ci, or 390ci except Boss 302ci and GT 350.
Note(s): Used after build date September 10, 1968. May have three yellow stripes for identification.

Interchange Number: 7
Part Number(s): C9ZZ5560D (either side)
Number of Leaves: 4
Rating: 690lb
ID Number(s): C9ZA5556H, DOZA5556J, or DOZA5556K
Usage: 1969–70 Mustang fastback and hardtop with 428ci engine with under-hood battery, all except GT 500 models
Note(s): May have two gold and one violet stripe for identification.

Interchange Number: 8
Part Number(s): C9ZZ5560C (either side)
Number of Leaves: 4
Rating: 730lb
ID Number(s): C9ZA5556F, DOZA5556G, DOZA5556H, or D7ZZ5556T
Usage: 1969–70 Mustang fastback and hardtop with 428ci engine with trunk-mounted battery, 1969–70 Mustang convertible with 428ci, with or without trunk-mounted battery (except GT 500 models and 1969–70 Boss 429ci)
Note(s): May have two yellow and two brown stripes for identification.

Interchange Number: 9
Part Number(s): C9ZZ5560B (either side)
Number of Leaves: 4
Rating: 695lb
ID Number(s): C9ZA5556C, C9ZA5556D, or D5ZZ5556X
Usage: 1969 Mustang fastback and convertible with 351ci or 390ci with GT handling package

Interchange Number: 10
Part Number(s): C9ZZ5560J (either side)
Number of Leaves: 4
Rating: 550lb
ID Number(s): C9ZA5556S, S9MS5556A, SOMS5556TS, DOZA5556L, DOZA5556M, or D1ZA5556HA
Usage: 1969–71 Mustang Boss 302ci, 1969–70 GT 350 Mustang (all body styles), and 1971–72 Boss 351ci Mustang
Note(s): 1971 Boss 302ci Mustang after October 9, 1970 only. May have two green and two brown stripes for identification.

Interchange Number: 11
Part Number(s): C5OZ5560F (either side)
Number of Leaves: 5
Rating: 748lb
ID Number(s): C4OA5556C, C4OA5556D, C5OA5556F, C4OA5560G, C4OA5560H, C4OA5560J, or C4OA5560K
Usage: 1964–65 Fairlane with 260ci or 289ci (except 271hp version) and 1964–65 Fairlane six-cylinder with automatic transmission—all body styles except station wagon

Interchange Number: 12
Part Number(s): C5OZ5560J (either side)
Number of Leaves: 5
Rating: 763lb
ID Number(s): C4OA5560E, C4OA5560F, C5OA5556E, C5OA5556F, or C5OA5556H
Usage: 1964–65 Fairlane 289ci 271hp (all applications) and 1964–65 Fairlane with 260ci or 289ci (except 271hp version with heavy-duty suspension)—all body styles except station wagon

Interchange Number: 13
Part Number(s): C6OZ5560B (either side)
Number of Leaves: 4
Rating: 750lb
ID Number(s): C6OA5560EC, C6OA5560ED, C6OA5556BK, C6OA5556AY, C7OA5556G, C7OA5556H, or C7OA5556E
Usage: 1966–67 Fairlane 289ci with or without heavy-duty suspension (all body styles except station wagon and Ranchero) and 1966–67 Comet 289ci with or without heavy-duty suspension

Interchange Number: 14
Part Number(s): C6OZ5560AL (either side)
Number of Leaves: 4
Rating: 780lb
ID Number(s): C6OA5560BS, C6OA5560BV, C6OA5556DN, C6OA5556DR, C6OA5556EE, C6OA5556EF, C6OA55556Y, C6OA5556Z, C6OA5556AN, C6OA5556AZ, C9OA5556AG, or C90A5556AH
Usage: 1966–67 Fairlane 500 390ci (except convertible, station wagon, and Ranchero); 1966–67 Fairlane 390ci with heavy-duty suspension (except 500 and GT, convertible, station wagon and Ranchero);1966–67 Comet 390ci except station wagon and convertible; 1969 Torino 302ci, 351ci, and 390ci with heavy-duty suspension (except station wagon, convertible, and Ranchero), 1969 Torino convertible 302ci or 351ci two-barrel with heavy-duty suspension, 1969 Montego (except station wagon and convertible) 302ci, 351ci, and 390ci with heavy-duty suspension; 1969 Montego convertible 302ci or 351ci two-barrel with heavy-duty suspension; 1970–71 Torino four-door 429ci with cross country suspension (except Cobra Jet and Super Cobra Jet); 1970–71 Torino 500 two-door 351ci four-barrel with cross country suspension; 1970–71 Torino GT two-door 302ci or 351ci with cross country suspension;1970–71 Torino convertible with six-cylinder or 302ci and cross country suspension; 1970–71 Montego four-door 429ci with cross country suspension (except Cobra Jet and Super Cobra Jet), 1970–71 Montego MX two-door 351ci four-barrel with cross country suspension; 1970–71 Cyclone two-door 302ci or 351ci with cross country suspension; and 1970–71 Montego convertible with six-cylinder or 302ci and cross country suspension

Interchange Number: 15
Part Number(s): C6OZ5560AB (either side)
Number of Leaves: 4
Rating: 820lb
ID Number(s): C6OA5560CN, C6OA5560CR, C9OA5556AE, or C9OA5556AF
Usage: 1966–67 Fairlane 500 390ci with heavy-duty suspension (except station wagon, Ranchero, and convertible), 1966–67 Comet 390ci two-barrel with heavy-duty suspension (except station wagon and convertible), 1967 Cyclone GT 390ci convertible, 1966 Fairlane and Comet convertible 289ci with heavy-duty suspension, 1967 Fairlane GT and GTA 390ci convertible, 1968–69 Torino 500 390ci with heavy-duty suspension (except station wagon, Ranchero, and convertible), 1970–71 Torino convertible 351ci with cross country suspension, and 1970–71 Montego convertible with 351ci engine and cross country suspension

Interchange Number: 16
Part Number(s): C6OZ5560Z (either side)
Number of Leaves: 4
Rating: 730lb
ID Number(s): C6OA5560CE or C6OA5560CF
Usage: 1966–67 Fairlane GT and Cyclone GT (except convertible) 390ci or 427ci

Interchange Number: 17
Part Number(s): C6DZ5560A (either side)
Number of Leaves: 5
Rating: 970lb
ID Number(s): C6DA55560K or C6DA5556V
Usage: 1966–67 Ranchero six-cylinder or 289ci engine

Interchange Number: 18
Part Number(s): C7OZ5560E (either side)
Number of Leaves: 5
Rating: 1050lb
ID Number(s): C2OA55560AC, C2OA55560AE, C2OA55560AF, C7OA55560M, C7OA55560AC, C7OA55560AD, C7OA55560AE, or C7OA55560AF
Usage: 1966–67 Ranchero 390ci engine and 1968 Ranchero 289ci, 302ci, or six-cylinder

Interchange Number: 19
Part Number(s): C7OZ5560F (either side)
Number of Leaves: 5
Rating: 1,140lb
ID Number(s): C6DA5556H, C6DA5556Y, C6DZ5556Z, or C70A5556R
Usage: 1966–67 Ranchero 390ci engine with heavy-duty suspension, 1968 Ranchero 289ci, 302ci, or six-cylinder with heavy-duty suspension, and 1968–69 Ranchero 390ci.

Interchange Number: 20
Part Number(s): C8OZ5560D (either side)
Number of Leaves: 4
Rating: 860lb
ID Number(s): C6OA5556CL, C6OA5556CM, C6OA5556CS, or C6OA5556CT
Usage: 1966–67 Fairlane 500 390ci convertible and 1966–67 Comet 390ci convertible.

Interchange Number: 21
Part Number(s): C8OZ5560B (either side)
Number of Leaves: 4
Rating: 735lb
ID Number(s): See notes
Usage: 1968 Torino or Torino GT 302ci or 390ci two-barrel (except convertible, fastback, station wagon, and Ranchero), 1968 Montego or Cyclone 302ci or 390ci two-barrel (except convertible, fastback, and station wagon)
Note(s): Identified by green and orange color stripes.

Interchange Number: 22
Part Number(s): C8OZ5560K (either side)
Number of Leaves: 4
Rating: 840lb
ID Number(s): C8OA5556S, C8OA5556T, C8OA5556U, or C8OA5556V
Usage: 1968 Torino 390ci four-barrel without GT handling package (except convertible, fastback, station wagon, and Ranchero) and 1968 Montego 390ci two-barrel without GT handling package (except convertible, fastback, and station wagon)

Interchange Number: 23
Part Number(s): C9OZ5560L (either side)
Number of Leaves: 4
Rating: 720lb
ID Number(s): C9OA5556AA, C90A5556AB, C9OA5556J, or C9OA5556R
Usage: 1968 Torino GT two-door hardtop and fastback 390ci four-barrel, 427ci, or 428ci Cobra jet; 1969 Torino 500 convertible with 351ci or 390ci; 1969 Torino 500 fastback 390ci; 1969 Torino GT convertible 302ci or 351ci; 1969 Torino GT fastback with 351ci or 390ci; 1969 Torino 500 fastback and convertible 302ci or 351ci with GT handling package; 1968 Cyclone GT two-door hardtop and fastback 390ci four-barrel, 427ci, or 428ci Cobra jet; 1969 Montego MX convertible with 351ci or 390ci; 1969 Montego MX 390ci; 1969 Cyclone GT convertible 302ci or 351ci; 1969 Cyclone GT fastback with 351ci or 390ci; and 1969 Montego MX two-door hardtop 302ci or 351ci with GT handling package

Interchange Number: 24
Part Number(s): C8OZ5560M (either side)
Number of Leaves: 4
Rating: 910lb
ID Number(s): C8OA5556AA, C80A5556AB, or D9RR5556AC
Usage: 1968–69 Torino and Montego convertible 302ci or six-cylinder with heavy-duty suspension 390ci

Interchange Number: 25
Part Number(s): C8OZ5560N (either side)
Number of Leaves: 5
Rating: 975lb
ID Number(s): C8OA5556AC, C80A5556AD
Usage: 1968–69 Torino and Montego convertible 390ci with heavy-duty suspension

Interchange Number: 26
Part Number(s): C8OZ5560A (either side)
Number of Leaves: 4
Rating: 795lb
ID Number(s): See notes
Usage: 1968–69 Torino GT and Cyclone GT two-door hardtop

Interchange Number: 27
Part Number(s): C9OZ5560J (either side)
Number of Leaves: 4
Rating: 702lb
ID Number(s): C9OA5556U or C9OA5556V
Usage: 1968–69 Torino and Montego convertible 428ci Cobra Jet with trunk-mounted battery, 1969 Torino GT 428ci Cobra Jet with under-hood battery, 1968–69 Montego 428ci Cobra Jet convertible with trunk-mounted battery, and 1969 Cyclone GT 428ci Cobra with under-hood battery

Interchange Number: 28
Part Number(s): C9OZ5560H (either side)
Number of Leaves: 4
Rating: 798lb
ID Number(s): C9OA5556S or C90A5556T
Usage: 1968–69 Torino GT and Cyclone GT 428ci Cobra Jet with trunk-mounted battery, except fastback

Interchange Number: 29
Part Number(s): C9OZ5560K (either side)
Number of Leaves: 4
Rating: 670lb
ID Number(s): C9OA5556Y or C90A5556Z
Usage: 1969 Torino GT and Cyclone GT fastback and two-door hardtop 302ci, 1969 Torino and Montego fastback 351ci or 390ci, and 1969 Torino and Montego 302ci with GT handling package

Interchange Number: 30
Part Number(s): DOOZ5560C (either side)
Number of Leaves: 4
Rating: 660lb
ID Number(s): See notes
Usage: 1970–71 Torino and Montego fastback, convertible, or four-door hardtop with 429ci; and 1970–71 Torino GT or Cyclone GT 429ci Cobra Jet and Super Cobra Jet (all body styles except Ranchero GT)
Note(s): Identified by two brown and two yellow stripes.

Interchange Number: 31
Part Number(s): DOOZ5560A (either side)
Number of Leaves: 5
Rating: 965lb
ID Number(s): DOOA5556A or DOOA5556B
Usage: 1970–71 Ranchero GT 429ci Cobra Jet and Super Cobra Jet
Note(s): May have one brown and two orange stripes for identification.

Interchange Number: 32
Part Number(s): DOOZ5560 (either side)
Number of Leaves: 4
Rating: 850lb
ID Number(s): DOOA5556C or DOOA5556D
Usage: 1970–71 Ranchero, all engines except 429ci

Interchange Number: 33
Part Number(s): C9OZ5560D (either side)
Number of Leaves: 4
Rating: 677lb
ID Number(s): C9OA5556F or C9OA5556L
Usage: 1969 Torino and Montego fastback 302ci (except GT or Cyclone), 1970–71 Torino GT fastback 302ci models, and 1970–71 Torino GT or Cyclone 351ci two-door hardtop

Interchange Number: 34
Part Number(s): C7WY5560A (either side)
Number of Leaves: 4
Usage: 1967 Cougar (except GT) and 1968 Cougar 390ci two-barrel, 428ci, and 427ci without handling package

Interchange Number: 35
Part Number(s): C7WY5560B (either side)
Number of Leaves: 4
Usage: 1967 Cougar GT; 1968 Cougar 390ci four-barrel; and 1968 Cougar hardtop 302ci, 390ci, and 428ci with handling package.

Interchange Number: 36
Part Number(s): C8WY5560A (either side)
Number of Leaves: 4
ID Number(s): C8WA5556B
Usage: 1968 Cougar six-cylinder 289ci or 302ci—all body styles.

Interchange Number: 37
Part Number(s): DOWY5560D (either side)
Number of Leaves: 4
Rating: 700lb
ID Number(s): C9WA5556AE, C9WA5556AF, DOWA5556G, or DOWA5556AF
Usage: 1969 Cougar hardtop 302ci, 351ci or 390ci (except GT and Eliminator) and 1970 Cougar hardtop 302ci or 351ci (except Eliminator)
Note(s): May have two violet, one silver or red-violet, and one brown stripe for identification.

Interchange Number: 38
Part Number(s): C9WY5560D (either side)
Number of Leaves: 4
Usage: 1969 Cougar hardtop 302ci, 351ci, or 390ci—all with GT package

Interchange Number: 39
Part Number(s): DOWY5560B (either side)
Number of Leaves: 4
Rating: 710lb
ID Number(s): C9WA5556F, DOWA5556C, DOWA5556D, C9WA5556V, C9WA5556AA, C9WA5556AB, or D1WA5556HA
Usage: 1969–70 Cougar Eliminator 302ci, 1969 Cougar (all body styles) with 428ci Cobra Jet with or without trunk-mounted battery, 1970 Cougar 428ci Cobra Jet, 1970 Cougar 351ci with competition handling package, late-1972 Cougar 351ci with competition handling package, and 1971 Cougar 351ci four-barrel or 429ci
Note(s): 1972 model usage begins at build date September 1, 1971. ID number C9WA5556F is rated at 720lb and originally was used on 1969 Eliminator and on 1969 428ci Cobra Jet models with trunk-mounted battery. ID number C9WA5556V is rated at 760lb. However, all will interchange.

Interchange Number: 40
Part Number(s): C9WY5560L (either side)
Number of Leaves: 4
Rating: 742lb
ID Number(s): C9WA5556AC or C9WA5556AD
Usage: 1969 Cougar convertible 351ci or 390ci without GT package

Interchange Number: 41
Part Number(s): C9WY5560C (either side)
Number of Leaves: 4
Usage: 1969 Cougar convertible 351ci or 390ci with GT package

Interchange Number: 42
Part Number(s): DOWY5560D (either side)
Number of Leaves: 4
Rating: 700lb
ID Number(s): DOWA5556G or DOWA5556H
Usage: 1970 Cougar hardtop 302ci or 351ci
Note(s): May be identified by two violet and one silver stripe.

Interchange Number: 43
Part Number(s): DOWY5560C (either side)
Number of Leaves: 4
Rating: 740lb
ID Number(s): DOWA5556E or DOWA5556F
Usage: 1970 Cougar convertible 302ci or 351ci

Interchange Number: 44
Part Number(s): DOWY5560A (either side)
Number of Leaves: 4
ID Number(s): DOWA5556A or DOWA5556B
Usage: 1970 Cougar convertible 428ci engine or 351ci with competition suspension and late-1972 Cougar 351ci Cobra Jet with competition suspension.
Note(s): May be identified by two violet and two green stripes. 1972 model usage begins at September 1, 1971.

Interchange Number: 45
Part Number(s): B9A5560A (either side)
Number of Leaves: 3
Usage: 1957–59 full-size Ford two-door hardtop or coupe

Interchange Number: 46
Part Number(s): B9A5560AC (either side)
Number of Leaves: (either side)
Number of Leaves: convertible, four-door hardtop, or four-door sedan

Interchange Number: 47
Part Number(s): COAA5560AK (either side)
Number of Leaves: 3
Usage: 1960 full-size Ford two-door hardtop or sedan

Interchange Number: 48
Part Number(s): COAA5560AC (either side)
Number of Leaves: 4
Usage: 1960 full-size Ford convertible, four-door hardtop, or four-door sedan

Interchange Number: 49
Part Number(s): C2AA5560F (either side)
Number of Leaves: 4
ID Number(s): Same as part number
Usage: 1961–62 full-size Ford convertible, four-door hardtop, or four-door sedan

Interchange Number: 50
Part Number(s): C2AA5560H (either side)
Number of Leaves: 4
ID Number(s): Same as part number
Usage: 1961–62 full-size Ford two-door hardtop or two-door sedan

Interchange Number: 51
Part Number(s): C8OZ5560F (either side)
Number of Leaves: 4
Rating: 850lb
ID Number(s): See notes
Usage: 1968 Torino and Montego convertible 302ci and 390ci two-barrel without GT package, and 1968 Torino fastback 302ci and 390ci two-barrel without GT package
Note(s): Identify by one green and one violet stripe.

Interchange Number: 52
Part Number(s): C3OZ5560H (either side)
Number of Leaves: 4
Rating: 744–782lb
ID Number(s): C3OA5560BE or C3OA5560BF
Usage: 1962–63 Fairlane—all body styles except 116in wheelbase and station wagon

Sway Bars, Front
Sway bars, or stabilizer bars, as they are sometimes referred to, are highly interchangeable, interchanging freely between family groups Fairlane and Comet and Cougar and Mustang.

The bars are identified by color stripes and the diameter of the bar. However, even if color stripe codes are correct, always measure the diameter of the bar because color stripes are too easily applied by dishonest sellers.

Be especially aware of fresh-looking paint.

The interchange below is for the correct diameter of bar, but all bars will interchange from that group physinterchange from that group physar that is smaller in diameter than your original unit, as this will create a dangerous handling condition. Nevertheless, you can use a larger-diameter bar and improve the handling.

Model Identification

Cougar	Interchange Number
1967–68	
289ci	
all except 271hp	14
271hp with maximum handling package	17
302ci	
with GT package	16
without GT package	14
maximum handling pack	17
390ci	
without GT package	15
with GT package	16
maximum handling package	17
428ci, all	17
1969	
302ci	
all except Eliminator	18
Eliminator	19, 20
with GT package	16
maximum handling package	17
351ci	
without GT package	18
with GT package	16
maximum handling package	17
390ci	
with special handling	18
without special handling	19
maximum handling package	17
428ci, all	17
1970	
302ci	
all except Eliminator	
without heavy-duty suspension	21
with heavy-duty suspension	18
Eliminator	19
351ci	
without heavy-duty suspension	21
with heavy-duty suspension	18
428ci, all	17

Cyclone	Interchange Number
1966–67	
289ci, all	3
390ci	
all except GT models	3
GT models	4
427ci, all	4
1968–69	
289ci or 302ci, all	6
351ci	
two-barrel	4
four-barrel	3
390ci with competition suspension	5
428ci, all	5

Interchange

Interchange Number: 1
Part Number(s): C3OZ5482C
Bar Diameter: 3/4in
Color Code(s): One green stripe
Usage: 1962–65 Fairlane, all except station wagon or with 289ci 271hp

Interchange Number: 2
Part Number(s): C3OZ5482D
Bar Diameter: 3/4in
Color Code(s): One red stripe
Usage: 1962–65 Fairlane station wagon V-8 and 1964–65 Fairlane 289ci 271hp
Note(s): Interchange Number 3 may fit.

Interchange Number: 3
Part Number(s): C6OZ5482A
Bar Diameter: 3/4in
Color Code(s): One red stripe
Usage: 1966–67 Fairlane 289ci or 390ci (except GT), 1966–67 Comet 289ci or 390ci (except Cyclone), 1968–69 Torino station wagon and Ranchero V-8, 1968–69 Montego station wagon V-8, and 1969 Torino and Montego with 351ci four-barrel (including Ranchero and station wagon)

Interchange Number: 4
Part Number(s): C6OZ5482E
Bar Diameter: 7/8in
Color Code(s): One violet stripe
Usage: 1966–67 Fairlane and Cyclone GT 390ci; 1968–69 Torino GT 390ci, 427ci, or 428ci without competition suspension package; 1967 Fairlane and Comet 427ci; and 1969 Torino and Montego 351ci two-barrel

Interchange Number: 5
Part Number(s): C9OZ5482C
Bar Diameter: 15/16in
Color Code(s): Four green stripes
Usage: 1969 Torino and Montego 390ci or 428ci with competition suspension package
Note(s): Very rare; might find on 428ci station wagon ambulance.

Interchange Number: 6
Part Number(s): C7WY5482A
Bar Diameter: 3/4in
Usage: 1968–69 Torino six-cylinder, 289ci, or 302ci without GT handling package (except station wagon and Ranchero) and 1968–69 Montego with six-cylinder, 289ci, or 302ci without GT handling package (except station wagon)

Interchange Number: 7
Part Number(s): DOOZ5482A
Bar Diameter: 3/4in
Color Code(s): One violet and two green stripes
Usage: 1970–71 Torino and Montego six-cylinder or 302ci without cross country suspension package (except station wagon)

Interchange Number: 8
Part Number(s): DOOZ5482C
Bar Diameter: 7/8in
Color Code(s): Three green and one red stripe
Usage: 1970–71 Torino and Montego six-cylinder or 302ci with cross country suspension package
Note(s): Station wagon and Ranchero used this bar with and without the cross country suspension package.

Interchange Number: 9
Part Number(s): DOOZ5482B
Bar Diameter: 3/4in
Color Code(s): One brown and one green stripe.
Usage: 1970–71 Torino and Montego 351ci or 429ci, all except with competition suspension, police car, or with Cobra Jet engine
Note(s): Will fit Ranchero and station wagon.

Interchange Number: 10
Part Number(s): DOOZ5482D
Bar Diameter: 15/16in
Color Code(s): One yellow and two green stripes
Usage: 1970–71 Torino GT and Cyclone GT with 429ci Cobra Jet, 1970–71 Torino police car, 1970–71 Montego police car, and 1970–71 Torino and Montego with 351ci or 429ci with competition suspension package.
Note(s): Will fit Ranchero and station wagon.

Interchange Number: 11
Part Number(s): C5ZZ5482B
Usage: 1964-1/2–66 Mustang 289ci except 271hp and GT 350

Interchange Number: 12
Part Number(s): C5ZZ5482A
Bar Diameter: 13/16in
Usage: 1964-1/2–66 Mustang 289ci 271hp except GT 350

Interchange Number: 13
Part Number(s): S1MS5482A
Usage: 1965–66 Mustang GT 350

Interchange Number: 14
Part Number(s): C7WY5482A
Bar Diameter: 3/4in
Usage: 1967–68 Mustang six-cylinder, 289ci, or 302ci (except 289ci 271hp and GT 350) and 1967–68 Cougar six-cylinder, 289ci or 302ci (except 289ci 271hp)

Interchange Number: 15
Part Number(s): C7ZZ5482B
Bar Diameter: 3/4in
Color Codes: One yellow and one blue stripe
Usage: 1967–68 Mustang and Cougar 390ci without GT package

Interchange Number: 16
Part Number(s): C7ZZ5482C
Bar Diameter: 7/8in
Color Code(s): One green stripe
Usage: 1967–68 Mustang and Cougar 390ci GT and 1968–69 Mustang and Cougar 302ci GT (except Boss and Eliminator)

Interchange Number: 17
Part Number(s): C9ZZ5482E
Usage: 1967–70 GT 350 and GT 500 Mustangs, 1967–69 Mustang 289ci, 302ci, 390ci, or 428ci with maximum handling package; 1970 Boss 302ci Mustang; 1969–70 Boss 429ci Mustang; 1967–69 Cougar 289ci, 302ci, 390ci, or 428ci with maximum handling package; and 1970 Eliminator 302ci

Interchange Number: 18
Part Number(s): C9ZZ5482B
Bar Diameter: 11/16in
Color Codes: One pink and one gold stripe
Usage: 1969 Mustang six-cylinder, 302ci two-barrel, or 351ci; 1970 Mustang 302ci two-barrel with heavy-duty suspension; 1969 Cougar six-cylinder, 302ci two-barrel, or 351ci; and 1970 Cougar 302ci two-barrel with heavy-duty suspension

Interchange Number: 19
Part Number(s): C9ZZ5482D
Bar Diameter: 7/8in
Color Code(s): One green stripe
Usage: 1969 Boss 302ci Mustang and Cougar 302ci Eliminator until build date April 14, 1969; 1969 Mustang Mach 1 with 351ci; and 1969 Mustang and Cougar 390ci with special handling package
Note(s): After build date, use Interchange Number 19. Interchange Number 16 may fit.

Interchange Number: 20
Part Number(s): C9ZZ5482C
Bar Diameter: 3/4in
Color Code(s): One yellow one blue stripe
Usage: Late-1969 Boss 302ci Mustang and Cougar Eliminator 302ci and 1969 Mustang and Cougar 390ci without special handling package
Note(s): For models built after build date April 14, 1969. For models before date, see Interchange Number 18. Interchange Number 17 will fit.

Interchange Number: 21
Part Number(s): DOZZ5482A
Usage: 1970 Mustang and Cougar six-cylinder, 302ci two-barrel, or 351ci without heavy-duty suspension

Interchange Number: 22
Part Number(s): C2AZ5482A
Usage: 1959–62 full-size Ford except 427ci, 406ci, or 390ci with high-performance package

Interchange Number: 23
Part Number(s): C2AZ5482B
Usage: 1959–62 full-size Ford with 427ci, 406ci, or 390ci with high-performance package

Steering Gear Box
Two types of gear boxes were used: manual and power-assisted. Interchange here is very good inside the car family group (i.e. Mustang and Cougar, and Montego and Torino).

Gear boxes are identified by a code that is stamped on a tag attached to the unit, as shown in the illustration. Several codes may be used within one single interchange. The codes given are just to be used for identification purposes only.

Model Identification

Cougar	Interchange Number
1967	
manual	8, 9, 10
power	11, 12
1968–70	
manual	13, 14
power	15

Cyclone	Interchange Number
1966–67	
manual	3
power	4
1968–71	
manual	1
power	5

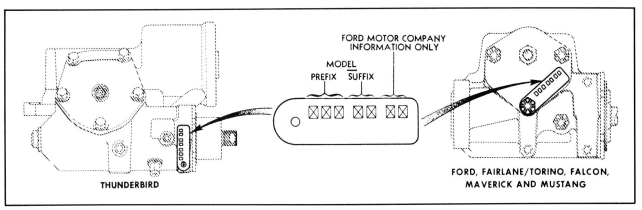

Steering gearbox identification tag.

Fairlane and Torino   *Interchange Number*
1959 manual 16
1960 manual 17
1961
     manual 18
     power 19
1962–64 manual 1
1966–67
     manual 3
     power 4
1968–71
     manual 1
     power 5

Mustang   *Interchange Number*
1964-1/2–67
     manual 7, 8, 9
     power 6, 11, 12
1968–70
     manual 13, 14
     power 15

Interchange

Interchange Number: 1
     Part Number(s): C7OZ3504A
     Type: Manual
     Code Number(s): HCA-AV or SMF-F
     Usage: 1962–63 Fairlane, 1968–71 Torino, 1968–71 Montego, and 1968–70 Falcon
     Note(s): 7-3/16in-long input shaft

Interchange Number: 2
     Part Number(s): C4OZ3504A
     Type: Manual
     Code Number(s): HCA-BU
     Usage: 1964–65 Fairlane
     Note(s): 39-1/2in-long input shaft.

Interchange Number: 3
     Part Number(s): C6DZ3504B
     Type: Manual
     Code Number(s): HCA-CA or SMS-C
     Usage: 1966–67 Fairlane, Comet, and Falcon
     Note(s): 39-1/2in-long input shaft.

Interchange Number: 4
     Part Number(s): C6DZ3504B
     Type: Power
     Code Numbers: HCA-BY, HCA-CD, or SMA-A
     Usage: 1966–67 Fairlane, Comet, and Falcon
     Note(s): 39-1/2in-long input shaft.

Interchange Number: 5
     Part Number(s): C5OZ3504B
     Type: Power
     Code Numbers: HCA-BV, HCV-BZ, HCV-CE, HCV-XX9, or SMA-A
     Usage: 1968–71 Torino, Montego, and Falcon
     Note(s): 7-3/16in-long input shaft.

Interchange Number: 6
     Part Number(s): C5ZZ3504C
     Type: Power
     Code Numbers: HCA-AX or SMB-B
     Usage: 1964-1/2–66 Mustang with 16:1 ratio
     Note(s): 41 7/8in-long input shaft.

Interchange Number: 7
     Part Number(s): C5ZZ3504A
     Type: Manual
     Code Number(s): HCC-AT or SMB-A
     Usage: 1964-1/2–67 Mustang with 19:1 ratio
     Note(s): 41-7/8in-long input shaft.

Interchange Number: 8
     Part Number(s): C5ZZ3504C
     Type: Manual
     Code Number(s): HCC-AW or SMB-B
     Usage: 1964-1/2–67 Mustang and 1967 Cougar with 16:1 ratio
     Note(s): 41-7/8in-long input shaft.

Interchange Number: 9
     Part Number(s): C7ZZ3504D
     Type: Manual
     Code Number(s): SMB-C
     Usage: 1967 Mustang and Cougar
     Note(s): 6-3/16in-long input shaft.

Interchange Number: 10
     Part Number(s): C7ZZ3504G
     Type: Manual
     Code Number(s): SMB-H
     Usage: 1967 Mustang and Cougar with 19:1 ratio
     Note(s): 41-7/8in-long input shaft and 1-1/8in sector shaft.

Interchange Number: 11
     Part Number(s): C7ZZ3504E
     Type: Power
     Code Numbers: SMB-J
     Usage: 1967 Mustang and Cougar with 16:1 ratio
     Note(s): 41-7/8in-long input shaft.

Interchange Number: 12
     Part Number(s): C7ZZ3504B
     Type: Power
     Code Numbers: SMB-E
     Usage: 1967 Mustang and Cougar with 16:1 ratio
     Note(s): 6-3/16 in-long input shaft.

Interchange Number: 13
Part Number(s): C7ZZ3504A
Type: Manual
Code Number(s): SMB-D
Usage: 1967–70 Mustang and Cougar with 19:1 ratio
Note(s): 6-7/8in-long input shaft.

Interchange Number: 14
Part Number(s): C7ZZ3504F
Type: Manual
Code Number(s): SMB-F
Usage: 1967–70 Mustang and Cougar with 16:1 ratio

Interchange Number: 15
Part Number(s): C7ZZ3504F
Type: Power
Code Numbers: SMB-K
Usage: 1967–70 Mustang and Cougar with16:1 ratio
Note(s): 6-3/16in-long input shaft.

Interchange Number: 16
Part Number(s): B9AA3504A
Type: Manual
Usage: 1959 full-size Ford

Interchange Number: 17
Part Number(s): COAR3504C
Type: Manual
Code Number(s): HCA-G, HCA-H, HCA-K, or HCA-L
Usage: 1960 full-size Ford

Interchange Number: 18
Part Number(s): C2AZ3504A
Type: Manual
Code Number(s): HCA-AH, HCA-Z, HCA-AE, or HCA-A
Usage: 1961–62 full-size Ford and Mercury
Note(s): Also used with dealer-installed power steering.

Interchange Number: 19
Part Number(s): C2AZ3504B
Type: Power
Code Number(s): HCA-AJ
Usage: 1961 full-size Ford and Mercury with power steering
Note(s): Can be adapted to earlier models.

Pump, Power Steering

Among the things that will effect the usage and interchange of power steering pumps are model, engine size, and whether or not air conditioning was used.

A pump is identified by a code number that is stamped into it on or on a tag. Many different code numbers may be found in one single interchange and should be used for identification purposes only.

Model Identification

Interchange

Interchange Number: 1
Part Number(s) C2AZ3A674A
Usage: 1959–64 full-size Ford or Mercury 352ci or 390ci
Note(s): Ford-built pump. Some used an Eaton pump. See Interchange Number 2.

Interchange Number: 2
Part Number(s): C2AZ3A674B
Usage: 1959–64 full-size Ford or Mercury 352ci or 390ci; 1960 full-size Ford or Mercury 352ci, 292ci, or six-cylinder; 1962–64 Fairlane six-cylinder; 1962–64 Falcon six-cylinder; 1963–65 Comet six-cylinder; 1962–63 Fairlane 260ci or 289ci with air conditioning; 1960 Thunderbird; and 1964-1/2–65 Mustang 170ci six-cylinder.
Note(s): Eaton-built pump. Some used a Ford pump. See Interchange Number 1. Has separate reservoir.

Interchange Number: 3
Part Number(s): C3AZ3A674A
Usage: 1963 full-size Ford, Fairlane, or Falcon 289ci without air conditioning
Note(s): Has separate reservoir.

Interchange Number: 4
Part Number(s): C4AZ3A674A
Usage: 1964 full-size Ford, Fairlane, or Falcon 289ci without air conditioning
Note(s): Has separate reservoir.

Interchange Number: 5
Part Number(s): C5OZ3A674ARM
ID Code: HBA-AE, HBA-AE1, HBA-AE2, HBA-AE3, or HBA-AE4
Usage: 1965 Fairlane 260ci or 289ci without air conditioning
Note(s): Ford-built pump. Some used Eaton pump. See Interchange Number 6.

Interchange Number: 6

    Part Number(s): C5OZ3A674B

    Usage: 1965 Fairlane, Falcon, Comet, or Mustang 260ci or 289ci without air conditioning

    Note(s): Eaton-built pump. Some used Ford pump. See Interchange Number 5.

Interchange Number: 7

    Part Number(s): C5OZ3A674BRM

    ID Code: HBA-AF, HBA-AF1, HBA-AF2, HBA-AF3, or HBA-AF4

    Usage: 1965 Fairlane 260ci or 289ci with air conditioning

Interchange Number: 8

    Part Number(s): C6OZ3A674BRM

    ID Code: HBA-AT or HBA-AT3

    Usage: 1966 Fairlane, Falcon, and Comet 289ci without air conditioning.

Interchange Number: 9

    Part Number(s): C6OZ3A674CRM

    ID Code: HBA-AU or HBA-AU3

    Usage: 1966 Fairlane, Falcon, and Comet 289ci with air conditioning

Interchange Number: 10

    Part Number(s): C5DZ3A674ARM

    ID Code: HBA-AC, HBA-AC1, HBA-AC2, HBA-AC3, HBA-AC4, or HBA-XC99

    Usage: 1966 Fairlane 390ci without air conditioning, 1966 Comet 390ci without air conditioning, 1965 Falcon 289ci without air conditioning, and 1965–66 Mustang 289ci without air conditioning

Interchange Number: 11

    Part Number(s): C5DZ3A674CRM

    ID Code: HBA-AD, HBA-AD1, HBA-AD2, HBA-AD3, HBA-AD4, or HBA-XD98

    Usage: 1966 Fairlane 390ci with air conditioning, 1966 Comet 390ci with air conditioning, 1965 Falcon 289ci with air conditioning, and 1965–66 Mustang 289ci with air conditioning

Interchange Number: 12

    Part Number(s): C7OZ3A674A

    ID Code: HBA-BF or HBA-BF1

    Usage: 1967 Fairlane, 1967 Comet, 1967 Falcon, 1967–68 Mustang except GT 350 and GT 500 models, 1967–68 Cougar, 1968 Torino, 1968 Montego, 1969 Mustang except Boss 429ci, 1969 Falcon six-cylinder, 1969 Torino 390ci or 428ci, 1969 Montego 390ci or 429ci, and 1969 Cougar 390ci or 428ci—all with or without air conditioning

Interchange Number: 13

    Part Number(s): C9OZ3A674A

    ID Code: HBA-BK or HBK-BK11

    Usage: 1969 Torino 302ci or 351ci, 1969 Montego 302ci or 351ci, 1969 Cougar 302ci or 351ci, and 1969 Falcon 302ci or 351ci—all with or without air conditioning

Interchange Number: 14

    Part Number(s): DOOZ3A674A

    ID Code: HBA-BM or HBA-BM11

    Usage: 1970–71 Torino and Montego—all engines except six-cylinders, with or without air conditioning

Interchange Number: 15

    Part Number(s): C7TZ3A674A

    ID Code: HBA-BH, HBA-BH1, HBA-BH99, SPA-H, or SPA-N

    Usage: 1967–68 Mustang GT 350 and GT 500 and 1967–69 full-size Ford—all with or without air conditioning

    Note(s): Use with Saginaw-built power steering gearbox.

Interchange Number: 16

    Part Number(s): DOZZ3A674C

    ID Code: HBA-BZ, HBA-BZ99, or HBA-CD

    Usage: 1969–70 Boss 429ci Mustang

This simulated-wood rim steering wheel can be found in a variety of models.

Interchange Number: 17

    Part Number(s): DOZZ3A674B

    ID Code: HBA-CC

    Usage: 1970 Mustang, Cougar, and Falcon 302ci or 351ci with or without air conditioning

1964–67 simulated-wood rim steering wheel.

1968–69 standard steering wheel was available in a wide range of makes and models.

Interchange Number: 18
　　Part Number(s): DOOZ3A674B
　　ID Code: HBA-BR or HBA-BR98
　　Usage: 1970–71 Torino and Montego six-cylinder, 1970 Mustang
　　　six-cylinder or 428ci Cobra Jet, 1970 Cougar 428ci Cobra Jet,
　　　1970–72 Maverick six-cylinder, 1971–72 Comet (compact)
　　　six-cylinder, 1970 Falcon six-cylinder, 1971–72 Maverick
　　　302ci, 1971–72 Comet (compact) 302ci—all with or without
　　　air conditioning
　　Note(s): Only up until build date August 8, 1972 on 1972 models.

1968–69 simulated-wood rim steering wheel.

1970 standard three-spoke steering wheel which was used in various models until 1972.

Steering Wheel

　　Steering wheels were moulded-in color to match the interior trim. However, interchange here is not based on color. Instead, all wheels are grouped under black or their basic part number. Wheels can be painted to match your trim or your can look for a matching color. Listed below is the bare steering wheel strip of the horn cap and/or shroud and what models the wheel was found in.

Model Identification

Cougar	Interchange Number
1967 standard	20
1968–69	
standard	6
wood rim	
1968	21
1969 walnut	7
1969 rosewood	23
1970	
standard	8
wood rim	9

Cyclone	Interchange Number
1966	
no rings	15
2 rings	16
4 rings	17
1967	
standard	18
wood grain	19
1968–69	
standard	6
wood rim	
1968	7
1969	7
1970	
standard	8
wood rim	9

Fairlane and Torino	Interchange Number
1959–60, all	24

1969–70 standard two-spoke steering wheel was used in various models.

Interchange Number: 2
    Part Number(s): C6OZ3600
    Type: Standard
    Usage: 1966 Fairlane and Falcon—all models and body styles

Interchange Number: 3
    Part Number(s): C7OZ3600
    Type: Standard (two-spoke)
    Usage: 1967 and Falcon—all models and body styles

Interchange

Interchange Number: 1
    Part Number(s): C5OZ3600
    Type: Standard
    Usage: 1965 Fairlane—all models and body styles

This was the standard steering wheel in 1964-1/2–65 Mustangs.

Shelby GT 350/500 and 1968 California Special used this steering wheel.

1969 Rosewood steering wheel.

Interchange Number: 4
Part Number(s): C5ZZ3600N
Type: Wood grain
Usage: 1965–66 Mustang, 1966 Fairlane, and 1966 full-size Ford

Interchange Number: 5
Part Number(s): C7OZ3600AJ
Type: Wood grain (three-spoke)
Usage: 1967 Fairlane, 1967 Mustang, 1967 full-size Ford.

Interchange Number: 6
Part Number(s): C8AZ3600A1A
Type: Standard (two-spoke)
Usage: 1968–69 Torino, 1968–69 Mustang, 1968–69 full-size Ford, 1968–69 Thunderbird, 1968–70 Falcon, 1968–69 full-size Mercury, 1968–69 Montego, and 1968–69 Cougar

Interchange Number: 7
Part Number(s): C9AZ3600B5A
Type: Wood grain-colored (three-spoke)
Usage: 1968–69 Torino, 1968–69 Mustang, 1968–69 full-size Ford, 1969 Thunderbird, 1969 Falcon, 1969 full-size Mercury, 1968–69 Montego, and 1969 Cougar
Note(s): Wood grain towards driver; color towards instrument panel. Not rosewood grain.

Interchange Number: 8
Part Number(s): D2AZ3600K
Type: Standard (two-spoke)
Usage: 1970–72 Torino, 1970–72 full-size Ford, 1970–72 Mustang, 1970–72 Montego, 1970–72 Cougar, 1970–72 full-size Mercury, 1970–72 Maverick, and 1971–72 Comet (compact)

Interchange Number: 9
Part Number(s): D2AZ3600BA
Type: Wood grain-colored
Usage: 1970–72 Torino, 1970–72 full-size Ford, 1970–72 Mustang, 1970–72 Montego, 1970–72 Cougar, 1970–72 full-size Mercury, 1970–72 Maverick, and 1971–72 Comet (compact)
Note(s): Wood grain towards driver; color towards instrument panel. Not rosewood grain.

Interchange Number: 10
Part Number(s): C5ZZ3600A
Type: Standard
Usage: 1964-1/2 Mustang (up to build date August 8, 1964)

Interchange Number: 11
Part Number(s): C5ZZ3600F
Type: Standard
Usage: 1965–66 Mustang except GT 350

Interchange Number: 12
Part Number(s): C7ZZ3600M
Type: Standard
Usage: 1967 Mustang except GT 350 and GT 500

Interchange Number: 13
Part Number(s): S2MS3A300A
Type: Real wood rim
Usage: 1966 GT 350 Mustang

Interchange Number: 14
Part Number(s): S7MS3600A
Type: Real wood rim
Usage: 1967–68 GT 350 and GT 500 Mustang

Interchange Number: 15
Part Number(s): C6GY3600A
Type: Standard, no rings
Usage: 1966 Comet—all models and body styles
Note(s): Rings on circumference of wheel.

Interchange Number: 16
Part Number(s): C6GY3600B
Type: Standard, two rings
Usage: 1966 Comet—all models and body styles
Note(s): Rings on circumference of wheel.

Interchange Number: 17
Part Number(s): C6GY3600C
Type: Standard, four rings
Usage: 1966 Comet—all models and body styles
Note(s): Rings on circumference of wheel.

Interchange Number: 18
Part Number(s): C7GY3600H
Type: Standard
Usage: 1967 Comet—all models and body styles

Interchange Number: 19
Part Number(s): C7GY3600AE
Type: Wood grain-colored
Usage: 1967 Comet—all models and body styles

Interchange Number: 20
Part Number(s): CWY3600A
Type: Standard
Usage: 1967 Cougar—all models and body styles

Interchange Number: 21
Part Number(s): C8MY3600A1A
Type: Wood grain and colored
Usage: 1968 Cougar—all models and body styles, 1969 Montego, 1968–69 Thunderbird
Note(s): Wood grain towards driver; color towards instrument panel.

Interchange Number: 22
Part Number(s): C8SZ3600A
Type: Wood grain and colored
Usage: 1968 Montego (all models and body styles) and 1968 Thunderbird with speed control only.
Note(s): Wood grain towards driver; color towards instrument panel.

Interchange Number: 23
Part Number(s): C9WY3600B5A
Type: Rosewood grain and colored
Usage: 1969 Cougar—all models and body styles

Interchange Number: 24
Part Number(s): COAA3600A001
Type: Standard
Usage: 1959–60 full-size Fairlane or Galaxie models—all body styles

Interchange Number: 25
Part Number(s): C1AA3600A001
Type: Standard
Usage: 1961 full-size Fairlane or Galaxie models—all body styles

Interchange Number: 26
Part Number(s): C4OZ3600A
Type: Standard
Usage: 1962–64 mid-sized Fairlane

Steering Column

Type and location of shift lever will greatly affect the interchange of the steering column. Those with a floor shifter, either automatic or manual, are usually interchangeable, but those with a three-speed manual or automatic on the column are not interchangeable.

Model Identification

Cougar
	Interchange Number
1967	
manual on column	26
floor shift	27
1968	
without tilt wheel	28
with tilt wheel	29
1969	
without tilt wheel	30
with tilt wheel	31
1970	
without tilt wheel	32
with tilt wheel	33

Cyclone
	Interchange Number
1966	
manual on column	5
auto on column	
without power steering	6
with power steering	7
on floor	
without power steering	8
with power steering	9
1967	
manual on column	10
auto on column	
without power steering	11
with power steering	12
floor shift	
without power steering	13
with power steering	14
1968	
manual on column	17
auto on column	16
floor shift	15
1969	
manual on column	19
auto on column	18
floor shift	20
1970	
manual on column	22
auto on column	23
floor shift	21

Fairlane and Torino
	Interchange Number
1962–65	
manual on column	3
auto on column	1, 2
floor shift	4
1966	
manual on column	5
auto on column	
without power steering	6
with power steering	7
on floor	
without power steering	8
with power steering	9
1967	
manual on column	10
auto on column	
without power steering	11
with power steering	12
floor shift	
without power steering	13
with power steering	14
1968	
manual on column	17
auto on column	16
floor shift	15
1969	
manual on column	19
auto on column	18
floor shift	20
1970	
manual on column	22
auto on column	23

Mustang
	Interchange Number
1964-1/2–66	
column	24
floor shift	25
1967	
manual on column	26
floor shift	27
1968	
without tilt wheel	28
with tilt wheel	29
1969	
without tilt wheel	30
with tilt wheel	31
1970	
without tilt wheel	32
with tilt wheel	33
GT 350 and GT 500	
with tilt	31
without tilt	30

Interchange

Interchange Number: 1
Part Number(s): C3OZ3514D
Type/Location: Automatic on column, except C4
Usage: 1962–63 Fairlane and 1962 Mercury Meteor

Interchange Number: 2
Part Number(s): C5OZ3514A
Type/Location: Automatic on column with C4
Usage: 1964–65 Fairlane

Interchange Number: 3
Part Number(s): C5OZ3514B
Type/Location: Manual on column
Usage: 1962–65 Fairlane and 1962 Mercury Meteor

Interchange Number: 4
Part Number(s): C5OZ3514C
Type/Location: Manual on floor or automatic on floor
Usage: 1964–65 Fairlane

Interchange Number: 5
Part Number(s): C6OZ3514A
Type/Location: Manual on column
Usage: 1966 Fairlane, 1966 Comet, 1966 Falcon

Interchange Number: 6
Part Number(s): C6OZ3514C
Type/Location: Automatic on column
Usage: 1966 Fairlane, 1966 Comet, 1966 Falcon without power steering

Interchange Number: 7
Part Number(s): C6OZ3514D
Type/Location: Automatic on column
Usage: 1966 Fairlane, Comet, and Falcon with power steering

Interchange Number: 8
Part Number(s): C6OZ3514E
Type/Location: Manual or automatic on the floor
Usage: 1966 Fairlane, Comet, or Falcon without power steering

Interchange Number: 9
Part Number(s): C6OZ3514F
Type/Location: Manual or automatic on the floor
Usage: 1966 Fairlane, Comet, and Falcon with power steering.

Interchange Number: 10
Part Number(s): C7OZ3514A
Type/Location: Manual on column
Usage: 1967 Fairlane, Comet, and Falcon

Interchange Number: 11
Part Number(s): C7OZ3514F or C7OZ3514J
Type/Location: Automatic on column
Usage: 1967 Fairlane, Comet, and Falcon without power steering
Note(s): C7OZ-J was used after build date 02-01–67.

Interchange Number: 12
Part Number(s): C7OZ3514D
Type/Location: Automatic on column
Usage: 1967 Fairlane, Comet, and Falcon with power steering

Interchange Number: 13
Part Number(s): C7OZ3514B
Type/Location: Manual or automatic on the floor
Usage: 1967 Fairlane, Comet, and Falcon without power steering
Note(s): Longer than unit with power steering.

Interchange Number: 14
Part Number(s): C7OZ3514C
Type/Location: Manual or automatic on the floor
Usage: 1967 Fairlane, Comet, and Falcon with power steering
Note(s): Unit without power steering is too long and will not fit this interchange.

Interchange Number: 15
Part Number(s): C8AZ3514A
Type/Location: Manual or automatic on the floor
Usage: 1968 Torino, Montego, full-size Ford with fixed wheel, and Falcon

Interchange Number: 16
Part Number(s): C8AZ3514B
Type/Location: Automatic on column
Usage: 1968 Torino, 1968 Montego, 1968 full-size Ford with fixed wheel, and 1968 Falcon

Interchange Number: 17
Part Number(s): C8AZ3514C
Type/Location: Manual on column
Usage: 1968 Torino, 1968 Montego, 1968 full-size Ford with fixed wheel, and 1968 Falcon

Interchange Number: 18
Part Number(s): C9OZ3514A
Type/Location: Automatic on column
Usage: 1969 Torino, 1969 Montego, and 1969 Falcon

Interchange Number: 19
Part Number(s): C9OZ3514C
Type/Location: Manual on column
Usage: 1969 Torino, 1969 Montego, and 1969 Falcon

Interchange Number: 20
Part Number(s): C9OZ3514B
Type/Location: Manual or automatic on the floor
Usage: 1969 Torino, 1969 Montego, and 1969 Falcon

Interchange Number: 21
Part Number(s): DOOZ3514A
Type/Location: Manual or automatic on floor
Usage: 1970–71 Torino and Montego

Interchange Number: 22
Part Number(s): DOOZ3514B
Type/Location: Manual on column
Usage: 1970–71 Torino and Montego.

Interchange Number: 23
Part Number(s): DOOZ3514C
Type/Location: Automatic on column
Usage: 1970–71 Torino and Montego

Interchange Number: 24
Part Number(s): C5DZ3514A
Type/Location: Manual on floor
Usage: 1964-1/2–66 Mustang and 1964–65 Falcon

Interchange Number: 25
Part Number(s): C5DZ3514B
Type/Location: Manual or automatic on floor
Usage: 1964-1/2–66 Mustang and 1964–65 Falcon

Interchange Number: 26
Part Number(s): C7ZZ3514A
Type/Location: Manual on column
Usage: 1967 Mustang and Cougar

Interchange Number: 27
Part Number(s): C7ZZ3514C
Type/Location: Manual or automatic on floor
Usage: 1967 Mustang and Cougar

Interchange Number: 28
Part Number(s): C8ZZ3514A
Type/Location: Manual or automatic on floor
Usage: 1968 Mustang and Cougar without tilt wheel

Interchange Number: 29
Part Number(s): C8ZZ3514B
Type/Location: Manual or automatic on floor
Usage: 1968 Mustang or 1968 Cougar with tilt wheel

Interchange Number: 30
Part Number(s): C9ZZ3514A
Type/Location: Manual or automatic on floor
Usage: 1969 Mustang and Cougar without tilt steering and 1969–70 GT 350 and GT 500 without tilt wheel

Interchange Number: 31
Part Number(s): C9ZZ3514B
Type/Location: Manual or automatic on floor
Usage: 1969 Mustang and Cougar with tilt steering and 1969–70 GT 350 and GT 500 with tilt wheel

Interchange Number: 32
Part Number(s): DOZZ3514C
Type/Location: Manual or automatic on floor
Usage: 1970 Mustang and Cougar without tilt steering
Note(s): Not for 1970 GT 350 and GT 500 models.

Interchange Number: 33
 Part Number(s): DOZZ3514B or DOZZ3514D
 Type/Location: Manual or automatic on floor
 Usage: 1970 Mustang and Cougar with tilt steering
 Note(s): Not for 1970 GT 350 and GT 500 models. DOZZ-D used
 after March 2, 1970.

Steering Knuckles

The type of front brakes will effect the interchanging of the spindles. Drum and disc brakes usually use a different set of spindles, but there are parts that can be used on both systems if the proper caliper brakes are used.

Model Identification

Cougar	*Interchange Number*
1967 drum/disc brakes	3
1968–69	
drum	3
disc	
all except Eliminator	4
Eliminator	8
1970	
drum	5
disc	
all except Eliminator	6
Eliminator	8

Cyclone	*Interchange Number*
1966–67, all	3
1968–69	
drum	3
disc	4
1970	
drum	5
disc	6

Fairlane and Torino	*Interchange Number*
1959, all	10
1961	
all except high-performance	11
high-performance	12
1962–63 drum	1
1964–65 drum	2
1966–67, all	3
1968–69	
drum	3
disc	4
1970	
drum	5
disc	6
557	

Mustang	*Interchange Number*
1964-1/2–66, all	7
1967 drum/disc brakes	3
1968–69	
drum	3
disc	
all except Boss	4
Boss 302ci	8
Boss 429ci	9
1970	
drum	5
disc	
all except Boss	6
Boss 302ci	8
Boss 429ci	9

Interchange

Interchange Number: 1
 Part Number(s): C3OZ3105A (right), C3OZ3106A (left)
 Usage: 1962–63 Fairlane and 1962 Mercury Meteor

Interchange Number: 2
 Part Number(s): C4OZ3105A (right), C4OZ3106A (left)
 Usage: 1964–65 Fairlane

Interchange Number: 3
 Part Number(s): C9OZ3105C (right), C9OZ3106C (left)
 Usage: 1966–67 Fairlane, Comet, Torino, Montego, Mustang, and Cougar—all with drum brakes
 Note(s): Will fit 1967 models with drum brakes if brackets for calipers are installed.

Interchange Number: 4
 Part Number(s): C8OZ3105A (right), C8OZ3106A (left)
 Usage: 1968–69 Torino, 1968–69 Montego, 1968–69 Falcon, 1968–69 Mustang except Boss 302ci or Boss 429ci, 1968–69 Cougar except Eliminator 302ci, and 1969–70 GT 350 and GT 500 Mustang—all with disc brakes

Interchange Number: 5
 Part Number(s): D3DZ3105A (right), D3DZ3106A (left)
 Usage: 1970–71 Torino, 1970–71 Montego, 1971–72 Maverick, 1971–72 Comet (compact), 1970 Mustang, and 1970 Cougar—all with drum brakes
 Note(s): Have 13/16in 20-thread at studs.

Interchange Number: 6
 Part Number(s): DOOZ3105B (right), DOOZ3106B (left)
 Usage: 1970–71 Torino, 1970–71 Montego, 1971–72 Maverick, 1971–72 Comet (compact), 1970 Mustang, and 1970 Cougar—all with disc brakes
 Note(s): Cast with the numbers DOZA3107C (right) and DOZA3108C (left).

Interchange Number: 7
 Part Number(s): C9ZZ3105C (right), C9ZZ3106C (left)
 Usage: 1964-1/2–66 Mustang with drum brakes and V-8 engine and 1965 Falcon with drum brakes

Interchange Number: 8
 Part Number(s): C9ZZ3105A (right), C9ZZ3106A (left)
 Usage: 1969–70 Boss 302ci, 1969–70 Cougar Eliminator 302ci with disk brakes.
 Note(s): Identify by casting numbers DOZA3107B (right), DOZA31078B (left)

Interchange Number: 9
 Part Number(s): C9ZZ3105B (right), C9ZZ3106B (left)
 Usage: 1969–70 Boss 429ci DISC BRAKES.
 Note(s): Identify by casting number DOZA3107C (right), DOZA31078C (left)

Interchange Number: 10
 Part Number(s): COSZ3105A (right), COSZ3106A (left)
 Usage: 1957–59 full-size Ford, 1958–60 Thunderbird. Drum brakes

Interchange Number: 11
 Part Number(s): COAZ3105B (right), COAZ3106B (left)
 Usage: 1960–61 full-size Ford and 1961 full-size Mercury, except with high-performance 390ci.
 Note(s): 1962–64 units will fit if bearing, washer, and retaining nuts are also swapped.

Interchange Number: 12
 Part Number(s): COAZ3105A (right), COAZ3106A (left)
 Usage: 1960–64 full-size Ford with high-performance 390ci, 406ci, or 427ci.

Chapter 7

Brake Systems and Parking Brakes

Master Cylinder

Brake type will effect the interchange of the master cylinder. Thus, a car with disc brakes cannot use a master cylinder from a car with drum brakes.

Master cylinders can be identified by a casting number, or, for a better definition, a pattern number. To some degree these numbers can be used for identification, but be warned to not rely solely on pattern numbers, as the same pattern number could be used on more than one master cylinder.

Model Identification

Cougar	*Interchange Number*
1967–70	
drum brakes	
without power brakes	6
with power brakes	19
disc brakes, all	24

Cyclone	*Interchange Number*
1966 drum brakes	
without power brakes	26
with power brakes	
289ci	14, 27
390ci	14
1967	
drum brakes	
without power brakes	7
with power brakes	15
disc brakes	
all except 427ci	20
427ci	21
1968–70	
drum brakes	
without power brakes	7
with power brakes	
1968–69	15
1970	16
disc brakes	
1968–69	
all except 427ci	20
427ci	21
1970, all	20

Fairlane and Torino	*Interchange Number*
1959 drum brakes	
without power brakes	1
with power brakes	8
1960–61 drum brakes	
without power brakes	2
with power brakes	9

1962–64 drum brakes	
without power brakes	2
with power brakes	10
1965 drum brakes	
without power brakes	3
with power brakes	13
1966 drum brakes	
without power brakes	26
with power brakes	
289ci	14, 27
390ci	14
1967	
drum brakes	
without power brakes	7
with power brakes	15
disc brakes	
all except 427ci	20
427ci	21
1968–70	
drum brakes	
without power brakes	7
with power brakes	
1968–69, all	15
1970, all	16
disc brakes	
1968–69	
all except 427ci	20
427ci	21
1970, all	20

Mustang	*Interchange Number*
1964-1/2–6 drum brakes	
without power brakes	2, 3
with power brakes	12, 17
1966 drum brakes	
without power brakes	4, 5
with power brakes	17, 18
1967–70 drum brakes	
without power brakes	6
with power brakes	19
disc brakes, all	24

Interchange

Interchange Number: 1
Part Number(s): B7A2140A
Type: Drum brakes
Pattern Number: FE23223
Usage: 1957–59 full-size Ford, 1957 Lincoln, and 1958–59 Edsel

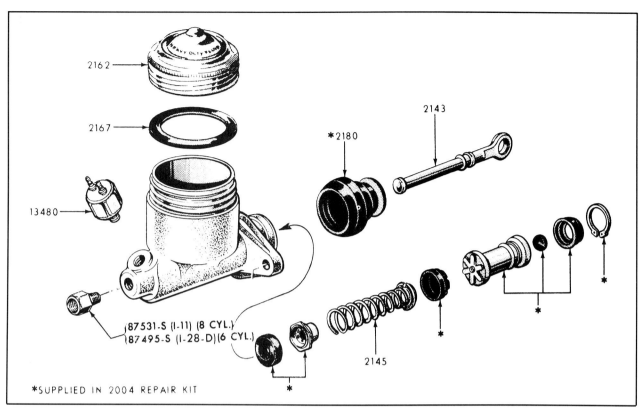

Typical master cylinder used from 1959–66.

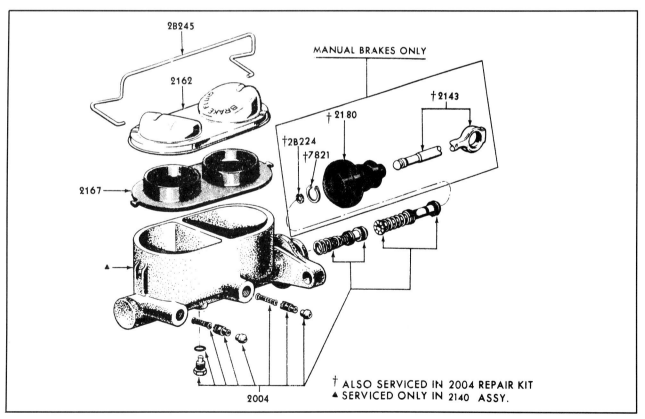

Typical Amstar cylinder used from 1967–70.

Interchange Number: 2
Part Number(s): C3AZ2140B
Type: Drum brakes
Pattern Number: FE32949
Usage: 1960–64 full-size Ford, 1962–64 Fairlane, 1960–64 Falcon, 1960–64 Comet, 1960–64 full-size Mercury, and 1964 1/2–65 Mustang.
Note(s): For 1964 models except Mustang, usage was up to build date December 10, 1963. For Mustang it was used up to August 17, 1964.

Interchange Number: 3
Part Number(s): C5AZ2140A
Type: Drum brakes
Pattern Number: FE50336
Usage: 1965 full-size Ford, 1965 Fairlane, 1965 Mustang (beginning build date August 18, 1964), 1965 Falcon, 1965 full-size Mercury, and 1965 Comet

Interchange Number: 4
Part Number(s): C6AZ2140D
Type: Drum brakes
Usage: 1966 Mustang up to November 23, 1965, 1966 full-size Ford or Mercury after January 2, 1966

Interchange Number: 5
Part Number(s): C6ZZ2140B
Type: Drum brakes
Usage: 1966 Mustang after November 23, 1965

Interchange Number: 6
Part Number(s): C9AZ2140D*
Type: Drum brakes
Pattern Number: FE23223
Usage: 1967–70 Mustang, 1967–70 Cougar, 1967–71 full-size Ford, and 1967–71 full-size Mercury
Note(s): *Replacement part number; original numbers: C7AZ2140H–67, C7AZ2140M–68, and C9AZ2140D–69–71.

Interchange Number: 7
Part Number(s): C9OZ2140A*
Type: Drum brakes
Usage: 1967 Fairlane, 1968–71 Torino, 1967 Comet, 1968–71 Montego, 1968–70 Falcon, 1970–71 Maverick, and 1971 Comet.
Note(s): *1967–68 Replacement part number; original part numbers: C7OZ2140H–67 and C8OZ2140M–68.

Interchange Number: 8
Part Number(s): B7A2140B
Type: Drum brakes (power assisted)
Pattern Number: FE23237
Usage: 1957–59 full-size Ford

Interchange Number: 9
Part Number(s): COZ2140B
Type: Drum brakes (power assisted)
Pattern Number: FE32949*
Usage: 1960–61 full-size Ford with V-8 only
Note(s): *Do not use pattern number as ID; also used without power brakes.

Interchange Number: 10
Part Number(s): C4OZ2140A*
Type: Drum brakes (power assisted)
Usage: 1962 full-size Ford, 1962 full-size Mercury, and 1963–64 Ford Fairlane
Note(s): *Replacement part number.

Interchange Number: 11
Part Number(s): C3AZ2140A
Type: Drum brakes (power assisted)
Usage: 1963 full-size Ford.

Interchange Number: 12
Part Number(s): C1SZ2140A
Type: Drum brakes (power assisted)
Usage: 1964 full-size Ford, 1961–64 Thunderbird, 1964 Falcon, and 1965 Mustang (up to build date August 17, 1964)

Interchange Number: 13
Part Number(s): C5OZ2140B
Type: Drum brakes (power assisted)
Usage: 1965 Fairlane
Note(s): Interchange Number 10 will fit.

Interchange Number: 14
Part Number(s): C6OZ2140A
Type: Drum brakes (power assisted)
Usage: 1966 Fairlane 390ci, 1966 Comet 390ci engine, and early-built Fairlane and Comet 289ci engine before January 4, 1966

Interchange Number: 15
Part Number(s): C9OZ2140A
Type: Drum brakes (power assisted)
Usage: 1967 Fairlane, 1968–69 Torino, 1967 Comet, 1968–69 Montego (all engines except 427ci), and 1968–70 Falcon

Interchange Number: 16
Part Number(s): DOGY2140A
Type: Drum brakes (power assisted)
Usage: 1970–71 Torino and Montego—all engines

Interchange Number: 17
Part Number(s): C5ZZ2140B
Type: Drum brakes (power assisted)
Usage: 1965–66 Mustang (except GT-350; used from build dates August 17, 1964, to January 3, 1966), 1965 Falcon, 1965 Comet, and 1965–66 full-size Ford

Interchange Number: 18
Part Number(s): C6AZ2140B
Type: Drum brakes (power assisted)
Usage: Late-built 1966 Mustang except GT 350, 1966 full-size Ford
Note(s): Begins at build date January 3, 1966.

Interchange Number: 19
Part Number(s): C7ZZ2140G
Type: Drum brakes (power assisted)
Usage: 1967–70 Mustang and Cougar

Interchange Number: 20
Part Number(s): C8OZ2140A
Type: Disc brakes (power assisted)
Usage: 1967 Fairlane, 1967 Comet, 1968–71 Torino, and 1968–71 Montego—all engines except 427ci
Note(s): Uses a 15/16in-diameter piston.

Interchange Number: 21
Part Number(s): C7OZ2140J
Type: Disc brakes (power assisted)
Usage: 1967 Fairlane or 1967 Comet with 427ci engine and 1968 Torino and Montego with 427ci
Note(s): Used a 1in-diameter piston

Interchange Number: 22
Part Number(s): C5ZZ2140C
Type: Disc brakes (power assisted)
Usage: 1965–66 Mustang (except GT-350) built before January 3, 1966

Interchange Number: 23
Part Number(s): C6ZZ2140C
Pattern Number: None
Usage: 1966 Mustang except GT-350. Built beginning at build date January 4, 1966

Interchange Number: 24
Part Number(s): C8ZZ2140A
Type: Disc brakes (power assisted)
Usage: 1967–71 Mustang and Cougar, except with 429ci Boss

Interchange Number: 25
Part Number(s): C9ZZ2140B
Type: Disc brakes (power assisted)
Usage: 1969–70 Boss 429ci Mustang

Interchange Number: 26
Part Number(s): C6OZ2140D
Type: Drums brakes
Usage: 1966 Fairlane, Comet, and Falcon without power assist

Interchange Number: 27
Part Number(s): C6OZ2140B
Type: Drums brakes (power assisted)
Usage: Late-built 1966 Fairlane, Comet, or Falcon 289ci with power assist
Note(s): Begins at build date January 4, 1966

Interchange Number: 28
Part Number(s): C6OZ2140D
Type: Drums brakes
Usage: 1966 Fairlane, Comet, and Falcon without power assist

Chamber, Power Booster

The power booster is interchangeable by its original part number or original replacement part number. Some units are stamped or tagged with an identification number. These numbers can be used for identification, but do not rely on them solely. When the ID number is known, it is given.

Model Identification

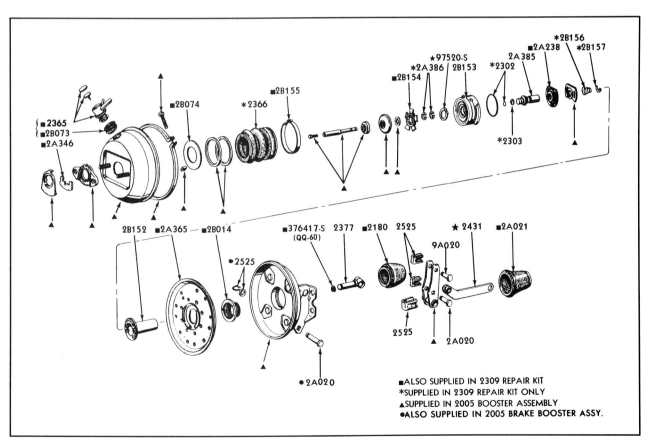

1964–66 booster chamber, all except Mustang.

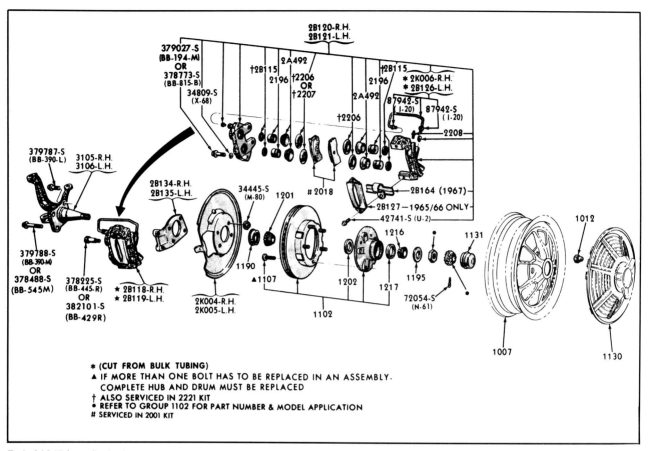

Typical 1967 front disc brakes.

Interchange

Interchange Number: 1
Part Number(s): B9A2005A
ID Number(s): 379494
Usage: 1959 full-size Ford with drum brakes

Interchange Number: 2
Part Number(s): COAZ2005A
Usage: 1960 full-size Ford with drum brakes

Interchange Number: 3
Part Number(s): C1AZ2005A
Usage: 1961 full-size Ford with drum brakes

Interchange Number: 4
Part Number(s): C2OZ2005A
ID Number(s): C4202-M
Usage: 1962–63 Fairlane and 1962–63 Mercury Meteor with drum brakes

Interchange Number: 5
Part Number(s): C5OZ2005B
ID Number(s): C4202-A
Usage: 1964–66 Fairlane (all engines except 390ci) and 1966 Comet (except 390ci), both with drum brakes

Interchange Number: 6
Part Number(s): C6OZ2005B
ID Number(s): C4202-J
Usage: 1966 Fairlane and Comet 390ci engine with drum brakes

Interchange Number: 7
Part Number(s): C7OZ2005D
ID Number(s): C4261-M
Usage: 1967 Fairlane, Falcon, and Comet—all engines with drum brakes

Interchange Number: 8
Part Number(s): C8OZ2005B
ID Number(s): C4261-C
Usage: 1968 Torino, Falcon, and Montego with drum brakes

Interchange Number: 9
Part Number(s): C9OZ2005B
Usage: 1969 Torino, 1969–70 Falcon, and 1969 Montego with drum brakes

Interchange Number: 10
Part Number(s): DOGY2005B
Usage: 1970–71 Torino and Montego, all engines with drum brakes

Interchange Number: 11
Part Number(s): C5ZZ2005C
Usage: 1964-1/2–65 Mustang up to build date May 24, 1965, with drum brakes

Interchange Number: 12
Part Number(s): C5ZZ2005D
Usage: 1965 Mustang beginning build date February 15, 1965, with drum brakes

Interchange Number: 13
Part Number(s): C6ZZ2005A
Usage: 1966 Mustang with drum brakes
Note(s): Interchange with linkage without master-cylinder.

Interchange Number: 14
Part Number(s): C7WY2005A
ID Number(s): C4262-G
Usage: 1967 Mustang and Cougar with drum brakes

Interchange Number: 15
Part Number(s): C8WY2005A
Usage: 1968 Mustang and Cougar with drum brakes

Interchange Number: 16
Part Number(s): C9ZZ2005B
Usage: 1969–70 Mustang and Cougar with drum brakes

Interchange Number: 17
Part Number(s): C7OZ2005C
ID Number(s): C4261-N
Usage: 1967 Fairlane, Falcon, and Comet, all engine sizes with disc brakes

Interchange Number: 18
Part Number(s): C8OZ2005A
ID Number(s): C4261-AJ
Usage: 1968 Torino, Falcon, and Montego with disc brakes

Interchange Number: 19
Part Number(s): C9OZ2005A
Usage: 1969 Torino, 1969–70 Falcon, and 1969 Montego with disc brakes

Interchange Number: 20
Part Number(s): DOOZ2005A
Usage: 1970–71 Torino and Montego with disc brakes

Interchange Number: 21
Part Number(s): C7ZZ2005C
ID Number(s): C4262-M
Usage: 1967 Mustang and Cougar with disc brakes

Interchange Number: 22
Part Number(s): C8ZZ2005C
ID Number(s): C4262-AD, C4262-AF
Usage: 1968 Mustang and Cougar with disc brakes

Interchange Number: 23
Part Number(s): C9ZZ2005A
ID Number(s): Stamped 6586
Usage: 1969 Mustang and Cougar with disc brakes, except 429ci Boss

Interchange Number: 24
Part Number(s): C9ZZ2005C
ID Number(s): 2508790
Usage: 1969–70 Boss 429ci Mustang.

Interchange Number: 25
Part Number(s): DOZZ2005C
Usage: 1970 Mustang, 1970 Cougar with disc brakes (except Boss 429ci)

Brake Drums

Brake drums are identified by their diameter and brake surface. There is difference a between front and rear drums, so they are not interchangeable.

Model Identification

Cougar	*Interchange Number*
1967	
front	
all except 390ci	4
390ci	5
rear	
all except GT models	14
GT models	15
1968	
front	5
rear	
all except GT models	14
GT models	15
1969	
front	5
rear	
all except GT models	14
GT models	15
1970	
front	6
rear	
all except GT models	14
GT models	15

Cyclone	*Interchange Number*
1966–67	
front	
all except 390ci	4
390ci	5
rear	
all except GT models	14
GT models	15
1968	
front	5
rear	
all except GT models	14
GT models	15
1969	
front	5
rear	
all except GT models	14
GT models	15
1970	
front	6
rear	
all except GT models	14
GT models	15

Interchange

Interchange Number: 1
    Part Number(s): BAJ1102D
    Dimensions: 11x2-1/2in
    Location: Front
    Usage: 1959 full-size Ford—all body styles

Interchange Number: 2
    Part Number(s): COAA1102C
    Dimensions: 11x2-1/2in
    Location: Front
    Usage: 1960 full-size Ford—all body styles except station wagon
    Note(s): Station wagon used 11x3-1/2in drums, which were also used on a handful of race-type cars.

Interchange Number: 3
    Part Number(s): C1AA1102A
    Dimensions: 11x2-1/2in
    Location: Front
    Usage: 1961 full-size Ford—all body styles

Interchange Number: 4
    Part Number(s): C3OZ1102C
    Dimensions: 10x2-13/16in (non-flared)
    Location: Front
    Usage: 1962–66 Fairlane*, 1962–63 Mercury Meteor, 1966–67 Comet*, 1964-1/2–66 Mustang, 1965–66 Falcon, and 1967 Cougar*.
    Note(s): *With six-cylinder or 289ci V-8 only.

Interchange Number: 5
    Part Number(s): C9OZ1102B
    Dimensions: 10x2-3/4in
    Location: Front
    Usage: 1966–67 Fairlane GT, 1966–67 Cyclone GT, 1968–69 Torino, 1968–69 Montego, 1969–70 Falcon, 1967–69 Mustang, and 1967–69 Cougar
    Note(s): All 1967–68 models with F70 tires. Standard 390ci engine and GT packages. Standard in all models in 1969

Interchange Number: 6
    Part Number(s): DOOZ1102A
    Dimensions: 10x2-3/4in
    Location: Front
    Usage: 1970–72 Torino, 1970–72 Montego, 1970–72 V-8 Mustang, 1970–72 V-8 Cougar, 1971–72 Maverick, and 1971–72 Comet

Interchange Number: 7
    Part Number(s): C1DZ1102B
    Dimensions: 9x2-1/2in
    Location: Front
    Usage: 1964-1/2–66 Mustang and 1960–65 Falcon

Interchange Number: 8
    Part Number(s): C7OZ1102A
    Dimensions: 10x2-9/16in
    Location: Front
    Usage: 1967–69 Mustang, 1967 Fairlane, 1968 Torino, 1967 Comet, 1968 Montego, and 1967–68 Falcon
    Note(s): Standard brakes for V-8 engine in Mustang or Falcon. Standard brakes for the rest except with GT package or heavy-duty brakes. Six-cylinder Mustangs used smaller-diameter drums and will not interchange.

Interchange Number: 9
    Part Number(s): B7A1126A
    Location: Rear
    Usage: 1959 full-size Ford except station wagon, retractable hard-top, or those with heavy-duty brakes

Interchange Number: 10
    Part Number(s): B7A1126B
    Location: Rear
    Usage: 1959 full-size Ford station wagon, retractable hardtop, and those with heavy-duty brakes
    Note(s): Stamped K41655

Interchange Number: 11
    Part Number(s): COAA1126A
    Dimensions: 11x2-3/4in
    Usage: 1960 full-size Ford and full-size Mercury.

Interchange Number: 12

Part Number(s): C3AZ1126A
Dimensions: 11-1/32x2-3/4in (non-flared)
Usage: 1961–64 full-size Ford, 1961–64 full-size Mercury, and 1961 Thunderbird.

Interchange Number: 13

Part Number(s): C2OZ1126E
Dimensions: 10x3-1/8in
Location: Rear
Usage: 1962–65 Fairlane and 1962–63 Mercury Meteor with heavy-duty brakes or station wagon

Interchange Number: 14

Part Number(s): C3OZ1126B
Dimensions: 10x2in
Location: Rear
Usage: 1962–65 Fairlane, 1963–67 Comet, 1968–71 Torino, 1968–71 Montego, 1967–72 Cougar, 1964-1/2–72 Mustang, 1963–70 Falcon, 1970–72 Maverick, 1971–72 Comet, and 1962–63 Mercury Meteor—all with standard brakes, except GT

Interchange Number: 15

Part Number(s): C2OZ1126B
Dimensions: 10x2-1/4in
Location: Rear
Usage: 1962–65 Fairlane, 1963–67 Comet, 1968–71 Torino, 1968–71 Montego, 1967–69 Cougar, 1965–72 Mustang, 1963–70 Falcon, 1970–72 Maverick, 1971–72 Comet, and 1962–63 Mercury Meteor—all with heavy-duty brakes and all 1966 Fairlane GT

Interchange Number: 16

Part Number(s): C3OZ1126A
Dimensions: 10x2-3/4in
Location: Rear
Usage: 1966 Fairlane station wagon, 1966 Ranchero, and 1967 Fairlane without finned drums

Interchange Number: 17

Part Number(s): C6OZ1126C
Dimensions: 10x2-3/4in
Location: Rear
Usage: 1967 Fairlane, 1966–67 Comet, 1968–71 Torino, and 1968–71 Montego
Note(s): With 390ci or 427ci engine in 1966–67. Drums are flared with fins.

Interchange Number: 18

Part Number(s): C8OZ1126A
Dimensions: 10x2in
Usage: 1968–71 Torino, 1968–71 Montego, 1973 Mustang, 1973 Cougar (flared drums)

Rotor, Disc Brakes

Model Identification

Cougar/Mustang	Interchange Number
1967, all	1
1968–69	
all except Boss and Eliminator	2
Boss 302ci and Eliminator	4
Boss 429ci	5

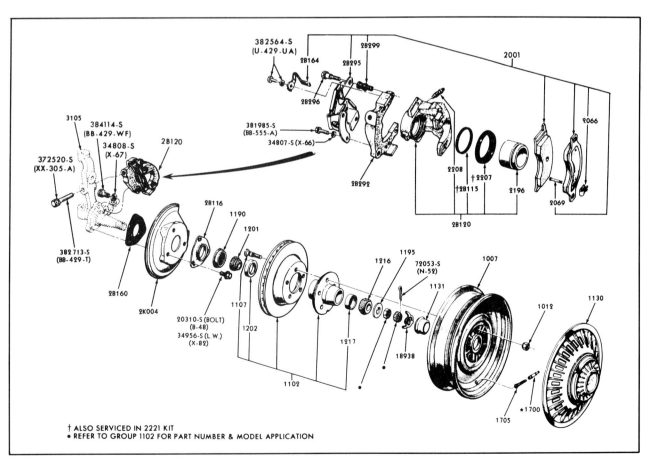

Typical 1968–70 front disc brakes.

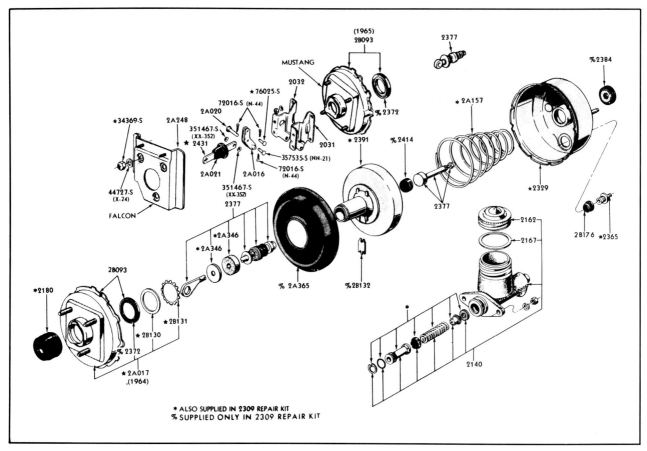

1965–66 Mustang booster chamber.

Interchange

Interchange Number: 1
Part Number(s): C5ZZ1102B
Usage: 1967 Fairlane, 1967 Comet, 1965–67 Mustang, 1967 Cougar, 1967 Falcon

Interchange Number: 2
Part Number(s): C8OZ1102A
Usage: 1968–69 Torino, 1968–69 Montego, 1968–69 Mustang except Boss, 1968–69 Cougar except Eliminator, 1968–70 Falcon

Interchange Number: 3
Part Number(s): DOOZ1102B
Usage: 1970–71 Torino, 1970–71 Montego, 1970 Mustang, 1970 Cougar

Interchange Number: 4
Part Number(s): C9ZZ1102A
Usage: 1969 Boss 302ci Mustang, 1969 Cougar Eliminator 302ci

Interchange Number: 5
Part Number(s): C9ZZ1102B
Usage: 1969 Boss 429ci Mustang

Pedals, Brake
Interchange of brake pedals is for the bare pedal without the cover. Interchange is usually limited to the same family group (i.e. Mustang and Cougar). There are two distinct pedals, according to the type of transmission. Cars with an automatic use a larger pedal than those with a manual. Also, brake type has some effect on interchangeability. Some pedals that were used with disc brakes will not fit a car with drum brakes, and vice versa.

Model Identification

Interchange

Interchange Number: 1
 Part Number(s): B8A2455A
 Usage: 1959–60 full-size Ford with manual transmission

Interchange Number: 2
 Part Number(s): C4AZ2455B
 Usage: 1961–64 full-size Ford with manual transmission, except 1963 with tilt steering column

Interchange Number: 3
 Part Number(s): C3OZ2455AE
 Usage: 1962–65 Fairlane, 1962–63 Mercury Meteor with manual transmission

Interchange Number: 4
 Part Number(s): C6OZ2455A
 Usage: 1966–67 Fairlane, 1966–67 Falcon, 1966–67 Comet with manual transmission

Interchange Number: 5
 Part Number(s): C8OZ2455B
 Usage: 1968 Torino, 1968 Falcon, 1968 Montego with manual transmission

Interchange Number: 6
 Part Number(s): C9OZ2455A
 Usage: 1969 Torino, 1969 Montego, and 1969–70 Falcon with manual transmission

Interchange Number: 7
 Part Number(s): DOOZ2455B
 Usage: 1970–71 Torino and Montego with manual transmission

Interchange Number: 8
 Part Number(s): C5ZZ2455J
 Usage: 1964-1/2–66 Mustang with manual transmissions, drum brakes only

Interchange Number: 9
 Part Number(s): C5ZZ2455G
 Usage: 1965–66 Mustang with manual transmissions, disc brakes only

Interchange Number: 10
 Part Number(s): C7ZZ2455G
 Usage: 1967 Mustang and Cougar with manual transmissions, drum brakes only

Interchange Number: 11
 Part Number(s): C7ZZ2455B
 Usage: 1967 Mustang and Cougar with manual transmissions, disc brakes only

Interchange Number: 12
 Part Number(s): C8ZZ2455E
 Usage: 1968 Mustang, 1968 Cougar with manual transmissions, drum brakes only

Interchange Number: 13
Part Number(s): C8ZZ2455C
Usage: 1968 Mustang and Cougar with manual transmissions, disc brakes only

Interchange Number: 14
Part Number(s): C9ZZ2455B
Usage: 1969–70 Mustang and Cougar with manual transmissions, drum brakes only

Interchange Number: 15
Part Number(s): C9ZZ2455D
Usage: 1969 Mustang (except Boss 429ci) and Cougar, both with manual transmissions and disc brakes only

Interchange Number: 16
Part Number(s): DOZZ2455B
Usage: 1970 Cougar and Mustang (except Boss 429ci) with manual transmission, disc brakes only

Interchange Number: 17
Part Number(s): C9ZZ2455E
Usage: 1969–70 Boss 429ci Mustang with manual transmission and disc brakes

Interchange Number: 18
Part Number(s): C3OZ2455AD
Usage: 1963–65 Fairlane and 1962–63 Mercury Meteor with automatic transmission (except 427ci)

Interchange Number: 19
Part Number(s): C6OZ2455B
Usage: 1966–67 Fairlane, Falcon, and Comet with automatic transmission

Interchange Number: 20
Part Number(s): C7OZ2455E
Usage: 1967 Fairlane, 1967 Comet with automatic transmission, disc brakes, and 427ci engine

Interchange Number: 21
Part Number(s): C8OZ2455A
Usage: 1968 Torino, Falcon, and Montego with automatic transmission

Interchange Number: 22
Part Number(s): C9OZ2455B
Usage: 1969 Torino, 1969 Montego with automatic transmission

Interchange Number: 23
Part Number(s): DOOZ2455B
Usage: 1970–71 Torino and Montego with automatic transmission

Interchange Number: 24
Part Number(s): C7ZZ2455J
Usage: 1964-1/2–67 Mustang and 1967 Cougar with automatic transmission, drum brakes only

Interchange Number: 25
Part Number(s): C5ZZ2455H
Usage: 1965–66 Mustang with automatic transmission, disc brakes only

Interchange Number: 26
Part Number(s): C7ZZ2455K
Usage: 1967 Mustang and Cougar with automatic transmission, disc brakes only

Interchange Number: 27
Part Number(s): C8ZZ2455B
Usage: 1968 Mustang and Cougar with automatic transmission, drum brakes only

Interchange Number: 28
Part Number(s): C8ZZ2455A
Usage: 1968 Mustang and Cougar with automatic transmission, disc brakes only

Interchange Number: 29
Part Number(s): C9ZZ2455C
Usage: 1969–70 Mustang and Cougar with automatic transmission, disc brakes only

Interchange Number: 30
Part Number(s): C9ZZ2455A
Usage: 1969 Mustang and Cougar with automatic transmission, disc brakes only

Interchange Number: 31
Part Number(s): DOZZ2455A
Usage: 1970 Cougar and Mustang with automatic transmission, disc brakes only

Interchange Number: 32
Part Number(s): B8A2455B
Usage: 1959–60 full-size Ford with automatic transmission

Interchange Number: 33
Part Number(s): C4AZ2455C
Usage: 1961–64 full-size Ford with manual transmission (except 1963 with tilt steering column)

Pad, Brake Pedal

Model Identification

Cougar	Interchange Number
1967–70	
manual transmission	
drum brakes	3
disc brakes	5
automatic transmission	
drum brakes	7
disc brakes	9

Cyclone	Interchange Number
1966–67	
manual transmission	
drum brakes	
without power brakes	3
with power brakes	4
disc brakes	5
automatic transmission	
drum brakes	
without power brakes	7
with power brakes	8
1968–70	
manual transmission	
drum brakes	3
disc brakes	5
automatic transmission	
drum brakes	7
disc brakes	9

Fairlane and Torino	Interchange Number
1959–61	
manual transmission	
drum brakes	
without power brakes	1
with power brakes	2
automatic transmission	
drum brakes	
without power brakes	6
with power brakes	10
1962–64	
manual transmission, drum brakes	11
automatic transmission, drum brakes	12
1966–67	
manual transmission	
drum brakes	
without power brakes	3
with power brakes	4
disc brakes	5

automatic transmission, drum brakes
  without power brakes 7
  with power brakes...8
1968–70
  manual transmission
    drum brakes 3
    disc brakes..5
  automatic transmission
    drum brakes 7
    disc brakes..9

Mustang   *Interchange Number*
1964-1/2–70
  manual transmission
    drum brakes 3
    disc brakes..5
  automatic transmission
    drum brakes 7
    disc brakes..9

Interchange

Interchange Number: 1
Part Number(s): B4A2454A
Usage: 1954–64 full-size Ford without power-assisted drum brakes but with manual transmission, all except 1962–64 Galaxie models

Interchange Number: 2
Part Number(s): B9A2455B
Usage: 1959–64 full-size Ford with power-assisted drum brakes with manual transmission

Interchange Number: 3
Part Number(s): C5ZZ2455G
Usage: 1965–67 Fairlane, 1968–72 Torino, 1966–67 Comet, 1968–72 Montego, 1964-1/2–72 Mustang, 1970–72 Maverick, 1971–72 Comet (compact), 1968–70 Falcon, and 1967–72 Cougar—all models with drum brakes (without power assist in 1965–66) with manual transmission

Interchange Number: 4
Part Number(s): C2OZ2454A
Usage: 1966–67 Fairlane and Comet with power drum brakes and manual transmission

Interchange Number: 5
Part Number(s): C5ZZ2455D
Usage: 1967 Fairlane, 1968–72 Torino, 1967 Comet, 1968–72 Montego, 1966–72 Mustang, 1970–72 Maverick, 1971–72 Comet (compact), and 1968–70 Falcon—all models with disc brakes and manual transmission
Note(s): Early-1964-1/2–65 Mustangs used part number C4DZ2455A. It was only slightly different and was used up to build date March 8, 1965. Later style is the replacement part.

Interchange Number: 6
Part Number(s): B4A2454B
Usage: 1959–60 full-size Ford without power-assisted drum brakes but with automatic transmission, all except 1962–64 Galaxie

Interchange Number: 7
Part Number(s): C6OZ2455A
Usage: 1965–67 Fairlane, 1968–72 Torino, 1966–67 Comet, 1968–72 Montego, 1964-1/2–72 Mustang, 1970–72 Maverick, 1971–72 Comet (compact), and 1968–70 Falcon—all models with drum brakes (without power assist in 1965–66) and automatic transmission

Interchange Number: 8
Part Number(s): C6OZ2454C
Usage: 1966–67 Fairlane and 1965–67 Comet with power-assisted drum brakes and automatic transmission

Interchange Number: 9
Part Number(s): D3ZZ2455A
Usage: 1967 Fairlane, 1968–72 Torino, 1967 Comet, 1968–72 Montego, 1966–72 Mustang, 1970–72 Maverick, 1971–72 Comet, and 1968–70 Falcon—all models with disc brakes and automatic transmission

Interchange Number: 10
Part Number(s): B4A2454C
Usage: 1959–60 full-size Ford with power-assisted drum brakes and automatic transmission, all except 1962–64 Galaxie

Interchange Number: 11
Part Number(s): B3OZ2454D
Usage: 1962–64 Fairlane with drum brakes and automatic transmission

Interchange Number: 12
Part Number(s): C3OZ2454E
Usage: 1962–64 Fairlane with drum brakes and manual transmission

Brake Assembly, Parking

Model Identification

Cougar   *Interchange Number*
1967–68...7
1969–70...8

Cyclone   *Interchange Number*
1966–67...4
1968–70...5

Fairlane and Torino   *Interchange Number*
1959–61...1
1962–65...2
1966–67...4
1968–70...5

Mustang   *Interchange Number*
1964-1/2–66..6
1967–68...7
1969–70...8

Interchange

Interchange Number: 1
Part Number(s): C1AA2780B
Usage: 1960–61 full-size Ford

Interchange Number: 2
Part Number(s): C2OZ2780A
Usage: 1962–65 Fairlane, 1962–63 Meteor

Interchange Number: 3
Part Number(s): CODZ2780A
Usage: 1960–65 Falcon and 1964–65 Comet

Interchange Number: 4
Part Number(s): C6OZ2780B
Usage: 1966–67 Fairlane, Falcon, and Comet

Interchange Number: 5
Part Number(s): DOOZ2780A
Usage: 1968–71 Torino and Montego

Interchange Number: 6
Part Number(s): C5ZZ2780B
Usage: 1964-1/2–66 Mustang

Interchange Number: 7
Part Number(s): C7ZZ2780B
Usage: 1967–68 Mustang and Cougar

Interchange Number: 8
Part Number(s): DOZZ2780A
Usage: 1969–70 Mustang and Cougar

Calipers

Disc brakes became available in 1965 on full-size and Mustang models. Then, across the board in 1967. Calipers are greatly interchangeable. In fact, after 1967, all but the full-size Ford, Mercury, Lincoln, and Thunderbird will interchange. There is a distinct difference between the calipers on the driver's and passenger's side of the car; they are not interchangeable.

Model Identification

Cougar	Interchange Number
1967	2
1968–70	3

Cyclone	Interchange Number
1967	2
1968–70	3

Fairlane and Torino	Interchange Number
1967	2
1968–70	3

Mustang	Interchange Number
1965–66	1
1967	2
1968–70	3

Interchange

Interchange Number: 1
Part Number(s): C5ZZ2B120C (right), C5ZZ2B121C (left)
Usage: 1965–66 Mustang; no other interchange

Interchange Number: 2
Part Number(s): C7OZ2B120C (right), C7OZ2B121C (left)
Usage: 1967 Mustang and Cougar and 1967 Fairlane, Comet, and Falcon

Interchange Number: 3
Part Number(s): C8OZ2B120C (right), C8OZ2B121C (left)
Usage: 1968–73 Mustang and Cougar and 1968–71 Torino, Montego, and Falcon

Chapter 8

Wheels, Wheel Covers, and Wheel Trim

Determining factors in interchanging wheels are the diameter, width, and offset. Of these, the offset is an important factor to watch for. You may find two wheels that have the same diameter and width, but each has a different offset. The offset is the distance that the wheel sets back from the brake drum or rotor. It can be measured by noting the distance from the centerline of the rim to the inner side of the wheel disc.

Wheels with the wrong offset can interfere with brake operations (especially with disc brakes) and cause tire clearance problems at the wheelwell lip. There is generally a "1 plus" rule in swapping wheels. This means you can usually, but not always, go up one size in the wheel without problems. For example, if your car is equipped with 14x5in wheels, you can usually install 14x6in wheels. Try to avoid large offset changes. For example, if you have a wheel with a 1/4in offset, you should not use a wheel with a 3in offset. Another factor to use as a guide is if the wheels were optional on your car, they will usually fit your car.

Also, you may notice some wheels have the same diameter, same width, and same bolt pattern size, yet they are still not interchangeable, due to size of the center hub hole. While you can install a wheel with a larger-diameter hole on a car with a smaller hub, the reverse is not true. This information (size of the hole) is not given, so be sure you measure, or better yet, try the wheel's fit before you buy.

You may note color listed in the interchange section below. This is not the color of the wheel but refers to a paint code stripe that was used as identification.

Wheels, Plain and Styled

Model Identification

Cougar	Interchange Number
1967	
plain steel	
14x5	6, 8
14x5-1/2	7
styled wheels	
14x5-1/2	17
1968–69	
plain steel	
14x5	6, 8
14x5-1/2	7
14x6	9
styled wheels	
twelve-slot	
14x6	
silver	19
chrome	20
five-spoke	22
1970	
plain wheels	
14x6	9

	Interchange Number
14x7	10
15x7	11
styled wheels	
14x6	23

Cyclone	Interchange Number
1966–67	
plain wheels	
14x5	6, 8
14x5-1/2	6, 7
styled wheels	
five-spoke	
14x5 (1966)	14, 15
14x 5-1/2 (1967)	17
1968–69	
plain wheels	
14x5	6, 8
14x5-1/2	7
14x6	9
styled wheels	
twelve-slot 14x6	
silver	19
chrome	20
five-spoke	22
1970	
plain wheels	
14x6	9
14x7	10
15x7	11
styled wheels	
14x6	23

Fairlane and Torino	Interchange Number
1959–61 plain wheels	
14x5	1
14x5-1/2	2
14x6	3
15x5	4
15x5-1/2	5
1962–65 plain wheels	
13x 4-1/2	12
14x5	6
1966–67	
plain wheels	
14x5-1/2	7, 2
styled wheels	
14x5 (1966)	14, 15
14x5-1/2 (1967)	16
1968–69	
plain wheels	
14x5	6, 8
14x6	9

styled wheels, twelve-slot 14x6
    black 18
    silver 19, 20
    chrome 21
1970
  plain wheels
    14x5 6
    14x7 10
    15x7 11
  styled wheels
    15x7 25

Mustang	**Interchange Number**

1964-1/2–66
  plain wheels
    13x4-1/2 12
    14x5 6
    15x5-1/2 5
    15x6 13
  styled wheels
    14x5 ....14, 15
1967
  plain wheels
    14x5 ....6, 9
    15x6 13
  styled wheels
    14x5-1/2 16
1968
  plain wheels
    14x5 ....6, 8
    14x5-1/2 7
    14x6 9
  styled wheels
    twelve-slot 14x6
      black 18
      silver 19, 20
      chrome 21
    Magnum 500
      15x7 Boss 302ci 24, 25
      15x7 Boss 429ci 26
1970
  plain wheels
    14x5 6
    14x7 10
    15x7 11
  styled wheels
    15x7 25
    GT 350/500 27

Interchange

Interchange Number: 1
  Part Number(s): B7A1015A
  Diameter/Width: 14x5in
  Usage: 1957–60 full-size Ford
  Note(s): Will fit 1962–65 Fairlane.

Interchange Number: 2
  Part Number(s): C2AZ1007C
  Diameter/Width: 14x5-1/2in
  Usage: 1960–64 full-size Ford, 1966 Fairlane GT, and 1966 Cyclone

Interchange Number: 3
  Part Number(s): C3AZ1007A
  Diameter/Width: 14x6in
  Usage: 1960–64 full-size Ford

Interchange Number: 4
  Part Number(s): COAA1007N
  Diameter/Width: 15x5in
  Usage: 1960 full-size Ford and full-size Mercury

Interchange Number: 5
  Part Number(s): C1AZ1007A
  Diameter/Width: 15x5-1/2in
  Usage: 1961–65 full-size Ford and 1964-1/2–66 Mustang

Interchange Number: 6
  Part Number(s): C8OZ1007G
  Diameter/Width: 14x5in
  Identification Marks(s): White paint
  Usage: 1962–67 Fairlane, 1966–67 Comet, 1968–71 Torino, 1968–71 Montego, 1964-1/2–69 Mustang, 1967–69 Cougar, and 1965–70 Falcon

Interchange Number: 7
  Part Number(s): C8OZ1007H
  Diameter/Width: 14x5-1/2in
  Identification Marks: Red paint
  Usage: 1967 Fairlane GT, 1967 Cyclone GT, 1968–69 Mustang, and 1968–69 Cougar

Interchange Number: 8
  Part Number(s): C8OZ1007C
  Diameter/Width: 14x5in
  Identification Mark(s): Stamped C8OA1007EW, C8OA1007FW, C8OA1007GW, or C8OA1007HW
  Usage: 1968 Torino, Montego, Mustang, and Cougar—all with disc brakes

Interchange Number: 9
  Part Number(s): C8ZZ1007D
  Diameter/Width: 14x6in
  Identification Mark(s): Stamped C8AZ1007AW, C8AZ1007BW, or C8AZ1007CW; or coded with red or tan paint
  Usage: 1968–69 Torino, 1968–69 Montego, 1967–70 Mustang, and 1968–70 Cougar, except Ranchero and 1969–70 Boss Mustang spare tire

Interchange Number: 10
  Part Number(s): DOOZ1007B
  Diameter/Width: 14x7in
  Identification Mark(s): White and violet paint
  Usage: 1970–71 Torino and Montego and 1970–72 Mustang and Cougar
  Note(s): *Warning:* 1972–74 14x6 wheels have the same color markings, so be sure to check the width.

Interchange Number: 11
  Part Number(s): DOOZ1007A
  Diameter/Width: 15x7in
  Identification Mark(s): Green paint, stamped "D"
  Usage: 1970–71 Torino and Montego and 1970–72 Mustang and Cougar

Interchange Number: 12
  Part Number(s): C1UU1007A
  Diameter/Width: 13x4-1/2in
  Usage: 1964-1/2–65 Mustang, 1962–64 Fairlane, 1964–65 Comet, and 1963–64 Falcon
  Note(s): Not a good choice for performance. Upgrade to Interchange Number 6.

Interchange Number: 13
  Part Number(s): C8AZ1007F
  Diameter/Width: 15x6in
  Identification Mark(s): *
  Usage: 1966–69 Shelby GT 350 Mustang and 1965–72 full-size Ford or Mercury
  Note(s): *Codes vary through model years. 1968 wheel stamped C8AA1007DW. 1969–72 coded with brown paint. 1965–67 model years used no code markings.

Styled Wheels

The first styled wheels were designed for the Mustang, but found their way onto other models. The 14x5in wheel appeared in 1965, and it featured a five-spoke design with a chrome rim and outline of the spokes. The inner sides of the spokes were painted gray up to build date

February 1, 1965. After this date, the same wheel design was used but the inward portions were painted gray-gold. The gray-gold-colored wheel was continued into the 1966 model year.

The next wheel design appeared in 1966. It, too, measured 14x5in and looked like the wheel used in 1965–66, but it also featured a chrome ring. This unit was phased into production in mid-1966 and pushed the non-trim-ring wheel out.

Width was increased to 5-1/2in for 1967. Thus, the wheel is not interchangeable on 1966 models. The pattern was the same, but the wheel was deeper inset and required a wider trim ring.

For 1968, the entire design was changed. This time it measured 14x6in and was designed for the Torino series but found its way onto the Mustang, Montego, and even the Cougar. The basic design consisted of a wheel with twelve small oval slots and was used in conjunction with a trim ring and hub cap. Two styles were used: the argent silver unit and the chrome-plated unit. The latter had the same design but did not use a trim ring. Lesser known was a third version of this wheel, which was painted gloss-black. These wheels continued into the 1969 model year.

Boss Mustangs used their own special wheels. These measured 15x7in and featured a five-spoke design and looked very similar to the popular Magnum 500 wheels. Two different finishes were used: argent silver and chrome-plated. Note that the 1970 Boss Mustangs used only the chrome-plated unit, which featured inserts that were painted flat black. This is the Magnum 500 wheel, which found its way onto other 1970–up models.

Interchange Number: 14
Part Number(s): C5ZZ1007B
Diameter/Width: 14x5in
Identification Mark(s): *
Usage: 1965–66 Mustang, 1966 Comet, 1966 Fairlane five-spoke design
Note(s): *Early models (up to February 1, 1965) had insert painted gray. After date, inserts painted gray-gold. Inserts can be repainted.

Interchange Number: 15
Part Number(s): C6ZZ1007A
Diameter/Width: 14x5in
Identification Mark(s): Has trim ring.
Usage: 1966 Mustang, 1966 Fairlane, and 1966 Comet five-spoke design

Interchange Number: 16
Part Number(s): C7ZZ1007B
Diameter/Width: 14x5-1/2in
Identification Marks: Uses trim ring
Usage: 1967 Fairlane and Mustang five-spoke design

1969–69 twelve-slot wheel with dull silver finish.

Interchange Number: 17
Part Number(s): C7GY1007A
Diameter/Width: 14x5-1/2in
Usage: 1967 Cougar and Comet
Note(s): Five-spoke design with five elongated slots. Similar to Magnum 500 wheel.

Interchange Number: 18
Part Number(s): C8OZ1007F
Diameter/Width: 14x6in
Identification Mark(s): *
Usage: 1968 Torino and Mustang
Note(s): *Twelve slots in spider. Painted reflective black. Interchange Number 19 can be modified to fit.

Interchange Number: 19
Part Number(s): C8OZ1007J
Diameter/Width: 14x6in
Identification Mark(s): Some stamped C8OA1007L or C8OA1007M
Usage: 1968–69 Torino, Mustang, Montego, and Cougar
Note(s): Twelve-slot with silver finish. Can be painted reflective black to fit Interchange Number 18.

1967 Ford-styled wheel.

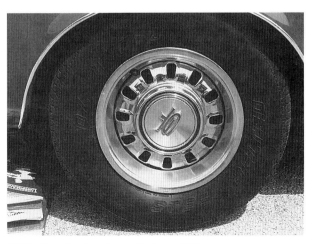

1968–69 twelve-slot wheel with chrome finish.

1968 cougar used a five-spoke design.

Interchange Number: 20
Part Number(s): C8OZ1007K
Diameter/Width: 14x6in
Identification Mark(s): Reflective silver finish
Usage: 1968–69 Torino and Mustang
Note(s): Twelve slots in spider.

Interchange Number: 21
Part Number(s): C8ZZ1007E
Diameter/Width: 14x6in
Identification Mark(s): Some stamped C8OA1007N, C8OA1007T, or C8OA1007Z
Usage: 1968–69 Torino, Mustang, Montego, and Cougar
Note(s): Twelve slots in spider chrome-plated wheel.

Interchange Number: 22
Part Number(s): C8WY1007A
Diameter/Width: 14x6in
Identification Mark(s): Stamped C8ZA1007C
Usage: 1968 Cougar and Montego
Note(s): Five-spoke wheel.

Interchange Number: 23
Part Number(s): C9WY1007B
Diameter/Width: 14x6in
Identification Mark(s): Stamped C9WA1007B1 or C9WA1007B2
Usage: 1969–70 Cougar and Montego
Note(s): Five-spoke wheel painted gray-gold.

Interchange Number: 24
Part Number(s): C9ZZ1007E
Diameter/Width: 15x7
Usage: 1969 Boss 302ci Mustang
Note(s): Wheels painted argent silver. Five-spoke design that looks like Magnum 500 wheel.

Interchange Number: 25
Part Number(s): C9ZZ1007D
Diameter/Width: 15x7in
Usage: 1969–70 Boss 302ci Mustang, 1970 Boss Mustang, 1970–71 Torino and Montego, and 1970–71 Mustang
Note(s): Wheels are chrome-plated five-spoke design with flat black insets. Magnum 500 wheel will not fit Boss 429ci; center hole is too small.

Interchange Number: 26
Part Number(s): C9ZZ1007H
Diameter/Width: 15x7in
Usage: 1969 Boss 429ci Mustang
Note(s): Wheels are chrome-plated five-spoke design. Will fit Interchange Number 24 but not vice versa.

Interchange Number: 27
Part Number(s): C9ZZ1007J
Diameter/Width: 15x7in
Usage: 1969–70 GT 350 and GT 500 Mustang

Wheel Covers

Wheel covers should not be confused with hubcaps. Hubcaps cover only the inner portion of the wheel and the lug nuts, while wheel covers hide the entire face of the wheel. Wheel covers are identified by their design and size (diameter). Sometimes a cover can be modified a little, such as changing the inner emblem, and it will work on another model. A description of the cover is given to help you identify the cover. If modification can adapt it to another model, the modification is described in the notes section. Note that the diameter given is for the wheel cover itself.

Wheel covers can identified by a number that is stamped on their back. When the number is known, it is given. But note that some identical covers may use more than one casting number, so use them only as a guide.

Model Identification

Cougar	Interchange Number
1967	
simulated mag wheel	13
simulated wire wheel	27, 28, 57, 59
multiple-ribbed	14
Dan Gurney Special	60

1969–70 five-spoke "Magnum 500" wheels.

1964-1/2–65 full Mustang wheel cover without spinners.

Interchange

Interchange Number: 1
Part Number(s): B9AA11307A
Diameter: 14in
Description: Center dome surround by spiraled bar pattern.
Usage: 1959 full-size Ford and 1959–60 Thunderbird

Interchange Number: 2
Part Number(s): C1AA1130A
Diameter: 14in
Description: Center dome outline with forty straight struts.
Usage: 1961 full-size Ford

Interchange Number: 3
Part Number(s): C3OZ1130D
Diameter: 14in
Description: Large center dome with thirty-six struts and the Ford crest in center of dome.
Usage: 1962–63 Fairlane with 14in wheels

Interchange Number: 4
Part Number(s): C3OZ1130G
Diameter: 14in
Description: Has multiple struts with tri-bar spinner in center of cover.
Usage: 1963 Fairlane

Interchange Number: 5
Part Number(s): C3OZ1130K
Diameter: 14in
Description: Has simulated wire cover with tri-bar spinner in the center.
Usage: 1963–64 Fairlane

Interchange Number: 6
Part Number(s): C4OZ1130C
Diameter: 14in
Description: Tri-spinner in center. Reads Fairlane Sports Coupe. Has dull finish.
Usage: 1964 Fairlane

Interchange Number: 7
Part Number(s): C4OZ1130L
Diameter: 14in
Description: Tri-spinner in center. Reads Fairlane Sports Coupe. Has bright finish.
Usage: 1964 Fairlane

Interchange Number: 8

Part Number(s): C4AZ1130H

Diameter: 14in

Description: Wire-spokes. Larger plain center dome; wires criss-cross.

Usage: 1964 Fairlane, 1964 full-size Ford, and 1964-1/2–66 (up to build date December 31, 1966)

Interchange Number: 9

Part Number(s): C5OZ1130A

ID Number(s): C5OA1130A

Diameter: 14in

Description: Raised center ribbed dome with Ford crest in center.

Usage: 1965–66 Fairlane

Interchange Number: 10

Part Number(s): C5OZ1130E

ID Number(s): C5OA1130C

Diameter: 14in

Description: Has red-colored center crest.

Usage: 1965 Fairlane

Interchange Number: 11

Part Number(s): C6OZ1130C

ID Number(s): C6OA1130C

Diameter: 14in

Description: Four-bar spinner in center with red-colored insert. Outer edge of cover is dominated by eight slots.

Usage: 1966 Fairlane

Interchange Number: 12

Part Number(s): C6OZ1130K

ID Number(s): C6OA1130E or C8OA1130M

Diameter: 14in

Description: Five-spoke simulated mag wheel with Ford name stamped in center of hub and bright-plated simulated lug nuts.

Usage: 1966–67 Fairlane, 1968–71 Torino, 1966–70 Mustang, 1966–68 Falcon, and 1971 Maverick

Note(s): Center cap has Ford or Mercury name. Must be changed accordingly.

Interchange Number: 13

Part Number(s): C6OZ1130N

ID Number(s): C6OA1130M

Diameter: 14in

Description: Five-spoke simulated mag wheel with plain center hub and bright-plated simulated lug nuts.

Usage: 1966–67 Fairlane, 1968–71 Torino, 1966–70 Mustang, 1966–68 Falcon, 1971 Maverick, 1966–67 Comet, 1968–71 Montego, and 1967–71 Cougar

Note(s): Interchange Number 12 will fit but center caps must be changed.

1967 Mustang wheel cover with twenty-one depressions.

Interchange Number: 14

Part Number(s): C7OZ1130F

ID Number(s): C7OA1130D

Diameter: 14in

Description: Simulated wire wheel with tri-bar-spinner center cap and Ford-blue-colored center.

Usage: 1967 Fairlane, Falcon, and Mustang

Interchange Number: 15

Part Number(s): C7OZ1130B

ID Number(s): C7OA1130B

Diameter: 14in

Description: Twelve indentations with high center dome imprinted with Ford name.

Usage: 1967 Fairlane

Interchange Number: 16

Part Number(s): C7OZ1130D

ID Number(s): C7OA1130A or C7OA1130E

Diameter: 14in

Description: Twelve indentations with high-dome center; blue center with Ford crest.

Usage: 1967 Fairlane

1966 slotted Mustang wheel cover.

1967 wire wheel cover with tri-bar spinners.

Interchange Number: 17
Part Number(s): C8OZ1130E
ID Number(s): C8OA1130E
Diameter: 14in
Description: Sixteen slots and Ford-blue center insert.
Usage: 1968 Torino

Interchange Number: 18
Part Number(s): C8OZ1130A
ID Number(s): C8OA1130A
Diameter: 14in
Description: Ford-blue ID center and sixty-four ribs.
Usage: 1968 Torino and Falcon
Note(s): See Interchange Number 19 for interchanging tips.

Interchange Number: 19
Part Number(s): C8OZ1130B
ID Number(s): C8OA1130B
Diameter: 14in
Description: Steel center imprinted with Ford crest. Outer edge of cover has sixty-four ribs.
Usage: 1968 Torino and Falcon
Note(s): Center may be changed with Interchange Number 18 or vice versa to allow for a greater interchange.

Interchange Number: 20
Part Number(s): C8OZ1130J
ID Number(s): C8OA1130N
Diameter: 14in
Description: Simulated wire wheel with round center hub.
Usage: 1968–71 Torino, 1968–70 Falcon, 1968–71 Mustang, 1968–71 Cougar, 1971 Maverick, 1971 Comet, and 1968–71 Montego

Interchange Number: 21
Part Number(s): C8OZ1130L
ID Number(s): C8OA1130L
Diameter: 15-3/8in
Description: Simulated wire wheel with round center hub with Ford-blue crest in center.
Usage: 1968 Torino.

Interchange Number: 22
Part Number(s): C9OZ1130A
ID Number(s): C9OA1130A
Diameter: 14in
Description: Center dome with red-colored crest. Outer lined by a ribbed pattern.
Usage: 1969 Torino and Falcon

Interchange Number: 23
Part Number(s): C9OZ1130B
ID Number(s): C9OA1130B
Diameter: 14in
Description: Large center dome with Ford crest in center dome supported by five bent-down legs.
Usage: 1969–71 Torino and 1969–70 Falcon

Interchange Number: 24
Part Number(s): DOOZ1130D
ID Number(s): DOOA1130D or DOOA1130H
Diameter: 15-1/4in
Description: Simulated styled wheel. Has a deep inset with five triangular-shaped slots. Wire wheel with red-colored center cap and argent silver background.
Usage: 1970–71 Torino with 14x7in wheels

Interchange Number: 25
Part Number(s): DOOZ1130G
ID Number(s): DOOA1130F or DOOA1130J
Diameter: 16-1/4in
Description: Simulated styled wheel. Has a deep inset with five triangular-shaped slots. Wire wheel with red-colored center cap and argent silver background.
Usage: 1970–71 Torino with 15x7in wheels.

Interchange Number: 26
Part Number(s): C6GY1130B (front), G4GY1130B (rear)
Diameter: 14in
Description: Simulated chrome wheels with plain center.
Usage: 1965–67 Comet
Note(s): Front cover has protruded center hub.

Interchange Number: 27
Part Number(s): C5GY1130A
Diameter: 14in
Description: Simulated wire wheels with tri-bar spinner and center cap with Mercury logo.
Usage: 1965–67 Comet and 1967 Cougar (dealer-installed)

Interchange Number: 28
Part Number(s): C7GY1130C
ID Number(s): C7WA1130G
Diameter: 14in
Description: Simulated wire wheels with round center hub and black center. Factory-installed option.
Usage: 1967 Comet and Cougar

Interchange Number: 29
Part Number(s): C8GY1130B
ID Number(s): C8GA1130G
Diameter: 14in
Description: Simulated wire wheels with round center hub and red-colored Mercury logo.
Usage: 1968 Montego

Interchange Number: 30
Part Number(s): C8GY1130A
ID Number(s): C8GA1130B
Diameter: 14in
Description: Round center hub with red-colored Mercury logo, outlined by fifty-two ribs.
Usage: 1968 Montego

Interchange Number: 31
Part Number(s): C8GY1130G
ID Number(s): G8GA1130F
Diameter: 14in
Description: Red-colored center hub with Mercury logo. Outlined by twenty-two chrome ribs.
Usage: 1968–69 Cyclone Spoiler Dan Gurney Special

Interchange Number: 32
Part Number(s): C6GY1130A (front), G4GY1130B (rear)
Diameter: 14in
Description: Simulated chrome wheels with plain center.
Usage: 1965–67 Comet

1967–69 Mustang wire wheel cover without spinner.

1968 Mustang wheel cover.

Interchange Number: 33

Part Number(s): DOGY1130A
ID Number(s): DOGA1130A
Diameter: 14in
Description: Large plain center imprint with Mercury name. Looks like a large pie pan.
Usage: 1970–71 Montego

Interchange Number: 34

Part Number(s): DOGY1130B
ID Number(s): DOGA1130B
Diameter: 15-3/8in
Description: Has black center with Mercury logo and eighteen ribs.
Usage: 1970–73 Montego and 1972–73 Cougar
Note(s): Ford unit will interchange if center logo is changed.

Interchange Number: 35

Part Number(s): C5ZZ1130C
ID Number(s): C4ZA1130E
Diameter: 14in
Description: Black center imprinted with Mustang and circular ribs divided by five simulated spokes. Stainless steel finish.
Usage: 1964-1/2 Mustang up to build date August 16, 1964

1967 cap used with five-spoke wheels on Fairlanes.

Interchange Number: 36

Part Number(s): C5ZZ1130J
ID Number(s): C4ZA1130J
Diameter: 14in
Description: Black center imprinted with Mustang and circular ribs divided by five simulated spokes. Stainless steel finish.
Usage: 1965 Mustang after build date August 16, 1964

Interchange Number: 37

Part Number(s): C5ZZ1130N
ID Number(s): C4ZA1130C
Diameter: 14in
Description: Black center imprinted with Mustang and circular ribs divided by five simulated spokes. Chrome finish.
Usage: 1965 Mustang optional wheel cover

Interchange Number: 38

Part Number(s): C5ZZ1130L
ID Number(s): C4ZA1130L
Diameter: 14in
Description: Black tri-bar spinner cap imprinted with Mustang in the center and has circular ribs divided by five simulated spokes. Stainless steel finish.
Usage: 1964-1/2 Mustang

Interchange Number: 39

Part Number(s): C5ZZ1130R
ID Number(s): C4ZA1130E
Diameter: 14in
Description: Black tri-bar spinner cap imprinted with Mustang in the center and has circular ribs divided by five simulated spokes. Chrome finish.
Usage: 1965 Mustang after build date October 25, 1964

Interchange Number: 40

Part Number(s): C4AZ1130L
ID Number(s): C4AA1130R
Diameter: 14in
Description: Wire-spoke cover with tri-bar spinner and red, white, and blue center cap.
Usage: 1964-1/2–65 Mustang, 1964 full-size Ford

Interchange Number: 41

Part Number(s): C6ZZ1130A
ID Number(s): C6ZA1130A
Diameter: 14in
Description: Raised center dome with Mustang logo. Accented in black and with five triangular cutouts.
Usage: 1966 Mustang

Interchange Number: 42

Part Number(s): C6ZZ1130B
ID Number(s): C6ZA1130C
Diameter: 14in
Description: Tri-bar spinner cap in center with Mustang logo. Accented in black and with five triangular cutouts.
Usage: 1966 Mustang

Interchange Number: 43

Part Number(s): C7ZZ1130G
ID Number(s): C7ZA1130H
Diameter: 14in
Description: Center imprinted with Mustang. Twenty-one depressions painted reflective gray.
Usage: 1967 Mustang

Interchange Number: 44

Part Number(s): C7ZZ1130B
ID Number(s): C7ZA1130B
Diameter: 14-1/8in
Description: Center imprinted with Mustang. Twenty-one depressions painted gray-gold metallic.
Usage: 1967 Mustang

Interchange Number: 45
Part Number(s): C7ZZ1130E
ID Number(s): C7ZA1130G
Diameter: 14in
Description: Simulated wire wheel. Red-colored center with Mustang logo.
Usage: 1967–68 Mustang and 1969 Mustang Grande.

Interchange Number: 46
Part Number(s): C7AZ1130H
ID Number(s): C7AA1130E
Diameter: 15in
Description: Simulated wire wheels. Tri-bar spinner cap with blue-colored center.
Usage: 1967 Mustang and full-size Ford

Interchange Number: 47
Part Number(s): C6AZ1130C
ID Number(s): C6AA1130E
Diameter: 16-1/4in
Description: Simulated five-spoke mag wheel. Bolts onto wheel. Has red center.
Usage: 1967–69 Mustang, 1966–68 full-size Ford, and 1969–70 Mustang GT-350 and GT 500.
Note(s): Standard cover on GT350 and GT 500 models. Extremely rare on GT-350 and GT-500.

Interchange Number: 48
Part Number(s): C8ZZ1130B
Diameter: 14in
Description: Red-colored center cap with Mustang logo. Sixteen indentations.
Usage: 1968 Mustang

Interchange Number: 49
Part Number(s): C8ZZ1130E
ID Number(s): C8ZA1130G
Diameter: 14in
Description: Simulated wire cover with red-colored center cap.
Usage: 1968 Mustang

Interchange Number: 50
Part Number(s): C6AZ1130K
ID Number(s): C6AA1130J, C6AA1130H, C6AA1130L
Diameter: 15in
Description: Simulated five-spoke mag wheel. Has a Ford-imprinted center and bright simulated lug nuts.
Usage: 1968 Mustang and 1966–70 full-size Ford

1968–69 cap used with twelve-slot wheels with the GT logo.

1969–70 "Magnum 500" wheels on Mustang feature the Pony logo.

Interchange Number: 51
Part Number(s): S8MS1132A
ID Number(s): Not used
Description: Simulated five-spoke mag wheel with Shelby Cobra center.
Usage: 1968 Mustang GT 350 and GT 500; standard cover on these models

Interchange Number: 52
Part Number(s): C9ZZ1130A
ID Number(s): C9ZA1130B
Diameter: 14in
Description: Has a star-shaped center and center cap imprinted with Mustang.
Usage: 1969 Mustang

Interchange Number: 53
Part Number(s): D0ZZ1130A
ID Number(s): D0ZA1130K
Diameter: 14-1/8in
Description: Has a chrome background and a raised center hub imprinted Mustang. Outer edge has sixteen depressions.
Usage: 1970 Mustang

Interchange Number: 54
Part Number(s): D0ZZ1130D
ID Number(s): D0ZA1130E or D0ZA1130L
Diameter: 15-1/4in
Description: Simulated styled wheel. Has a deep inset with five triangle-shaped slots on a wire wheel with a red-colored center cap and black background.
Usage: 1970 Mustang with 14x7in wheels
Note(s): Interchange Number 24 will fit if repainted.

Interchange Number: 55
Part Number(s): D0ZZ1130E
ID Number(s): D0ZA1130F or D0ZA1130M
Diameter: 15-1/8in
Description: Simulated styled wheel. Has a deep inset with five triangle-shaped slots on a wire wheel with a red-colored center cap and black background.
Usage: 1970 Mustang with 14x6in wheels

Interchange Number: 56
Part Number(s): D0ZZ1130F
ID Number(s): D0ZA1130G, D0ZA1130N
Diameter: 16-1/4in
Description: Simulated styled wheel. Has a deep inset with five triangle-shaped slots on a wire wheel with a red-colored center cap and black background.
Usage: 1970 Mustang with 15x7in wheels
Note(s): Interchange Number 25 will fit if repainted.

Interchange Number: 57
Part Number(s): C7WY1130C
ID Number(s): C7WA1130G
Diameter: 14in
Description: Simulated wire wheel with black center cap.
Usage: 1967 Cougar and Comet

Interchange Number: 58
Part Number(s): C7WY1130A
ID Number(s): C7WA1130C
Diameter: 14in
Description: Plain center with multiple-rib pattern.
Usage: 1967 Cougar

Interchange Number: 59
Part Number(s): C5GY1130C
Diameter: 14in
Description: Simulated wire wheel with tri-bar center spinner cap. Dealer-installed option.
Usage: 1967 Cougar and 1965–67 Comet

Interchange Number: 60
Part Number(s): C7WY1130E
ID Number(s): C7WA1130A
Diameter: 14in
Description: Has eleven triangular slots around center hub.
Usage: 1967 Cougar with Dan Gurney Special package

Interchange Number: 61
Part Number(s): C8WY1130B
ID Number(s): C8WA1130A
Diameter: 14in
Description: Has fifty-three ribs with center cap imprinted with Cougar.
Usage: 1968 Cougar

Interchange Number: 62
Part Number(s): C8WY1130D
ID Number(s): C8WA1130C
Diameter: 15-3/8in
Description: Has twenty-two black and chrome ribs, with red XR7 logo of Coke-bottle-top-shaped center cap.
Usage: 1968 Cougar XR7

Interchange Number: 63
Part Number(s): C8WY1130G
ID Number(s): C8WA1130F
Diameter: 15-3/8in
Description: Has twenty-two chrome ribs.
Usage: 1968 Cougar with Dan Gurney Special package

Interchange Number: 64
Part Number(s): C9WY1130C
ID Number(s): C8WA1130C1 or C8WA1130C2
Diameter: 14in
Description: Simulated road wheel with five oval slots and blue-colored center with Cougar name.
Usage: 1969–70 Cougar

Interchange Number: 65
Part Number(s): C9WY1130B
ID Number(s): C9WA1130B
Diameter: 15in
Description: Has a multiple-rib pattern with center red XR7 crest.
Usage: 1969 Cougar XR7

Interchange Number: 66
Part Number(s): C9GY1130D
ID Number(s): ED-C8GA1130F
Diameter: 15-3/8in
Description: Has twenty-two chrome ribs with plain center with medallion.
Usage: 1969 Cougar with Dan Gurney Special package

Interchange Number: 67
Part Number(s): DOWY1130B
ID Number(s): DOWA1130B or DOWA1130F
Diameter: 15-1/4in
Description: Simulated road wheel. Has a deep inset with five tri-angle-shaped slots and black crest with Mercury emblem in center cap.
Usage: 1970 Cougar with 14x6in wheels

Interchange Number: 68
Part Number(s): DOWY1130D
ID Number(s): DOWA1130D
Diameter: 15-3/8in
Description: Multiple-rib pattern with Mercury crest in the center dome.
Usage: 1970–72 Cougar

Interchange Number: 69
Part Number(s): DOWY1130A
ID Number(s): DOWA1130A
Diameter: 15-3/8in
Description: Has fifty-three ribs with black center XR7 emblem and black-accented center ring.
Usage: 1970 Cougar XR7
Note(s): Similar to 1969 unit, but center emblem and accent ring are different.

Interchange Number: 70
Part Number(s): C5OZ1130B
ID Number(s): C5OWA1130A
Diameter: 14in
Description: Simulated wire wheel with tri-bar spinner center cap.
Usage: 1965–66 Fairlane and 1964-1/2–66 Mustang built before January 1, 1966

Hubcaps

The caps listed here are for the styled wheels. Standard hubcaps are not given, as they are not a popular choice with restorers nor that common on the cars with a musclecar image. There are certain exceptions, such as the 1968–69 cars that used hubcap with trim rings on standard rims, that are listed.

Hubcaps can be identified by a number stamped on the underside. Diameter is the diameter of the cap itself and not for wheel size.

Model Identification

Mustang   **Interchange Number**

1964-1/2–66
   all except GT 350 1
   GT 350 ....2, 3, 4
1967
   all except GT 350 and GT 500........................1, 7
   GT 350 and GT 500..................................8, 9
1968–69
   slotted wheels
      without GT package 10
      with GT package 11
   Boss 302ci 14
   Boss 429ci 13
   GT 350 and GT 500.................................16
1970
   all except GT 350 and GT 500........................14
   GT 350 and GT 500.................................16

Interchange

Interchange Number: 1
Part Number(s): C5ZZ1130W
ID Number(s): C5ZA1130J
Diameter: 2-1/2in
Description: Center cap imprinted with Ford Mustang and Mustang logo.
Usage: 1965–67 Mustang with styled wheels, except GT 350 and GT 500

Interchange Number: 2
Part Number(s): S1MS1130A
Diameter: 3in
Description: Chrome cap, imprinted with Carroll Shelby logo.
Usage: 1965 GT 350 with Cragar SS 15in wheels

Interchange Number: 3
Part Number(s): S2MS1007B or S2MS1007C
Description: Tri-spoke-spinner-look with Cobra logo.
Diameter: 2-3/4in
Usage: 1965–66 GT 350 with Shelby-styled wheels

Interchange Number: 4
Part Number(s): S2MS1130C
Description: Round diecast with rough texture face, with Carroll Shelby logo.
Diameter: 3in
Usage: Late-1965–66 GT350 with Shelby wheel S2MS1007A

Simple but effective was the wide track option in 1970 models that included a simple hubcap and wheel trim ring on wide wheels.

Interchange Number: 5
Part Number(s): C6OZ1130L
ID Number(s): C6OA1130F
Description: Center hub with red-colored center and Ford emblem.
Diameter: 2-3/4in
Usage: 1966 Fairlane with styled steel wheels

Interchange Number: 6
Part Number(s): C7OZ1130C
ID Number(s): C7OA1130C
Description: Center hub with red-colored center and Ford emblem. Push-in type.
Diameter: 2-1/2in
Usage: 1967 Fairlane

Interchange Number: 7
Part Number(s): C7ZZ1130W
ID Number(s): C7ZA1130J
Description: Center cap (1967 wheel-type) is knob-type with Mustang logo in center. Push-in mount.
Diameter: 3-3/4in
Usage: 1967 Mustang

Interchange Number: 8
Part Number(s): S7MS1130B
Description: Center cap imprinted with snake and Shelby Cobra. Thick round ring.
Diameter: 2-1/2in
Usage: 1967 Mustang GT 350 and GT 500, including GT500 KR and GT 350H. Use with S7MS1007D wheels.

Interchange Number: 9
Part Number(s): S7MS1130C
Description: Center cap imprinted with snake and Shelby Cobra. Thin round ring.
Diameter: 2-3/4in
Usage: 1967 Mustang GT 350 and GT 500, including GT 500 KR and GT 350H. Use with S7MS1007C wheels.

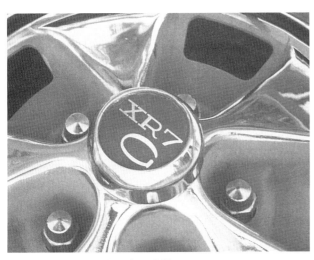

The 1968 Cougar XR7G used special logo caps.

Interchange Number: 10
Part Number(s): C8OZ1130G
ID Number(s): C8OA1130H or C8OA1130J
Description: Plain center cap without logo (see Diameter).
Diameter: 7-1/2in (use size as an ID guide)
Usage: 1968–70 Torino, 1968–70 Mustang, 1968–70 Cyclone Spoiler, and 1971–72 Cougar—all with slotted wheels but without GT packages

Interchange Number: 11
Part Number(s): C8OZ1130C
ID Number(s): C8OZ1130C or C8OZ1130D
Description: Hub cap with GT logo in the middle.
Diameter: 7-1/2in
Usage: 1968–70 Mustang GT and Torino GT with slotted wheels

Interchange Number: 12
Part Number(s): C9OZ1130D
Description: Center cap imprinted with Ranchero Rio Grande. Black center with bull's-head logo
Diameter: 2-3/4in
Usage: 1969 Ranchero with Rio Grande package

Interchange Number: 13
Part Number(s): C9ZZ1130F
Description: Center cap imprinted with Mustang horse logo (see Diameter).
Diameter: 2-3/16in
Usage: 1969 Mustang Boss 429ci with Magnum-styled wheels
Note(s): Similar to that used in Interchange Number 14 but smaller diameter.

Interchange Number: 14
Part Number(s): C9ZZ1130E
Description: Center cap imprinted with Mustang horse logo (see Diameter).
Diameter: 2-3/4in
Usage: 1969–70 Boss 302ci Mustang, 1970 Boss 429ci Mustang, and 1970–71 Mustangs with Magnum 500 wheels

Interchange Number: 15
Part Number(s): DOOZ1130F
Description: Center cap imprinted with Ford crest with chrome background.
Diameter: 2-3/4in
Usage: 1970–71 Torino with Magnum 500 wheels

Interchange Number: 16
Part Number(s): C9ZZ1130D
ID Number(s): C9ZA1130B
Description: Black center with Cobra (snake) logo. Push-in type, made of plastic.
Diameter: 2-3/4in
Usage: 1969–70 Mustang GT 350 and GT 500

Interchange Number: 17
Part Number(s): C6GY1130A
ID Number(s): C6GA1130D
Description: Solid black center cap.
Diameter: 2-1/2in
Usage: 1966 Comet

Interchange Number: 18
Part Number(s): C7WY1130
ID Number(s): C7WA1130E
Description: Solid black center with Mercury emblem.
Diameter: 2-3/4in
Usage: 1967 Comet, 1968 Montego, and 1967–68 Cougar (except 1968 Cougar XR7)—all with styled wheels

Interchange Number: 19
Part Number(s): C8WY1130F
Description: Center cap imprinted with XR7
Diameter: 2-1/2in
Usage: 1968 Cougar XR7 with styled wheels

Interchange Number: 20
Part Number(s): C9GY1130C
Description: Center cap with solid black center and Mercury emblem (head).
Diameter: 2-1/2in
Usage: 1968–69 Montego

Interchange Number: 21
Part Number(s): C9GY1130E
ID Number(s): C9GA1130G
Description: Solid black center cap with red Mercury crest.
Diameter: 2-1/2in
Usage: 1969–70 Montego and full-size Mercury with styled wheels
Note(s): Not for 1969 Spoiler models or those with slotted wheels.

Interchange Number: 22
Part Number(s): C9WY1130A
ID Number(s): C9WA1130D
Description: Center cap with blue-colored center with Cougar medallion (cat).
Diameter: 2-1/2in
Usage: 1969–70 Cougar with styled wheels

Interchange Number: 23
Part Number(s): DOGY1130G
ID Number(s): None
Description: Solid black center cap and red Mercury crest (phased into production).
Diameter: 2-3/4in
Usage: 1970 Montego (except Spoiler) and full-size Mercury with Magnum 500 wheels
Note(s): Spoiler used 1969 10-1/2in Torino plain hubcap. See 1968–69 Torino.

Trim Rings

Bright trim rings were used with different applications, such as styled steel wheels and certain wide-stance wheels. Trim rings are greatly interchangeable and are identified by diameter and finish. In addition, some trim rings are stamped with an identification number. If this number is used or known, it is given. The dimensions are outside diameter and inside diameter.

Model Identification

Cougar	Interchange Number
1967	2
1968	
with five-spoke wheels	2
XR7	6
1969 Eliminator	2
1970 with spoke wheels	22

Cyclone	Interchange Number
1966, all	1
1967, all	2
1968–69	
all except Spoiler	2
Spoiler	3
1970	
all except Magnum 500 wheels	21
Magnum 500	22
Spoiler	10

Fairlane and Torino	Interchange Number
1966, all	1
1967, all	2
1968–69	
slotted wheels	3
Ranchero, with Rio Grande	2
1970	
14x7	4
15x7	5

Interchange

Interchange Number: 1

Part Number(s): C6ZZ1210A
Diameter: 15-3/8in outside diameter, 12-3/16in inside diameter
Usage: 1966 styled wheels on Comet, Fairlane, and Mustang

Interchange Number: 2

Part Number(s): C7ZZ1210A
Diameter: 15-3/8in outside diameter, 12-15/16in inside diameter
Usage: 1967 styled wheels on Comet, Fairlane, Mustang, and Cougar; 1969 Montego and Cougar with styled wheels; and 1969–70 Cougar Eliminator

Interchange Number: 3

Part Number(s): C8ZZ1210B
ID Number(s): C8OA1210B
Diameter: 15-3/8in outside diameter, 12in inside diameter, 2in wide
Usage: 1968–69 Torino and Mustang, 1968 Montego and Cougar, and 1969–70 Cyclone Spoiler
Note(s): Use with slotted wheels.

Interchange Number: 4

Part Number(s): DOZZ1210B
ID Number(s): DOZA1210B or DOZA1210E
Diameter: 15-1/4in outside diameter, 11in inside diameter, 2-3/4in wide
Finish: Brushed chrome
Usage: 1970–71 Torino and Montego, 1971 Cougar, and 1970–71 Mustang—all with 14x7in wheels

Interchange Number: 5

Part Number(s): DOZA1210C
ID Number(s): DOAZ1210D or DOAZ1210G
Diameter: 16-1/4in outside diameter, 10-15/16in inside diameter, 2-11/16in wide
Finish: Brushed chrome
Usage: 1970–72 Montego, 1972 Cougar, 1970–72 Torino, and 1970–72 Mustang—all with 15x7in wheels

Interchange Number: 6

Part Number(s): C8ZZ1210B
ID Number(s): C8ZA1210B
Diameter: 15-3/8in outside diameter, 12in inside diameter, 2in wide
Usage: 1968–69 Mustang and Cougar (except Eliminator) with styled steel wheels

Chapter 9

Electrical Systems

Motor, Starter

The starter motor is a Ford-built unit; thus, it can be found on many different Ford, Mercury, and Lincoln models, so there is a great interchange available. Starters can be identified by a number stamped on the side of the housing. While a starter may "physically fit," it may not have the power to turn over a high-performance engine fast enough to start it. Note that while it may start the engine in the middle of summer, it may not even budge it in the sub-freezing temperatures of winter, so all interchange is based on the output of the starter, ensuring that the output is the same as, or more than, the original unit.

You may notice that more than one identification number may be used in the interchange below. These numbers were usually changed each year to identify them for that model and model year, but their physical characteristics are the same and will fit.

Model Identification

289ci	Interchange Number
1962–64, all	2
1965–67, all	3

302ci	Interchange Number
1968–70, all	3

351ci	Interchange Number
1969–70, all	3

352ci	Interchange Number
1959–61, all	1

Starter motor can be identified by a number stamped on the end of the case just above the starter drive.

390ci	Interchange Number
1961, all	1
1962–70, all	4, 5

427ci	Interchange Number
1962–68, all	4

428ci	Interchange Number
1966–70	
Cobra Jet and Super Cobra Jet	6
all others	4

429ci	Interchange Number
1969–70	7

Interchange

Interchange Number: 1
Part Number(s): FAY11002A
ID Number(s): FAC11002C, FAR11002A, B6A11002B, or B9S11002A
Usage: 1956–61 full-size Ford, Mercury, and Lincoln with V-8, incuding 352ci and 390ci

Interchange Number: 2
Part Number(s): C2OZ11002A
ID Number(s): C2OF11001A, C2OF11001B, C2OF11001C, C2OF11001D, C2OF11001E, or C2OF11001F (1962–63); C3OF11001A or C2OF11001C (1963–64)
Usage: 1962–64 Fairlane, 1963–64 Comet, 1963–64 full-size Ford, 1962–63 Mercury Meteor, and 1964-1/2 Mustang—all 289ci or 260ci
Note(s): Unit has three splines on the drive. Interchange Number 3 will fit, but has four splines.

Interchange Number: 3
Part Number(s): D4OZ11002A
ID Number(s): C4ZF11011A, C4OF11001A*, or C6AF1001A (1964–66); C7AF11001B* or C7AF1101D (1967–69); DOAF1101C or DOAF11001B* (1970–71); D2AF11001CA* or D2AF11001DA (1972–73)
Usage: 1965–67 Fairlane and Comet, 1965–73 Mustang, 1965–74 full-size Ford, 1967–73 Cougar, 1971–73 full-size Mercury, 1968–73 Torino, 1968–73 Montego, 1965–70 Falcon, 1970–73 Maverick, and 1971–73 Comet (compact style)—all 289ci, 302ci, or 351ci engines; also six-cylinder in 1970–73 Maverick and 1971–73 Comet (compact)
Note(s): This unit will fit 1962–64 models in Interchange 2 of this section, but drive has four splines, not three. Those ID numbers marked with an * are for those with automatic transmissions only.

Interchange Number: 4
Part Number(s): C3OZ11002C
ID Number(s): C3OF11001B or C4OF11001B (1963–64); C5AF11001A (1965–66); C7AF11001C (1967–68); C9AF11001B (1969); DOOF11001A, DOAF11001A, DOAF1101E, or DODF11001A (1970–71)
Usage: 1966–67 Fairlane 390ci or 200ci six-cylinder with automatic transmission; 1968–69 Torino 390ci; 1967 Comet 390ci or 200ci six-cylinder with automatic transmission; 1968–69 Comet 390ci; 1966–69 Mustang 390ci; 1967–69 Cougar 390ci; 1963–70 full-size Ford or Mercury 390ci, 427ci, or 428ci; 1970–71 Maverick 200ci six-cylinder with automatic transmission; 1971 Comet (compact) 200ci six-cylinder with automatic transmission; 1967 Fairlane and Comet 427ci; 1968–69 Torino and Montego 427ci; and 1970 Cougar and Mustang 428ci (except Cobra Jet or Super Cobra Jet)
Note(s): Not for cars sold in California in 1968.

Interchange Number: 5
Part Number(s): C6AZ11002A
ID Number(s): C7AF11001E
Usage: 1968 Torino, Mustang, Cougar, and Montego 390ci sold in California
Note(s): Interchange Number 4 will fit and was the replacement unit.

Interchange Number: 6
Part Number(s): C4TZ11002B
ID Number(s): C8AF11001A or DOTF11001A
Usage: 1968–69 Torino GT and Cyclone GT and 1968–70 Mustang GT and Cougar GT 428ci Cobra Jet or 428ci Super Cobra Jet
Note(s): Tip—also look on 1966–73 Ford trucks with 330ci, 361ci, or 391ci engines. They have the same starter and are more common.

Interchange Number: 7
Part Number(s): D5AZ11002A
ID Number(s): C9AF11001A (1969–72)
Usage: 1969–72 Torino, 1969–71 Mustang, 1969–71 Cougar, 1969–72 full-size Ford, 1969–72 full-size Mercury, and 1969–71 Thunderbird—all with 429ci engines (includes Boss 429ci)
Note(s): Tip—a unit from a 1969–72 460ci engine will fit and has the following codes: C9AF11001A, C8VF11001A, DOVF1100A, and D2VF11000AA.

Distributor

Engine size, type of transmission, emissions controls, and in some cases, horsepower output are factors that effect the interchangeability of distributors.

Distributors can be easily identified by an ID number stamped onto the side of the housing. Note that several different ID numbers may be used. This is because the distributor was changed during the middle of the year or because several different model years will interchange.

Model Identification

Distributor housing is stamped with an identification number.

121

Interchange

Interchange Number: 1
    Part Number(s): COAZ12127B
    ID Number(s): COAF12127B, C5AF12127BR, or C6TF12127BJ
    Usage: 1959–65 full-size Ford or Mercury 352ci four-barrel, except high-performance
    Note(s): Each of the above ID numbers was used with different carburetors as follows: Motorcraft, Rochester, and Holley.

Interchange Number: 2
    Part Number(s): COAZ12127K
    ID Number(s): COAF12127J, COAF12127H, COAF12127K or COAF12127AV
    Usage: 1960 full-size Ford 352ci special high-performance, 1961–63 full-size Ford 390ci special high-performance (includes multi-carb engines), and 1961–62 full-size Ford and Mercury 406ci (except with multiple carbs).
    Note(s): Distributor has stamped weights.

Interchange Number: 3
    Part Number(s): C3AZ12127AH
    ID Number(s): COAF12127D*, COAF12127E, C2AF12127A, C3AF12127AH, C5AF12127BF, C3AF12127AD, C2AF12127D, C1SF12127A, or C3SF12127D*
    Usage: 1960–63 full-size 352ci two-barrel and 1961–63 full-size 390ci, except special high-performance.
    Note(s): *Originally used with automatic transmissions, but all will interchange.

Interchange Number: 4
    Part Number(s): C7ZZ12127A
    ID Number(s): C5AF12127M, C7AZ12127F, C5GF12127A, C7ZF121217F, C70F12127B, or C7AF12127AE
    Usage: 1963–67 289ci—all models except 271hp and GT 350 Mustang

Interchange Number: 5
    Part Number(s): C5OZ12127E
    ID Number(s): C3OF12127D, C3OF12127F, or C5OF12127E
    Usage: 1963–66 289ci 271hp four-barrel and 1965–66 GT 350 without supercharger

Interchange Number: 6
    Part Number(s): C7OZ12127D
    ID Number(s): C7OF12127D
    Usage: 1967 289ci two-barrel with manual transmission and Thermo-Emission systems (mandatory in California)

Interchange Number: 7
    Part Number(s): C7OF12127E
    ID Number(s): C7OF12127E, C7ZF12127E, or C7ZF12127
    Usage: 1967 289ci two-barrel and four-barrel with automatic transmissions and Thermo-Emission systems

Interchange Number: 8
    Part Number(s): C8OZ12127C
    ID Number(s): C8AF12127F or C8OF12127C
    Usage: 1968 302ci two-barrel with automatic transmission

Interchange Number: 9
    Part Number(s): C8ZZ12127D
    ID Number(s): C8ZF12127D
    Usage: 1968 302ci two-barrel with manual transmission

Interchange Number: 10
    Part Number(s): C8ZZ12127A
    ID Number(s): C8ZF12127A or C8ZF12127B
    Usage: 1968 302ci four-barrel with manual transmission

Interchange Number: 11
    Part Number(s): C8ZZ12127D
    ID Number(s): C8ZF12127D
    Usage: 1968 302ci four-barrel with automatic transmission

Interchange Number: 12
    Part Number(s): C9AZ12127R
    ID Number(s): C9AF12127R
    Usage: 1969 Torino, Montego, Mustang, and Cougar 302ci two-barrel with automatic transmission and air conditioning; and 1970 full-size 302ci with automatic transmission

Interchange Number: 13
    Part Number(s): C9AZ12127M
    ID Number(s): C9AF12127MN
    Usage: 1969 Torino, Montego, Mustang, and Cougar 302ci two-barrel with automatic transmission, without air conditioning

Interchange Number: 14
    Part Number(s): D1ZZ12127A
    ID Number(s): C9ZF12127B, C9ZF12127E, or D1FZ12127
    Usage: 1969–71 302ci four-barrel (Boss and Eliminator)

Interchange Number: 15
    Part Number(s): DOOZ12127AL
    ID Number(s): DOAF12127T or DOOF12127AC
    Usage: 1970–71 302ci two-barrel with automatic transmission— all models except Maverick and Comet (compact)

Interchange Number: 16
    Part Number(s): DOOZ12127M
    ID Number(s): C9OF12127M or DOOF12127M
    Usage: 1969 351ci two-barrel Windsor—all transmissions

Interchange Number: 17
    Part Number(s): DOOZ12127N
    ID Number(s): C9OF12127N or DOOF12127N
    Usage: 1969 351ci four-barrel Windsor with manual transmission

Interchange Number: 18
    Part Number(s): DOOZ12127R
    ID Number(s): C9OF12127T, C90F12127Z, or DOOF12127R
    Usage: 1969 302ci four-barrel Windsor with automatic transmission

Interchange Number: 19
    Part Number(s): D2ZZ12127A
    ID Number(s): DOOF12127T, D2ZF12127AA
    Usage: 1970–72 351ci two-barrel Cleveland with manual transmission

Interchange Number: 20
    Part Number(s): DOAZ12127V
    ID Number(s): DOAF12127 Vor DOAF12127AC
    Usage: 1970 351ci two-barrel Windsor with automatic transmission

Interchange Number: 21
Part Number(s): DOOZ12127U
ID Number(s): DOOF12127U
Usage: 1970–71 351ci two-barrel Cleveland with automatic transmission

Interchange Number: 22
Part Number(s): DOOZ12127V
ID Number(s): DOOF12127V
Usage: 1970–71 351ci four-barrel Cleveland with manual transmission

Interchange Number: 23
Part Number(s): DOOZ1217G
ID Number(s): DOOF12127Z
Usage: 1970 351ci four-barrel Cleveland with automatic transmission

Interchange Number: 24
Part Number(s): C6OZ12127J
ID Number(s): C6OF12127J
Usage: 1966 Fairlane GT and Cyclone GT 390ci
Note(s): Non-GT will not have the proper power range, and performance will greatly suffer.

Interchange Number: 25
Part Number(s): C7AZ12127U
ID Number(s): C7AF12127H or C7AF12127U*
Usage: 1967 Fairlane GT 390ci, 1967 Cyclone GT 390ci, 1967 Mustang GT 390ci, and 1967 Cougar GT 390ci
Note(s): *Originally used with automatic transmissions. Automatic will fit manual-equipped cars, but not vice versa.

Interchange Number: 26
Part Number(s): C7OZ12127F
ID Number(s): C7OF12127F
Usage: 1967–69 390ci four-barrel with automatic transmission (see Notes)
Note(s): In 1967 models this was used in California-sold cars only; in 1968–69 it was used on GT only. A non-GT distributor will not have the proper power range, and performance will suffer.

Interchange Number: 27
Part Number(s): C8OZ12127D
ID Number(s): C8OF12127D
Usage: 1968 390ci four-barrel in GT with manual transmission
Note(s): A non-GT distributor will not have the proper power range, and performance will suffer.

Interchange Number: 28
Part Number(s): C9AZ12127D
ID Number(s): C9OF12127J, C9AF12127D
Usage: 1969 390ci four-barrel in GT with manual transmission
Note(s): A non-GT distributor will not have the proper power range and performance will suffer.

Interchange Number: 29
Part Number(s): COAZ12127L
ID Number(s): C3AF12127AE or C5AF12127E
Usage: 1965–67 427ci, 1961–63 406ci twin four-barrel without transistor ignition

Interchange Number: 30
Part Number(s): C5AZ12127F
ID Number(s): C3AF12127AF or C3AF12127F
Usage: 1961–63 406ci or 1963–67 427ci with transistor ignition

Interchange Number: 31
Part Number(s): C7OZ12127F
ID Number(s): C7OF12127F
Usage: 1968 427ci four-barrel up to build date February 6, 1968

Interchange Number: 32
Part Number(s): C8OZ12127G
ID Number(s): C8OF12127G
Usage: 1968 427ci four-barrel after build date February 6, 1968

Interchange Number: 33
Part Number(s): C7OZ12127F
ID Number(s): C7OF12127F
Usage: 1967–69 Mustang and Cougar and 1968–69 Montego and Torino—all with 428ci Cobra Jet and automatic transmission; and 1969 full-size Ford and Mercury police car with 428ci engine
Note(s): Interchange Number 34 will fit.

Interchange Number: 34
Part Number(s): C8OZ12127H
ID Number(s): C8OF12127H
Usage: 1967–69 Cougar and Mustang and 1968–69 Montego and Torino—all with 428ci Cobra Jet and manual transmission

Interchange Number: 35
Part Number(s): C8OZ12127d
ID Number(s): C8OF12127D
Usage: 1969 Torino, Montego, Cougar, and Mustang—all with 428ci Cobra Jet automatic transmission or four-speed, both with emissions.

Interchange Number: 36
Part Number(s): DOZZ12127C
ID Number(s): DOZF12127C
Usage: 1970 Mustang and Cougar with 428ci Cobra Jet and manual transmission

Interchange Number: 37
Part Number(s): DOZZ12127D
ID Number(s): DOZF12127D
Usage: 1970 Cougar and Mustang 428ci Cobra Jet with automatic transmission

Interchange Number: 38
Part Number(s): C9ZZ12127D
ID Number(s): C9AF12127U* or C9AF12127D
Usage: 1969–70 Boss 429ci
Note(s): *Originally used until build date February 28, 1969; will not fit models after this build date, but later unit will fit earlier models.

Interchange Number: 39
Part Number(s): DOOZ12127J
ID Number(s): DOOF12127J or DOOF12127AA
Usage: 1970–71 Torino, Montego, Mustang, and Cougar—all with 429ci Cobra Jet and manual transmission

Interchange Number: 40
Part Number(s): D1AZ12127N
ID Number(s): DOOF12127Y or D1AF12127NA
Usage: 1970–71 Montego, Torino, Cougar, and Mustang—all with 429ci Cobra Jet and automatic transmission

Interchange Number: 41
Part Number(s): C9AZ12127F
ID Number(s): C8VF12127C
Usage: 1970–71 Montego and Torino with 429ci and manual transmission (except with Cobra Jet) and 1970 full-size Ford and Mercury 429ci

Interchange Number: 42
Part Number(s): DOAZ12127Z
ID Number(s): DOAF12127Z
Usage: 1970–71 Montego and Torino with 429ci and manual transmission (except with Cobra Jet) and 1970 full-size Ford and Mercury 429ci

Interchange Number: 43
Part Number(s): C7AZ12127E
ID Number(s): C7AF12127E
Usage: 1967 390ci four-barrel with manual transmission without emission control systems (except GT) and 1966–67 428ci manual transmission without emissions.

Interchange Number: 44

Part Number(s): C7AZ12127F

ID Number(s): C7AF12127F, C7MF12127G

Usage: 1967 390ci four-barrel automatic transmission without emissions (except GT models), 1967 410ci auto transmission without emissions, and 1967 428ci automatic without emissions (except police car)

Interchange Number: 45

Part Number(s): C7SZ12127H

ID Number(s): C7MF12127H or C7AF12127H

Usage: 1967 390ci four-barrel automatic transmission with emissions (except GT)

Interchange Number: 46

Part Number(s): C8AZ12127S

ID Number(s): C8AF12127S

Usage: 1968 390ci four-barrel with manual transmission (except GT) and 1968–69 428ci manual transmission (except Cobra Jet, Super Cobra Jet, or police car)

Interchange Number: 47

Part Number(s): C8AZ12127R

ID Number(s): C8AF12127R

Usage: 1968 390ci four-barrel with automatic transmission (except GT) and 1968–69 428ci with automatic transmission (except Cobra Jet, Super Cobra Jet, or police car)

Coil, Ignition

Simple interchange because only two coil types are used, regardless of engine size or output. The only concern is the type of ignition system. Conventional types used part number B6A12029B for all models covered in this guide, while those with transistor ignitions used part number C3TZ12029A. The two cannot interchange, so be sure yours is the proper unit.

Alternator and Generator

Early Ford and Mercury models (those up to 1963 and the 1964-1/2 Mustang) used a generator. Beginning with 1964 models (except the Mustang), all models came with an alternator instead of a generator. Mustangs begin using an alternator around mid-August 1964, with what is consider the true 1965 Mustang. However, before 1964, the alternator was available as an option on other models.

Both the generator and alternator can be identified by a number stamped on the housing. Note that there are different levels (outputs) of alternators and generators, and if you've added more accessories to your car than what it was originally equipped with, a higher output unit could be a wise interchange. Part Number, ID number, and output are given.

Typical yellow-top Ford coil.

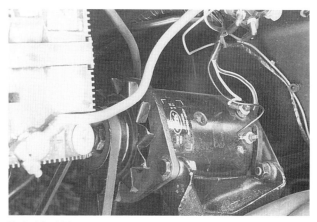

Typical Ford Motors generator.

Model Identification

1959–64	Interchange Number
generators	
30amp	1
35amp	2
40amp	
Delco-built	3
Ford-built	4
50amp	5
alternators	
42amp	7
50amp	9
60amp	11

1965–70 Alternators	Interchange Number
38amp	8
42amp	8
50amp	10
65amp	12

Interchange

Interchange Number: 1

Part Number(s): C1TZ10002A

Output: 30amp (Ford-built generator)

ID Number(s): COAF10000B, COAF10000F, COAF10000G, FHA10000A, 2900643, 2900694, C1AF10000B, C1AF10000C, C1AF10000E, C1TF10000BV, C2AF10000C, C2AF10000D, C2AF10000E, C2AF10000F, C2OF10000A, C2OF10000G, C2OF10000H, C2TF10000H, C2TF10000U, C3OF10000B, C4OF10000A, C2OF10000B, C1TF10000A, C1TF10000K, C1TF10000L, C1TF10000M, C1TF10000N, C1TF10000AA, C1TF10000AD, C1TF10000AH, C1TF10000AK, or C2DF10000B

Usage: 1959–64—all models (except Falcon and Comet) and all engines (except 427ci and 430ci)

Interchange Number: 2

Part Number(s): COAZ10002C

Output: 35amp (Ford-built generator)

ID Number(s): COAF10000D, COAF10000K, 2900232, 2900693, COAF10000A, C0SF10000A, C1AF1000D, C1SF1000A, C1AF1000A, or C2AF10000B

Usage: 1959–60 352ci or 292ci with air conditioning

Interchange Number: 3

Part Number(s): COAF10002B

Output: 40amp (Delco/Remey-built generator, low-cut-in type)

ID Number(s): COAF10000C or C1AF10000G

Usage: 1959–62 full-size or mid-size models with V-8.

Interchange Number: 4

Part Number(s): B6A1002E
Output: 40amp (Autolite-built generator)
ID Number(s): C1AF10000L, FAU10000A, FAV10000A, FAV10000B, FCD10000A, FCT10000A, FGM10000B, C3AF10000B, GGA6006P, or GGA6006R
Usage: 1962–64 full-size with 352ci or 390ci

Interchange Number: 5

Part Number(s): B6A10002D
Output: 50amp (Bosch-built generator)
ID Number(s): FCC10000A or FCR10000A
Usage: 1956–60 full-size models

Interchange Number: 6

Part Number(s): C2AZ10346A
Output: 40amp (Leece Neville-built alternator)
ID Number(s): C2AF10300B, C2AF10300C, C2OF10300B, C2OF10300C, 90164, 90165, 90166, 90167, or 6000-AC
Usage: 1962–64—all models and all engines except 427ci and 406ci

Interchange Number: 7

Part Number(s): C4AZ10300D
Output: 42amp (Ford-built alternator)
ID Number(s): C3OF10346E or C4TF10300BD
Usage: 1963–64 full-size or mid-size models with V-8 engine, except 352ci, 390ci, or 427ci in full-size

Interchange Number: 8

Part Number(s): D2AZ10346C
Output: 38amp and 42amp (Motorcraft-built alternator)
ID Number(s): 42amp—C5AF10300A, C5AF10300B, C5AF10300C, C5AF10300D, C5AF10300, C6AF10300A, C6AF10300B, C6AF10300C, C6AF10300D, C6AF10300, C9AF10300A, DOAF10300C, DOAF10300F, DOAF10300G, D2AF10300AA, D2AF10300AB, D2OF10300DA,

Alternators have an identification number stamped on the housing.

D2OF10300DB, D2ZF10300AC, C6AF10346A, C6AF10346B, C6DF10346A, DOAF10346E, D2AF10346CA, D2OF10346DA, and D2OF10346GA; 38amp—C5DF10300A, C5DF10300B, CDF10300A, C6DF10300B, C6TF10300A, C9ZF10300A, DOZF10300B, D2ZF10300AA, D2ZF10300AB, C5DF10346A, and C5DF10346B
Usage: 1965–72—all models and engines
Note(s): Two alternators are grouped together, as the 42amp unit phased the 38amp out. When interchanging, a 42amp unit can take the place of a 38amp unit, but a 38amp unit should never be used in place of a 42amp unit. Lower-rated 38amp units were used usually on six-cylinders and small (289ci or 302ci) V-8s with no accessories.

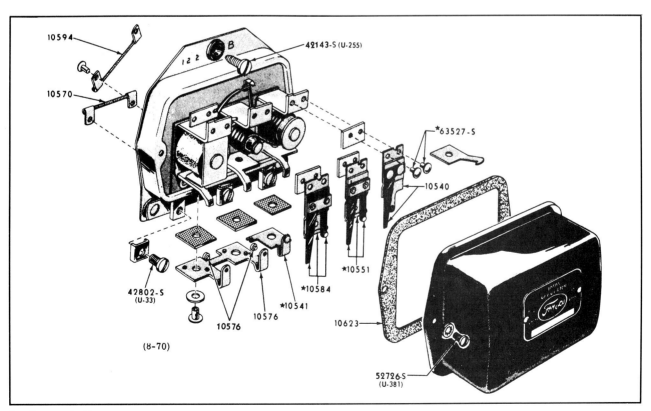

Regulator used with generators.

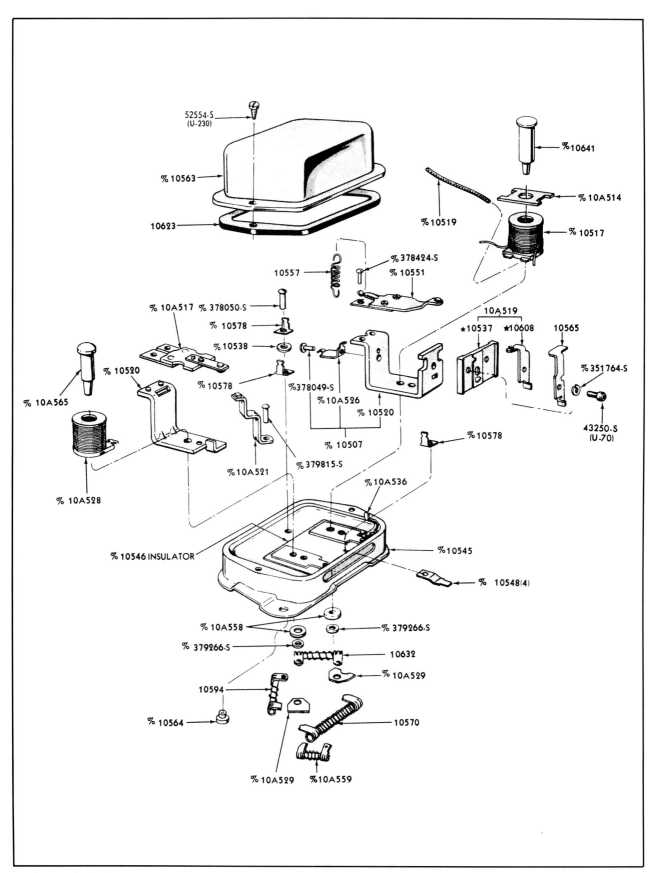

52554-S
(U-230)

% 10563

10623

10557

% 378424-S
% 10551

% 10A517 % 378050-S

% 10578

% 10538

% 10A565

% 10520

% 10A565

% 10578

% 378049-S

% 10A526

% 10520

% 10507

% 10A521

% 379815-S

% 10A528

%10641

% 10A514

% 10517

% 10519

10A519

★10537 ★10608 10565

% 351764-S

43250-S
(U-70)

% 10578

% 10A536

% 10546 INSULATOR

%10545

% 10548(4)

% 10A558

% 379266-S

% 379266-S

10632

% 10A529

10594

% 10564

10570

% 10A529   %10A559

Regulator used with alternator.

126

Interchange Number: 9

Part Number(s): B8TZ10346G
Output: 50amp (Leece Neville-built alternator)
ID Number(s): B9AF10300B, B9MF10300A, B9MF10300B, B9MF10300E, B9TF10300D, B9TF10300E, B9MF10300F, 90027, 90029, 90031, 90032, 90035, 90049, 5428-GA, B9TF10300G, B9TF10300H, 90017, 90018, 5468-GA, B97999GAX,
Usage: 1959–60 full-size V-8 only

Interchange Number: 10

Part Number(s): DOAZ10346A
Output: 50amp (Motorcraft-built alternator)
ID Number(s): C5AF10300F, C6AF10300F, C6AF10300G, C6TF10300E, C6TF10300F, C8LF10300B, C9AF10300B, C9SF10300A, C9SF10300B, C9ZF10300B, C9ZF10300C, DOAF10300E, DOAF10300H, DOLF10300A, DOSF10300A, DOZF10300A, DOZF10300C, DIZF10300AA, D2AF10300BA, D2AF10300BB, D2OF10300BA, D2OF10300BB, D2OF10300EA, D2OF10300EB, D2OF10300FA, D2OF10300FB, D2SF10300AA, C6TF10346B, C6TF10346C, C8SF10346B, C9ZF10346B, DOAF10346F, DOSZ10346A, DOZF10346B, D2AF10346DA, D2OF10346AA, D2OF10346EA, D2OF10346FA, D2OF10346HA, D2OF10346JA, D2ZF10346BA, or D2XX910346XZ
Usage: 1965–72—all models and engines
Note(s): Those units with C9ZF or DOZF prefixes are special high-temp versions and were originally installed on Cobra Jet, Super Cobra Jet, and Boss models, and are designed to better resist high under-hood temperatures.

Interchange Number: 11

Part Number(s): C2TZ10346B
Output: 60amp (Leece Neville-built alternator)
ID Number(s): C1MF10300A, C2AF10300A, C2OF10300D, 90109, 90156, 90157, 2074-AB, C4AF10300B, C4MF10300A, C4OF10300A, 90237, 90238, 90239, 2178-AA, or C3ZZ10346F
Usage: 1962–64 full-size or mid-sized, all engines except 427ci

Interchange Number: 12

Part Number(s): D2TZ10346D
Output: 65amp (Motorcraft-built alternator)
ID Number(s): C9AF10300D, DOAF10300A, or C7AF10300A
Usage: 1967–70—all models and engines

Regulator, Voltage

Manufacture and output of the generator will effect the interchanging of regulator. But output makes little difference in the interchanging of alternators.

Ford-built 30amp or 40amp generators used a regulator with part number C3TZ1505B; it can be identified by these numbers: 2700015, C1TF10505A, C2AF10505A, C1TZ10505A, C2TF10505B, or C3TZ10505B, which are stamped into the case of the regulator.

Autolite-built 40amp generators used a regulator with the part number C1TF10505D; it is stamped B7A10505A, COAF1050B, CITF10505D, or C1TZ10505D.

Delco/Remey-built generators used a regulator listed as part number COAF10505B and stamped COAF10505B.

As previously stated above, output of an alternator has little effect on the interchangeability of regulator, but the alternator's manufacture does.

Motorcraft-built alternators used a regulator listed as part number D4TZ10316A; it is stamped C3TF10316B, C3SZ10316B, C3XF10316C, C4TF10316B, C4TF10316D, C4UF10316A, C4UF10316B, C5AF10316A, C5TF10316A, C8AF10316A, C8TF10316A, DOAF10316A, D2AF1036AA, or D2TF10316AA.

Tray, Battery

Model and the original battery's output have effects on the interchangeability of the battery tray or carrier. Also, certain options and engine sizes will affect the interchange in some models. These will be listed under the heading Restrictions.

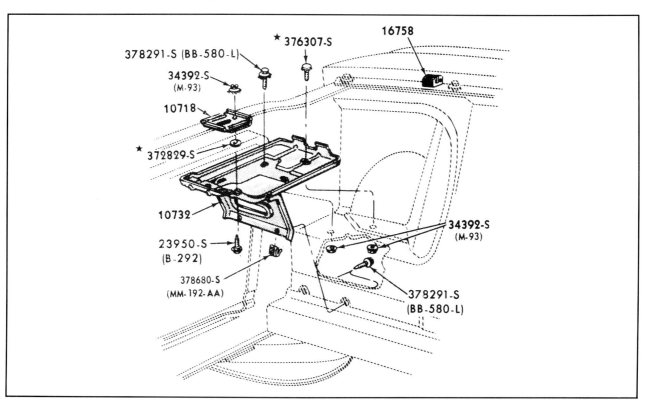

1964-1/2–68 Mustang battery tray.

Model Identification

Cougar	Interchange Number
1967–70	
under-hood battery	
all except Eliminator	
45amp battery	8
55amp battery	9
70amp	10
Eliminator	11
trunk-mounted 85amp	14

Cyclone	Interchange Number
1964–65, all	4
1966–67	
45amp battery	5
55amp battery	6
70amp or 80amp battery	3
1968–69	
under-hood battery	
45amp battery	
all except 351ci with air conditioning	5
351ci with air conditioning	7
55amp battery	
all except 351ci with air conditioning	6
351ci with air conditioning	12
70amp or 80amp battery	3
trunk-mounted 85amp	13
1970	
45amp or 55amp	15
70amp	16

Fairlane and Torino	Interchange Number
1959–60, all	17
1961, all	18
1962–65, all	1
1966–67	
45amp battery	5
55amp battery	6
70 or 80amp battery	3
1968–69	
under-hood battery	
45amp battery	
all except 351ci with air conditioning	5
351ci with air conditioning	7
55amp battery	
all except 351ci with air conditioning	6
351ci with air conditioning	12
70amp or 80amp battery	3
trunk-mounted 85amp	13
1970	
45amp or 55amp	15
70amp	16

Mustang	Interchange Number
1964-1/2–66, all	2
1967–70	
under-hood battery	
all except Eliminator	
45amp battery	8
55amp battery	9
70amp battery	10
Eliminator	11
trunk-mounted 85amp	14

Interchange

Interchange Number: 1
Part Number(s): C3AZ10764C
Usage: 1962–65 Fairlane, 1964–65 Falcon with air conditioning, and 1963–64 full-size Ford 289ci V-8
Restrictions: None.

Interchange Number: 2
Part Number(s): C5ZZ10732C
Usage: 1964-1/2–66 Mustang
Restrictions: None.

Interchange Number: 3
Part Number(s): C5AZ10764D
Usage: 1966–67 Fairlane GT 390ci and 427ci or Fairlane 289ci with air conditioning, 1966–67 Comet 390ci or 427ci, 1966–68 Thunderbird*, and 1968–69 Torino and Montego with 70amp or 80amp battery
Restrictions: *Only on Thunderbirds built after February 1, 1965.

Interchange Number: 4
Part Number(s): C3DZ10732G
Usage: 1964–65 Comet and 1960–64 Falcon without air conditioning

Interchange Number: 5
Part Number(s): C6OZ10732D
Usage: 1966–67 Comet, 1968–69 Montego, 1966-967 Fairlane, 1968–69 Torino, and 1966–70 Falcon
Restrictions: 45amp battery only. Not for 390ci or 428ci engines. Not used with 351ci and air conditioning in 1969 models. Early-1969 Montego models only before build date August 12, 1968, with 351ci engine.

Interchange Number: 6
Part Number(s): C7OZ10732B
Usage: 1966–67 Comet and Fairlane and 1968–69 Torino and Montego
Restrictions: 55amp battery only. Not for 390ci or 428ci engines. Not for 1969 models with 351ci and air conditioning. Early-1969 Montego models with 351ci only before build date August 12, 1968.

Interchange Number: 7
Part Number(s): C9OZ10764A
Usage: 1969 Torino and Montego with 351ci and air conditioning
Restrictions: Used with air conditioning on 351ci only with 45amp battery.

Interchange Number: 8
Part Number(s): C7ZZ10732C
Usage: 1967–70 Mustang and Cougar (except Boss and Eliminator)
Restrictions: 45amp battery only.

Interchange Number: 9
Part Number(s): C7ZZ10732D
Usage: 1967–70 Mustang and Cougar (except Boss and Eliminator)
Restrictions: 55amp battery only.

Interchange Number: 10
Part Number(s): C9ZZ10732A
Usage: 1967–70 Mustang, except Boss, and Cougar (except Boss and Eliminator)
Restrictions: 70amp battery only. Standard with 427ci.

Interchange Number: 11
Part Number(s): C9ZZ10732B
Usage: 1969–70 Boss Mustang and Cougar Eliminator
Restrictions: These models only; no other interchange.

Interchange Number: 12
Part Number(s): C9OZ10764B
Usage: 1969 Torino and Montego with 351ci and air conditioning and 55amp battery

Interchange Number: 13
Part Number(s): C9OZ10762B
Usage: 1969 Torino GT or 1969 Cyclone with Drag Pack. Trunk-mounted battery.

Interchange Number: 14
Part Number(s): C9ZZ10732B
Usage: 1969–70 Mustang and Cougar, hardtop only with trunk-mounted 85amp battery

Interchange Number: 15
  Part Number(s): DOOZ10732A
  Usage: 1970–71 Torino and Montego and 1971–73 Mustang and Cougar
  Restrictions: 45amp or 55amp battery only.

Interchange Number: 16
  Part Number(s): DOOZ10732B
  Usage: 1970–71 Torino and Montego, 1971–73 Mustang and Cougar
  Restrictions: 70amp battery only.

Interchange Number: 17
  Part Number(s): COAB10732A
  Usage: 1959–60 full-size Ford

Interchange Number: 18
  Part Number(s): C2SZ10732A
  Usage: 1961–64 full-size Ford (except 289ci) and 1961–64 Thunderbird

Cyclone	Interchange Number
1966–70 two-speed	8

Fairlane and Torino	Interchange Number
1959	
vacuum-powered	3
electrical power	5
1960–61	
vacuum-powered	4
electric-powered	6, 7
1962 single-speed	2
1963–65 single-speed	1
1966–70 two-speed	8

Mustang	Interchange Number
1964-1/2–65	
single speed	1
two-speed	9
1966 two-speed	10
1967–68 two-speed	8
1969–70 two-speed	11

Motor, Windshield Wiper

Interchange for wiper motor is quite large. Things that will affect the interchange are the number of wiper speeds and the type. Earlier models use both electrical- and vacuum-powered wiper assemblies.

Wiper motors are identified by a stamped ID number. You will notice that more than one ID number may be listed. This just means that more than one model year will interchange.

Model Identification

Cougar	Interchange Number
1967–68 two-speed	8
1969–70 two-speed	11

Interchange

Interchange Number: 1
  Number of Speeds: Single
  Part Number(s): C3UZ17508C
  ID Number(s): C3OF17504A, C3OF17504L, C3OF17508A, C3OF17508B, C3OF17508D, C3UF17508A, C4ZF17504A, C30F17508A, C3OF17508B, C3OF17508D, C3OF17504A, or C5OF17508A
  Usage: 1963–65 Fairlane and 1964-1/2–65 Mustang
  Note(s): Ford-built unit.

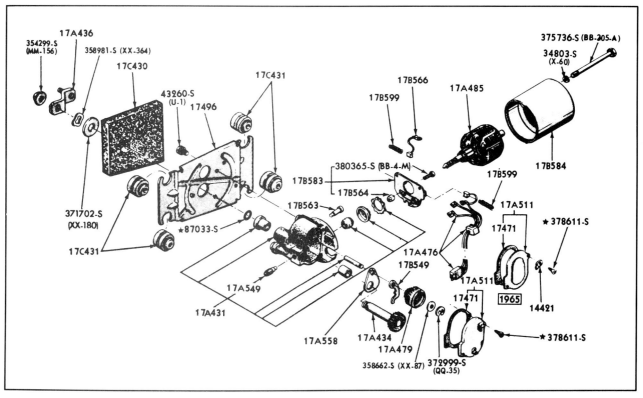

1960–68 two-speed wiper motor.

Interchange Number: 2
Number of Speeds: Single
Part Number(s): C2AZ17508A
ID Number(s): C2AF17508D, C2OF17508B, C2OF17508C, C2OF17508F, C2OF17508H, C2OF17508K, C2OF17508L, or C2OF17508R
Usage: 1962 Fairlane and full-size Ford after build date June 15, 1962

Interchange Number: 3
Number of Speeds: Single (vacuum)
Part Number(s): B9A17508A
Usage: 1959 full-size Ford
Note(s): Used on base models; usually not found on higher-trim models

Interchange Number: 4
Number of Speeds: Single
Part Number(s): COAB17508B (vacuum)
ID Number(s): COAB17508B
Usage: 1960 full-size Ford
Note(s): Used on base models; usually not found on higher trim models

Interchange Number: 5
Number of Speeds: Two (electric)
Part Number(s): B9A17508C
Usage: 1959 full-size Ford

Interchange Number: 6
Number of Speeds: Two (electric)
Part Number(s): COAF17508E
ID Number(s): COAF17508E
Usage: 1960–61 full-size Ford
Note(s): Up to build date October 3, 1960, in 1961 models.

Interchange Number: 7
Number of Speeds: Two
Part Number(s): C2AZ17508B
ID Number(s): C2AF17508C, C2AF17508E, or C2AF17508S
Usage: Late-1961–64 full-size Ford
Note(s): Begins at build date October 3, 1960.

Interchange Number: 8
Number of Speeds: Two
Part Number(s): C6OZ17508D
ID Number(s): C9OF17504A, C6OF17504A, C7DF17504A, C7MF17504A, C7MF17504B, C7OF17504A, C7OF17504B, C7ZF17504A, C7ZF17504C, C7ZF17504D, C8MF17504A, C8OF17504A, C9OF17504A, DOOF17504A, DOOF17504B, D1DF17504AA, D2DF17504AA, D2OF17504AB, C7AF17C504A, CAF17C504A, C9OF17C504A, C9OF17C504A, C9OF17C504B, C6Of17508A, C7MF17508A, C70F17508A, or C7ZF17508A
Usage: 1965–67 Fairlane, 1966–67 Comet, 1968–72* Torino, 1968–72* Montego, 1966–69 full-size Ford, 1966–69 full-size Mercury, 1967–68 Mustang and Cougar, and 1966–68 Falcon
Note(s): *With non-concealed wipers only in 1972 models.

Interchange Number: 9
Number of Speeds: Two-speed
Part Number(s): C3DZ17508A
ID Number(s): C3DF17504A, C3DF17504C, C3DF17504E, 3DF17504G, C3DF17504H, C3DF17504J, C3DF17504K, C3DF17504L, or C4ZF17504B
Usage: 1964-1/2–65 Mustang and 1963–65 Falcon

Interchange Number: 10
Number of Speeds: Two
Part Number(s): C6ZZ17508A
ID Number(s): C6ZF7504A
Usage: 1966 Mustang

Interchange Number: 11
Number of Speeds: Two
Part Number(s): DOZZ17508A
ID Number(s): DOZZ17504A, C9ZF17508A, C9ZF17C504A, C9ZF17504A, C9ZF17504B, C9ZF17504C, C9ZF17504D
Usage: 1969–70 Mustang and Cougar

Arms, Wiper Blade
Wiper-blade arms interchange between many models, and few things will affect the interchange, with the exception of a few models that have different arms for each side of the car. Most, however, interchange from the driver's to the passenger's side.

Many arms were made adjustable; thus, you may have to readjust the arms before you swap them to a different family group of cars. For example, if you retrieve the arms from a full-size car and place them on your Mustang, you will have to make adjustments to the arms.

Model Identification

Cougar	Interchange Number
1967–70	4

Cyclone	Interchange Number
1966–69	4
1970	5

Fairlane and Torino	Interchange Number
1959–61	1, 2
1962–64	3
1965–69	4
1970	5

Mustang	Interchange Number
1964-1/2–70	4

Interchange

Interchange Number: 1
Part Number(s): COAZ17526A (fits either side)
Length: Adjustable from 10.38in to 14.87in
Usage: 1959–late-1961 full-size Ford and Mercury
Note(s): Used up to build date November 16, 1960.

Interchange Number: 2
Part Number(s): C2AZ17526A (right), C2AZ17527A (left)
Length: Adjustable from 10.38in to 14.87in*
Usage: Late-1961–64 full-size Ford
Note(s): *Used with 43/64in-inside-diameter pivot shaft. Use begins at build date November 16, 1960.

Interchange Number: 3
Part Number(s): C2OZ17526A (fits either side)
Length: 13-1/2in
Usage: 1962–64 Fairlane

Interchange Number: 4
Part Number(s): C1AZ17526A (fits either side)
Length: Adjustable from 12-7/64in to 16-23/32in
Usage: 1965–67 Fairlane, 1968–69 Torino, 1964-1/2–70 Mustang, 1967–70 Cougar, 1966–67 Comet, 1968–69 Montego, 1965–68 full-size Ford, 1965–68 full-size Mercury, 1965 Thunderbird, and 1966–67 Falcon

Interchange Number: 5
Part Number(s): DOOZ17526A (right), DOOZ17527A (left)
Usage: 1970 Torino and Montego
Note(s): 1971 models are similar but will not interchange.

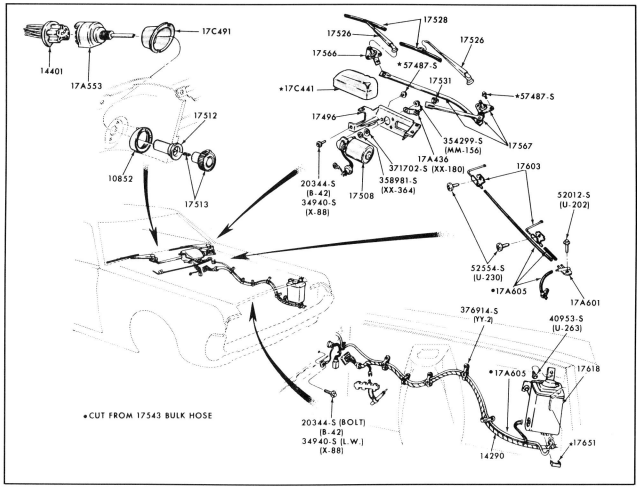

1969–70 Mustang/Cougar wiper system.

Arms/Pivot Shaft, Windshield Wiper

These are the arms that connect the wiper-blade arms to the motor or motor linkage. Driver's side and passenger's side are unique and are not interchangeable. Also, model and model year effect the interchange.

Model Identification

Cougar	Interchange Number
1967–68	11
1969–70	12

Cyclone	Interchange Number
1966–67	6
1968–69	7
1970	8

Fairlane and Torino	Interchange Number
1959–60	1
1961	1, 2
1962	3
1963	4
1964–65	5
1966–67	6
1968–69	7
1970	8

Mustang	Interchange Number
1964-1/2–65	9, 10
1966, all	10
1967–68	11
1969–70	12

Interchange

Interchange Number: 1
Part Number(s): COAB17566B (right), COAB17567B (left)
Usage: 1959 to very-early-1961 models. 1960 (up to build date November 16, 1960)
Note(s): Use with 1/2in-outside-diameter knurled driver only.

Interchange Number: 2
Part Number(s): C1AB17566A (right), C1AB17567A (left)
Usage: Early-1961–late-1961
Note(s): Used from build dates November 16, 1960, to July 30, 1961.

Interchange Number: 3
Part Number(s): C2OZ17566A (right), C2OZ17567A (left)
Usage: 1962 Fairlane

Interchange Number: 4
Part Number(s): C3OZ17566A (right), C3OZ17567A (left)
Usage: 1963 Fairlane

Interchange Number: 5
Part Number(s): C4OZ17566A (right), C4OZ17567A (left)
Usage: 1964–65 Fairlane

Interchange Number: 6
Part Number(s): C6OZ17566A (right), C6OZ17567B (left)
Usage: 1966–67 Fairlane, Comet, and Falcon

Interchange Number: 7
Part Number(s): C8OZ17566A (right), C6OZ17567B* (left)
Usage: 1968–69 Torino and Montego
Note(s): *Driver's side uses same unit used in 1966–67 models; see Interchange Number 6.

Interchange Number: 8
Part Number(s): DOOZ17566A (right), DOOZ17567A* or DOOZ17567B# (left)
Usage: 1970 Torino and Montego (see Note for usage restrictions)
Note(s): *Used to build date February 2, 1970. #Used from February 2, 1970. The later unit can be found on early-built 1971 Torinos and Montegos up to November 2, 1970.

Interchange Number: 9
Part Number(s): C5ZZ17566B (right), C5ZZ17567B (left)
Usage: 1964-1/2–late-1965 Mustang
Note(s): Used up to build date May 3, 1965.

Interchange Number: 10
Part Number(s): C5ZZ17566C (right), C5ZZ17567C (left)
Usage: Late 1965–66 Mustang
Note(s): Beginning at build date May 3, 1965.

Interchange Number: 11
Part Number(s): C7ZZ17566A (right), C5ZZ17567C* (left)
Usage: 1967–68 Mustang and Cougar (see Notes for more usage)
Note(s): *Driver's side can be found in 1965–66 Mustangs; see Interchange Number 10 for further details.

Interchange Number: 12
Part Number(s): C9ZZ17566A (right), C9ZZ17567A (left)
Usage: 1969–70 Mustang and Cougar

Jar, Windshield Washer

Model Identification

Cougar	Interchange Number
1967	3, 5

Bag-type windshield washer jar.

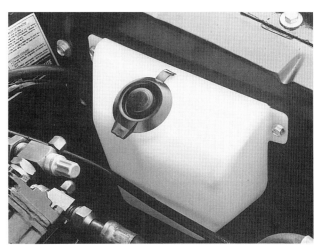

1968 models used this type of washer jar.

	Interchange Number
1968	5
1969–70	7
Cyclone	**Interchange Number**
1966–67	3, 5
1968	5
1969–70	6
Fairlane and Torino	**Interchange Number**
1959–60	1, 2
1961–67	
dealer-installed	2
factory-installed	3, 5
1968	5
1969–70	6
Mustang	**Interchange Number**
1964-1/2–67	3, 5
1968	5
1969–70	7

Interchange

Interchange Number: 1
Part Number(s): COAB17618B
Usage: 1959–60 full-size Ford V-8 without alternator and 1960 full-size Ford six-cylinder without air conditioning

Interchange Number: 2
Part Number(s): C1RZ17618A
Usage: 1960–61 full-size Ford V-8 with alternator, 1960 full-size Ford six-cylinder with air conditioning, 1962–65 Fairlane, and 1960–65 Falcon
Note(s): Dealer-installed type.

Interchange Number: 3
Part Number(s): C1AZ17618E
Usage: 1962–67* Fairlane, 1966–67 full-size Ford, 1964-1/2–67* Mustang, 1965–67* Thunderbird, 1965–67* Falcon, 1965–67# Comet, and 1967# Cougar
Note(s): *Used until build date March 1, 1967, on these models. #Used until build date November 1, 1966, on these models. Bag type with cover. Used in 1966 Comet convertible only. All body styles, all other years.

Interchange Number: 4
Part Number(s): C5MY17618B
Usage: 1966 Comet convertible and 1965–67* full-size Mercury
Note(s): Rectangular plastic with cover. Also see Interchange Number 3 this section. *Used between build dates September 1, 1964, and December 1, 1966, only; also used in some 1967 Comets before November 1, 1966.

Interchange Number: 25
Part Number(s): C7ZZ17A553A
Number of Terminals: Five
ID Number(s): C7ZB17A553B
Usage: 1967 Mustang

Interchange Number: 26
Part Number(s): C8ZZ17A553A
Number of Terminals: Five
ID Number(s): C8ZB17A553A
Usage: 1968 Mustang

Interchange Number: 27
Part Number(s): C9ZZ17A553A
Number of Terminals: Seven
ID Number(s): C9ZB17A553A
Usage: 1969 Mustang and Cougar with two-speed wipers

Interchange Number: 28
Part Number(s): DOZZ17A553A
Number of Terminals: Seven
ID Number(s): C9ZF17A553B, C9ZF17A553C, or DOZB17A553B
Usage: 1969–70 Mustang and Cougar with intermittent wipers

Interchange Number: 29
Part Number(s): DOZZ17A553B
Number of Terminals: Seven
ID Number(s): DOZB17A553A
Usage: 1970 Mustang and Cougar, 1970–73 Maverick, and 1971–73 Comet (compact)—all with two-speed wipers

Interchange Number: 30
Part Number(s): C7WY17A553A
Usage: 1967 Cougar with two-speed wipers (except XR7)

Interchange Number: 31
Part Number(s): C7WY17A553B
Usage: 1967 Cougar XR7 only

Interchange Number: 32
Part Number(s): C8WY17A553A
Number of Terminals: Five
Usage: 1968 Cougar with two-speed wipers (except XR7)

Interchange Number: 33
Part Number(s): C8WY17A553B
Number of Terminals: Five
Usage: 1968 Cougar XR7 only

Interchange Number: 34
Part Number(s): B9AA17A553C
Usage: 1959 full-size Ford with single-speed wipers

Interchange Number: 35
Part Number(s): B9AA17A553A
Usage: 1959 full-size Ford with two-speed wipers

Interchange Number: 36
Part Number(s): COAA17A553A
Usage: 1960 full-size Ford with single-speed wipers

Interchange Number: 37
Part Number(s): COAA17A553B
Usage: 1960 full-size Ford with two-speed wipers

Interchange Number: 38
Part Number(s): C1AA17A553A
Usage: 1961 full-size Ford with single-speed wipers

Interchange Number: 39
Part Number(s): C1AA17A553B
Usage: 1961 full-size Ford with two-speed wipers

Motor, Heater

Interchange here is fairly common, but the factor to watch for is whether the car you're interchanging from or to is or was equipped with factory-installed air conditioning. A special motor is used with factory-equipped air conditioned cars, and it will not fit a car without factory air conditioning.

Model Identification

Cougar	Interchange Number
1967–68	
without air conditioning	6
with air conditioning	13
1969–70 without air conditioning	
with forced air	7
without forced air	8

Cyclone	Interchange Number
1965 without air conditioning	5
1966–70	
without air conditioning	4
with air conditioning	
factory	11
dealer	12

767 Fairlane and Torino	Interchange Number
1959–60	
without air conditioning	1
with air conditioning	
1961 without air conditioning	1, 2
1962–64 without air conditioning	3
1965–70	
without air conditioning	4
with air conditioning	
factory	11
dealer	12

Mustang	Interchange Number
1964-1/2, all	5
1965 without air conditioning	5, 6
1966–68	
without air conditioning	6
with air conditioning	13
1969–70 without air conditioning	
with forced air	7
without forced air	8

Interchange

Interchange Number: 1
Part Number(s): B6A18527B
Usage: 1959–61 full-size Ford up to build date May 1, 1961, without air conditioning
Note(s): Recirculating type. Has 1/4in shaft diameter.

Interchange Number: 2
Part Number(s): C2AZA18527A
Usage: 1961–62 full-size Ford after build date May 1, 1961 without air conditioning
Note(s): Recirculating type. Has 5/16in-diameter shaft.

Interchange Number: 3
Part Number(s): C2OZ18527B
Usage: 1962–64 Fairlane and full-size Ford without air conditioning

Interchange Number: 4
Part Number(s): DOAZ18504B or D1OZ18527A
Usage: 1965–67 Fairlane, 1966–67 Comet, 1968–71 Torino, 1968–71 Montego, 1966–69 Falcon, 1971 Mustang, and 1971 Cougar
Note(s): Up to build date April 2, 1971, on 1971 models. Also Torino and Montego without forced ventilation system.

Interchange Number: 5
Part Number(s): CODZ18527A
Usage: 1964-1/2–65 Mustang, 1960–65 Falcon, and 1960–65 Comet, all up to build date April 1, 1965

Interchange Number: 6
Part Number(s): C5ZZ18527B
Usage: 1965–68 Mustang and 1967–68 Cougar
Note(s): After build date April 1, 1965, on 1965 Mustang.

Interchange Number: 7
Part Number(s): C9ZZ18527A
Usage: 1969–70 Mustang and Cougar and 1970 Maverick—all without forced-air ventilation system

Interchange Number: 8
Part Number(s): C9ZZ18527B
Usage: 1969–70 Mustang and 1968–70 Cougar without forced-air ventilation or air conditioning

Interchange Number: 9
Part Number(s): C9OZ18527A
Usage: 1968–70 Torino and Montego with forced-air ventilation but without air conditioning

Interchange Number: 10
Part Number(s): C3AZ18527B
Usage: 1963–65 Fairlane and 1963–64 full-size Ford with air conditioning

Interchange Number: 11
Part Number(s): C8OZ18527A
Usage: 1966–67 Fairlane and Comet, 1968–71 Torino and Montego, and 1966–70 Falcon—all with integrated factory air conditioning

Interchange Number: 12
Part Number(s): C8OZ18527C
Usage: 1966–67 Fairlane and Comet, 1968–71 Torino and Montego, and 1966–70 Falcon—all with dealer-installed air conditioning

Interchange Number: 13
Part Number(s): C7ZZ18527A
Usage: 1967–68 Mustang and Cougar with integrated air conditioning

Interchange Number: 14
Part Number(s): C8ZZ18527A
Usage: 1967–68 Mustang and Cougar with hang-on air conditioning

Interchange Number: 15
Part Number(s): C9ZZ18527A
Usage: 1969–73 Mustang and Cougar with integrated air conditioning

Interchange Number: 16
Part Number(s): C9ZZ18527B
Usage: 1969–71 Mustang and Cougar, 1970–71 Maverick, and 1971 Comet (subcompact)—all with hang-on air conditioning

Interchange Number: 17
Part Number(s): C8ZZ18527B
Usage: 1968 Mustang and Cougar with hang-on air conditioning with variable speed switch

Core, Heater

Model Identification

Interchange

Interchange Number: 1
Part Number(s): C2AZ18476A
Usage: 1962 Fairlane and full-size without air conditioning

Interchange Number: 2
Part Number(s): C3AZ18476A
Usage: 1963–65 Fairlane and 1963 full-size without air conditioning

Interchange Number: 3
Part Number(s): C6OZ18476B
Usage: 1966–67 Fairlane and Comet, 1968–74 Torino and Montego, 1971 Mustang and Cougar, and 1966–70 Falcon—all without air conditioning

Interchange Number: 4
Part Number(s): C5DZ18476A
Usage: 1964-1/2–68 Mustang, 1967–68 Cougar, and 1965 Falcon without air conditioning

Interchange Number: 5
Part Number(s): C9ZZ18476A
Usage: 1969–70 Mustang and Cougar, 1970–73 Maverick, 1971–73 Comet (compact) without air conditioning

Interchange Number: 6
Part Number(s): C6OZ18476B
Usage: 1966 Fairlane, Comet, and Falcon with air conditioning

Interchange Number: 7
Part Number(s): C7OZ18476A
Usage: 1967 Fairlane, 1968–70 Torino, 1967 Comet, 1968–70 Montego, 1967–70 Falcon—all with air conditioning
Note(s): Core from 1971 Torino and Montego will not interchange.

Interchange Number: 8
Part Number(s): C7ZZ18476A
Usage: 1967–68 Mustang and Cougar with air conditioning

Interchange Number: 9
Part Number(s): C9ZZ18476B
Usage: 1969–73 Mustang, 1968–73 Cougar, 1970–73 Maverick, and 1971–73 Comet (subcompact)—all without air conditioning

Interchange Number: 10
Part Number(s): C0AF18476B
Usage: 1959–62 full-size Ford without air conditioning

Interchange Number: 11
Part Number(s): C0AF18476C
Usage: 1959–62 full-size Ford with air conditioning

The air conditioning compressor part number is stamped on a tag on the compressor. This unit was made for 1967 (C7AA) models, although it will fit other years.

Compressor, Air Conditioning

Many interchanges are available here because engine size and model usage are not concerns. However, 1969–70 models with hang-on-type air conditioning differed from those with an integrated air conditioning system, and the compressors will not interchange.

Model Identification

Cougar	Interchange Number
1967–68, all	1
1969–70, factory-installed	
1969	2
1970	3

Cyclone	Interchange Number
1966–68, all	1
1969–70, factory-installed	
1969	2
1970	3

Fairlane and Torino	Interchange Number
1959–61, all	4
1963–68, all	1
1969–70, factory-installed	
1969	2
1970	3

Mustang	Interchange Number
1964-1/2–68, all	1
1969–70, factory-installed	
1969	2
1970	3

Interchange

Interchange Number: 1
Part Number(s): C3AZ19703F
Usage: 1963–67 Fairlane, 1963–67 Comet, 1968 Torino, 1968 Montego, 1965–68 Mustang, 1962–68 Thunderbird, 1963–68 full-size Ford and Mercury, 1963–68 Falcon, 1967–68 Cougar (all with air conditioning systems), 1969–71 Torino, 1969–71 Montego, 1969–71 Mustang, 1969–71 Cougar, 1970–71 Maverick, and 1971 Comet (subcompact)—all with hang-on air conditioning

Interchange Number: 2
Part Number(s): C9AZ19703A
Usage: 1969 Torino, 1969 Montego, 1969 Mustang, 1969 Thunderbird, 1969 full-size Ford, 1969 full-size Mercury, and 1969 Cougar—all with integrated air conditioning systems
Note(s): This unit will fit those from earlier models, but Interchange Number 1 will not fit these vehicles.

Interchange Number: 3
Part Number(s): D3AZ19703B
Usage: 1970–72 Torino, 1970–72 Montego, 1970–72 full-size Ford, 1970–72 full-size Mercury, 1970–72 Mustang, 1970–72 Maverick, 1970–72 Cougar, and 1971–72 Comet (subcompact)—all with integrated air conditioning systems only

Interchange Number: 4
Part Number(s): C2AZ19703A
Usage: 1959–62 full-size Ford, 1961–62 full-size Mercury, and 1960–62 Thunderbird—except six-cylinder models

Condenser, Air Conditioning

Type of air conditioning system will greatly influence the interchanging of condensers. Those with hang-on (dealer-installed) or integrated (factory) will not interchange.

Model Identification

Cougar	Interchange Number
1967–68	
factory-installed	8
dealer-installed	6
1969–70	
factory-installed	9
dealer-installed	6

Cyclone	Interchange Number
1966–67	
factory-installed	
289ci	
1966	10
1967	12
390ci	4
dealer-installed	
1966	11
1967	6
1968–69	
factory-installed	5
dealer-installed	6
1970	
factory-installed	7
dealer-installed	6

Fairlane and Torino	Interchange Number
1959–60	13
1961	14
1962–64	15
1966–67	
factory-installed	
289ci	
1966	10
1967	12
390ci	4
dealer-installed	
1966, all	11
1967, all	6
1968–69	
factory-installed	5
dealer-installed	6
1970	
factory-installed	7
dealer-installed	6

Interchange

Interchange Number: 1
Part Number(s): C4AZ19712B
Usage: 1964–65 Fairlane, 1964–65 Comet, 1964-1/2–66 Mustang, 1964–65 Falcon, and 1964 full-size Ford—all with hang-on air conditioning

Interchange Number: 2
Part Number(s): C5OZ19712A
Usage: 1965 Fairlane with integrated air conditioning only

Interchange Number: 3
Part Number(s): C3OZ19712A
Usage: 1963–64 Fairlane and 1963 Meteor with factory-installed air conditioning

Interchange Number: 4
Part Number(s): C6OZ19712B
Usage: 1966–67 Fairlane GT and Fairlane 390ci and 1966–67 Cyclone and Comet 390ci—all with air conditioning

Interchange Number: 5
Part Number(s): C8OZ19712A
Usage: 1968–69 Torino, 1968–69 Montego, and 1968–70 Falcon—all with integrated air conditioning

Interchange Number: 6
Part Number(s): C7AZ19712A
Usage: 1967 Fairlane, 1967 Comet, 1968–71 Torino, 1968–71 Montego, 1967–71 Mustang, 1967–71 Cougar, 1970–71 Maverick, 1971 Comet (subcompact), 1967–71 full-size Ford, 1967–71 full-size Mercury, 1967–70 Falcon—all with hang-on air conditioning

Interchange Number: 7
Part Number(s): D1OZ19712A
Usage: 1970–71 Torino and Montego with integrated air conditioning

Interchange Number: 8
Part Number(s): C7ZZ19712A
Usage: 1967–68 Mustang and Cougar with integrated air conditioning

Interchange Number: 9
Part Number(s): C9ZZ19712A
Usage: 1969–70 Mustang and Cougar with integrated air conditioning

Interchange Number: 10
Part Number(s): C6OZ19712A
Usage: 1966 Comet 289ci, Fairlane 289ci, and Falcon—all with integrated factory air conditioning

Interchange Number: 11
Part Number(s): C6OZ19712C
Usage: 1966 Comet 289ci, Fairlane 289ci, and Falcon—all with hang-on air conditioning

Interchange Number: 12
Part Number(s): C7OZ19712A
Usage: 1967 Comet 289ci, Fairlane 289ci, and Falcon—all with integrated factory air conditioning

Interchange Number: 13
Part Number(s): COAF19712A
Usage: 1959–60 full-size Ford with air conditioning

Interchange Number: 14
Part Number(s): C1AF19712C
Usage: 1961–62 full-size Ford with air conditioning (except six-cylinder)

Interchange Number: 15
Part Number(s): C3OZ19712A
Usage: 1962–64 Fairlane with air conditioning

Horn Assembly

From 1958–73, horns are the same regardless of model or model year—all Ford and Mercurys used the same horns. The high-tone horn is part number B8AZ13832B, and the low-tone horn is part number B8AZ13833B.

Lever, Turn Signal

Model Identification

Interchange

Interchange Number: 1
Part Number(s): COKF13305AP
Usage: 1959–62 full-size Ford, except Galaxie 500 XL

Interchange Number: 2
Part Number(s): C2OA13305AP
Usage: 1962 Fairlane

Interchange Number: 3
Part Number(s): C3OZ13305A
Usage: 1963–64 Fairlane and 1964 Falcon

Interchange Number: 4
Part Number(s): DOAZF13305A
Usage: 1965–67 Fairlane, 1968–73 Torino, 1966–67 Comet, 1968–73 Montego, 1964–70 Mustang, 1967–70 Cougar, 1965–70 Falcon, 1965–73 full-size Ford, 1966–73 full-size Mercury, 1965–73 Thunderbird, 1970–72 Maverick, and 1971–72 Comet (subcompact)—all without speed control

Interchange Number: 5
Part Number(s): D1VY13305A
Usage: 1967–69 Mustang, 1967–69 Cougar, 1967–69 full-size Ford, 1966–69 full-size Mercury, and 1970 Thunderbird—all with speed control

Switch, Headlamp

Many switches interchange. However, those models with hidden headlamps used a special switch, and those without hidden headlamps will not interchange, or vice versa.

Like most other Ford switches, the headlamp switch uses a number for identification. When this number is known or used it is given.

Model Identification

Cougar	Interchange Number
1967	4
1968	10
1969	11
1970	12

Cyclone	Interchange Number
1966–67	4
1968–70	
exposed headlamps	1
hidden headlamps	2

Fairlane and Torino	Interchange Number
1959–60	13
1961	14
1962–64	15
1965–66	3
1967	4
1968–70	
exposed headlamps	1
hidden headlamps	2

Mustang	Interchange Number
1964-1/2	5
1965	6, 7
1966, all	6
1967–68	7
1969	8
1970	9

Interchange

Interchange Number: 1
Part Number(s): C5AZ11654A
ID Number(s): C5AB11654A or C5AB11654B
Usage: 1965–72 full-size Ford, 1965–72 full-size Mercury, 1968–72 Torino, 1968–72 Montego, and 1971–72 Mustang (except convertible)—all with exposed headlamps

Interchange Number: 2
Part Number(s): C8AZ11654A
ID Number(s): C8AB11654C, C8AB11654XC
Usage: 1965–70 full-size Ford, 1968–71 full-size Mercury, 1971–71 Torino, and 1970–71 Montego—all with hide-away headlamps

Interchange Number: 3
Part Number(s): C5OZ11654A
ID Number(s): C5OB11654A
Usage: 1965–66 Fairlane

Interchange Number: 4
Part Number(s): C5GY11654C
ID Number(s): C5GB11654A
Usage: 1967 Fairlane, 1965–67 Comet, and 1967 Cougar

Interchange Number: 5
Part Number(s): C5ZZ11654A
ID Number(s): C5ZB11654
Usage: 1964-1/2 Mustang

Interchange Number: 6
Part Number(s): C5DZ11654A
ID Number(s): C5DB11654A
Usage: 1965 Mustang (up to build date November 16, 1964), 1966 Mustang, 1971 Mustang, 1972 Mustang (all except fastback), and 1970–72 Maverick (after build date January 3, 1972)

Interchange Number: 7
Part Number(s): C5ZZ11654B
ID Number(s): C5ZB11654A
Usage: 1965 Mustang (after build date November 16, 1964) and 1967–68 Mustang

Interchange Number: 8
Part Number(s): C9ZZ11654A
ID Number(s): C9ZB11654C
Usage: 1969 Mustang; no other interchange

Interchange Number: 9
Part Number(s): DOZZ11654A
ID Number(s): DOZB11654B
Usage: 1970 Mustang; no other interchange

Interchange Number: 10
Part Number(s): C8WY11654A
Usage: 1968 Cougar; no other interchange

Interchange Number: 11
Part Number(s): C9WY11654A
Usage: 1969 Cougar; no other interchange

Interchange Number: 12
Part Number(s): DOWY11654A
Usage: 1970 Cougar; no other interchange

Interchange Number: 13
Part Number(s): COAF11654C
Usage: 1959–60 full-size Ford

Interchange Number: 14
Part Number(s): C2AF11654A
Usage: 1961–62 full-size Ford

Interchange Number: 15
Part Number(s): C2OB11654A
Usage: 1962–64 Fairlane

Motor, Convertible Top

Model Identification

Cougar	Interchange Number
1967–70	1

Cyclone	Interchange Number
1966–70	1

Fairlane and Torino	Interchange Number
1959–61	2
1966–70	1

Mustang	Interchange Number
1964-1/2–70	1

Interchange

Interchange Number: 1
Part Number(s): D1AZ76533A
Usage: 1966–67 Fairlane, 1968–71 Torino, 1966–67 Comet, 1968–71 Montego, 1964–65 Falcon, 1964-1/2–73 Mustang, and 1967–70 Cougar

Interchange Number: 2
Part Number(s): COAB76533AODA
Usage: 1958–61 full-size Ford and 1957–59 full-size Mercury (see notes)
Note(s): This is the 1960–61 part number; it will fit earlier models but motors used before 1960 will not fit 1960–61 models.

Switch, Convertible Top

Breakdown here is by car family and major design changes, but don't rule out switches from station wagons. The power tailgate window switch on the station wagon is the same unit that controls the top on some convertible models, provided it is the single-control type.

Model Identification

Cougar	Interchange Number
1967	5
1968	6
1969–70	7

Interchange

Interchange Number: 1
Part Number(s): C6OZ15668A
Usage: 1966–67 Fairlane, Comet, and Falcon convertible and station wagon

Interchange Number: 2
Part Number(s): C8OZ15668A (marked C8OB15668A)
Usage: 1968–69 Torino and Montego convertible and station wagon

Interchange Number: 3
Part Number(s): DOOZ15668A (marked DOOB15668A)
Usage: 1970–71 Torino and Montego convertible and station wagon

Interchange Number: 4
Part Number(s): C4DZ15668A
Usage: 1964-1/2–66 Mustang and 1964–65 Falcon convertible and wagon

Interchange Number: 5
Part Number(s): C7ZZ15668A
Usage: 1967 Mustang and Cougar

Interchange Number: 6
Part Number(s): C8ZZ15668A (marked C8ZB15668A)
Usage: 1968 Mustang and Cougar with convertible or sliding top

Interchange Number: 7
Part Number(s): C9ZZ15668A (marked C9ZB15668C)
Usage: 1969–70 Mustang and Cougar with convertible or sliding top

Interchange Number: 8
Part Number(s): COAF15668A
Usage: 1959–61 full-size Ford and 1960–61 full-size Ford wagon with power tailgate window

Chapter 10

Sheet Metal/Body and Exterior Trim

Hood

The hood should be interchanged without any trim nameplates or the hinges. Some models, such as the Fairlane GT, used a special hood that featured simulated hood scoops. It is noted that the interchange is for these models only; however, the GT hood will fit non-GT. The interchange is based on the original model's usage.

Some hoods may have to be modified to fit correctly. This is especially true with ram-air-type hoods. Some models with the shaker-style hood will require a portion of the hood to be cut out to provide clearance for the scoop. Unless you know exactly how to do this, I would recommend that a professional perform the surgery on your hood. This is the procedure Ford used when they installed the shaker-hood assembly. If a standard hood can be modified to fit another application, it is listed in the notes of the interchange section.

Model Identification

Interchange

Interchange Number: 1
Part Number(s): B9A16612A
Usage: 1959 full-size Ford—all models and body styles

Interchange Number: 2
Part Number(s): COAB1662P
Usage: 1960 full-size Ford—all models and body styles

Interchange Number: 3
Part Number(s): C2AZ16612B
Usage: 1961–62 full-size Ford—all models and body styles

Standard hood can be modified to accommodate Ram Air.

Interchange Number: 4
   Part Number(s): C2OZ16612B
   Usage: 1962 Fairlane—all models, all body styles

Interchange Number: 5
   Part Number(s): C3OZ16612A
   Usage: 1963–64 Fairlane—all models, all body styles

Interchange Number: 6
   Part Number(s): C5OZ16612A
   Usage: 1965 Fairlane—all models, all body styles

Interchange Number: 7
   Part Number(s): C6OZ16612C
   Usage: 1966–67 Fairlane—all models, all body styles, except GT and GTA models

Interchange Number: 8
   Part Number(s): C6OZ16612A
   Usage: 1966 Fairlane GT and GTA only
   Note(s): Interchange with scoop.

Interchange Number: 9
   Part Number(s): C7OZ16612B
   Usage: 1967 Fairlane GT and GTA only

Interchange Number: 10
   Part Number(s): C8OZ16612B
   Usage: 1968–69 Torino—all models and body styles (see notes for GT usage)
   Note(s): GT with a hood scoop used the same hood, and the hood was drilled to allow the installation of the scoop. Also used with ram air. The hood was cut (see illustration) in specific locations.

Interchange Number: 11
   Part Number(s): DOOZ16612D
   Usage: 1970–71 Torino GT and Cobra without ram air (uses twin simulated air scoops)

Interchange Number: 12
   Part Number(s): DOOZ16612C
   Usage: 1970–71 Torino (all models and body styles except Torino GT and Cobra without ram air); is used in Torinos with ram air (see Note regarding usage)
   Note(s): Standard hood was cut open to provide clearance for the shaker scoop. See illustration.

Interchange Number: 13
   Part Number(s): C5ZZ16612B
   Usage: 1964-1/2–66 Mustang, except GT 350 models

Interchange Number: 14
   Part Number(s): SMS216612A
   Usage: 1966 GT 350 Shelby Mustang (includes center air scoop)

The 1969–70 GT 350/500 Mustang hood used five special functional scoops, three from the front and two at the rear.

Interchange Number: 15
   Part Number(s): C7ZZ16612C
   Usage: 1967–68 Mustang without hood-mounted turn indicators, except GT 350 and GT 500 models

Interchange Number: 16
   Part Number(s): C7ZZ16612D
   Usage: 1967–68 Mustang with hood-mounted turn indicators except GT 350 and GT 500 models

Interchange Number: 17
   Part Number(s): S7MS16612B
   Usage: 1967 Shelby Mustang (fiberglass hood)

Interchange Number: 18
   Part Number(s): S8MS16612A
   Usage: 1968 GT 350 and GT 500 without ram air (fiberglass hood)

Interchange Number: 19
   Part Number(s): S8MS16612B
   Usage: 1968 GT 350 and GT 500 with ram air (fiberglass hood)
   Note(s): 1968 GT 500 KR was standard with this hood.

Interchange Number: 20
   Part Number(s): DOZZ16612A
   Usage: 1969–70 Mustang—all models except Boss 429ci, GT 350, and GT 500 (see notes for ram-air installation)
   Note(s): Will fit GT and those with hood scoop but without ram air, provided holes are drilled for the installation of the scoop. On those models with through-the-hood air cleaner (ram air), this hood was cut open in the center just above the air cleaner.

Interchange Number: 21
   Part Number(s): C9ZZ16612B
   Usage: 1969–70 GT 350 and GT 500 models only

Interchange Number: 22
   Part Number(s): C6GY16612D
   Usage: 1966–67 Cyclone, all except 1967 Comet with 427ci (includes simulated air vents)

Interchange Number: 23
   Part Number(s): C7GY16612D
   Usage: 1967 Comet with 427ci engine (lightweight)

Interchange Number: 24
   Part Number(s): C8GY16612B
   Usage: 1968–69 Montego—all models, all body styles; see Notes for Cyclone usage
   Note(s): Standard hood must be drilled and cut as shown in the illustration for installation of hood scoop on Cyclone models

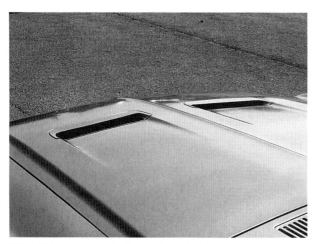

1967–68 Mustang hood with hood-mounted signal lamps.

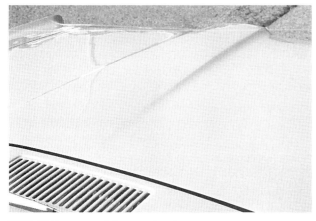
1967–68 Cougars used the same hood.

Interchange Number: 25
Part Number(s): DOGY16612C
Usage: 1970–71 Montego—all models and body styles except 1970–71 Cyclone Spoiler, Cyclone GT, and 1971 Cyclone models
Note(s): Not used with ram air.

Interchange Number: 26
Part Number(s): DOGY16612D
Usage: 1970–71 Montego with ram air, 1970–71 Cyclone GT and Cyclone Spoiler (with or without ram air), and 1971 Cyclone (with or without ram air)

Interchange Number: 27
Part Number(s): C7WY16612A
Usage: 1967–68 Cougar, except with 428ci Cobra Jet (see notes for hood scoop installation on XR7)
Note(s): Eight 1/2in holes must be drilled in standard hood installation of scoop, and two 1-1/8in-diameter holes at the front for the locking pins.

Interchange Number: 28
Part Number(s): C8WY16612A
Usage: 1968 Cougar with 428ci Cobra Jet

Interchange Number: 29
Part Number(s): C9WY16612A
Usage: 1969 Cougar—all models (see notes for hood-scoop installation)
Note(s): Ten holes must be drilled during installation of hood scoop.

Interchange Number: 30
Part Number(s): DOWY16612A
Usage: 1970 Cougar—all models (see notes for hood-scoop installation)
Note(s): Ten holes must be drilled in hood to mount the hood scoop. To use with ram air, the hood must be cut open, as shown.

Interchange Number: 31
Part Number(s): C9ZZ16612E
Usage: 1969–70 Boss 429ci

Hinges, Hood

Model Identification

Cougar	Interchange Number
1967–70	7

Cyclone	Interchange Number
1966–69	5
1970	6

Fairlane and Torino	Interchange Number
1959–60	1
1961	2
1962	3
1963–65	4
1966–69	5
1970	6

Mustang	Interchange Number
1964-1/2–66	4
1967–70	7

Interchange

Interchange Number: 1
Part Number(s): COAB16796A (right), COAB1697A (left)
Usage: 1959–60 full-size Ford—all models and body styles

Interchange Number: 2
Part Number(s): C3AZ16796A (right), C3AZ1697A (left)
Usage: 1961–64 full-size Ford and full-size Mercury—all models and body styles

Interchange Number: 3
Part Number(s): C2OZ16796A (right), C2OZ1697A (left)
Usage: 1962 Fairlane—all models and body styles

Interchange Number: 4
Part Number(s): C3OZ16796A (right), C3OZ1697A (left)
Usage: 1963–65 Fairlane, 1964–65 Comet, 1964-1/2–66 Mustang, and 1964–65 Falcon—all models and body styles

Interchange Number: 5
Part Number(s): C6OZ16796B (right), C6OZ1697B (left)
Usage: 1966–67 Fairlane, 1966–67 Comet, 1966–70 Falcon, 1968–69 Torino, and 1968–69 Montego—all models and all body styles

Interchange Number: 6
Part Number(s): DOOZ16796B (right), DOOZ1697B (left)
Usage: 1970–71 Torino and Montego—all models and body styles

Interchange Number: 7
Part Number(s): C9ZZ16796A (right), C9ZZ1697A (left)
Usage: 1967–70 Mustang and Cougar—all models, all body styles

Springs, Hood Hinge
Hood-hinge springs are universal fit, meaning that a spring on the right side will fit the left side. Only seven different springs were used, so there is large interchange available.

Model Identification

Cougar	Interchange Number
1967–70	4

Cyclone	Interchange Number
1966–69	
all except with fiberglass hood	4
with fiberglass hood	5
1970	7

Fairlane and Torino	Interchange Number
1959–60	1
1961	2
1962	3
1963–65	
all except fiberglass hood	4
with fiberglass hood	5
1970	7

Mustang	Interchange Number
1964-1/2–70	
all except 1967–68 GT 350 and GT 500	4
1967–68 GT 350 and GT 500	6

Interchange

Interchange Number: 1
Part Number(s): COAB16789B
Usage: 1959–60 full-size Ford

Interchange Number: 2
Part Number(s): C1AZ16789B
Free Length: 8in
Usage: 1961–64 full-size Ford and full-size Mercury

Interchange Number: 3
Part Number(s): C2OZ16789A
Free Length: 6.58in
Usage: 1962 Fairlane and 1963 Falcon

Interchange Number: 4
Part Number(s): C3OZ16789A
Free Length: 5-13/32in
Usage: 1963–67 Fairlane, 1964–70 Falcon, 1964–67 Comet, 1968–69 Torino, 1968–69 Montego, 1964-1/2–70 Mustang, and 1967–70 Cougar
Note(s): With this exception: do not use with fiberglass hoods.

Interchange Number: 5
Part Number(s): CGY16789A
Usage: 1966–67 Fairlane, 1966–67 Comet with fiberglass hood.
Note(s): Low-tension spring.

Interchange Number: 6
Part Number(s): S7MS16789B
Usage: 1967–68 GT 350, GT 500, and GT 500 KR—all with fiberglass hoods
Note(s): Low-tension spring.

Interchange Number: 7
Part Number(s): DOOZ16789B
Free Length: 6-59/34in
Usage: 1970–71 Torino and Montego

Fenders, Front

Due to natural evolutionary design changes, very few front fenders interchange. There were also sometimes special models like the Talladega that used special fenders, so regular Torino fenders will not interchange.

Interchange is for the bare unit without nameplates, wheelwell trim, or any side mouldings. Note, however, that these factors will have to be weighted in when interchanging used parts, as side trim and nameplates require that holes be drilled. The pre-drilled holes may not match up to your existing fenders. To mount the fender, existing holes may have to be filled or new ones drilled to accommodate your specific usage. Remember, it is always easier to drill new holes than it is to cover up existing ones. So look for a fender that matches your particular application or without any other trim, if possible.

Model Identification

Interchange

Interchange Number: 1
Part Number(s): B9AB16005F (right), B9AB160006F (left)
Usage: 1959 full-size Ford—all body styles and models

Interchange Number: 2
Part Number(s): COAB16005D (right), COAB160006D (left)
Usage: 1960 full-size Ford—all body styles and models
Note(s): 1960 Edsel will also interchange, but problems can exist with pre-drilled holes.

Interchange Number: 3
Part Number(s): C1AZ16005AE (right), C1AZ160006AE (left)
Usage: 1961–62 full-size Ford—all body styles and models

Interchange Number: 4
Part Number(s): C2OZ16005B (right), C2OZ160006B (left)
Usage: 1962 Fairlane—all models and body styles

Interchange Number: 5
Part Number(s): C3OZ16005A (right), C3OZ160006A (left)
Usage: 1963–64 Fairlane—all body styles and models

Interchange Number: 6
Part Number(s): C5OZ16005A (right), C5OZ160006A (left)
Usage: 1965 Fairlane—all body styles and models

Interchange Number: 7
Part Number(s): C6OZ16005A (right), C6OZ16006A (left)
Usage: 1966–67 Fairlane—all body styles and models

Interchange Number: 8
Part Number(s): C8OZ16005C (right), C8OZ16006C (left)
Usage: 1968–69 Torino—all models and body styles except Talladega

Interchange Number: 9
Part Number(s): DOOZ16005B (right), DOOZ160006B (left)
Usage: 1970–71 Torino—all models and body styles

Interchange Number: 10
Part Number(s): C5ZZ16005A (right), C5ZZ16006A (left)
Usage: 1964-1/2–66 Mustang

Interchange Number: 11
Part Number(s): C7ZZ16005B (right), C7ZZ16006B (left)
Usage: 1967 Mustang

Interchange Number: 12
Part Number(s): C8ZZ16005A (right), C8ZZ16006A (left)
Usage: 1968 Mustang

Interchange Number: 13
Part Number(s): C9ZZ16005C (right), C9ZZ16006C (left)
Usage: 1969 Mustang—all models except Boss 302ci, Boss 429ci, GT 350, and GT 500

Interchange Number: 14
Part Number(s): C9ZZ16005F (right), C9ZZ16006F (left)
Usage: 1969 Boss 302ci with F60x15in tires
Note(s): *Warning:* due to tire-clearance problems, regular fenders must *never* be used on a Boss 302ci.

Interchange Number: 15
Part Number(s): DOZZ16005C (right), DOZZ16006C (left)
Usage: 1970 Mustang—all except Boss 302ci, Boss 429ci, GT 350, and GT 500 or with optional F70x14in or F60x15in tires

Interchange Number: 16
Part Number(s): DOZZ16005B (right), DOZZ16006B (left)
Usage: 1970 Mustang with F70x14in or F60x15in tires, all except for Boss 429ci and GT 350 and GT 500 models
Note(s): Will fit 1970 Boss 302ci.

Interchange Number: 17
Part Number(s): DOZZ16005E (right), DOZZ16006E (left)
Usage: 1970 Mustang Boss 429ci only; no other interchange

Interchange Number: 18
Part Number(s): C9ZZ16005C (right), C9ZZ16006C (left)
Usage: 1969–70 GT 350 and GT 500 models (have special side scoops)

Interchange Number: 19
Part Number(s): C5GY16005A (right), C5GY16006A (left)
Usage: 1965 Comet—all models and body styles

Interchange Number: 20
Part Number(s): C7GY16005B (right), C7GY16006B (left)
Usage: 1966 Comet (all models and body styles) and 1967 Comet station wagon only

Interchange Number: 21
Part Number(s): C7GY16005A (right), C7GY16006A (left)
Usage: 1967 Comet—all models and body styles, except station wagon

Interchange Number: 22
Part Number(s): C8GY16005A (right), C8GY16006A (left)
Usage: 1968 Montego—all models and body styles

Interchange Number: 23
Part Number(s): C9GY16005A (right), C9GY16006A (left)
Usage: 1969 Montego—all models and body styles, except Spoiler II

Interchange Number: 24
Part Number(s): C9GY16005B (right), C9GY16006B (left)
Usage: 1969 Cyclone Spoiler II (special extended type)

Interchange Number: 25
Part Number(s): DOGY16005A (right), DOGY16006A (left)
Usage: 1970–71 Montego—all models and body styles

Interchange Number: 26
Part Number(s): C7WY16005A (right), C7WY16006A (left)
Usage: 1967 Cougar

Interchange Number: 27
Part Number(s): C8WY16005A (right), C8WY16006A (left)
Usage: 1968 Cougar

Interchange Number: 28
Part Number(s): C9WY16005A (right), C9WY16006A (left)
Usage: 1969 Cougar

Interchange Number: 29
Part Number(s): DOWY16005A (right), DOWY16006A (left)
Usage: 1970 Cougar

Interchange Number: 30
Part Number(s): C9ZZ16005E (right), C9ZZ16006E (left)
Usage: 1969 Mustang Boss 429ci

Interchange Number: 31
Part Number(s): C9OZ16005A (right), C9OZ16006A (left)
Usage: 1969 Torino Talladega

Door, Front
Doors of most models were changed only when a major design evolution occurred, so the interchange is larger than it may at first appear. Body style will greatly affect the interchange. A door from a two-door sedan will not fit a two-door hardtop.

Interchange is the complete door minus interior door panel and any exterior trim mouldings. When interchanging from convertible to hardtop or vice versa, remove the glass and all its hardware. Although the doors will fit, the glass may not. Because trim requires holes to be drilled in the sheet metal, trim should be considered in interchanging used doors. A plain door (without trim) is always the best bet, as holes can be easily drilled. But filling holes from a door with trim to a car without trim is more difficult.

Model Identification

Cougar	Interchange Number
1967–68, all	21
1969–70, all	22

Cyclone	Interchange Number
1965	
two-door sedan	17
two-door hardtop and convertible	18
1966–67	
two-door sedan	19
two-door hardtop and convertible	20
1968–69, all	11
1970, all	13

Fairlane and Torino	Interchange Number
1959, all	1
1960, all	2
1961, all	3
1962–64	
two-door sedan	4
two-door hardtop	5
1965	
two-door sedan	6
two-door hardtop	7
1966–67	
two-door sedan	9
two-door hardtop and convertible	8
Ranchero	10
1968–69, all (including Ranchero)	11
1970, all	12

Mustang	Interchange Number
1964-1/2–66, all	14
1967–68, all	15
1969–70, all	16

Interchange

Interchange Number: 1
Part Number(s): B9A6420124A (right), B9A6420125A (left)
Usage: 1959 full-size Ford—all two-door models except Thunderbird

Interchange Number: 2
Part Number(s): COA6420124M (right), COA6420125M (left)
Usage: 1960 full-size Ford—all two-door models except Thunderbird

Interchange Number: 3
Part Number(s): C1A6420124L (right), C1A6420125L (left)
Usage: 1961 full-size Ford—all two-door models except Thunderbird

Interchange Number: 4
Part Number(s): C3OZ6220124B (right), C3OZ6220125A (left)
Usage: 1962–64 Fairlane two-door sedan

Interchange Number: 5
Part Number(s): C3OZ6520124B (right), C3OZ620125A (left)
Usage: 1963–64 Fairlane two-door hardtop

Interchange Number: 6
Part Number(s): C5OZ6220124B (right), C5OZ6220125A (left)
Usage: 1965 Fairlane two-door sedan

Interchange Number: 7
Part Number(s): C5OZ6520124B (right), C5OZ620125A (left)
Usage: 1965 Fairlane two-door hardtop

Interchange Number: 8
Part Number(s): C6OZ6320124B (right), C6OZ6320125A (left)
Usage: 1966–67 Fairlane two-door hardtop and convertible

Interchange Number: 9
Part Number(s): C6OZ6220124B (right), C3OZ6220125A (left)
Usage: 1966–67 Fairlane two-door sedan

Interchange Number: 10
Part Number(s): C7DZ6620124B (right), C6DZ66620125B (left)
Usage: 1966–67 Ranchero

Interchange Number: 11
Part Number(s): C8OZ6320124A (right), C8OZ6320125A (left)
Usage: 1968–69 Torino and Montego—all body styles except station wagon or four-door models; will fit Ranchero

Interchange Number: 12
Part Number(s): DOOZ6520124B (right), DOOZ6520125A (left)
Usage: 1970–71 Torino—all body styles except four-door and station wagon (see notes)
Note(s): 1971 models used slightly different doors, but will physically fit. The window stop is different.

Interchange Number: 13
Part Number(s): DOGY6520124A (right), DOGY6520125A (left)
Usage: 1970–71 Montego—all body styles except four-door and station wagon. (see notes)
Note(s): 1971 models used slightly different doors, but will physically fit. The window stop is different.

Interchange Number: 14
Part Number(s): C5ZZ6520124B (right), C5ZZ6520125B (left)
Usage: 1964-1/2–66 Mustang—all body styles

Interchange Number: 15
Part Number(s): C7ZZ6520124C (right), C7ZZ6520125C (left)
Usage: 1967–68 Mustang—all body styles

Interchange Number: 16
Part Number(s): DOZZ6520124A (right), DOZZ6520125A (left)
Usage: 1969–70 Mustang—all body styles

Interchange Number: 17
Part Number(s): C4DZ6220124B (right), C4DZ6220125B (left)
Usage: 1964–65 Comet and Falcon two-door sedans

Interchange Number: 18
Part Number(s): C4DZ6320124B (right), C4DZ6320125B (left)
Usage: 1964–65 Comet and Falcon two-door hardtop and convertible only

Interchange Number: 19
Part Number(s): C7GY6220124A (right), C7GY6220125A (left)
Usage: 1966–67 Comet two-door sedans only

Interchange Number: 20
Part Number(s): C7GY6320124B (right), C7GY6320125B (left)
Usage: 1966–67 Comet two-door hardtop and convertible

Interchange Number: 21
Part Number(s): C7WY6520124C (right), C7GY6520125C (left)
Usage: 1967–68 Cougar—all body styles

Interchange Number: 22
Part Number(s): C97WY6520124A (right), C7GY6520125A (left)
Usage: 1969–70 Cougar—all body styles

Hinges, Door

Model Identification

Cougar	Interchange Number
1967–68	
upper	8
lower	19
1969–70	
upper	9
lower	20

Cyclone	Interchange Number
1965	
upper	10
lower	21
1966–67	
upper	11
lower	22
1968–69	
upper	5
lower	16
1970	
upper	6
lower	17

Fairlane and Torino	Interchange Number
1959–61	
upper	1
lower	12
1962–63	
upper	2
lower	13
1964	
upper	3
lower	14
1965	
upper	4
lower	15
1967–69	
upper	5
lower	16
1970	
upper	6
lower	17

Mustang	Interchange Number
1964-1/2–66	
upper	7
lower	18
1967–68	
upper	8
lower	19
1969–70	
upper	9
lower	20

Interchange

Interchange Number: 1
Part Number(s): COAB6422800A (right), COAB6422801A (left)
Hinge Location: Upper
Usage: 1959–63 full-size Fords—all models and body styles

Interchange Number: 2
Part Number(s): C2OB6422800A (right), C2OB6422801A (left)
Hinge Location: Upper
Usage: 1962–63 Fairlane—all models and body styles

Interchange Number: 3
   Part Number(s): C4OZ6222800A (right), C4OZ6422801A (left)
   Hinge Location: Upper
   Usage: 1964 Fairlane—all models and body styles

Interchange Number: 4
   Part Number(s): C5OZ6222800A (Fits either side)
   Hinge Location: Upper
   Usage: 1965 Fairlane—all models and body styles
   Note(s): Reverse pin to used be on other side of car.

Interchange Number: 5
   Part Number(s): C6OZ6222800B (right), C6OZ6422801B (left)
   Hinge Location: Upper
   Usage: 1966–67 Fairlane, 1968–69 Torino, 1968–69 Montego, and 1966–70 Falcon—all models and body styles
   Note(s): Will not fit 1966–67 Comet models.

Interchange Number: 6
   Part Number(s): D1OZ6522800B (right), C6OZ6422801B (left)
   Hinge Location: Upper
   Usage: 1970–71 Torino and Montego, 1971–73 Mustang and Cougar, 1971–74 Pinto—all models and body styles (see notes regarding 1970 models)
   Note(s): 1971 upper hinge on the driver's side will not fit 1970 models, but those on the passenger's side will fit either year, so either use the 1970 hinge on the driver's side or the 1971 door and the 1971 hinges on the 1970 models.

Interchange Number: 7
   Part Number(s): C5ZZ6522800B (right), C5ZZ6422801B (left)
   Hinge Location: Upper
   Usage: 1964-1/2–66 Mustang—all models and body styles

Interchange Number: 8
   Part Number(s): C7ZZ6522800C (right), C7ZZ6522801C (left)
   Hinge Location: Upper
   Usage: 1967–68 Mustang and Cougar—all models and body styles

Interchange Number: 9
   Part Number(s): DOZZ6522800A (right), DOZZ6522801A (left)
   Hinge Location: Upper
   Usage: 1969–70 Mustang and Cougar—all models and body styles

Interchange Number: 10
   Part Number(s): C4DZ6222800A (right), C4DZ6222801A (left)
   Hinge Location: Upper
   Usage: 1964–65 Comet and Falcon—all models and body styles

Interchange Number: 11
   Part Number(s): CGY6222800B (right), CGY6222801B (left)
   Hinge Location: Upper
   Usage: 1966–67 Comet—all models and body styles

Interchange Number: 12
   Part Number(s): C3AZ6222810A (right), C3AZ6222811A (left)
   Hinge Location: Lower
   Usage: 1959–63 full-size Fords—all models and body styles

Interchange Number: 13
   Part Number(s): C2OB6422810A (right), C2OB6422811A (left)
   Hinge Location: Lower
   Usage: 1962–63 Fairlane—all models and body styles

Interchange Number: 14
   Part Number(s): C4OZ6222810A (right), C4OZ6422811A (left)
   Hinge Location: Lower
   Usage: 1964 Fairlane—all models and body styles

Interchange Number: 15
   Part Number(s): C5OZ6222810A (right), C5OZ622811A (left)
   Hinge Location: Lower
   Usage: 1965 Fairlane—all models and body styles

Interchange Number: 16
   Part Number(s): C6OZ6222810C (right), C6OZ6422811C (left)
   Hinge Location: Lower
   Usage: 1966–67 Fairlane, 1968–69 Torino, 1968–69 Montego, 1966–70 Falcon—all models and body styles; will not fit 1966–67 Comet

Interchange Number: 17
   Part Number(s): D1OZ6522810A (right), D1OZ6422811A (left)
   Hinge Location: Lower
   Usage: 1970–71 Torino and Montego, 1971–73 Mustang and Cougar, and 1971–74 Pinto—all models and body styles

Interchange Number: 18
   Part Number(s): C5ZZ6522810B (right), C5ZZ6522811B (left)
   Hinge Location: Lower
   Usage: 1964-1/2–66 Mustang—all models and body styles

Interchange Number: 19
   Part Number(s): C7ZZ6522810C (right), C7ZZ6522811C (left)
   Hinge Location: Lower
   Usage: 1967–68 Mustang and Cougar—all models and body styles (see notes)
   Note(s): 1968 hinge will fit 1967 models, but 1967 hinge will not fit 1968 models.

Interchange Number: 20
   Part Number(s): C9ZZ6522810A (right), C9ZZ6522811A (left)
   Hinge Location: Lower
   Usage: 1969–70 Mustang and Cougar—all models and body styles

Interchange Number: 21
   Part Number(s): C4DZ6222810A (right), C4DZ6222811A (left)
   Hinge Location: Lower
   Usage: 1964–65 Comet and Falcon—all models and body styles

Interchange Number: 22
   Part Number(s): CGY6222810B (right), CGY6222811B (left)
   Hinge Location: Lower
   Usage: 1966–67 Comet—all models and body styles

Door Handle, Outside

Exterior door handles are largely interchangeable and will cross model lines and years. Handles are unique to each side of the car. Thus, a handle from a driver door will not fit a passenger door. Although the handles listed in this interchange are for two-door models only, sometimes the rear door handles of a four-door sedan will fit, but first the button and the pin should be removed. If this is the case, it is noted.

Model Identification

Cougar	Interchange Number
1967–68	7
1969–70	5

Cyclone	Interchange Number
1965	6
1966–70	5

Fairlane and Torino	Interchange Number
1959–60	1
1961	2
1962–64	3
1965	4
1966–70	5

Mustang	Interchange Number
1964-1/2–66	6
1967–68	7
1969–70	6

Interchange

Interchange Number: 1
   Part Number(s): COAB6222404A (right), COAB6222405A (left)
   Usage: 1959–60 full-size Fords—all front doors of all models

Interchange Number: 2
Part Number(s): C1AB6222404B (right), C1AB6222405B (left)
Usage: 1961 full-size Fords—all front doors of all models

Interchange Number: 3
Part Number(s): C3OZ62222404A (right), C3OZ6222405A (left)
Usage: 1962–64 Fairlane—all front doors of all models. Rear doors will fit with modification listed above.

Interchange Number: 4
Part Number(s): C5OZ62222404A (right), C5OZ6222405A (left)
Usage: 1965 Fairlane—all front doors of all models
Note(s): Rear doors will fit with modification listed above.

Interchange Number: 5
Part Number(s): C6OZ62222404A (right), C6OZ6222405A (left)
Usage: 1966–67 Fairlane and Comet, 1966–70 Falcon, 1968–71 Torino and Montego, and 1969–70 Cougar—all front doors of all models
Note(s): Rear doors will fit with modification listed above.

Interchange Number: 6
Part Number(s): C4DZ62222404A (right), C3OZ6222405A (left)
Usage: 1964-1/2–66 Mustang, 1964–65 Comet and Falcon, and 1969–70 Mustang—all front doors of all models
Note(s): Rear doors will fit with modification listed above.

Interchange Number: 7
Part Number(s): C7ZZ62222404A (right), C7ZZ6222405A (left)
Usage: 1967–68 Mustang and Cougar, 1970–74 Maverick, and 1971–74 Comet (compact)—all front doors of all models

Roof Assembly

This interchange is the complete roof assembly, including the rear pillars. Body style will greatly affect the interchange. If interchanging from a used roof, look for a plain steel roof. Vinyl-covered roofs can hide rust and other signs of damage. Plus, those with a vinyl roof will require more prep work to get the roof ready.

Model Identification

The hardtop 1959 Ford convertible required a special folding roof assembly.

The roof assembly for a 1964-1/2–66 Mustang fastback is the same all three years.

Interchange

Interchange Number: 1
Part Number(s): B9AB6450202B
Body Style: Two-door or four-door sedan
Usage: 1959 full-size Ford, except Galaxie

Interchange Number: 2
Part Number(s): B9AB6550200B
Body Style: Two-door hardtop
Usage: 1959 Galaxie models, except retractable top

Interchange Number: 3
Part Number(s): B9A5150209A (front), B9A5150200A (rear)
Body Style: Two-door retraceable hardtop
Usage: 1959 full-size Fords with retractable hardtop

Interchange Number: 4
Part Number(s): B9AB6650200A
Body Style: Pickup
Usage: 1959 Ranchero; no other interchange

Interchange Number: 5
Part Number(s): COAB6450202A
Body Style: Two-door or four-door sedan
Usage: 1960–61 Fairlane, 1960–61 Custom 300, and 1961
    Mercury Meteor 600

Interchange Number: 6
Part Number(s): COAB6350202B
Body Style: Two-door hardtop
Usage: 1960–61 Starliner and 1960 Edsel

Interchange Number: 7
Part Number(s): COAB6250202B
Body Style: Two-door hardtop
Usage: 1960–61 Galaxie, except Starliner models

Interchange Number: 8
Part Number(s): C2OB6250202A
Body Style: Two-door or four-door sedan
Usage: 1962–63 Fairlane and Meteor

Interchange Number: 9
Part Number(s): C3OB6550202A
Body Style: Two-door hardtop
Usage: 1963–65 Fairlane and 1963 Mercury Meteor

Interchange Number: 10
Part Number(s): C4OB6250202A
Body Style: Two-door or four-door sedan
Usage: 1964–65 Fairlane

Interchange Number: 11
Part Number(s): C6OZ6250202B
Body Style: Two-door sedan
Usage: 1966–67 Fairlane and 1968–69 Torino

Interchange Number: 12
Part Number(s): C6DZ6650202A
Body Style: Pickup
Usage: 1966–67 Ranchero

Interchange Number: 13
Part Number(s): C6OZ6350202B
Body Style: Two-door hardtop
Usage: 1966–67 Fairlane and Comet

Interchange Number: 14
Part Number(s): C8OZ6350202A
Body Style: Two-door hardtop
Usage: 1968–69 Torino and Montego

Interchange Number: 15
Part Number(s): C8OZ6550202A
Body Style: Two-door fastback
Usage: 1968–69 Torino and Montego

Interchange Number: 16
Part Number(s): DOOZ6550202A
Body Style: Two-door hardtop
Usage: 1970–71 Torino and Montego

Interchange Number: 17
Part Number(s): DOOZ6350202B
Body Style: Two-door fastback
Usage: 1970–71 Torino and Montego

Interchange Number: 18
Part Number(s): C5ZZ6550202A
Body Style: Two-door hardtop
Usage: 1964-1/2–66 Mustang

Interchange Number: 19
Part Number(s): C5ZZ6350202A
Body Style: Two-door fastback
Usage: 1964-1/2–66 Mustang

Interchange Number: 20
Part Number(s): C7ZZ6550202A
Body Style: Two-door hardtop
Usage: 1967–68 Mustang

Interchange Number: 21
Part Number(s): C7ZZ6350202A
Body Style: Two-door fastback
Usage: 1967–68 Mustang

Interchange Number: 22
Part Number(s): C9ZZ6550202A
Body Style: Two-door hardtop
Usage: 1969–70 Mustang

Interchange Number: 23
Part Number(s): C9ZZ6350202A
Body Style: Two-door fastback
Usage: 1969–70 Mustang

Interchange Number: 24
Part Number(s): C3DZ6350202A
Body Style: Two-door hardtop
Usage: 1964–65 Comet and 1963–65 Falcon

Interchange Number: 25
Part Number(s): C3DZ6250202A
Body Style: Two-door sedan
Usage: 1964–65 Comet and 1963–65 Falcon

Interchange Number: 26
Part Number(s): C7WY6550202A
Body Style: Two-door hardtop
Usage: 1967–68 Cougar

Interchange Number: 27
Part Number(s): C9WY6550202A
Body Style: Two-door hardtop
Usage: 1969–70 Cougar

Interchange Number: 28
Part Number(s): C7GY6250202A
Body Style: Two-door sedan
Usage: 1966–67 Comet

Interchange Number: 29
Part Number(s): DOOZ6650202A
Body Style: Pickup
Usage: 1968–71 Ranchero

Quarter Panel

Interchange listed here is based on a cutout quarter panel from an original car. A new replacement panel can also be used using the same interchange. Note that body style greatly influences the interchange, as does minor changes in model year. If you are salvaging a used panel,

The 1967 and 1968 Cougars use the same sheet metal.

try to pick a unit that is as close as possible to your original unit in trim and emblem usage. Otherwise, you may have to fill pre-drilled holes before you can use it. Better yet is to find a clean unit that is free of any trim or emblems and then drill the holes that are needed. Part Numbers are given in pairs (one for each side) in the interchange below.

Model Identification

Interchange

Interchange Number: 1
    Part Number(s): B9A6327846A (right), B9A6327847A (left)
    Usage: 1959 full-size Ford two-door sedan

Interchange Number: 2
    Part Number(s): B9A7627846A (right), B9A7627847A (left)
    Usage: 1959 full-size Ford convertible, except retractable hardtop

Interchange Number: 3
    Part Number(s): B9A5127846A (right), B9A5127847A (left)
    Usage: 1959 full-size Ford with retractable hardtop

Interchange Number: 4
    Part Number(s): B9A6527846A (right), B9A6527847A (left)
    Usage: 1959 full-size Ford two-door hardtop

Interchange Number: 5
Part Number(s): B9A6627846A (right), B9A6627847A (left)
Usage: 1959 Ranchero

Interchange Number: 6
Part Number(s): COAB6427846B (right), COAB6427847B (left)
Usage: 1960 full-size Ford two-door—all body styles (see notes regarding Ranch wagon usage)
Note(s): The right side panel of the two-door Ranch wagon will fit, but the left side will not fit.

Interchange Number: 7
Part Number(s): C1AB6427846C (right), C1AB6427847C (left)
Usage: 1961 full-size Ford two-door, all body styles (see notes regarding Ranch wagon usage, and upper body panels)
Note(s): The right side panel of the two-door Ranch wagon will fit. But the left side will not fit. Upper panels were different for each body style, except Galaxie two-door sedan and Galaxie two-door hardtop, which used the same set of upper panels. However, Starliner models will not interchange, nor will Fairlane (full-size) models.

Interchange Number: 8
Part Number(s): C3OZ6227846A (right), C3OZ6227847A (left)
Usage: 1962–63 Fairlane two-door sedan

Interchange Number: 9
Part Number(s): C3OZ6527846A (right), C3OZ6527847A (left)
Usage: 1963 Fairlane two-door hardtop

Interchange Number: 10
Part Number(s): C4OZ6227846A (right), C4OZ6227847A (left)
Usage: 1964 Fairlane two-door sedan

Interchange Number: 11
Part Number(s): C4OZ6527846A (right), C4OZ65227847A (left)
Usage: 1964 Fairlane two-door hardtop

Interchange Number: 12
Part Number(s): C5OZ6227846A (right), C5OZ6227847A (left)
Usage: 1965 Fairlane two-door sedan

Interchange Number: 13
Part Number(s): C5OZ6527846A (right), C5OZ6527847A (left)
Usage: 1965 Fairlane two-door hardtop

Interchange Number: 14
Part Number(s): C6OZ7627846A (right), C6OZ7627847A (left)
Usage: 1966–67 Fairlane convertible

Interchange Number: 15
Part Number(s): C6OZ6227840A (right), C6OZ6227841A (left)
Usage: 1966 Fairlane two-door sedan

Interchange Number: 16
Part Number(s): C6OZ6327840A (right), C6OZ6327841A (left)
Usage: 1966 Fairlane two-door hardtop

Interchange Number: 17
Part Number(s): C7OZ6227840A (right), C7OZ6227841A (left)
Usage: 1967 Fairlane two-door sedan

Interchange Number: 18
Part Number(s): C7OZ6327840A (right), C7Z6327841A (left)
Usage: 1967 Fairlane two-door hardtop

Interchange Number: 19
Part Number(s): C7OZ6627846A (right), C7OZ6627847A (left)
Usage: 1966–67 Ranchero

Interchange Number: 20
Part Number(s): C8OZ6327840A (right), C6OZ6327841A (left)
Usage: 1968–69 Torino two-door fastback

Interchange Number: 21
Part Number(s): C9OZ6527840A (right), C9OZ6527841A (left)
Usage: 1968–69 Torino hardtop

Interchange Number: 22
Part Number(s): C8OZ7627846A (right), C8OZ6527847A (left)
Usage: 1968–69 Torino convertible

Interchange Number: 23
Part Number(s): C9OZ6627846A (right), C9OZ6627847A (left)
Usage: 1968–69 Ranchero

Interchange Number: 24
Part Number(s): DOOZ6327840A (right), DOOZ6327841A (left)
Usage: 1970–71 Torino fastback

Interchange Number: 25
Part Number(s): DOOZ6527840A (right), DOOZ6527841A (left)
Usage: 1970–71 Torino hardtop

Interchange Number: 26
Part Number(s): C5ZZ6527846A (right), C5ZZ6527847A (left)
Usage: 1964-1/2–66 Mustang hardtop

Interchange Number: 27
Part Number(s): C5ZZ6327846A (right), C5ZZ6327847A (left)
Usage: 1965–66 Mustang fastback

Interchange Number: 28
Part Number(s): C5ZZ7627846A (right), C5ZZ7627847A (left)
Usage: 1964-1/2–66 Mustang convertible

Interchange Number: 29
Part Number(s): C5ZZ6527846A (right), C5ZZ6527847A (left)
Usage: 1964-1/2–66 Mustang hardtop

Interchange Number: 30
Part Number(s): C7ZZ6527840A (right), C7ZZ6527841A (left)
Usage: 1967 Mustang hardtop

Interchange Number: 31
Part Number(s): C7ZZ6327840A (right), C7ZZ6327841A (left)
Usage: 1967 Mustang fastback

Interchange Number: 32
Part Number(s): C7ZZ7627840A (right), C7ZZ7627841A (left)
Usage: 1967 Mustang convertible

Interchange Number: 33
Part Number(s): C8ZZ6527840A (right), C8ZZ6527841A (left)
Usage: Early-1968 Mustang hardtop
Note(s): Used up to build date February 15, 1968. Has depression for side reflector.

Interchange Number: 34
Part Number(s): C8ZZ6327840B (right), C8ZZ6327841B (left)
Usage: Early-1968 Mustang fastback
Note(s): Used up to build date February 15, 1968. Has depression for side reflector. Also, there is a change in the quarter vents.

Interchange Number: 35
Part Number(s): C8ZZ7627840B (right), C8ZZ7627841B (left)
Usage: Early-1968 Mustang convertible
Note(s): Used up to build date February 15, 1968. Has depression for side reflector.

Interchange Number: 36
Part Number(s): C8ZZ6527840B (right), C8ZZ6527841B (left)
Usage: Late-1968 Mustang hardtop.
Note(s): Used after build date February 15, 1968. No depression for side reflector.

Interchange Number: 37
Part Number(s): C8ZZ6327840B (right), C8ZZ6327841B (left)
Usage: Late 1968 Mustang fastback.
Note(s): Used after build date February 15, 1968. No depression for side reflector. Also, there is a change in the quarter vents.

Interchange Number: 38
Part Number(s): C8ZZ7627840B (right), C8ZZ7627841B (left)
Usage: Late-1968 Mustang convertible
Note(s): Used after build date February 15, 1968. No depression for side reflector.

Interchange Number: 39
Part Number(s): C9ZZ6527840A (right), C9ZZ6527841A (left)
Usage: 1969 Mustang hardtop

151

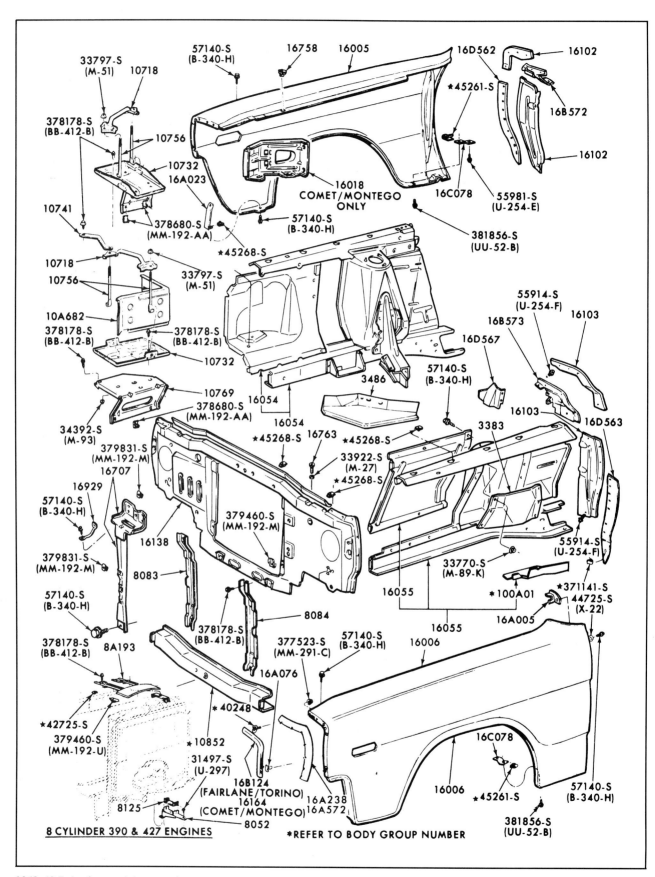

33797-S (M-51)
10718
378178-S (BB-412-B)
10756
10732
16A023
10741
378680-S (MM-192-AA)
10718
10756
10A682
378178-S (BB-412-B)
378178-S (BB-412-B)
10732
34392-S (M-93)
10769
378680-S (MM-192-AA)
379831-S (MM-192-M)
16707
16929
57140-S (B-340-H)
379831-S (MM-192-M)
16138
8083
57140-S (B-340-H)
378178-S (BB-412-B)
8A193
*42725-S
379460-S (MM-192-U)
*10852
31497-S (U-297)
16B124 (FAIRLANE/TORINO)
16164 (COMET/MONTEGO)
8125
8052

8 CYLINDER 390 & 427 ENGINES

57140-S (B-340-H)
16758
16005
16D562
16102
*45261-S
16B572
16102
55981-S (U-254-E)
16C078
381856-S (UU-52-B)
16018 COMET/MONTEGO ONLY
57140-S (B-340-H)
*45268-S
16054
3486
16054
*45268-S
16763
*45268-S
33922-S (M-27)
*45268-S
57140-S (B-340-H)
379460-S (MM-192-M)
16055
8084
377523-S (MM-291-C)
57140-S (B-340-H)
16A076
*40248
16A238
16A572
16006

55914-S (U-254-F)
16B573
16D567
16103
16103
16D563
55914-S (U-254-F)
3383
33770-S (M-89-K)
*100A01
16A005
*371141-S
44725-S (X-22)
3383
57140-S (B-340-H)
16006
16C078
16055
*45261-S
57140-S (B-340-H)
381856-S (UU-52-B)

**REFER TO BODY GROUP NUMBER

1968–69 Torino front-end sheet metal.

152

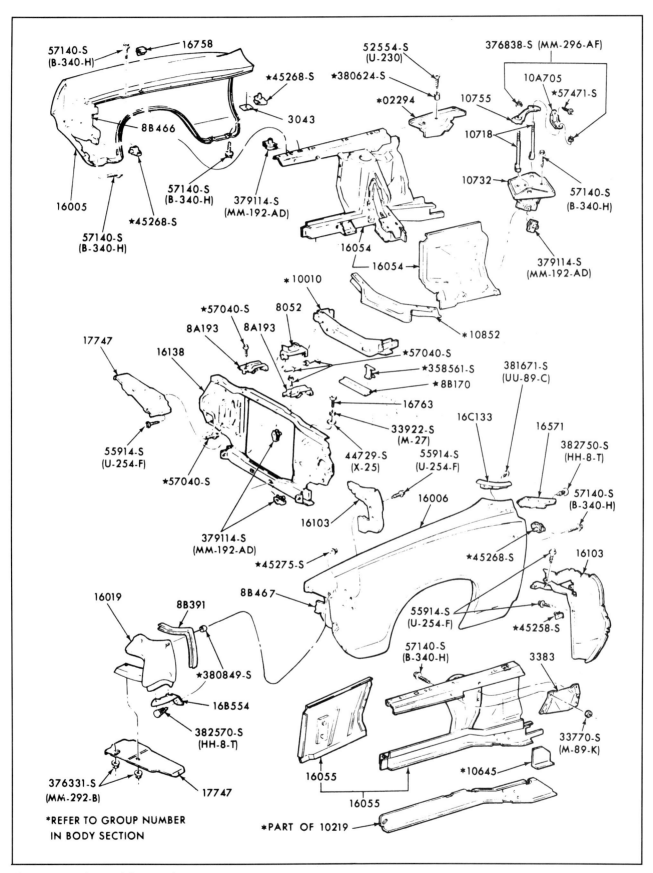

57140-S (B-340-H)
16758
*45268-S
3043
8B466
16005
57140-S (B-340-H)
*45268-S
57140-S (B-340-H)
379114-S (MM-192-AD)

52554-S (U-230)
*380624-S
*02294
10755
16054
16054

376838-S (MM-296-AF)
10A705
*57471-S
10718
10732
57140-S (B-340-H)
379114-S (MM-192-AD)

*10010
*57040-S
8A193   8A193
8052
16138
17747
*57040-S
55914-S (U-254-F)
379114-S (MM-192-AD)
*57040-S
*358561-S
*8B170
16763
33922-S (M-27)
44729-S (X-25)
55914-S (U-254-F)
16103
*10852
381671-S (UU-89-C)
16C133
16571
382750-S (HH-8-T)
57140-S (B-340-H)
16006
*45268-S
16103

16019
8B391
*380849-S
16B554
382570-S (HH-8-T)
376331-S (MM-292-B)
17747
8B467
*45275-S
55914-S (U-254-F)
*45258-S
57140-S (B-340-H)
16055
16055
*PART OF 10219
*10645
3383
33770-S (M-89-K)

*REFER TO GROUP NUMBER IN BODY SECTION

1970–71 Torino front-end sheet metal.

153

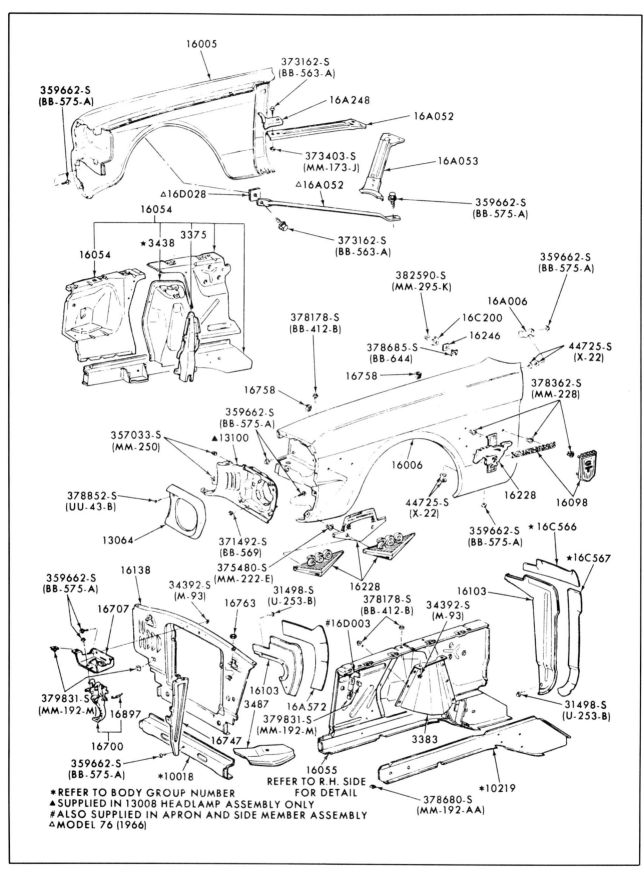

16005

373162-S
(BB-563-A)

359662-S
(BB-575-A)

16A248

16A052

373403-S
(MM-173-J)

16A053

△16A052

359662-S
(BB-575-A)

△16D028

16054

3375

★3438

16054

373162-S
(BB-563-A)

359662-S
(BB-575-A)

382590-S
(MM-295-K)

16A006

378178-S
(BB-412-B)

16C200

16246

44725-S
(X-22)

378685-S
(BB-644)

16758

16758

378362-S
(MM-228)

359662-S
(BB-575-A)

357033-S
(MM-250)

▲13100

378852-S
(UU-43-B)

16006

16228

16098

13064

371492-S
(BB-569)

375480-S
(MM-222-E)

44725-S
(X-22)

359662-S
(BB-575-A)

★16C566

★16C567

16228

16138

34392-S
(M-93)

16763

31498-S
(U-253-B)

378178-S
(BB-412-B)

34392-S
(M-93)

16103

359662-S
(BB-575-A)

#16D003

16707

16103

31498-S
(U-253-B)

379831-S
(MM-192-M)

16897

16A572

379831-S
(MM-192-M)

3487

3383

16700

16747

359662-S
(BB-575-A)

*10018

16055

REFER TO R.H. SIDE
FOR DETAIL

*10219

378680-S
(MM-192-AA)

★REFER TO BODY GROUP NUMBER
▲SUPPLIED IN 13008 HEADLAMP ASSEMBLY ONLY
#ALSO SUPPLIED IN APRON AND SIDE MEMBER ASSEMBLY
△MODEL 76 (1966)

1964-1/2–66 Mustang front-end sheet metal.

154

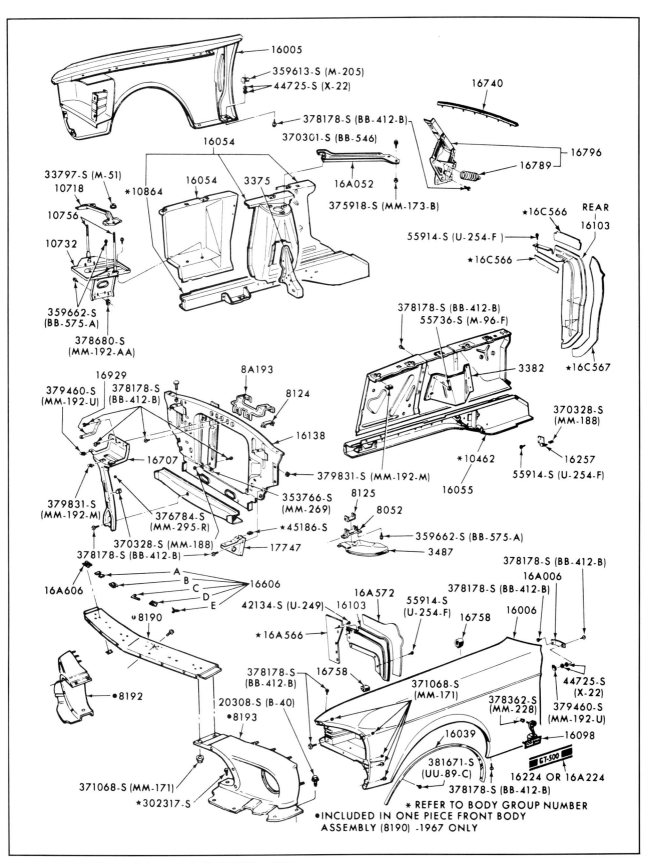

16005
359613-S (M-205)
44725-S (X-22)
378178-S (BB-412-B)
370301-S (BB-546)
16054
16A052
375918-S (MM-173-B)
16740
16796
16789
33797-S (M-51)
10718
10756
10732
16054
*10864
3375
359662-S (BB-575-A)
378680-S (MM-192-AA)
*16C566
REAR
16103
55914-S (U-254-F)
*16C566
*16C567
378178-S (BB-412-B)
55736-S (M-96-F)
3382
370328-S (MM-188)
16257
55914-S (U-254-F)
*10462
16055
16929
379460-S (MM-192-U)
378178-S (BB-412-B)
8A193
8124
16138
16707
379831-S (MM-192-M)
379831-S (MM-192-M)
376784-S (MM-295-R)
353766-S (MM-269)
8125
8052
*45186-S
370328-S (MM-188)
17747
359662-S (BB-575-A)
378178-S (BB-412-B)
3487
16A606
A
B
C
D
E
16606
•8190
42134-S (U-249)
16103
*16A566
16758
16A572
55914-S (U-254-F)
378362-S (MM-228)
378178-S (BB-412-B)
16A006
378178-S (BB-412-B)
16006
16758
44725-S (X-22)
379460-S (MM-192-U)
•8192
378178-S (BB-412-B)
16758
371068-S (MM-171)
16039
16098
20308-S (B-40)
•8193
371068-S (MM-171)
*302317-S
381671-S (UU-89-C)
16224 OR 16A224
378178-S (BB-412-B)
GT-500
* REFER TO BODY GROUP NUMBER
•INCLUDED IN ONE PIECE FRONT BODY ASSEMBLY (8190) -1967 ONLY

1967–68 Mustang front-end sheet metal. GT 350/500, which has slightly different nose than standard Mustang is shown.

155

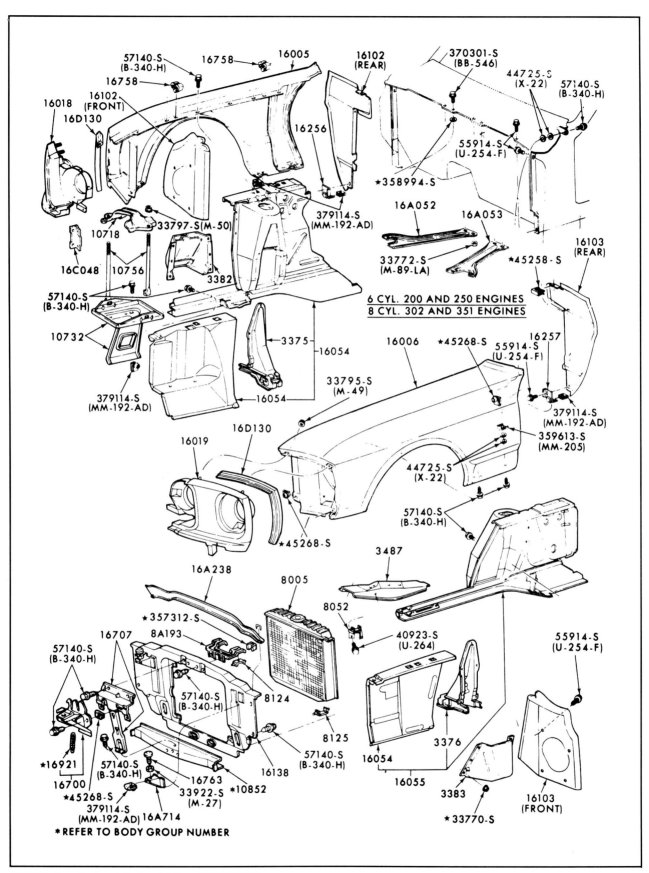

57140-S
(B-340-H)
16758
16102
(FRONT)
16018
16D130
16102
(REAR)
16005
16256
370301-S
(BB-546)
44725-S
(X-22)
57140-S
(B-340-H)
55914-S
(U-254-F)
*358994-S
16758
16A052
16A053
33772-S
(M-89-LA)
*45258-S
16103
(REAR)
33797-S(M-50)
10718
379114-S
(MM-192-AD)
16C048
10756
3382
57140-S
(B-340-H)
10732
3375
16054
16006
*45268-S
55914-S
(U-254-F)
16257
379114-S
(MM-192-AD)
6 CYL. 200 AND 250 ENGINES
8 CYL. 302 AND 351 ENGINES
359613-S
(MM-205)
379114-S
(MM-192-AD)
33795-S
(M-49)
16054
16D130
16019
44725-S
(X-22)
57140-S
(B-340-H)
*45268-S
3487
16A238
8005
8052
40923-S
(U-264)
55914-S
(U-254-F)
*357312-S
57140-S
(B-340-H)
8A193
16707
57140-S
(B-340-H)
57140-S
(B-340-H)
8124
8125
3376
16054
*16921
16700
57140-S
(B-340-H)
16763
*10852
57140-S
(B-340-H)
16138
16055
3383
16103
(FRONT)
*45268-S
379114-S
(MM-192-AD)
33922-S
(M-27)
16A714
*33770-S
*REFER TO BODY GROUP NUMBER

1969 Mustang front-end sheet metal. Except GT 350/500.

156

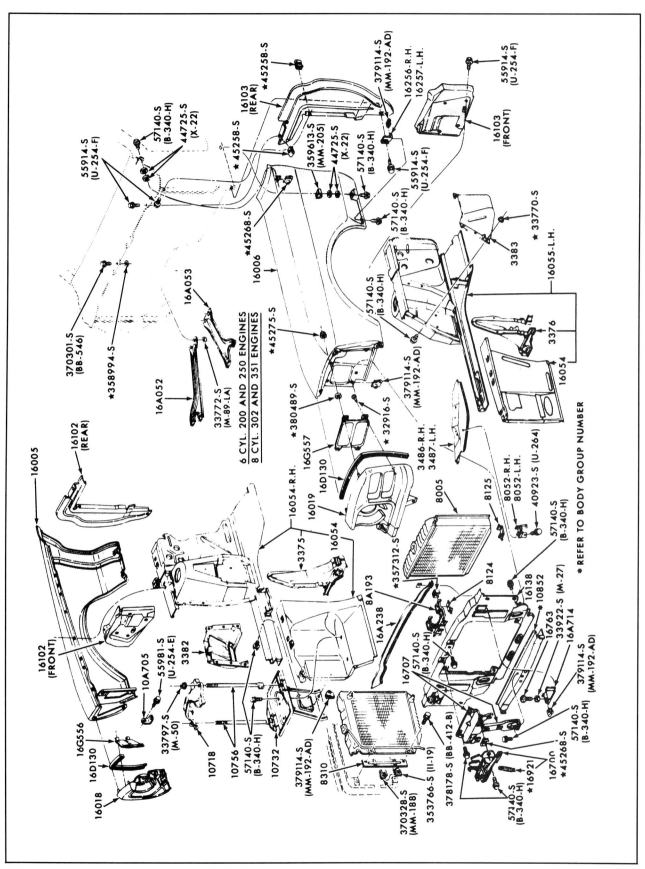

1970 Mustang front-end sheet metal. Except GT 350/500.

55914-S (U-254-F)

57140-S (B-340-H)
44725-S (X-22)

45258-S
16103 (REAR)

45258-S

★45268-S

16006

45275-S

359613-S (MM-205)
44725-S (X-22)
57140-S (B-340-H)

55914-S (U-254-F)

379114-S (MM-192-AD)
16256-R.H.
16257-L.H.

55914-S (U-254-F)

16103 (FRONT)

57140-S (B-340-H)

33770-S
3383
★33770-S
16055-L.H.

57140-S (B-340-H)

3376
16054

6 CYL. 200 AND 250 ENGINES
8 CYL. 302 AND 351 ENGINES

370301-S (BB-546)
★358994-S

16A053

16A052
33772-S (M-89-LA)
16A102 (REAR)

★380489-S
16G557

379114-S (MM-192-AD)
32916-S

3486-R.H.
3487-L.H.

8052-R.H.
8052-L.H.
8125
40923-S (U-264)

57140-S (B-340-H)

16005
16102 (REAR)

16054-R.H.

16019
16D130
16054

★357312-S

8005

8124

16138
10852
33922-S (M-27)
16A714

3375
16054

8A193
8A238
16A238

16707

57140-S (B-340-H)

16102 (FRONT)

10A705
55981-S (U-254-E)
3382
33797-S (M-50)
10718
10756
57140-S (B-340-H)
10732

379114-S (MM-192-AD)
8310

16G556
16D130
16018

16763
★16921
16700
★45268-S

57140-S (B-340-H)

379114-S (MM-192-AD)

★ REFER TO BODY GROUP NUMBER

370328-S (MM-188)
353766-S (II-19)
378178-S (BB-412-B)
57140-S (B-340-H)

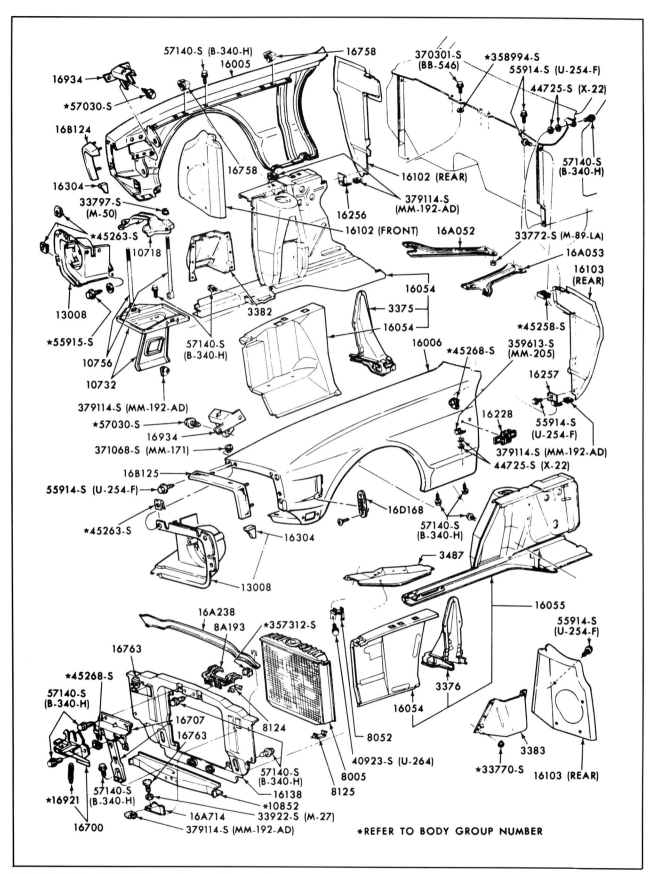

1969–70 GT 350 or GT 500 Mustang front end-sheet metal.

158

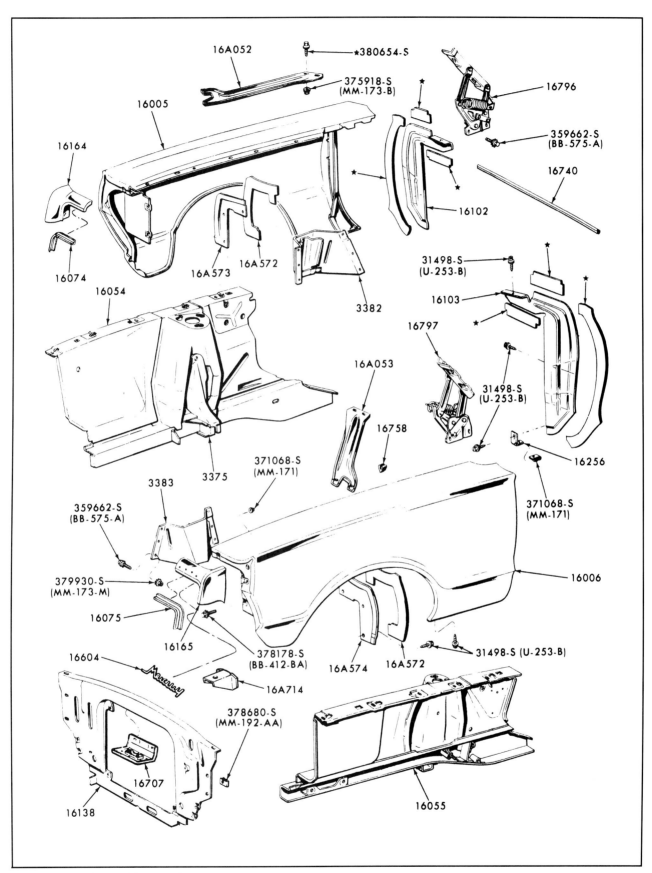

16A052

★380654-S

375918-S
(MM-173-B)

16005

16164

16796

359662-S
(BB-575-A)

16740

16102

16074

16A573

16A572

3382

31498-S
(U-253-B)

16103

16054

16797

31498-S
(U-253-B)

16A053

16758

16256

371068-S
(MM-171)

371068-S
(MM-171)

3383

3375

359662-S
(BB-575-A)

16006

379930-S
(MM-173-M)

16075

16165

378178-S
(BB-412-BA)

16A574

16A572

31498-S (U-253-B)

16604

16A714

378680-S
(MM-192-AA)

16707

16055

16138

1967–68 Cougar front end-sheet metal.

159

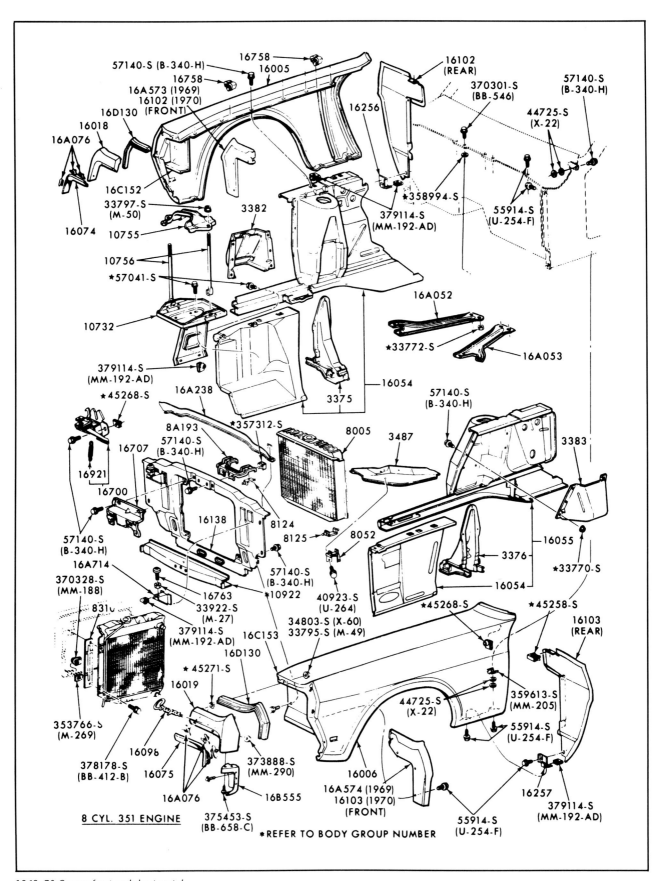

1969–70 Cougar front-end sheet metal.

Interchange Number: 40
Part Number(s): C9ZZ6327840A (right), C9ZZ6327841A (left)
Usage: 1969 Mustang fastback (except Boss 302ci) and 1969–70 GT 350 and GT 500 fastback,
Note(s): Features built-in scoop.

Interchange Number: 41
Part Number(s): C9ZZ6327840B (right), C9ZZ7637841B (left)
Usage: 1969 Boss 302ci
Note(s): Has no built-in side scoop. No other interchange.

Interchange Number: 42
Part Number(s): C9ZZ7627840A (right), C9ZZ7627841A (left)
Usage: 1969 Mustang convertible and 1969–70 GT 350 and GT 500 convertible

Interchange Number: 43
Part Number(s): DOZZ6527840A (right), DOZZ6527841A (left)
Usage: 1970 Mustang hardtop

Interchange Number: 44
Part Number(s): DOZZ7627840B (right), DOZZ7627841B (left)
Usage: 1970 Mustang convertible, all except GT 350 and GT 500

Interchange Number: 45
Part Number(s): DOZZ6327840B (right), DOZZ6327841B (left)
Usage: 1970 Mustang fastback, except GT 350 and GT 500

Interchange Number: 46
Part Number(s): DOZZ7627840ZZ (right), DOZZ7627841ZZ (left)
Usage: 1970 GT 350 and GT 500

Interchange Number: 47
Part Number(s): C5GY6227846A (right), C5GY6227841A (left)
Usage: 1965 Comet two-door sedan

Interchange Number: 48
Part Number(s): C5GY6327846A (right), C5GY6327841A (left)
Usage: 1965 Comet two-door hardtop

Interchange Number: 49
Part Number(s): C5GY7627846A (right), C5GY7627841A (left)
Usage: 1965 Comet convertible

Interchange Number: 50
Part Number(s): C7GY6327846A (right), C7GY6327841A (left)
Usage: 1966–67 Comet two-door hardtop

Interchange Number: 51
Part Number(s): C7GY6227846A (right), C7GY6227841A (left)
Usage: 1966–67 Comet two-door sedan

A regular Mustang quarter panel will fit the 1968 California Special, as the side scoops are add-on.

1969 Mustang fastbacks, except the Boss 302, have side scoops. These are for the GT 350 models.

Interchange Number: 52
Part Number(s): C7GY7627846A (right), C7GY7627841A (left)
Usage: 1966–67 Comet convertible

Interchange Number: 53
Part Number(s): C8GY7627846A (right), C8GY67627841A (left)
Usage: 1968–69 Montego convertible

Interchange Number: 54
Part Number(s): C9GY6527846B (right), C9GY6327841B (left)
Usage: 1968–69 Montego two-door hardtop

Interchange Number: 55
Part Number(s): C9GY6327846B (right), C9GY6327841B (left)
Usage: 1968–69 Montego fastback

Interchange Number: 56
Part Number(s): DOGY6527846A (right), DOGY6527841A (left)
Usage: 1970–71 Montego two-door hardtop

Interchange Number: 57
Part Number(s): DOGY6327846A (right), DOGY6327841A (left)
Usage: 1970–71 Montego fastback

Interchange Number: 58
Part Number(s): DOGY7627846A (right), DOGY7627841A (left)
Usage: 1970–71 Montego convertible

Interchange Number: 59
Part Number(s): C7WY6527846A (right), C7WY6527841A (left)
Usage: 1967–68 Cougar two-door hardtop

Interchange Number: 60
Part Number(s): C7WY7627846A (right), C7WY7627841A (left)
Usage: 1967–68 Cougar convertible

Interchange Number: 61
Part Number(s): C9WY6527846A (right), C9WY6527841A (left)
Usage: 1969 Cougar two-door hardtop

Interchange Number: 62
Part Number(s): C9WY7627846A (right), C7WY7627841A (left)
Usage: 1969 Cougar convertible

Interchange Number: 63
Part Number(s): DOWY6527846A (right), DOWY6527841A (left)
Usage: 1970 Cougar two-door hardtop, all except Eliminator

Interchange Number: 64
Part Number(s): DOWY6527846C (right), DOWY6527841B* or DOWY6527841C (left)
Usage: 1970 Cougar Eliminator
Note(s): Left panel changed during model year run; change date is May 1, 1970. *Panel used before that date. The later unit can fit earlier models, but the earlier panel will not fit later models.

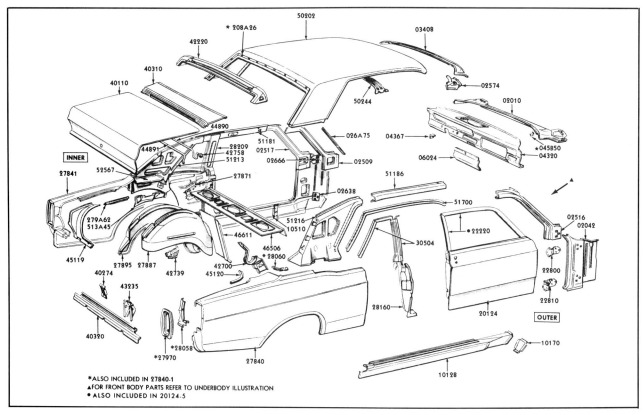

1966–67 Fairlane two-door hardtop sheet metal.

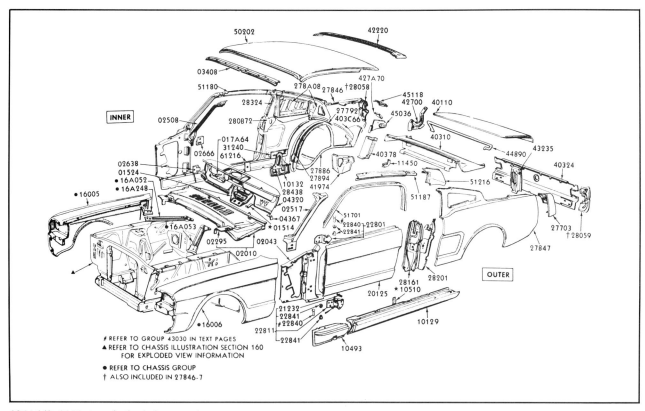

1964-1/2–66 Mustang fastback sheet metal.

162

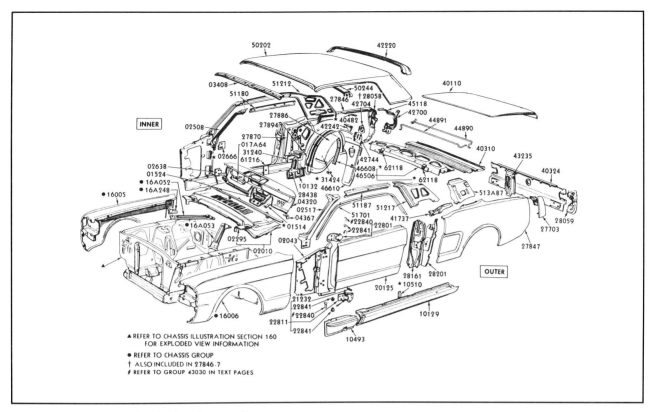

1964-1/2–66 Mustang two-door hardtop sheet metal.

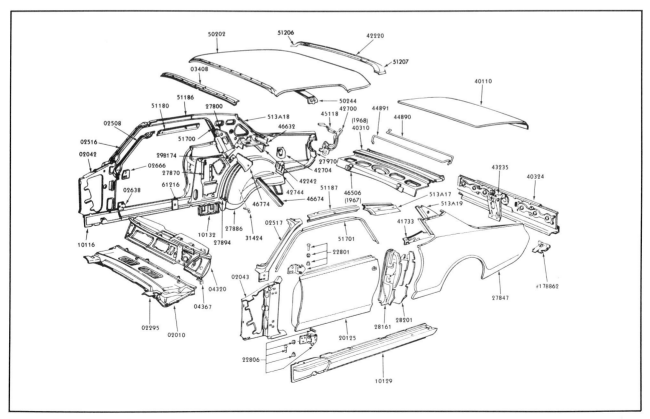

1967–68 Cougar hardtop sheet metal.

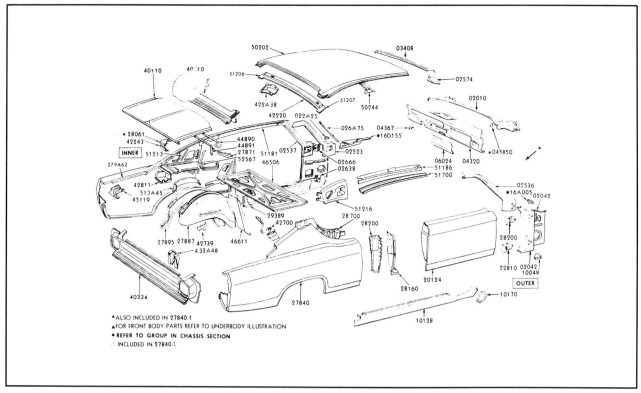

1968–69 Torino fastback.

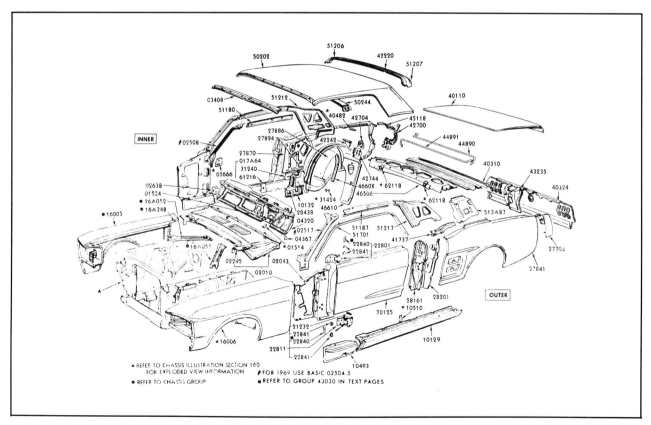

1967–68 Mustang hardtop sheet metal.

164

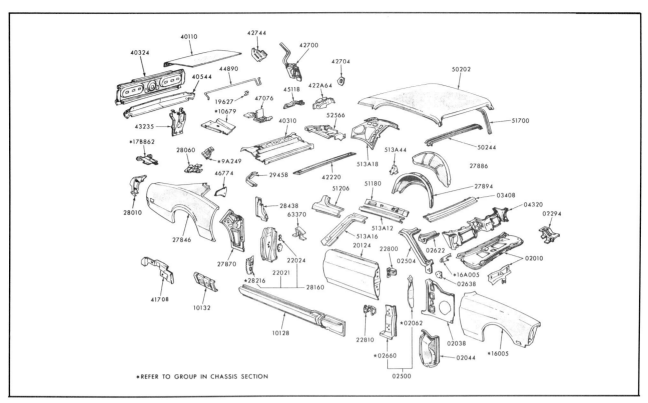

1969–70 Cougar hardtop sheet metal.

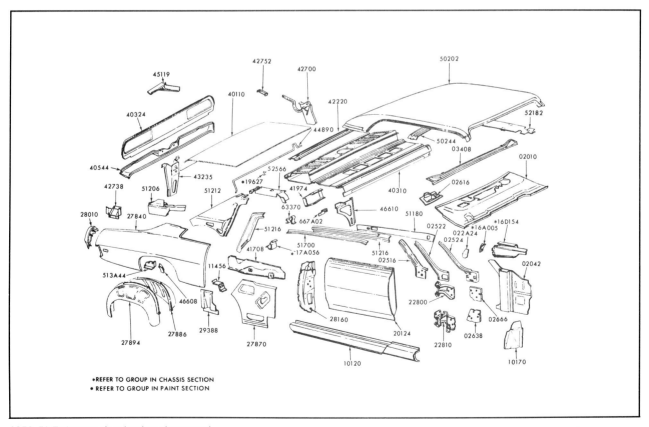

1970–71 Torino two-door hardtop sheet metal.

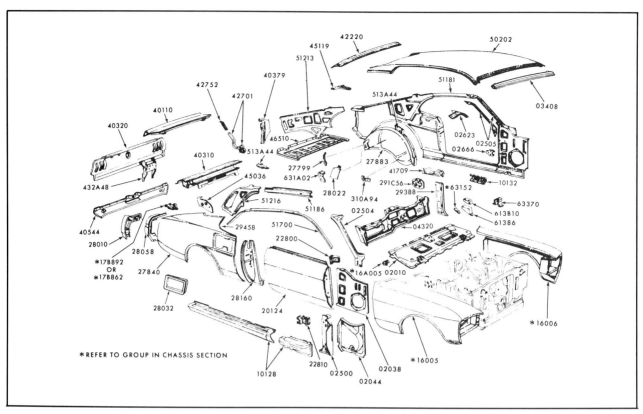

1969–70 Mustang fastback sheet metal.

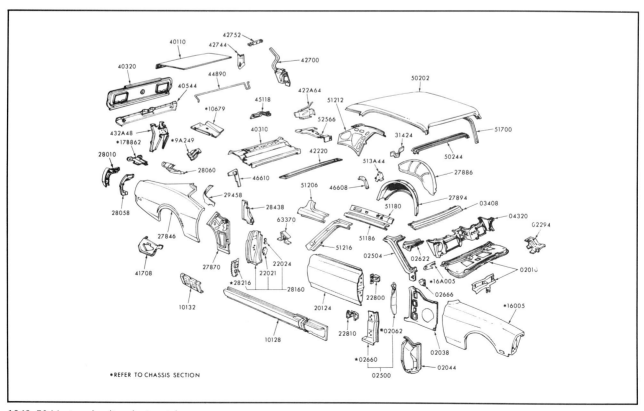

1969–70 Mustang hardtop sheet metal.

Interchange Number: 65
Part Number(s): DOWY7627846A (right), DOWY7627841A (left)
Usage: 1970 Cougar two-door convertible built before May 1, 1970

Interchange Number: 66
Part Number(s): DOWY7627846B (right), DOWY7627841B (left)
Usage: 1970 Cougar two-door convertible built after May 1, 1970

Interchange Number: 67
Part Number(s): DOOZ7627846B (right), DOOZ7627841B (left)
Usage: 1970–71 Torino convertible

Interchange Number: 68
Part Number(s): DOOZ7662846A (right), DOOZ6627841A (left)
Usage: 1970–71 Ranchero

Deck Lid
Some body styles will greatly influence the interchangeability of deck lids. Fastbacks use a much narrower deck lid than do other body styles. You should find a deck lid that is clean and free of damage, rust, and if possible, any additional trim. Interchange below is without hinges, nameplates, or trim.

Model Identification

Cougar	Interchange Number
1967–68, all	28
1969–70, all	29

Cyclone	Interchange Number
1965, all	25
1966–67, all	26
1968–69	
all except fastback	27
fastback	10
1970	
all except fastback	12
fastback	13

Fairlane and Torino	Interchange Number
1959	
all except retractable hardtop	2
retractable hardtop	1
1960, all	3
1961	
Galaxie except convertible	5
Galaxie convertible	4
all except Galaxie	4
1962–63, all	6

1964, all	7
1965, all	8
1966–67, all	9
1968–69	
all except fastback	11
fastback	10
1970	
all except fastback	12
fastback	13

Mustang	Interchange Number
1964-1/2–66	
all except fastback	15
fastback	14
1967–68	
all except fastback and 1968 GT/CS, 1968 High Country, and GT 350 and GT 500 convertible and fastback	17
1968 California Special	18
1968 High Country	18
GT 350 and GT 500	
fastback	19
convertible	20

Fastback Mustangs used a special deck lid. Shown is the 1965–66 style.

All body styles of 1966–67 Fairlanes used the deck lid.

1964-1/2–66 Mustang hardtop or convertible used the same deck lid.

Deck lids are the same in 1967 and 1968 for hardtop or convertible.

1969–70 Mustang convertible and hardtops used this deck lid.

Interchange

Interchange Number: 1
Part Number(s): B9A5140110A
Usage: 1959 full-size Ford with retractable hardtop

Interchange Number: 2
Part Number(s): B9A6440110B
Usage: 1959 full-size Ford—all body styles except retractable hardtop

Interchange Number: 3
Part Number(s): COAB6340110F
Usage: 1960 full-size Ford—all body styles

Interchange Number: 4
Part Number(s): C1AB6340110B
Usage: 1961 full-size Ford in these body styles—Fairlane/Custom four-door sedan, Starliner two-door hardtop, two-door sedan, and Galaxie convertible

Interchange Number: 5
Part Number(s): C1AB6240110B
Usage: 1961 Galaxie two- and four-door sedan and hardtop

Interchange Number: 6
Part Number(s): C2OZ6240110B
Usage: 1962–63 Fairlane—all models and body styles

Interchange Number: 7
Part Number(s): C4OZ6240110B
Usage: 1964 Fairlane—all models and body styles

Interchange Number: 8
Part Number(s): C5OZ6240110A
Usage: 1965 Fairlane—all models and body styles

Interchange Number: 9
Part Number(s): C6OZ6240110C
Usage: 1966–67 Fairlane—all models and body styles

Interchange Number: 10
Part Number(s): C8OZ6340110A
Usage: 1968–69 Torino and Montego fastback only

Interchange Number: 11
Part Number(s): C9OZ5440110A
Usage: 1968–69 Torino—all models and body styles except fastback

Interchange Number: 12
Part Number(s): DOOZ6540110A
Usage: 1970–71 Torino and Montego—all body styles except fastback

Interchange Number: 13
Part Number(s): D1OZ6540110A
Usage: 1970–71 Torino and Montego fastback only

Interchange Number: 14
Part Number(s): C5ZZ6340110A
Usage: 1965–66 Mustang fastback only

Interchange Number: 15
Part Number(s): C5ZZ6540110A
Usage: 1964-1/2–66 Mustang—all models and body styles except fastback

Interchange Number: 16
Part Number(s): C7ZZ6340110C
Usage: 1967–68 Mustang fastback only

Interchange Number: 17
Part Number(s): C7ZZ6540110C
Usage: 1967–68 Mustang—all body styles except fastback and all models except GT 350, GT 500, and GT/CS

Example of the 1967–68 Mustang fastback deck lid.

168

Interchange Number: 18
Part Number(s): S8MS6540110A
Usage: 1968 Mustang GT/CS and High Country
Note(s): Interchange Number 20 may fit.

Interchange Number: 19
Part Number(s): S8MS6340110A
Usage: 1967–68 GT 350 and GT 500 fastback

Interchange Number: 20
Part Number(s): S8MS7640110A
Usage: 1967–68 GT 350 and GT 500 convertible

Interchange Number: 21
Part Number(s): DOZZ6340110A
Usage: 1969–70 Mustang fastback only, all except GT 350 and GT 500

Interchange Number: 22
Part Number(s): C9ZZ6540110A
Usage: 1969–70 Mustang—all body styles except fastback and all models except GT 350 and GT 500

Interchange Number: 23
Part Number(s): C9ZZ7640110A
Usage: 1969–70 GT 350 and GT 500 convertible

Interchange Number: 24
Part Number(s): C9ZZ6340110C
Usage: 1969–70 GT 350 and GT 500 fastback

Interchange Number: 25
Part Number(s): C5GY6540110C
Usage: 1965 Comet—all models and body styles

Interchange Number: 26
Part Number(s): C6GY6540110A
Usage: 1966–67 Comet—all models and body styles

Interchange Number: 27
Part Number(s): C9GY6540110A
Usage: 1968–69 Montego—all models and body styles except fastback

Interchange Number: 28
Part Number(s): C7WY6540110A
Usage: 1967–68 Cougar—all models and body styles

Interchange Number: 29
Part Number(s): C9WY6540110A
Usage: 1969–70 Cougar—all models and body styles

Tailgate (Ranchero Only)

Model Identification
1959...1
1966–70...2

Interchange

Interchange Number: 1
Part Number(s): B9A5940709A
Usage: 1959 Ranchero (see notes)
Note(s): 1959 full-size Ford station wagon tailgate can be adapted to fit by doing the following: 1) Remove glass and glass regulator. 2) Cover the top opening over with the proper moulding.

Interchange Number: 2
Part Number(s): C6DZ6640709D
Usage: 1966–71 Ranchero (see notes)
Note(s): 1966 Ranchero is based on Falcon body.

Hinges, Deck Lid/Tailgate

All hinges listed here are the bare hinges with mounting bracket but without torque rods. Some body styles will effect the interchange. Some hinges are universal fit, meaning one hinge will fit either side of the car, while others have specific usage and cannot swap sides.

The 1969–70 GT 350/500 models used two special deck lids: one for the rag top, and the other for the fastback, as shown here.

Model Identification

Cougar	Interchange Number
1967–70, all	16

Cyclone	Interchange Number
1966–67, all	17
1968–69	
all except fastback	6
fastback	7
1970, all	8

Fairlane and Torino	Interchange Number
1959 Ranchero	18
1960, all	1
1961, all	2
1962, all	3
1963–65, all	4
1966–67	
all except Ranchero	5
Ranchero	19
1968–69	
all except fastback and Ranchero	6
fastback	7
Ranchero	19
1970	
all except Ranchero	8
Ranchero	19

Mustang	Interchange Number
1964-1/2–66	
all except fastback	9
fastback	10
1967–68	
all except fastback	11
fastback	12
1969–70	
fastback	13
all except fastback	
1969, all	14
1970, all	15

Interchange

Interchange Number: 1
Part Number(s): COAB6442700B (fits either side)
Usage: 1960 full-size Ford, except station wagon

Interchange Number: 2
Part Number(s): C2AZ6242700A (right), C2AZ6242701A (left)
Usage: 1961–64 full-size Ford, except station wagon

Interchange Number: 3
Part Number(s): C2OZ6242700A (right), C2OZ6242701A (left)
Usage: 1962 Fairlane—all body styles

Interchange Number: 4
Part Number(s): C3OZ6242700A (right), C3OZ6242701A (left)
Usage: 1963–65 Fairlane—all body styles except station wagon

Interchange Number: 5
Part Number(s): C6OZ6242700A (right), C6OZ6242701A (left)
Usage: 1966–67 Fairlane and Falcon—all body styles except station wagon and Ranchero

Interchange Number: 6
Part Number(s): C8OZ6242700B (right), C8OZ6242701B (left)
Usage: 1968–69 Torino and Montego and 1968–70 Falcon—all body styles except fastback, station wagon, and Ranchero

Interchange Number: 7
Part Number(s): C8OZ6342700B (right), C8OZ632701B (left)
Usage: 1968–69 Torino and Montego fastback only

Interchange Number: 8
Part Number(s): C9AZ6242700B (right), C9AZ6242701B (left)
Usage: 1970–71 Torino and Montego and 1969–73 full-size Ford and full-size Mercury—all body styles except station wagon and Ranchero. Will fit fastback

Interchange Number: 9
Part Number(s): C4DZ6242700A (right), C4DZ622701A (left)
Usage: 1964-1/2–66 Mustang and 1964–65 Falcon—all body styles except fastback

Interchange Number: 10
Part Number(s): C5ZZ6342700A (right), C5ZZ632701A (left)
Usage: 1965–66 Mustang fastback only

Interchange Number: 11
Part Number(s): C7ZZ6342700D (right), C7ZZ632701D (left)
Usage: 1967–68 Mustang fastback only

Interchange Number: 12
Part Number(s): C7ZZ6542700C (right), C7ZZ652701C (left)
Usage: 1967–68 Mustang, all except fastback

Interchange Number: 13
Part Number(s): C9ZZ6342700A (right), C9ZZ632701A (left)
Usage: 1969–70 Mustang fastback only

Interchange Number: 14
Part Number(s): C9ZZ6542700A (right), C9ZZ652701A (left)
Usage: 1969 Mustang—all body styles except fastback (see notes for more interchanges)
Note(s): 1970 hinges (Interchange Number 15) will fit, but *always* replace with a pair of 1970 hinges.

Interchange Number: 15
Part Number(s): DOZZ6542700A (right), DOZZ654701A (left)
Usage: 1970 Mustang—all body styles except fastback
Note(s): Will fit 1969 Mustangs, if replaced in pairs.

Interchange Number: 16
Part Number(s): C7WY6542700A (right), C7WY6542701A (left)
Usage: 1967–70 Cougar—all body styles

Interchange Number: 17
Part Number(s): C6GY6542700A (right), C6GY6542701A (left)
Usage: 1966–67 Comet—all body styles except station wagon

Interchange Number: 18
Part Number(s): B9A7143000A (right), B9AB7143001A (left)
Usage: 1959 Ranchero and full-size Ford station wagon

Interchange Number: 19
Part Number(s): C6DZ7143000A (right), C6DZ7143001A (left)
Usage: 1966–71 Ranchero, 1966–67 Fairlane station wagon, 1968–71 Torino station wagon, 1966–71 Falcon station wagon, 1966–67 Comet station wagon, and 1968–71 Montego station wagon (see notes)
Note(s): All station wagons are those built after March 21, 1966, and with single-action tailgate only.

Bumper, Front
Interchange here is the basic bumper bar without any back struts or supports. Bumper bars are generally interchangeable between their own model and model year. However, there are cases on which other model years will interchange.

Model Identification

Cougar	Interchange Number
1967–68	21
1969–70	22

Cyclone	Interchange Number
1965	17
1966–67	18
1968–69	
all except Spoiler II	19
Spoiler II	23
1970	20

Fairlane and Torino	Interchange Number
1959	1
1960	2
1961	3
1962	4
1963	5
1964	6
1965	7
1966–67	8
1968–69	
all except Talladega or Ranchero	9
Talladega	10
Ranchero	11
1970	12

Mustang	Interchange Number
1964-1/2–66, all	13
1967–68, all	14
1969–70	
all except GT 350 and GT 500	15
GT 350 and GT 500	16

Interchange

Interchange Number: 1
Part Number(s): B9A17757A
Usage: 1959 full-size Ford—all body styles except Thunderbird

Interchange Number: 2
Part Number(s): COA17757B
Usage: 1960 full-size Ford—all body styles except Thunderbird

Interchange Number: 3
Part Number(s): C3MZ17757A
Usage: 1961–62 full-size Ford and 1963 full-size Mercury—all body styles

Interchange Number: 4
Part Number(s): C2OZ17757A
Usage: 1962 Fairlane—all body styles

Interchange Number: 5
Part Number(s): C3OZ17757B
Usage: 1963 Fairlane—all body styles

Interchange Number: 6
Part Number(s): C4OZ17757A
Usage: 1964 Fairlane—all body styles

Interchange Number: 7
Part Number(s): C5OZ17757A
Usage: 1965 Fairlane—all body styles

Interchange Number: 8
Part Number(s): C6OZ17757A
Usage: 1966–67 Fairlane—all body styles

Interchange Number: 9
Part Number(s): C8OZ17757A
Usage: 1968–69 Torino—all body styles except 1969 Talladega and Ranchero

Interchange Number: 10
Part Number(s): C9OZ17757C
Usage: 1969 Talladega (special flush-fit bumper)

Interchange Number: 11
Part Number(s): C9OZ17757B
Usage: 1968–69 Ranchero; no other interchange

Interchange Number: 12
Part Number(s): DOOZ17757A
Usage: 1970–71 Torino—all models and body styles

Interchange Number: 13
Part Number(s): C5ZZ17757A
Usage: 1964-1/2–66 Mustang—all models and body styles

Interchange Number: 14
Part Number(s): C7ZZ17757A
Usage: 1967–68 Mustang—all models and body styles

Interchange Number: 15
Part Number(s): C9ZZ17757A
Usage: 1969–70 Mustang—all models and body styles except GT 350 and GT 500

Interchange Number: 16
Part Number(s): C9ZZ17757B
Usage: 1969–70 GT 350 and GT 500 models only—all body styles

Interchange Number: 17
Part Number(s): C5GY17757A
Usage: 1965 Comet—all models and body styles

Interchange Number: 18
Part Number(s): C65GY17757A
Usage: 1966–67 Comet—all models and body styles

Interchange Number: 19
Part Number(s): C8GY17757A
Usage: 1968–69 Montego—all models and body styles, except Spoiler II

Interchange Number: 20
Part Number(s): DOGY17757A
Usage: 1970–71 Montego—all models and body styles

Interchange Number: 21
Part Number(s): C7WGY17757A
Usage: 1967–68 Cougar—all models and body styles

Interchange Number: 22
Part Number(s): DOWY17757A
Usage: 1969–70 Cougar—all models and body styles

Interchange Number: 23
Part Number(s): C9GY17757E
Usage: 1969 Cyclone spoiler II (flush-fitting)

Bumper, Rear

Interchange here is the basic bumper bar without any back struts or supports. Rear bumpers are more interchangeable than their front counterparts, as some Torinos and Montegos used the same bumpers.

Model Identification

Interchange

Interchange Number: 1
Part Number(s): B9AB17906A
Usage: 1959 full-size Ford—all body styles

Interchange Number: 2
Part Number(s): COAB17906C (one-piece)
Usage: 1960–61 full-size Ford—all body styles except those with "Continental spare kit."
Note(s): A few models came with a three-piece bumper.

Interchange Number: 3
Part Number(s): C3OZ17906A
Usage: 1962–64 Fairlane—all models and body styles

Interchange Number: 4
Part Number(s): C5OZ17906A
Usage: 1965 Fairlane—all models and body styles

Interchange Number: 5
Part Number(s): C6OZ17906A
Usage: 1966–67 Fairlane—all models and body styles except Ranchero and station wagon

Interchange Number: 6
Part Number(s): C8OZ17906A
Usage: 1968–69 Torino (all body styles except Ranchero and station wagon) and 1968–69 Montego fastback only

Interchange Number: 7
Part Number(s): DOOZ17906A
Usage: 1970–71 Torino—all body styles except Ranchero and station wagon

Interchange Number: 8
Part Number(s): DOOZ17906B
Usage: 1966–71 Ranchero, 1966–67 Fairlane station wagon, 1968–69 Torino station wagon, 1966–67 Comet station wagon, and 1968–71 Montego station wagon
Note(s): 1966–70 Falcon station bumper will also fit, even though the part number (C6OZ17906B) is different.

Interchange Number: 9
Part Number(s): C5ZZ17906A
Usage: 1964-1/2–66 Mustang—all models and body styles

Interchange Number: 10
Part Number(s): C7ZZ17906A
Usage: 1967–68 Mustang—all models and body styles

Interchange Number: 11
Part Number(s): C9ZZ17906A
Usage: 1969–70 Mustang—all models and body styles

Interchange Number: 12
Part Number(s): C5GY17906A
Usage: 1965 Comet—all models and body styles except station wagon

Interchange Number: 13
Part Number(s): C6GY17906A
Usage: 1966 Comet—all models and body styles except station wagon

Interchange Number: 14
Part Number(s): C7GY17906A
Usage: 1967 Comet—all models and body styles except station wagon

Interchange Number: 15
Part Number(s): C8GY17906A
Usage: 1968–69 Montego—all models and body styles except station wagon and fastback

Interchange Number: 16
Part Number(s): DOGY17906A
Usage: 1970–71 Montego—all models and body styles except station wagon

Interchange Number: 17
Part Number(s): C7WY17906A
Usage: 1967–68 Cougar—all models and body styles

Interchange Number: 18
Part Number(s): C9WY17906A
Usage: 1969–70 Cougar—all models and body styles

Interchange Number: 19
Part Number(s): C9GY17906B
Usage: 1968–69 Montego fastback

Grille

Grilles are usually changed each year and differ between some models and submodels. However, some grilles can be modified (painted) to adapted them to other models. If this is the case, it is noted under the heading Modifications/Notes.

Model Identification

Regular 1966 Fairlane grille can be painted to match the GT style. Regular grille is shown.

1959 full-size Fords used a bright-plated grille.

1964-1/4–65 Mustang with fog lamps used a special grille.

Interchange

Interchange Number: 1
Part Number(s): B9A8200A
Usage: 1959 full-size Fords—all models and body styles except Thunderbird

Interchange Number: 2
Part Number(s): C0AZ8200A
Usage: 1960 full-size Fords—all models and body styles except Thunderbird

Interchange Number: 3
Part Number(s): C1AZ8200B
Usage: 1961 full-size Fords—all models and body styles except Thunderbird

Interchange Number: 4
Part Number(s): C2OZ8200A
Usage: 1962 Fairlane—all models and body styles

Interchange Number: 5
Part Number(s): C3OZ8200A
Usage: 1963 Fairlane—all models and body styles

1969 Mustang grille.

Interchange Number: 6
Part Number(s): C4OZ8200A
Usage: 1964 Fairlane—all models and body styles

Interchange Number: 7
Part Number(s): C5OZ8200A, Main section
Usage: 1965 Fairlane—all models and body styles

Interchange Number: 8
Part Number(s): C6OZ8200A (main section), C6OZ13064A (left bezel), C6OZ13064B (right bezel)
Usage: 1966 Fairlane—all models and body styles except GT and GTA models

Interchange Number: 9
Part Number(s): C6OZ8200B (main section), C6OZ13064A (left bezel), C6OZ13064B (right bezel)
Usage: 1966 Fairlane GT and GTA models
Modification/Note(s): Interchange Number 8 will fit if background pattern is painted to duplicate the GT look. Paint must be baked-on to adhere to the aluminum properly.

Interchange Number: 10
Part Number(s): C7OZ8200A (main section), C7OZ13064A (left bezel), C7OZ13064B (right bezel)
Usage: 1967 Fairlane—all models and body styles except GT

Interchange Number: 11
Part Number(s): C7OZ8200B (main section), C7OZ13064C (left bezel), C7OZ13064D (right bezel)
Usage: 1967 Fairlane GT
Modification/Note(s): Black-accented grille. Interchange Number 10 will fit if background egg-crate pattern is painted to duplicate the GT look.

1968 Mustang grille without fog lamps.

1969–70 GT 350/500 Mustang grille.

173

Interchange Number: 12
Part Number(s): C8OZ8200B (main section), C8OZ13064A (left bezel), C8OZ13064B (right bezel)
Usage: 1968 Torino—all models and body styles including GT (see notes)
Modification/Note(s): Original GT grille. Replacement grille for all models. Paint original non-GT grille to match.

Interchange Number: 13
Part Number(s): C9OZ8200A (main section), C9OZ13064J (left bezel), C9OZ13064K (right bezel)
Usage: 1969, all true Fairlane (not for GT and Torino-based models)

Interchange Number: 14
Part Number(s): C9OZ8200B (main section), C9OZ13064G (left bezel), C9OZ13064H (right bezel)
Usage: 1969, all true Torinos including GT models, Ranchero Custom and Ranchero GT, and Country Squire wagons; not for Cobra

Interchange Number: 15
Part Number(s): C9OZ8200D (main section), C9OZ13064M (left bezel), C9OZ13064L (right bezel)
Usage: 1969 Cobra models only
Modification/Note(s): Interchange Number 13 will fit if painted flat black.

Interchange Number: 16
Part Number(s): D10Z8200A (main section), DOOZ13064B (left bezel), DOOZ13064A (right bezel)
Usage: 1970 true Fairlane until build date December 30, 1969 (does not include GT and Cobra)

Interchange Number: 17
Part Number(s): DO0Z8200C (main section), DOOZ13064D (left bezel), DOOZ13064C (right bezel)
Usage: 1970 Torino (all year long), except Cobra, and 1970 Fairlane, after build date December 30, 1970
Modifications/Note(s): Main section can be used with hidden headlamps.

Interchange Number: 18
Part Number(s): DO0Z8200E (main section), DOOZ13064F (left bezel), DOOZ13064E (right bezel)
Usage: 1970 Cobra fastback

Interchange Number: 19
Part Number(s): C5ZZ8200C# or C5ZZ8200D* (main section), C5ZZ13064B (right bezel), C5ZZ13064A (left bezel)
Usage: 1964-1/2–65 Mustang (see notes)
Modifications/Notes: #With fog lamps; *without fog lamps. Bezels also used on 1966 Mustangs.

1967–68 Cougar grille.

1970 Cougar XR7 center grille.

Interchange Number: 20
Part Number(s): C6ZZZ8200A (main section), C5ZZ13064B (right bezel), C5ZZ13064A (left bezel)
Usage: 1966 Mustang (see notes)
Modifications/Notes: Bezels used on 1964-1/2–65 Mustangs.

Interchange Number: 21
Part Number(s): C7ZZZ8200A (main section)
Usage: 1967 Mustang—all except GT 350 and GT 500 models

Interchange Number: 22
Part Number(s): S7MS8220B
Usage: 1967 Mustang GT 350 and GT 500 only

Interchange Number: 23
Part Number(s): C8ZZ8200A
Usage: 1968 Mustang—all without fog lamps except GT 350, GT 500, GT/CS, and High Country

Interchange Number: 24
Part Number(s): C8ZZ8200B
Usage: 1968 Mustang—all without fog lamps except GT 350, GT 500, GT/CS, and High Country

Interchange Number: 25
Part Number(s): S8MS8220A
Usage: 1968 Mustang GT 350 and GT 500, GT/CS, and High Country

Interchange Number: 26
Part Number(s): C9ZZ8200A or C9ZZ8200C*
Usage: 1969 Mustang, all but GT 350 and GT 500 (see Notes)
Modifications/Note(s): *Grille has a bright frame. The other grille has a black frame.

Interchange Number: 27
Part Number(s): C9ZZ8200B
Usage: 1969–70 GT 350 and GT 500

Interchange Number: 28
Part Number(s): DOZZ8200A
Usage: 1970 Mustang—all without sport lamps except GT 350 and GT 500

Interchange Number: 29
Part Number(s): DOZZ8200B
Usage: 1970 Mustang—all with fog lamps except GT 350 and GT 500

Interchange Number: 30
Part Number(s): C5GY8200A
Usage: 1965 Comet—all models and body styles (see notes)
Note(s): For Cyclone, paint outer frame black and add center rectangular moulding.

Interchange Number: 31
Part Number(s): C6GY8200B
Usage: 1966 Cyclone models only

Interchange Number: 32
Part Number(s): C7GY8200B
Usage: 1967 Cyclone only

Interchange Number: 33
Part Number(s): See notes
Usage: 1968 Cyclone only
Modifications/ Note(s): Three-part design: none. C8GY8150B (right), C8GY8151B (left), Outer ends C8GY8200B (center).

Interchange Number: 34
Part Number(s): C9GY8150A (right), C9GY8151A (left) C9GY8200A (center)
Usage: 1969 Montego—all body styles except fastback

Interchange Number: 35
Part Number(s): C9GY8150B (right), C9GY8151B (left), C9GY8200B (center)
Usage: 1969 Montego fastback only, except Spoiler II

Interchange Number: 36
Part Number(s): C9OZ8200C
Usage: 1969 Spoiler II and Talladega—all except Sport Special

Interchange Number: 37
Part Number(s): C9OZ8200D
Usage: 1969 Spoiler II and Talladega Sport Special; has horizontal bars

Interchange Number: 38
Part Number(s): DOGY8224A (right), DOGY8224B (left), DOGY8200C (center)
Usage: 1970 Cyclone—all models and body styles
Modifications/Note(s): Outer ends are the same as on the 1971 Cyclone. For hide-away headlamps, use DOGY1304C (right) and DOGY1304D (left)

Interchange Number: 39
Part Number(s): C7WY8150B (right), C7WY8151B (left), C7WY8A047A (center)
Usage: 1967–68 Cougar—all except GTE

Interchange Number: 40
Part Number(s): C7WY8150C (right), C7WY8151C (left), C7WY8A047A (center)
Usage: 1968 Cougar GTE

Interchange Number: 41
Part Number(s): C9WY8150A (right), C7WY8151A (left), C9WY8200A (center)
Usage: 1969 Cougar—all except Eliminator

Interchange Number: 42
Part Number(s): C9WY8150C (right), C9WY8151C (left), C9WY8A047A (center)
Usage: 1969 Cougar Eliminator only

Interchange Number: 43
Part Number(s): DOWY8150A (right), DOWY8151A (left), DOWY16C706A (center), DOWY16A678A (on hood)
Usage: 1970 Cougar—all except Eliminator and XR7

Interchange Number: 44
Part Number(s): DOWY8150B (right), DOWY8151B (left), DOWY16C706B (center), DOWY16A678A (on hood)
Usage: 1970 Cougar XR7 only

Interchange Number: 45
Part Number(s): DOWY8150C (right), DOWY8151C (left), DOWY16C706C (center), DOWY16A678A (on hood)
Usage: 1970 Cougar Eliminator only
Note(s): Interchange Number 43 can be painted black and adapted for usage here.

Mirror, Exterior

Interchange is the entire mirror assembly and should include the mounting brackets. Inside mirror can be found in Chapter 11.

Mirrors are a general Ford Motor Company part, and there is a wide range of interchange available. Mirrors are identified by the basic functional (manual control or remote control), by the shape, and by an engineering number stamped on the bottom of the base. This number can be used for identification.

Model Identification

Cougar	*Interchange Number*
1967–68	
non-remote control	5
remote control	
rectangular head	7
racing mirror	18
1969	
non-remote control	5
remote control	
rectangular head	
all except XR7	20
XR7	n/a
racing mirror	19
1970	
non-remote control	5
remote control	
rectangular head	
all except XR7	20
XR7	n/a
racing mirror	21

Cyclone	*Interchange Number*
1965	
non-remote control	1, 2
remote control	6
1966	
non-remote control	2
remote control	6, 7
1967	
non-remote control	5
remote control	7
1968	
non-remote control	5
remote control with rectangular head	8
1969	
non-remote control	5
remote control	
rectangular head	8
racing mirror	9
1970	
non-remote control	5
remote control	
rectangular head	10
racing mirror	17

On the bottom of the mirror's base is the engineering number.

The conical-style mirror used on 1964 and 1965 Fords.

The standard mirror used on various models beginning in 1967.

Fairlane and Torino   Interchange Number

1959–65
    non-remote control
        conical 1
        round 2, 3
    remote control 6
1966
    non-remote control 4
    remote control 6, 7
1967
    non-remote control 5
    remote control 7
1968
    non-remote control 5
    remote control with rectangular head 8
1969
    non-remote control 5
    remote control
        rectangular head 8
        racing mirror 9
1970
    non-remote control 5
    remote control
        rectangular head 10
        racing mirror 11

Mustang   Interchange Number

1964-1/2–65
    non-remote control
        conical 1
        round head 4
    remote control 6
1966
    non-remote control 4
    remote control 6
1967
    non-remote control 5
    remote control 7
1968
    non-remote control 5
    remote control
        all except GT 350 and GT 500.......................7
        GT 350 and GT 500 18
1969
    non-remote control 5
    remote control
        all except Boss, Mach I, GT 350 and GT 500 12
        racing mirror 13
1970
    non-remote control 5
    remote control
        rectangular head 14
        racing mirror 15

Round head-style mirror standard in 1966 models.

Interchange

Interchange Number: 1
    Part Number(s): B5AZ17696A
    Type/Shape: Conical
    Engineering Number: C3RA17682D
    Type: Non-remote
    Usage: 1955–65 full-size Ford, 1960–65 Falcon, 1962–65 Fairlane, 1960–62 Thunderbird, 1960–65 full-size Mercury, 1963–65 Comet, and 1964-1/2–65 Mustang

Interchange Number: 2
    Part Number(s): C1SZ17696A
    Type/Shape: Round head
    Engineering Number: C3AB17682B
    Type: Non-remote
    Usage: 1963–66 full-size Ford, 1963–66 Falcon, 1961–62 Thunderbird, 1963–66 Fairlane, and 1965–66 Comet (except Capri)

Interchange Number: 3
Part Number(s): C2OZ17696A
Type/Shape: Round head
Engineering Number: C2RA17682A
Type: Non-remote
Usage: 1960–65 full-size Ford, 1960–65 Falcon, and 1962–65 Fairlane

Interchange Number: 4
Part Number(s): C3RZ17696A
Type/Shape: Round head
Engineering Number: C3RA17696A
Type: Non-remote
Usage: 1966 full-size Ford, 1966 Falcon, 1965–66 Mustang, 1966 Thunderbird, 1966 Fairlane, 1966 Bronco, and 1966 Falcon

Interchange Number: 5
Part Number(s): C8AZ17682B
Type/shape: Rectangular head
Engineering Number: C7AB17683A, C7AB17683B, C7TB17683U, and C7TB17683AB
Type: Non-remote
Usage: 1967–73 full-size Ford, 1967–70 Falcon, 1967 Fairlane, 1968–71 Torino, 1967 Comet, 1968–71 Montego, 1967–73 Mustang, 1967–73 Cougar, 1967–70 Thunderbird, 1967 Bronco, and 1967–73 full-size Mercury

Interchange Number: 6
Part Number(s): C5ZZ17682A
Type/Shape: Round head
Engineering Number: C3RA17682A, C3RA17217683C, C4RA17682A, C5RA17682A, C5ZB17682A, and C6OB17682A
Type: Remote control
Usage: 1963–66 Fairlane, 1963–66 full-size Ford, 1963–66 Falcon, 1964–66 Thunderbird, 1964-1/2–66 Mustang, and 1965 Comet (except Caliente)

Interchange Number: 7
Part Number(s): C7AZ17696E
Type/Shape: Rectangular head
Engineering Number: C7AB17683B, C7AB17683D, C7AB17683G, C7AB17683H, C7AB17683J, or C7OB17683B
Type: Remote control
Usage: 1967 Fairlane, 1967 full-size Ford, 1967 Falcon, 1967 Mustang, 1967 Comet, 1967 Cougar, and 1967 full-size Mercury

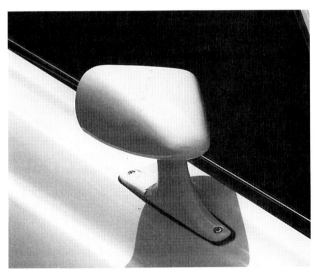

1970 Torino racing mirror. Showing is the passenger's side unit, which matches the driver's in looks.

1969 Mustang racing-style mirror.

Interchange Number: 8
Part Number(s): C8OZ17682C
Type/Shape: Rectangular head
Engineering Number: C8OB17683G
Type: Remote control
Usage: 1968–69 Torino and Montego—all body styles except four-door and station wagon

Interchange Number: 9
Part Number(s): C9OZ17682C
Type/Shape: Racing mirror
Engineering Number: C9OB17683AW or C9OB17683CW
Type: Remote control
Usage: 1969 Torino and Montego—all body styles except four-door and station wagon

Interchange Number: 10
Part Number(s): DOOZ17682A
Type/Shape: Rectangular head
Engineering Number: DOOB17683F
Type: Remote control
Usage: 1970 Torino and Montego—all body styles except four-door, station wagon, and two-door sedan

Interchange Number: 11
Part Number(s): DOOZ17682C
Type/Shape: Racing mirror
Engineering Number: DOOB17683GW
Type: Remote control
Usage: 1970 Torino—all body styles except four-door, station wagon, and two-door sedan; will not fit Montego

Interchange Number: 12
Part Number(s): C9ZZ17682B
Type/Shape: Rectangular head
Engineering Number: C9ZB17683D or C9ZB17683F
Type: Remote control
Usage: 1969 Mustang (base models only in fastback and all convertible); not for Mach I, Boss, or Shelby Mustangs.

Interchange Number: 13
Part Number(s): C9ZZ17682C or C9ZZ17682E*
Type/Shape: Racing
Engineering Number: C9ZB17683CW, C9ZB17683EW, or C9ZB17683GW*
Type: Remote control
Usage: 1969 Mustang—all body styles and models
Note(s): *After build date February 24, 1969

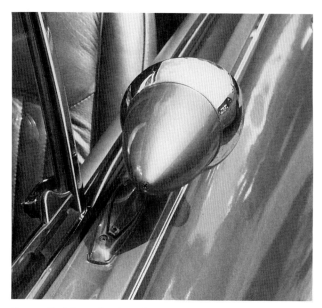

Cougar "bullet nose" racing mirror.

Interchange Number: 14
Part Number(s): DOZZ17682A
Type/Shape: Rectangular head
Engineering Number: DOZB17683A
Type: Remote control
Usage: 1970 Mustang—all models except Shelby

Interchange Number: 15
Part Number(s): DOZZ17682B
Type/Shape: Racing
Engineering Number: DOZB17683BW
Type: Remote control
Usage: 1970 Mustang

Interchange Number: 16
Part Number(s): C6GY17682A
Type/Shape: Rectangular head
Engineering Number: C6GB17682A
Type: Remote control
Usage: 1966 Comet—all models

Interchange Number: 17
Part Number(s): DOGY17682A
Type/Shape: Racing mirror
Engineering Number: DOGB17682GW
Type: Remote control
Usage: 1970 Montego two-door hardtop only

Interchange Number: 18
Part Number(s): C8WY17682H
Type/Shape: Racing mirror
Engineering Number: S8MS17683AP
Type: Remote control
Usage: 1968 Mustang GT 350 and GT 500 and 1968 Cougar XR7G

Interchange Number: 19
Part Number(s): C9WY17682D
Type/Shape: Racing mirror
Engineering Number: C9WB17683EW or C9WB17682HW
Type: Remote control
Usage: 1969 Cougar—all models

Interchange Number: 20
Part Number(s): C9WY17682B
Type/Shape: Rectangular head
Engineering Number: C9WB17683A or DOWB17683C
Type: Remote control
Usage: 1969–70 Cougar base models only; not for XR7

Interchange Number: 21
Part Number(s): DOWY17682B
Type/Shape: Racing mirror
Engineering Number: DOWB17683DW
Type: Remote control
Usage: 1970 Cougar—all models

Glass

General Interchange

Interchange here is "physical fit." There are two types of glass used: tinted and non-tinted. Tinted glass came in two forms: all-tinted glass; and with only the windshield tinted and the other glass untinted. Tinted glass was standard on air conditioned cars unless the customer specifically requested it not be. The interchanges do not consider tint, but you should match the glass to the rest of the car. For example, if your 1969 Cyclone GT has all-tinted glass, you should not replace the passenger's door glass with non-tinted glass.

Body style will greatly influence the interchangeability of the glass, especially door glass. But in certain models, even windshield or back glass can be affected by the body style.

Windshield

Model Identification

Cougar	Interchange Number
1967, all	13
1968, all	14
1969, all	15
1970, all	18

Cyclone	Interchange Number
1965 hardtop and convertible	19
1966–67	
sedan	8
hardtop and convertible	9
1968–69, all	10
1970	
all except fastback	12
fastback	11

Fairlane and Torino	Interchange Number
1959	
all except convertible	1
convertible	2
1960–61	
sedan	4
hardtop	3
convertible	5
1962–65	
sedan	6
hardtop	7
1966–67	
sedan	8
hardtop and convertible	9
1968–69, all	10
1970	
all except fastback	12
fastback	11

Mustang	Interchange Number
1964-1/2–67, all	13
1968, all	14

Interchange

Interchange Number: 1
NAGS Number: W571
Usage: 1959 full-size Ford—all body styles except convertible and folding hardtop

Interchange Number: 2
NAGS Number: W572
Usage: 1959 full-size Ford convertible and folding hardtop

Interchange Number: 3
NAGS Number: W598
Usage: 1960–61 full-size Ford two-door hardtop only

Interchange Number: 4
NAGS Number: W599
Usage: 1960–61 full-size Ford—all except two-door hardtop and convertible

Interchange Number: 5
NAGS Number: W615
Usage: 1960–61 full-size Ford convertible

Interchange Number: 6
NAGS Number: W619
Usage: 1962–65 Fairlane—all body styles except two-door hardtop

Interchange Number: 7
NAGS Number: W634
Usage: 1963–65 Fairlane two-door hardtop only

Interchange Number: 8
NAGS Number: W666
Usage: 1966–67 Fairlane, Comet, and Ranchero—all body styles except two-door hardtop and convertible

Interchange Number: 9
NAGS Number: W667
Usage: 1966–67 Fairlane and Comet two-door hardtop and convertible only

Interchange Number: 10
NAGS Number: W700
Usage: 1968–69 Torino and Montego, 1968–69 Ranchero—all two-door models, including hardtop, fastback, convertible, and pickup

Interchange Number: 11
NAGS Number: W735
Usage: 1970–71 Torino and Montego fastback only

Interchange Number: 12
NAGS Number: W736
Usage: 1970–71 Torino, Montego, and Ranchero—all body styles except fastback and station wagon, includes hardtop, convertible, and pickup

Interchange Number: 13
NAGS Number: W654
Usage: 1964-1/2–67 Mustang and 1967 Cougar—all body styles
Note(s): Interchange Number 14 will fit if you swap with 1968 mirror; will be visually incorrect.

Interchange Number: 14
NAGS Number: W703
Usage: 1968 Mustang and Cougar—all body styles

Interchange Number: 15
NAGS Number: W720
Usage: 1969 Mustang fastback only; no other interchange
Note(s): Interchange Number 17 may fit.

Body style may affect the windshield moldings.

Interchange Number: 16
NAGS Number: W721
Usage: 1969 Mustang (all body styles except fastback) and 1969 Cougar (all body styles)
Note(s): Interchange Number 18 may fit.

Interchange Number: 17
NAGS Number: W738
Usage: 1970 Mustang fastback only; no other interchange
Note(s): Interchange Number 15 may fit.

Interchange Number: 18
NAGS Number: W739
Usage: 1970 Mustang (all body styles except fastback) and 1970 Cougar (all body styles)
Note(s): Interchange Number 16 may fit.

Interchange Number: 19
NAGS Number: W635
Usage: 1965 Comet and Falcon—all two-door hardtop and convertible

Vent, Glass

Model Identification

Cougar	Interchange Number
1967–68, all	7

Cyclone	Interchange Number
1965 hardtop and convertible	8
1966–67	
sedan	5
hardtop and convertible	6

Fairlane and Torino	Interchange Number
1959, all	1
1960–61 hardtop and convertible	2
1962–65	
sedan	3
hardtop	4
1966–67	
sedan	5
hardtop and convertible	6

Mustang	Interchange Number
1964-1/2–68, all	7

Interchange

Interchange Number: 1
NAGS Number: 2250T
Usage: 1959 full-size Ford—all body styles

Interchange Number: 2

NAGS Number: 2314T

Usage: 1960–61 full-size Ford and full-size Mercury two-door hardtop and convertible only

Interchange Number: 3

NAGS Number: 2393T

Usage: 1962–65 Fairlane—all body styles except two-door hardtop

Interchange Number: 4

NAGS Number: 2427T

Usage: 1963–65 Fairlane two-door hardtop only

Interchange Number: 5

NAGS Number: V3516 (right), V3517 (left)

Usage: 1966–67 Fairlane, Comet, and Ranchero—all body styles except two-door hardtop and convertible; and 1968–71 Torino and Montego four-door sedans and station wagon (see notes)

Note(s): Station wagon only for 1970–71 models.

Interchange Number: 6

NAGS Number: V3539 (right), V3540 (left)

Usage: 1966–67 Fairlane and Comet two-door hardtop and convertible

Interchange Number: 7

NAGS Number: V3289 (right), V3290 (left)

Usage: 1964-1/2–68 Mustang and 1967–68 Cougar—all body styles

Interchange Number: 8

NAGS Number: 2312T

Usage: 1963–65 Comet and Falcon—all body styles except two-door hardtop and convertible

Interchange Number: 9

NAGS Number: 2430T

Usage: 1963–65 Comet and Falcon two-door hardtop and convertible models only

Door Side Glass

Model Identification

Cougar	Interchange Number
1967–68	
two-door hardtop	26
convertible	27
1969, all	28
1970	
bond-on type	31
bolt-on type	32

Cyclone	Interchange Number
1965	
sedan	35
hardtop and convertible	8
1966–67	
sedan	8
hardtop	11
convertible	9
1968	
all except sedan and convertible	12
convertible	14
1969	
all except sedan and convertible	15
convertible	17
1970	
all except convertible and fastback	18
convertible	19
fastback	20

Fairlane and Torino	Interchange Number
1959	
sedan	3
hardtop	1
convertible	2
1960–61	
sedan	4
hardtop	5
convertible	5
1962–65	
sedan	6
hardtop	7
1966–67	
sedan	8
hardtop	11
convertible	9
Ranchero	10
1968	
all except sedan, convertible, or Ranchero	12
convertible	14
Ranchero	13
1969	
all except sedan, convertible, or Ranchero	15
convertible	17
Ranchero	16
1970	
all except convertible, fastback, and Ranchero	18
convertible	19
Ranchero	21
fastback	20

Mustang	Interchange Number
1964-1/2–66	
hardtop	23
fastback	22
convertible	24
1967–68	
hardtop	26
fastback	25
convertible	27
1969	
all except fastback	28
fastback	29, 30
1970	
all except fastback	31, 32
fastback	29, 30

Interchange

Interchange Number: 1

NAGS Number: 4225T (fits either side)

Usage: 1959 full-size Ford two-door hardtop only; no other interchange

Interchange Number: 2

NAGS Number: 4228T (fits either side)

Usage: 1959 full-size Ford convertible, includes folding hardtop

Interchange Number: 3

NAGS Number: 4230T (fits either side)

Usage: 1959 full-size Ford two-door sedan only; no other interchange

Interchange Number: 4

NAGS Number: 4276T (fits either side)

Usage: 1960–61 full-size Ford two-door sedan only; no other interchange

Interchange Number: 5

NAGS Number: 4278T (fits either side)

Usage: 1960–61 full-size Ford two-door hardtop and convertible only

Interchange Number: 6

NAGS Number: 4357T (fits either side)

Usage: 1962–65 Fairlane two-door sedan only

Interchange Number: 7
NAGS Number: 2421T (fits either side)
Usage: 1963–65 Fairlane two-door hardtop only

Interchange Number: 8
NAGS Number: D3518 (right), D3519 (left)
Usage: 1966–67 Fairlane and Comet two-door sedan only

Interchange Number: 9
NAGS Number: D3546 (right), D3547 (left)
Usage: 1966–67 Fairlane and Comet convertible only

Interchange Number: 10
NAGS Number: D3537 (right), D3538 (left)
Usage: 1966–67 Ranchero

Interchange Number: 11
NAGS Number: D3541 (right), D3542 (left)
Usage: 1966–67 Fairlane and Comet two-door hardtop only

Interchange Number: 12
NAGS Number: D3537 (right), D3538 (left)
Usage: 1968 Torino and Montego two-door hardtop and fastback models

Interchange Number: 13
NAGS Number: D3537 (right), D3538 (left)
Usage: 1968 Ranchero

Interchange Number: 14
NAGS Number: D3922 (right), D3923 (left)
Usage: 1968 Torino and Montego convertible (see notes for exceptions)
Note(s): *Warning*—a change occurred in side glass midway through the model year. The NAGS number is the same for both sets, but they are not interchangeable, so go by these build dates: October 7, 1967 (Torino) and October 17, 1967 (Montego)

Interchange Number: 15
NAGS Number: D4129 (right), D4130 (left)
Usage: 1969 Torino and Montego two-door hardtop and fastback

Interchange Number: 16
NAGS Number: D4139 (right), D4140 (left)
Usage: 1969 Ranchero; no other interchange

Interchange Number: 17
NAGS Number: D4135 (right), D4136 (left)
Usage: 1969 Torino and Montego convertible

Interchange Number: 18
NAGS Number: D4328 (right), D4329 (left)
Usage: 1970–71 Torino and Montego two-door hardtop

Interchange Number: 19
NAGS Number: D4135 (right), D4136 (left)
Usage: 1970–71 Torino and Montego convertible

Interchange Number: 20
NAGS Number: D4323 (right), D4324 (left)
Usage: 1970–71 Torino and Montego fastback only

Interchange Number: 21
NAGS Number: D4378 (right), D4379 (left)
Usage: 1970–71 Ranchero

Interchange Number: 22
NAGS Number: D3330 (right), D3331 (left)
Usage: 1965–66 Mustang fastback

Interchange Number: 23
NAGS Number: D3295 (right), D3296 (left)
Usage: 1964-1/2–66 Mustang hardtop

Interchange Number: 24
NAGS Number: D3291 (right), D3292 (left)
Usage: 1964-1/2–66 Mustang convertible

Interchange Number: 25
NAGS Number: D3752 (right), D3753 (left)
Usage: 1967–68 Mustang fastback

Interchange Number: 26
NAGS Number: D3755 (right), D7566 (left)
Usage: 1967–68 Mustang and Cougar two-door hardtop only

Interchange Number: 27
NAGS Number: D3759 (right), D3580 (left)
Usage: 1967–68 Mustang and Cougar convertible

Interchange Number: 28
NAGS Number: D4121 (right), D4122 (left)
Usage: 1969 Mustang hardtop and convertible and 1969 Cougar (all body styles)

Interchange Number: 29
NAGS Number: D4116 (right), D4117 (left)
Usage: 1969–70 Mustang fastback with bond-on window

Interchange Number: 30
NAGS Number: D4280 (right), D4281 (left)
Usage: 1969–70 Mustang fastback with bolt-on design (see notes for exceptions)
Note(s): Change in glass occurred at build date October 1, 1969. Windows use same NAGS number but are different. Go by build date when interchanging.

Interchange Number: 31
NAGS Number: D4384 (right), D4385 (left)
Usage: 1970 Mustang hardtop and convertible and 1970 Cougar (all body styles); bond-on design

Interchange Number: 32
NAGS Number: D4282 (right), D4282 (left)
Usage: 1970 Mustang hardtop and convertible, 1970 Cougar (all body styles); bolt-on design

Interchange Number: 33
NAGS Number: 2486T
Usage: 1964–65 Comet and Falcon two-door hardtop

Interchange Number: 34
NAGS Number: 2431T
Usage: 1964–65 Comet and Falcon convertible

Interchange Number: 35
NAGS Number: 4271T
Usage: 1964–65 Comet and Falcon two-door sedan
Note(s): 1962–63 Falcons will also interchange, as will station wagon and 1965 Ranchero.

Quarter Window, Glass

Interchange

Interchange Number: 1
NAGS Number: 2251T
Usage: 1959 full-size Ford two-door hardtop only; not for folding hardtop

Interchange Number: 2
NAGS Number: 2252T
Usage: 1959 full-size Ford two-door folding hardtop only; no other interchange

Interchange Number: 3
NAGS Number: 4229T
Usage: 1959 full-size Ford two-door sedan

Interchange Number: 4
NAGS Number: 4235T
Usage: 1959 full-size Ford convertible—all except folding hardtop

Interchange Number: 5
NAGS Number: 4279T
Usage: 1960–61 Ford Starliner two-door hardtop

Interchange Number: 6
NAGS Number: 2316T
Usage: 1960–61 full-size Ford convertible

Interchange Number: 7
NAGS Number: 4227T
Usage: 1960–61 full-size Ford two-door sedan only

Interchange Number: 8
NAGS Number: 4358T
Usage: 1962–65 Fairlane two-door sedan

Interchange Number: 9
NAGS Number: 2428T
Usage: 1963–65 Fairlane two-door hardtop

Interchange Number: 10
NAGS Number: Q3520 (right), Q3521 (left)
Usage: 1966–67 Fairlane and Comet two-door sedans

Interchange Number: 11
NAGS Number: Q3543 (right), Q3544 (left)
Usage: 1966–67 Fairlane and Comet two-door hardtop

Interchange Number: 12
NAGS Number: Q3548 (right), Q3549 (left)
Usage: 1966–67 Fairlane and Comet convertible

Interchange Number: 13
NAGS Number: Q3905 (right), Q3906 (left)
Usage: 1968 Torino and Montego fastback only

Interchange Number: 14
NAGS Number: Q3908 (right), Q3909 (left)
Usage: 1968 Torino and Montego two-door hardtop

Interchange Number: 15
NAGS Number: Q3913 (right), Q3914 (left)
Usage: 1968 Torino and Montego convertible

Interchange Number: 16
NAGS Number: Q4131 (right), Q4132 (left)
Usage: 1969 Torino and Montego fastback only

Interchange Number: 17
NAGS Number: Q4133 (right), Q4134 (left)
Usage: 1968 Torino and Montego two-door hardtop

Interchange Number: 18
NAGS Number: Q4137 (right), Q4138 (left)
Usage: 1969 Torino and Montego convertible

Interchange Number: 19
NAGS Number: Q4325 (right), Q4326 (left)
Usage: 1970–71 Torino fastback only

Interchange Number: 20
NAGS Number: Q4330 (right), Q4331 (left)
Usage: 1970–71 Torino two-door hardtop

Interchange Number: 21
NAGS Number: Q4342 (right), Q4343 (left)
Usage: 1970–71 Torino convertible

Interchange Number: 22
NAGS Number: Q4358 (right), Q4359 (left)
Usage: 1970–71 Montego two-door hardtop
Note(s): *Warning*—will not fit Torino or vice versa.

Interchange Number: 23
NAGS Number: Q3297 (right), Q3298 (left)
Usage: 1964-1/2–66 Mustang hardtop

Interchange Number: 24
NAGS Number: Q3293 (right), Q3294 (left)
Usage: 1964-1/2–66 Mustang convertible

Interchange Number: 25
NAGS Number: Not used; see notes
Usage: 1966 GT 350 Mustang
Note(s): Plexiglass. No NAGS number.

Interchange Number: 26
NAGS Number: Q3757 (right), Q3758 (left)
Usage: 1967–68 Mustang mirrors will not fit Cougar

Interchange Number: 27
NAGS Number: Q3761 (right), Q3762 (left)
Usage: 1967–68 Mustang convertible; will not fit Cougar

Interchange Number: 28
NAGS Number: Q4123 (right), Q4124 (left)
Usage: 1969 Mustang hardtop and convertible; will not fit Cougar

Interchange Number: 29
NAGS Number: Q4118 (right), Q4119 (left)
Usage: 1969–70 Mustang fastback

Interchange Number: 30
NAGS Number: Q4284 (right), Q4285 (left)
Usage: 1970 Mustang hardtop and convertible (see notes for exceptions)
Note(s): Change occurred in glass at build date January 19, 1970. NAGS number is the same on both sets, but part number changes. Use build date when interchanging.

Interchange Number: 31
NAGS Number: Q3763 (right), Q3764 (left)
Usage: 1967–68 Cougar two-door hardtop

Interchange Number: 32
NAGS Number: Q4126 (right), Q4127 (left)
Usage: 1969 Cougar two-door hardtop

Interchange Number: 33
NAGS Number: Q4123 (right), Q4124 (left)
Usage: 1969 Cougar convertible

Interchange Number: 34
NAGS Number: Q4286 (right), Q4287 (left)
Usage: 1970 Cougar two-door hardtop (see notes for exceptions)
Note(s): Change occurred in glass at build date January 19, 1970. NAGS number is the same for both sets, but part number changes. Use build date when interchanging.

Interchange Number: 35
NAGS Number: Q4284 (right), Q4285 (left)
Usage: 1970 Cougar convertible (see notes)
Note(s): Change occurred in glass at build date January 19, 1970. NAGS number is the same for both sets, but part number changes. Use build date when interchanging.

Interchange Number: 36
NAGS Number: 4464T
Usage: 1965 Comet two-door sedan; no other interchange

Interchange Number: 37
NAGS Number: 2487T
Usage: 1964–65 Comet and 1963–65 Falcon two-door hardtop only

Interchange Number: 38
NAGS Number: 2432T
Usage: 1964–65 Comet and Falcon convertible

Back Window, Glass

Model Identification

Interchange

Interchange Number: 1
NAGS Number: B3014
Usage: 1959 full-size Ford two-door hardtop or sedan, except folding hardtop convertible

Interchange Number: 2
NAGS Number: B488
Usage: 1957–59 full-size Ford with folding hardtop convertible roof

Interchange Number: 3
NAGS Number: B3023
Usage: 1960 full-size Ford two-door hardtop

Interchange Number: 4
NAGS Number: B3022
Usage: 1960 Fairlane (full-size) two-door or four-door sedan; Galaxie will not fit

Interchange Number: 5
NAGS Number: B3027
Usage: 1960 full-size Ford (Galaxie) two-door or four-door sedan

Interchange Number: 6
NAGS Number: B3074
Usage: 1961 full-size Ford two-door sedan

Interchange Number: 7
NAGS Number: B3072
Usage: 1961 Starliner two-door hardtop

Interchange Number: 8
NAGS Number: B3073
Usage: 1961 Galaxie two- and four-door hardtop

Interchange Number: 9
NAGS Number: B3124
Usage: 1962–63 Fairlane two- and four-door sedan

Interchange Number: 10
NAGS Number: B3170
Usage: 1963–65 Fairlane two-door hardtop only

Interchange Number: 11
NAGS Number: B3285
Usage: 1964–65 Fairlane two- and four-door sedan

Interchange Number: 12
NAGS Number: B3522
Usage: 1966–67 Fairlane and Comet two-door sedan only

Interchange Number: 13
NAGS Number: B3545
Usage: 1966–67 Fairlane and Comet two-door hardtop only

Interchange Number: 14
NAGS Number: B526T
Usage: 1966–67 Ranchero

Interchange Number: 15
NAGS Number: B3907
Usage: 1968–69 Torino and Montego fastback only

Interchange Number: 16
NAGS Number: B3910
Usage: 1968–69 Torino and Montego two-door hardtop only

Interchange Number: 17
NAGS Number: 1099T
Usage: 1968–71 Ranchero

Interchange Number: 18
NAGS Number: B4327, B4560*
Usage: 1970–71 Torino and Montego fastback only
Note(s): *With rear window defroster.

Interchange Number: 19
NAGS Number: B4332, B4561*
Usage: 1970–71 Torino and Montego two-door hardtop only
Note(s): *With rear defroster.

Interchange Number: 20
NAGS Number: B3332
Usage: 1965–66 Mustang fastback only

Interchange Number: 21
NAGS Number: B3754
Usage: 1967–68 Mustang fastback only

Interchange Number: 22
NAGS Number: B4120
Usage: 1969–70 Mustang fastback only

Interchange Number: 23
NAGS Number: B3299
Usage: 1964-1/2–68 Mustang hardtop only

Interchange Number: 24
NAGS Number: B4125
Usage: 1969–70 Mustang hardtop only

Interchange Number: 25
NAGS Number: B3765
Usage: 1967–68 Cougar two-door hardtop only

Interchange Number: 26
NAGS Number: B4128
Usage: 1969–70 Cougar two-door hardtop only

Interchange Number: 27
 NAGS Number: B3333
 Usage: 1965 Comet two- and four-door sedan only

Interchange Number: 28
 NAGS Number: B3198
 Usage: 1965 Comet and Falcon two-door hardtop only

Mouldings

General Interchange

There are many different types of mouldings used on Ford cars. Thus, to help you more easily find the type of moulding you're looking for, different mouldings are grouped together.

When interchanging moulding, it is always a good idea to interchange with all the holding clips. Interchange range varies.

Glass mouldings are quite large, while bodyside moulding may have a somewhat narrower range. Note that body style may affect some moulding usage. Also, when interchanging used mouldings, inspect them carefully for signs of pitting, scratches, or abuse. Mouldings are easily bent, so remove them carefully.

Mouldings, Windshield

Model Identification

Cougar	Interchange Number
1967–68	
upper moulding	
two-door hardtop	9
convertible	10
side moulding	
two-door hardtop	25
convertible	26
lower moulding, all	38
1969–70	
upper moulding	
two-door hardtop	12
convertible	13
side moulding	
two-door hardtop	28
convertible	29
lower moulding	
two-door hardtop	39
convertible	40

Cyclone	Interchange Number
1965	
upper moulding	
sedan	14
two-door hardtop	15
convertible	16
side moulding	
sedan	30
two-door hardtop	31
convertible	32
1966–67	
upper moulding	
sedan	5
two-door hardtop	6
convertible	7
side moulding	
two-door hardtop	20
convertible	21
lower moulding, all	36
1968–69	
upper moulding	
sedan	5
two-door hardtop and fastback	6
convertible	7

side moulding	
two-door hardtop and fastback	20
convertible	21
lower moulding, all	36
1970 two-door hardtop	
upper moulding	8
side moulding	22
lower moulding	37

Fairlane and Torino	Interchange Number
1961 upper moulding	
all except fastback and convertible	1
fastback	2
1962–65 upper moulding	
sedan	3
two-door hardtop	4
1966–67	
upper moulding	
sedan	5
two-door hardtop	6
convertible	7
side moulding	
two-door hardtop	20
convertible	21
lower moulding, all	36
1968–69	
upper moulding	
sedan	5
two-door hardtop and fastback	6
convertible	7
side moulding	
two-door hardtop and fastback	20
convertible	21
lower moulding	36
1970	
upper moulding	
all except convertible and fastback	8
convertible	7
side moulding	
all except convertible and fastback	22
convertible	23
fastback	24
lower moulding	37

Mustang	Interchange Number
1964-1/2–68	
upper moulding	
all except convertible	9
convertible	10
side moulding	
all except convertible	25
convertible	26
lower moulding	38
1969–70	
upper moulding	
two-door hardtop	12
fastback	11
convertible	13
side moulding	
two-door hardtop	28
fastback	27
convertible	29
lower moulding	
all except convertible	39
convertible	40

Interchange

Interchange Number: 1
 Part Number(s): C1AB6203144A
 Location: Upper moulding
 Usage: 1961–62 full-size Ford—all body styles except convertible, two-door fastback, and station wagon

184

Interchange Number: 2
Part Number(s): COAB6303144E
Location: Upper moulding
Usage: 1961–62 full-size Ford two-door fastback only

Interchange Number: 3
Part Number(s): C2OZ6203144A
Location: Upper moulding
Usage: 1962–65 Fairlane—all body styles except two-door hard-top

Interchange Number: 4
Part Number(s): C3OZ6503144A
Location: Upper moulding
Usage: 1963–65 Fairlane two-door hardtop only

Interchange Number: 5
Part Number(s): C6OZ6203144A
Location: Upper moulding
Usage: 1966–67 Fairlane, 1968–69 Torino, 1966–67 Comet, 1968–69 Montego, and 1966–68 Ranchero—all body styles except two-door hardtop, fastback, and convertible

Interchange Number: 6
Part Number(s): C6OZ6303144A
Location: Upper moulding
Usage: 1966–67 Fairlane, 1968–69 Torino, 1966–67 Comet, 1968–69 Montego, and 1969 Ranchero, two-door hardtop and fastback models only

Interchange Number: 7
Part Number(s): C8OZ7603144A (right), C8OZ7603145A (left)
Location: Upper moulding
Usage: 1966–67 Fairlane, 1968–71 Torino, 1966–67 Comet, 1968–71 Montego. All models, convertible only.

Interchange Number: 8
Part Number(s): DOOZ6503144A
Location: Upper moulding
Usage: 1970–71 Torino, Montego, and Ranchero—all body styles except station wagon, fastback, and convertible

Interchange Number: 9
Part Number(s): C5ZZ6503144A (right), C5ZZ6503145A (left)
Location: Upper moulding
Usage: 1964-1/2–68 Mustang and 1967–68 Cougar—all except convertible

Interchange Number: 10
Part Number(s): C5ZZ7603144A (right), C5ZZ7603145A (left)
Location: Upper moulding
Usage: 1964-1/2–68 Mustang and 1967–68 Cougar, convertible only

Interchange Number: 11
Part Number(s): C9ZZ6303144A
Location: Upper moulding
Usage: 1969–70 Mustang fastback only

Interchange Number: 12
Part Number(s): C9ZZ6503144A
Location: Upper moulding
Usage: 1969–70 Mustang and Cougar, two-door hardtop only

Interchange Number: 13
Part Number(s): C9ZZ7603144A (right), C9ZZ7603145A (left)*
Location: Upper moulding
Usage: 1969–70 Mustang and Cougar, convertible only
Note(s): *Two different sets of trim were used. Above was used until build date April 29, 1969. After that date, part numbers C9ZZ7603144B (right) and C9ZZ7603145B (left) were used. So, 1970 trim will not fit early-built 1969 models, but will fit after this date, so interchange by build date. Later style will fit earlier models if later style header panel is also changed.

Interchange Number: 14
Part Number(s): CODB6403144A
Location: Upper moulding
Usage: 1963–65 Comet and 1960–65 Falcon—all models except two-door hardtop and convertible

Interchange Number: 15
Part Number(s): C3DZ6303144A
Location: Upper moulding
Usage: 1963–65 Comet and 1960–65 Falcon, two-door hardtop only

Interchange Number: 16
Part Number(s): C3DZ76303144A
Location: Upper moulding
Usage: 1963–65 Comet and 1960–65 Falcon, convertible only

Interchange Number: 17
Part Number(s): COAB6403136B (right), COAB6403137B (left)
Location: Side moulding
Usage: 1960–62 full-size Ford—all body styles except convertible

Interchange Number: 18
Part Number(s): C2OZ6203136A (right), COZ6203137A (left)
Location: Side moulding
Usage: 1962–65 Fairlane—all body styles except two-door hard-top

Interchange Number: 19
Part Number(s): C3OZ6503136A (right), C3Z6503137A (left)
Location: Side moulding
Usage: 1962–65 Fairlane two-door hardtop only

Interchange Number: 20
Part Number(s): C8OZ6503136A (right), C8Z6503137A (left)
Location: Side moulding
Usage: 1966–67 Fairlane and Comet, 1968–69 Torino and Montego, and 1966–69 Ranchero, two-door hardtop and fastback only

Interchange Number: 21
Part Number(s): C8OZ7603136A (right), C8Z7603137A (left)
Location: Side moulding
Usage: 1966–67 Fairlane and Comet and 1968–69 Torino and Montego, convertible only

Interchange Number: 22
Part Number(s): DOOZ6503136A (right), DOOZ6503137A (left)
Location: Side moulding
Usage: 1970–71 Torino, Montego, and Ranchero—all body styles except fastback, convertible, and station wagon

Interchange Number: 23
Part Number(s): DOOZ7603136A (right), DOOZ7603137A (left)
Location: Side moulding
Usage: 1970–71 Torino and Montego, convertible only

Interchange Number: 24
Part Number(s): DOOZ6303136A (right), DOOZ6303137A (left)
Location: Side moulding
Usage: 1970–71 Torino fastback (includes top moulding)

Interchange Number: 25
Part Number(s): C5ZZ6503136A (right), C5ZZ6503137A (left)
Location: Side moulding
Usage: 1964-1/2–68 Mustang and 1967–68 Cougar—all body styles except convertible

Interchange Number: 26
Part Number(s): C5ZZ7603136A (right), C5ZZ7603137A (left)
Location: Side moulding
Usage: 1964-1/2–68 Mustang and 1967–68 Cougar, convertible only

Interchange Number: 27
Part Number(s): C9ZZ6303136A (right), C9ZZ6303137A (left)
Location: Side moulding
Usage: 1969–70 Mustang fastback only

Interchange Number: 28
Part Number(s): C9ZZ6503136A (right), C9ZZ6503137A (left)
Location: Side moulding
Usage: 1969–70 Mustang and Cougar—all body styles except convertible

Interchange Number: 29
Part Number(s): C9ZZ7603136A (right), C9ZZ7603137A (left)
Location: Side moulding
Usage: 1969–70 Mustang and Cougar, convertible only

Interchange Number: 30
Part Number(s): C1AB6403136A (right), C1AB6403137A (left)
Location: Side moulding
Usage: 1964–65 Comet, 1961–65 Falcon—all body style, except two-door hardtop and convertible

Interchange Number: 31
Part Number(s): C1AB6503136A (right), C1AB6503137A (left)
Location: Side moulding
Usage: 1964–65 Comet, 1961–65 Falcon, two-door hardtop only

Interchange Number: 32
Part Number(s): C1AB7603136A (right), C1AB7603137A (left)
Location: Side moulding
Usage: 1964–65 Comet and 1961–65 Falcon, convertible only

Interchange Number: 33
Part Number(s): C0AB6403148A
Location: Lower moulding
Usage: 1960–62 full-size Ford—all body styles

Interchange Number: 34
Part Number(s): C2OB6203148A
Location: Lower moulding
Usage: 1962–65 Fairlane—all body styles except two-door hardtop

Interchange Number: 35
Part Number(s): C3OZ6503148A
Location: Lower moulding
Usage: 1963–65 Fairlane two-door hardtop only

Interchange Number: 36
Part Number(s): C6OZ203148A (right), C0Z6203149A (left)
Location: Lower moulding
Usage: 1966–67 Fairlane and Comet, 1968–69 Torino and Montego, 1968–70 Falcon, and 1966–69 Ranchero—all body styles and models

Interchange Number: 37
Part Number(s): D3AZ6503243A
Location: Lower moulding
Usage: 1970–72 Torino and Montego, 1970–72 full-size Ford and full-size Mercury, 1970–72 Lincoln and Mark III, 1971–72 Mustang and Cougar—all models and body styles (see notes for usage)
Note(s): Universal fit; cut to fit. Tip: when interchanging, always opt for a larger (wider) car than the model you're interchanging for.

Interchange Number: 38
Part Number(s): C5ZZ6503148B
Location: Lower moulding
Usage: 1964-1/2–68 Mustang and 1967–68 Cougar—all body styles

Interchange Number: 39
Part Number(s): D0ZZ6503148B (right), D0ZZ6503149B (left)
Location: Lower moulding
Usage: 1969–70 Mustang and Cougar—all body styles except convertible

Interchange Number: 40
Part Number(s): C9ZZ7603148A (right), C9ZZ7603149A (left)
Location: Lower moulding
Usage: 1969–70 Mustang and Cougar, convertible only

Interchange Number: 41
Part Number(s): C0DB6403148B
Location: Lower moulding
Usage: 1964–65 Comet and 1960–65 Falcon—all body styles

Mouldings, Drip Rail

Model Identification

Cougar	Interchange Number
1967–68 two-door hardtop	22
1969–70 two-door hardtop	
without vinyl top	23
with vinyl top	24

Cyclone	Interchange Number
1966–67	
sedan	6
hardtop	7
1968–69	
hardtop	10
fastback	9
1970	
two-door hardtop	
without vinyl top	12
with vinyl top	13

Fairlane and Torino	Interchange Number
1959–61	
all except fastback	1
fastback	2
1962–63	
sedan	3
hardtop	5
1964–65	
sedan	4
hardtop	5
1966–67	
sedan	6
hardtop	7
Ranchero	8
1968–69	
hardtop	10
fastback	9
Ranchero	11
1970	
two-door hardtop	
without vinyl top	12
with vinyl top	13
fastback	14
Ranchero	15

Mustang	Interchange Number
1964-1/2–66	
two-door hardtop	17
fastback	16
1967–68	
two-door hardtop	17
fastback	18
1969–70	
two-door hardtop	
without vinyl top	19
with vinyl top	20
fastback	21

Interchange

Interchange Number: 1
Part Number(s): C0AB7551728A (right), C0AB7551729A (left)
Usage: 1960–61 full-size Ford—all body styles except fastback

Interchange Number: 2
Part Number(s): C0AB6351726A (right), C0AB6351727A (left)
Usage: 1960–61 full-size Ford fastback only

Interchange Number: 3
  Part Number(s): C2OB6251726A (right), C2OB621727A (left)
  Usage: 1962–63 Fairlane two- and four-door sedan only

Interchange Number: 4
  Part Number(s): C4OZ6251726A (right), C2OB625727A (left)
  Usage: 1964–65 Fairlane two- and four-door sedan only

Interchange Number: 5
  Part Number(s): C3OZ6551726A (right), C3OZ6551727A (left)
  Usage: 1963–65 Fairlane two-door hardtop only

Interchange Number: 6
  Part Number(s): C6OZ6251726A (front right), C6OZ6251727A
    (front left), C6OZ6251726D (right rear), C6OZ6251727D
    (left rear)
  Usage: 1966–67 Fairlane and Comet, two-door sedan only

Interchange Number: 7
  Part Number(s): C6OZ6351726A (right), C6OZ635727A (left)
  Usage: 1966–67 Fairlane and Comet, two-door hardtop only

Interchange Number: 8
  Part Number(s): C6DZ6651726A (right), C6DZ665727A (left)
  Usage: 1966–67 Ranchero

Interchange Number: 9
  Part Number(s): C8OZ6351726A (right), C8OZ635727A (left)
  Usage: 1968–69 Torino and Montego, fastback body style only

Interchange Number: 10
  Part Number(s): C8OZ6551726A (right), C8OZ655727A (left)
  Usage: 1968–69 Torino and Montego, two-door hardtop only

Interchange Number: 11
  Part Number(s): C8OZ6651726A (right), C8OZ665727A (left)
  Usage: 1968–69 Ranchero

Interchange Number: 12
  Part Number(s): DOOZ6551726A (right), DOOZ655727A (left)
  Usage: 1970–71 Torino and Montego, two-door hardtop without
    vinyl roof

Interchange Number: 13
  Part Number(s): DOOZ6551726B (right), DOOZ655727B (left)
  Usage: 1970–71 Torino and Montego, two-door hardtop with
    vinyl roof

Interchange Number: 14
  Part Number(s): DOOZ6351726A (right), DOOZ635727A (left)
  Usage: 1970–71 Torino fastback only

Interchange Number: 15
  Part Number(s): DOOZ6651726A (right), DOOZ665727A (left)
  Usage: 1970–71 Ranchero

Interchange Number: 16
  Part Number(s): C5ZZ6351726A (right), C5ZZ635727A (left)
  Usage: 1965–66 Mustang fastback only

Interchange Number: 17
  Part Number(s): C5ZZ6551726B (right), C5ZZ655727B (left)
  Usage: 1965–68 Mustang hardtop

Interchange Number: 18
  Part Number(s): C7ZZ6351726A (right), C7ZZ635727A (left)
  Usage: 1967–68 Mustang fastback only

Interchange Number: 19
  Part Number(s): C9ZZ6551726C (right), C9ZZ655727C (left)
  Usage: 1969–70 Mustang hardtop without vinyl roof

Interchange Number: 20
  Part Number(s): C9ZZ6551726D (right), C9ZZ655727D (left)
  Usage: 1969–70 Mustang hardtop with vinyl roof

Interchange Number: 21
  Part Number(s): C9ZZ6351726A (right), C9ZZ635727A (left)
  Usage: 1969–70 Mustang fastback only

Interchange Number: 22
  Part Number(s): C7WY6551726A (right front), C7WY655727A
    (left front), C7WY6551728B (right rear), C7WY655729B (left
    rear)
  Usage: 1967–68 Cougar two-door hardtop

Interchange Number: 23
  Part Number(s): C9WY6551726C (right), C9WY655727C (left)
  Usage: 1969–70 Cougar two-door hardtop without vinyl roof

Interchange Number: 24
  Part Number(s): C9WY6551726D (right), C9WY655727D (left)
  Usage: 1969–70 Cougar two-door hardtop with vinyl roof

Interchange Number: 25
  Part Number(s): C5GY6251726A (right), C5GY625727A (left)
  Usage: 1965 Comet—all except two-door hardtop

Interchange Number: 26
  Part Number(s): C4DZ6351726A (right), C4DZ635727A (left)
  Usage: 1964–65 Comet and Falcon, two-door hardtop only

Mouldings, Rear Window

Model Identification

Interchange

Interchange Number: 1
    Part Number(s): COAZ62423A00A
    Location: Upper moulding
    Usage: 1960–63 full-size Ford—all body styles except fastback, convertible, and station wagon

Interchange Number: 2
    Part Number(s): COAB6342430E
    Location: Upper moulding
    Usage: 1960–63 full-size Ford fastback

Interchange Number: 3
    Part Number(s): C2OB6242430A
    Location: Upper moulding
    Usage: 1962–63 Fairlane two- and four-door sedan only

Interchange Number: 4
    Part Number(s): C3OZ6542430A
    Location: Upper moulding
    Usage: 1963–65 Fairlane two-door hardtop only

Interchange Number: 5
    Part Number(s): C4OZ6242430A
    Location: Upper moulding
    Usage: 1964–65 Fairlane two- and four-door sedan only

Interchange Number: 6
    Part Number(s): C6OZ6242430A (right), C6OZ6242431A (left)
    Location: Upper moulding
    Usage: 1966–67 Fairlane, Comet, and Falcon, two-door sedan only

Interchange Number: 7
    Part Number(s): C6DZ6642430A (right), C6DZ6642431A (left)
    Location: Upper moulding
    Usage: 1966–67 Ranchero

Interchange Number: 8
    Part Number(s): C6OZ6542430A (right), C6OZ6542431A (left)
    Location: Upper moulding
    Usage: 1966–67 Fairlane and Comet, two-door hardtop only

Interchange Number: 9
    Part Number(s): C8OZ6342430A (right), C8OZ6342431A (left)
    Location: Upper moulding
    Usage: 1968–69 Torino and Montego, fastback only

Interchange Number: 10
    Part Number(s): C8OZ6542430A (right), C8OZ6542431A (left)
    Location: Upper moulding
    Usage: 1968–69 Torino and Montego, two-door hardtop only

Interchange Number: 11
　　Part Number(s): C8OZ6642430A (right), C8OZ6642431A (left)
　　Location: Upper moulding
　　Usage: 1968–69 Ranchero

Interchange Number: 12
　　Part Number(s): DOOZ6342430A (right), DOOZ6342431A (left)
　　Location: Upper moulding
　　Usage: 1970–71 Torino fastback

Interchange Number: 13
　　Part Number(s): DOOZ6542430A (right), DOOZ6542431A (left)
　　Location: Upper moulding
　　Usage: 1970–71 Torino and Montego, two-door hardtop

Interchange Number: 14
　　Part Number(s): DOOZ6642430A
　　Location: Upper moulding
　　Usage: 1970–71 Ranchero

Interchange Number: 15
　　Part Number(s): C5ZZ6342430A (right), C5ZZ6342431A (left)
　　Location: Upper moulding
　　Usage: 1965–66 Mustang fastback

Interchange Number: 16
　　Part Number(s): C5ZZ6542430A (right), C5ZZ6542431A (left)
　　Location: Upper moulding
　　Usage: 1964-1/2–66 Mustang hardtop

Interchange Number: 17
　　Part Number(s): C7ZZ6342430A
　　Location: Upper moulding
　　Usage: 1967–68 Mustang fastback

Interchange Number: 18
　　Part Number(s): C7ZZ6542430A
　　Location: Upper moulding
　　Usage: 1967–70 Mustang hardtop

Interchange Number: 19
　　Part Number(s): C9ZZ6342430A (right), C9ZZ6342431A (left)
　　Location: Upper moulding
　　Usage: 1969–70 Mustang fastback (see notes for 1970 models)
　　Note(s): These above mouldings are bright. In 1970, black-colored mouldings were also used, listed as Part Numbers DOZZ6342430A (right) and DOZZ6342431A (left). Either will interchange physically.

Interchange Number: 20
　　Part Number(s): C7WY6542430A (right), C7WY6542431A (left)
　　Location: Upper moulding
　　Usage: 1967–68 Cougar two-door hardtop

Interchange Number: 21
　　Part Number(s): C9WY6542430A (right), C9WY6542431A (left)
　　Location: Upper moulding
　　Usage: 1969–70 Cougar two-door hardtop

Interchange Number: 22
　　Part Number(s): C1AB6242492D (right), C1AB6242493D (left)
　　Location: Side moulding
　　Usage: 1961 full-size Ford, all but fastback style and convertible

Interchange Number: 23
　　Part Number(s): C2OZ6242492A (right), C2OZ6242493A (left)
　　Location: Side moulding
　　Usage: 1962–63 Fairlane two- and four-door sedan only

Interchange Number: 24
　　Part Number(s): C3YY6542492A (right), C3YY6542493A (left)
　　Location: Side moulding
　　Usage: 1962–65 Fairlane two-door hardtop only

Interchange Number: 25
　　Part Number(s): C4OZ6242492A (right), C4OZ6242493A (left)
　　Location: Side moulding
　　Usage: 1964–65 Fairlane two- and four-door sedan only

Interchange Number: 26
　　Part Number(s): C6OZ6242492A (right), C6OZ6242493A (left)
　　Location: Side moulding
　　Usage: 1966–67 Fairlane and Comet, two-door sedan only

Interchange Number: 27
　　Part Number(s): C8OZ6542492A (right), C8OZ6542493A (left)
　　Location: Side moulding
　　Usage: 1968–69 Torino and Montego, two-door hardtop only

Interchange Number: 28
　　Part Number(s): C8OZ6642492C (right), C8OZ6642493C (left)
　　Location: Side moulding
　　Usage: 1968–69 Ranchero without vinyl roof

Interchange Number: 29
　　Part Number(s): C8OZ6642492D (right), C8OZ6642493D (left)
　　Location: Side moulding
　　Usage: 1968–69 Ranchero with vinyl roof

Interchange Number: 30
　　Part Number(s): DOOZ6542492A (right), DOOZ6542493A (left)
　　Location: Side moulding
　　Usage: 1970–71 Torino and Montego, two-door hardtop only

Interchange Number: 31
　　Part Number(s): DOOZ6642492A (right), DOOZ6642493A (left)
　　Location: Side moulding
　　Usage: 1970–71 Ranchero

Interchange Number: 32
　　Part Number(s): C5ZZ6542492A (right), C5ZZ6542493A (left)
　　Location: Side moulding
　　Usage: 1964-1/2–66 Mustang hardtop

Interchange Number: 33
　　Part Number(s): C7ZZ6542492A (right), C7ZZ6542493A (left)
　　Location: Side moulding
　　Usage: 1967–68 Mustang hardtop

Interchange Number: 34
　　Part Number(s): C9ZZ6542492A (right), C9ZZ6542493A (left)
　　Location: Side moulding
　　Usage: 1969 Mustang hardtop

Interchange Number: 35
　　Part Number(s): C7ZZ6342492A (right), C7ZZ6342493A (left)
　　Location: Side moulding
　　Usage: 1967–69 Mustang fastback only

Interchange Number: 36
　　Part Number(s): C1AB6342404
　　Location: Lower moulding
　　Usage: 1961 full-size Ford fastback

Interchange Number: 37
　　Part Number(s): C2OB6242404A
　　Location: Lower moulding
　　Usage: 1962–65 Fairlane two- and four-door sedan

Interchange Number: 38
　　Part Number(s): C6OZ6242404A
　　Location: Lower moulding
　　Usage: 1966–67 Fairlane and Comet, two-door sedan only

Interchange Number: 39
　　Part Number(s): C6OZ6342404A (right), C6OZ6342405A (left)
　　Location: Lower moulding
　　Usage: 1966–67 Fairlane and Comet, two-door hardtop only (includes side pieces)

Interchange Number: 40
　　Part Number(s): C6DZ6642404A (right), C6DZ6642405A (left)
　　Location: Lower moulding
　　Usage: 1966–67 Ranchero

Interchange Number: 41
　　Part Number(s): C8OZ6342404A (right), C8OZ6342405A (left)
　　Location: Lower moulding
　　Usage: 1968–69 Torino and Montego, fastback only

Interchange Number: 42
Part Number(s): C8OZ6542404A (right), C8OZ6542405A (left)
Location: Lower moulding
Usage: 1968–69 Torino and Montego, two-door hardtop only

Interchange Number: 43
Part Number(s): C8OZ6642404A (right), C8OZ6642405A (left)
Location: Lower moulding
Usage: 1968–69 Ranchero

Interchange Number: 44
Part Number(s): DOOZ6342404A (right), DOOZ6342405A (left)
Location: Lower moulding
Usage: 1970–71 Torino and Montego—all body styles except convertible, fastback, and pickup

Interchange Number: 45
Part Number(s): DOOZ6342404A (right), DOOZ6342405A (left)
Location: Lower moulding
Usage: 1970–71 Torino fastback only

Interchange Number: 46
Part Number(s): DOOZ6642404A (right), DOOZ6642405A (left)
Location: Lower moulding
Usage: 1970–71 Ranchero

Interchange Number: 47
Part Number(s): C5ZZ6342404A (right), C5ZZ6342405A (left)
Location: Lower moulding
Usage: 1965–66 Mustang fastback only

Interchange Number: 48
Part Number(s): C7ZZ6342404A
Location: Lower moulding
Usage: 1967–68 Mustang fastback only

Interchange Number: 49
Part Number(s): C5ZZ6542404A
Location: Lower moulding
Usage: 1964-1/2–66 Mustang hardtop

Interchange Number: 50
Part Number(s): C7ZZ6542404A (right), C7ZZ6542405A (left)
Location: Lower moulding
Usage: 1967–68 Mustang hardtop without vinyl roof

Interchange Number: 51
Part Number(s): C9ZZ6542404A
Location: Lower moulding
Usage: 1969 Mustang hardtop

Interchange Number: 52
Part Number(s): C9ZZ6342404A (right), C9ZZ634205A (left)
Location: Lower moulding
Usage: 1969–70 Mustang fastback (see notes for 1970 model usage)
Note(s): Above units are bright-plated. In 1970, black-colored mouldings DOZZ634204B (right), DOZZ634205B (left) were used. Both will fit.

Interchange Number: 53
Part Number(s): DOZZ6342404A (right), DOZZ634205A (left)
Location: Lower moulding
Usage: 1970 Mustang hardtop

Interchange Number: 54
Part Number(s): C7WY6542404A (right), C7WYZ6542405A (left)
Location: Lower moulding
Usage: 1967–68 Cougar two-door hardtop

Interchange Number: 55
Part Number(s): C9WY6542404A (right), C9WYZ6542405A (left)
Location: Lower moulding
Usage: 1969–70 Cougar two-door hardtop

Interchange Number: 56
Part Number(s): C6DZ62423A20A (fits either side)
Location: Lower, with vinyl top or two-tone paint
Usage: 1966–67 Fairlane two-door sedan

Interchange Number: 57
Part Number(s): C7OZ63423A20A (right), C7OZ63423A21A (left)
Location: Lower with vinyl top or two tone paint
Usage: 1966–67 Fairlane two-door hardtop

Interchange Number: 58
Part Number(s): C8OZ65423A20A (right), C8OZ65423A21A (left)
Location: Lower, with vinyl top or two-tone paint
Usage: 1968–69 Torino and Montego, two-door hardtop (see notes)
Note(s): Fords used this bright trim with vinyl top and two-tone colors on most models. Mercury used it only with two-tone paint.

Interchange Number: 59
Part Number(s): C8OZ76423A20A (right), C8OZ76423A21A (left)
Location: Lower with vinyl top or two-tone paint
Usage: 1968–69 Torino and Montego, convertible only

Interchange Number: 60
Part Number(s): DOOZ65423A20A (right), DOOZ65423A21A (left)
Usage: 1970–71 Torino and Montego two-door hardtop with two-tone paint (do not use with vinyl roof)

Interchange Number: 61
Part Number(s): DGY65423A20A (right), DGY65423A21A (left)
Location: Lower with vinyl top or two-tone paint
Usage: 1970–71 Torino and Montego two-door hardtop with vinyl roof without Halo mouldings

Interchange Number: 62
Part Number(s): C9ZZ65423A20C (right), C9ZZ65423A21C (left)
Location: Lower with vinyl top or two-tone paint
Usage: 1969 Mustang hardtop
Note(s): Moulding must be painted to match roof.

Interchange Number: 63
Part Number(s): DOZZ65423A20A (right), DOZZ65423A21A (left)
Location: Lower with vinyl top or two-tone paint
Usage: 1970 Mustang hardtop with vinyl top but without decorative design; also used with two-tone paint

Interchange Number: 64
Part Number(s): DOZZ65423A20B (right), DOZZ65423A21B (left)
Location: Lower with vinyl top or two-tone paint
Usage: 1970 Mustang hardtop with vinyl top with decorative design

Interchange Number: 65
Part Number(s): C9ZZ76423A20C (right), C9ZZ76423A21C (left)
Location: Lower with vinyl top or two-tone paint
Usage: 1969–70 Mustang and Cougar, convertible only

Interchange Number: 66
Part Number(s): C7WY765423A20B (right), C7WY65423A21B (left)
Location: Lower with vinyl top or two-tone paint
Usage: 1967–68 Cougar with vinyl roof or two-tone paint only

Interchange Number: 67
Part Number(s): C9WY765423A20B (right), C9WY65423A21B (left)
Location: Lower, with vinyl top or two-tone paint
Usage: 1969–70 Cougar with vinyl roof or two-tone paint only (see notes)
Note(s): Chrome strip. Paint to match top.

Wheelwell, Mouldings

Wheel lip mouldings, both front and back, are not interchangeable between make or models. Thus, wheel trim from a Montego will not fit a Torino. Nor will Mustang mouldings fit a Torino. However, there are lots of interchanges between the various submodels. For example, Torino station wagons used the same front wheelwell trim, as did higher-grade Torino GTs.

Model Identification

Cougar   *Interchange Number*
1967–68
    all except seven-liter
        front 15
          rear 36
    seven-liter (429ci)
        front 16
          rear 37
1969–70
    front...17
    rear
    1969...38
    1970 ....39, 10, 23

Cyclone   *Interchange Number*
1965
    front...10
    rear 30, 31
1966
    front...11
    rear 32
1967
    front...12
    rear 33
1968–69
    front...13
    rear 34
1970
    front...14
    rear 35

Fairlane and Torino   *Interchange Number*
1966
    front...1
    rear 18
1967
    front...2
    rear
        all except Ranchero 19
        Ranchero 20
1968–69
    front 3, 4
    rear 21, 22
1970
    front 5, 6
        all except Ranchero 23, 24
        Ranchero 25

Mustang   *Interchange Number*
1967–68
    front...7
    rear 26
1969
    front...8
    rear 27
1970
    front...9
    rear
        hardtop and convertible 28
        fastback 29

Interchange

Interchange Number: 1
Part Number(s): C6OZ16038A (right), C6OZ16039A (left)
Location: Front
Usage: 1966 Fairlane—all models and body styles

Interchange Number: 2
Part Number(s): C7OZ16038A (right), C7OZ16039A (left)
Location: Front
Usage: 1967 Fairlane—all models and body styles

Interchange Number: 3
Part Number(s): C9OZ16038A (right), C6OZ16039A (left)
Location: Front
Usage: 1968 Fairlane two- and four-door, 1969 Fairlane and Torino 500 four-door sedan and two-door hardtop, 1969 Ranchero 500, 1969 Torino 500 station wagon, and 1969 Fairlane 500 convertible
Note(s): It is important that these exact models be used, as different models used different trim each year. If your model is not listed here, it used Interchange Number 4.

Interchange Number: 4
Part Number(s): C9OZ16038B (right), C6OZ16039B (left)
Location: Front
Usage: 1968–69 Torino GT (all body styles), 1969 Ranchero GT, 1968 Fairlane and Torino 500 four-door sedan, 1968 Torino fastback (all models), 1968 Torino 500 two-door hardtop, 1968 Ranchero 500, 1968 Torino 500 station wagon, 1968 Torino 500 convertible (all models), 1969 Cobra (all body styles), 1969 Torino two-door hardtop (base models), and 1969 Ranchero (base models)
Note(s): It is important that these exact models be used, as different models used different trim each year. If your model is not listed here it used Interchange Number 3.

Interchange Number: 5
Part Number(s): D0OZ16038B (right), D0OZ16039B (left)
Location: Front
Usage: 1970 Torino Brougham four-door and two-door hardtop and 1970 Torino GT fastback and convertible
Note(s): Trim was changed at build date July 30, 1969, to part numbers D0OZ16038D (right) and D0OZ16039D (left). The later units will fit earlier models but the earlier style will not fit later models.

Interchange Number: 6
Part Number(s): D0OZ16038C (right), D0OZ16039C (left)
Location: Front
Usage: All 1970–71 Torino models except 1970 Torino Brougham four-door and two-door hardtop and Torino GT fastback and convertible

Interchange Number: 7
Part Number(s): C7ZZ16038B (right), C7ZZ16039B (left)
Location: Front
Usage: 1967–68 Mustang—all body styles

Interchange Number: 8
Part Number(s): C9ZZ16038A (right), C9ZZ16039A (left)
Location: Front
Usage: 1969 Mustang—all body styles

Interchange Number: 9
Part Number(s): D0ZZ16038A (right), D0ZZ16039A (left)
Location: Front
Usage: 1970 Mustang—all body styles

Interchange Number: 10
Part Number(s): C5GY16038A (right), C5GY16039A (left)
Location: Front
Usage: 1965 Comet—all body styles except station wagon

Interchange Number: 11
Part Number(s): C6GY16038A (right), C6GY16039A (left)
Location: Front
Usage: 1966 Comet—all body styles except station wagon

Interchange Number: 12
Part Number(s): C7GY16038A (right), C7GY16039A (left)
Location: Front
Usage: 1967 Comet—all body styles except station wagon

Interchange Number: 13

Part Number(s): C9GY16038A (right), C9GY16039A (left)
Location: Front
Usage: 1968–69 Montego—all body styles, including station wagon

Interchange Number: 14

Part Number(s): D0GY16038A (right), D0GY16039A (left)
Location: Front
Usage: 1970–71 Montego—all body styles, including station wagon

Interchange Number: 15

Part Number(s): C7WY16038C (right), C7WY16039C (left)
Location: Front
Usage: 1967–68 Cougar—all models and body styles except 1968 with 429ci (seven-liter)

Interchange Number: 16

Part Number(s): C8WY16038A (right), C8WY16039A (left)
Location: Front
Usage: 1968 Cougar with 429ci engine; no other interchange

Interchange Number: 17

Part Number(s): C9WY16038B (right), C9WY16039B (left)
Location: Front
Usage: 1969–70 Cougar—all models and body styles

Interchange Number: 18

Part Number(s): C6OZ6229164A (right), C6OZ6229165A (left)
Location: Rear
Usage: 1966 Fairlane—all body styles except station wagon

Interchange Number: 19

Part Number(s): C7OZ6229164A (right), C7OZ6229165A (left)
Location: Rear
Usage: 1966 Fairlane—all body styles except station wagon and Ranchero

Interchange Number: 20

Part Number(s): C7OZ7129164A (right), C7OZ7129165A (left)
Location: Rear
Usage: 1966–67 Ranchero and 1967 Fairlane station wagon

Interchange Number: 21

Part Number(s): C9OZ5429164A (right), C9OZ5429165A (left)
Location: Rear
Usage: 1968 Fairlane two- and four-door, 1969 Fairlane and Torino 500 four-door sedan and two-door hardtop, 1969 Ranchero 500, 1969 Torino 500 station wagon, and 1969 Fairlane 500 convertible
Note(s): It is important that these exact models be used, as different models used different trim each year. If your model is not listed here, it used Interchange Number 22.

Interchange Number: 22

Part Number(s): C9OZ5429164B (right), C9OZ5429165B (left)
Location: Rear
Usage: 1968–69 Torino GT (all body styles), 1969 Ranchero GT, 1968 Fairlane and Torino 500 four-door sedan, 1968 Torino fastback (all models), 1968 Torino 500 two-door hardtop, 1968 Ranchero 500, 1968 Torino 500 station wagon, 1968 Torino 500 convertible (all models), 1969 Cobra (all body styles), 1969 Torino two-door hardtop (base models), and 1969 Ranchero (base models)
Note(s): If your model is not listed here, it used Interchange Number 21.

Interchange Number: 23

Part Number(s): D0OZ659164A (right), D0OZ6529165A (left)
Location: Rear
Usage: 1970 Torino Brougham four-door and two-door hardtop and 1970 Torino GT fastback and convertible

Interchange Number: 24

Part Number(s): D0OZ6529164B (right), D0OZ6529165B (left)
Location: Rear
Usage: All 1970–71 Torino models except 1970–71 Torino Brougham four-door and two-door hardtop, 1970 Torino GT fastback and convertible, 1970–71 station wagon (all models), and 1970–71 Ranchero

Interchange Number: 25

Part Number(s): D0OZ6629164A (right), D0OZ6629165A (left)
Location: Rear
Usage: All 1970–71 Rancheros; no other interchange; station wagon will not fit

Interchange Number: 26

Part Number(s): C7ZZ6529164A (right), C7ZZ6529165A (left)
Location: Rear
Usage: 1967–68 Mustang—all models and body styles

Interchange Number: 27

Part Number(s): C9ZZ6529164A (right), C9ZZ6529165A (left)
Location: Rear
Usage: 1969 Mustang—all models and body styles

Interchange Number: 28

Part Number(s): D0ZZ6529164A (right), D0ZZ6529165A (left)
Location: Rear
Usage: 1970 Mustang hardtop and convertible

Interchange Number: 29

Part Number(s): D0ZZ6329164A (right), D0ZZ6329165A (left)
Location: Rear
Usage: 1970 Mustang fastback

Interchange Number: 30

Part Number(s): C5GY6329164A (right), C5GY6329165A (left)
Location: Rear
Usage: 1965 Cyclone two-door hardtop only; other hardtops will not interchange

Interchange Number: 31

Part Number(s): C5GY5429164A (right), C5GY5429165A (left)
Location: Rear
Usage: 1965 Comet Caliente two-door hardtop or four-door sedan only and all 1965 Comet convertible models

Interchange Number: 32

Part Number(s): C6GY5429164A (right), C6GY5429165A (left)
Location: Rear
Usage: 1966 Comet—all body styles except station wagon

Interchange Number: 33

Part Number(s): C7GY5429164A (right), C7GY5429165A (left)
Location: Rear
Usage: 1967 Comet—all body styles except station wagon

Interchange Number: 34

Part Number(s): C96GY5429164A (right), C96GY5429165A (left)
Location: Rear
Usage: 1968–69 Montego—all body styles except station wagon

Interchange Number: 35

Part Number(s): D0GY6529164A (right), D0GY6529165A (left)
Location: Rear
Usage: 1970–71 Montego two-door hardtop only; four-doors and station wagon will not fit

Interchange Number: 36

Part Number(s): C7WY6529164A (right), C7WY6529165A (left)
Location: Rear
Usage: 1967–68 Cougar—all models and body styles except 1968 with 429ci (seven-liter)

Interchange Number: 37

Part Number(s): C8WY6529164A (right), C8WY6529165A (left)
Location: Rear
Usage: 1968 Cougar with 429ci engine; no other interchange

Interchange Number: 38
Part Number(s): C9WY6529164A (right), C9WY6529165A (left)
Location: Rear
Usage: 1969 Cougar—all models and body styles

Interchange Number: 39
Part Number(s): DOWY6529164A (right), DOWY6529165A (left)
Location: Rear
Usage: 1970 Cougar—all models and body styles

Mouldings, Rocker Panel

Model Identification

Cougar	Interchange Number
1967–68, all	17
1969, all	18
1970, all	19

Cyclone	Interchange Number
1965, all	11
1966, all	12
1967, all	13
1968	
all except fastback	14
fastback	16
1969	
all except fastback	
without wheelwell mouldings	14
with wheelwell mouldings	15
fastback	16
1970, all	21

Fairlane and Torino	Interchange Number
1965, all	1
1966, all	2
1969, all except Torino 500 and GT models	3
1970, all	4

Mustang	Interchange Number
1964-1/2–66, all	5
1967–68, all	6
1969, all	7
1970	
all except Mach I or Grande	8
Mach I	9
Grande	10

Interchange

Interchange Number: 1
Part Number(s): C5OZ6210176A (right), C5OZ6210177A (left)
Usage: 1965 Fairlane—all models and body styles

Interchange Number: 2
Part Number(s): C6OZ6210176B (right), C6OZ6210177B (left)
Usage: 1966 Fairlane—all models and body styles, except station wagon

Interchange Number: 3
Part Number(s): C9OZ5410176A (right), C9OZ5410177A (left)
Usage: 1969 Base Torino two-door hardtop and four-door sedans only; not used on GT or 500

Interchange Number: 4
Part Number(s): DOOZ6510176A (right), DOOZ6510177A (left)
Usage: 1970 Torino GT—all body styles except Ranchero GT and 1970 Torino Brougham two-door or four-door hardtop
Note(s): 1971 trim will fit but is visually incorrect with GT lettering.

Interchange Number: 5
Part Number(s): C5ZZ6510176A (right), C5ZZ6510177A (left)
Usage: 1964-1/2–66 Mustang—all body styles

Interchange Number: 6
Part Number(s): C7ZZ6510176A (right), C7ZZ6510177A (left)
Usage: 1967–68 Mustang—all body styles

Interchange Number: 7
Part Number(s): C9ZZ6510176A (right), C9ZZ6510177A (left)
Usage: 1969 Mustang—all body styles

Interchange Number: 8
Part Number(s): DOZZ6510176B (right), DOZZ6510177B (left)
Usage: 1970 Mustang—all body styles and models except Mach I and Grande

Interchange Number: 9
Part Number(s): DOZZ6310176A (right), DOZZ6310177A (left)
Usage: 1970 Mustang Mach I only; no other interchange

Interchange Number: 10
Part Number(s): DOZZ6510176A (right), DOZZ6510177A (left)
Usage: 1970 Mustang Grande models only; no other interchange
Note(s): Black insert.

Interchange Number: 11
Part Number(s): C5GY6310176A (right), C5GY6310177A (left)
Usage: 1965 Cyclone two-door hardtop; no other interchange

Interchange Number: 12
Part Number(s): C6GY6310176A (right), C6GY6310177A (left)
Usage: 1966 Cyclone two-door hardtop and convertible; no other interchange

Interchange Number: 13
Part Number(s): C7GY6310176A (right), C7GY6310177A (left)
Usage: 1967 Cyclone two-door hardtop convertible; no other interchange

Interchange Number: 14
Part Number(s): C9GY5410176B (right), C9GY5410177B (left)
Usage: 1968–69 Montego two-door hardtop, four-door sedan, and convertible—all models
Note(s): Used only in 1969 models without wheelwell trim mouldings.

Interchange Number: 15
Part Number(s): C9GY5410176A (right), C9GY5410177A (left)
Usage: 1969 Montego two-door hardtop, four-door sedan, and convertible—all models with wheelwell trim mouldings

Interchange Number: 16
Part Number(s): C9GY6310176A (right), C9GY6310177A (left)
Usage: 1968–69 Montego fastback

Interchange Number: 17
Part Number(s): C8WY6510177B (fits either side)
Usage: 1967–68 Cougar—all body styles

Interchange Number: 18
Part Number(s): C9WY6510176B (right), C9WY6510177B (left), C9WY6510176C (right), C9WY6510177C (left)*
Usage: 1969 Cougar—all body styles (see notes)
Note(s): Two different styles used. *Has five black stripes and an air scoop. Not used on XR7 and convertible. Other has single black stripe; use on all convertibles and all XR7.

Interchange Number: 19
Part Number(s): DOWY6510176A (right), DOGY6510177A (left)
Usage: 1970 Cougar—all body styles
Note(s): Has single black stripe.

Interchange Number: 20
Part Number(s): DOGY6510176A (right), DOGY6510177A (left)
Usage: 1970–71 Montego MX and Montego MX Brougham—all body styles, except station wagon

Exterior Decoration

General Overview

This section covers the exterior decor emblems. Due to the vast number of emblems on each car, the interchange is broken down by location (grille, fender, etc.). Part numbers given appear on the back of the emblem.

Emblems, Grille

Model Identification

1964-1/2–65 Mustang grille and running horse emblem.

1966 Mustang grille emblem with fog lamps.

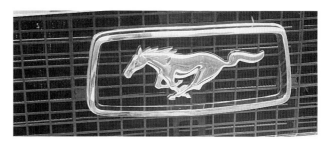

1968 Mustang grille emblem.

1967 Fairlane GT grille emblem.

1969–70 Snake emblem for GT 350 or GT 500 Mustangs.

1970 Torino GT grille emblem.

1970 Mustang grille emblem.

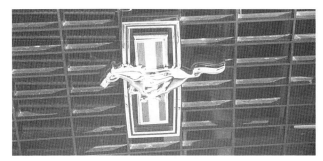
1969 Mustang grille emblem.

1967–68 Cougar center emblem.

Hood lettering for the 1964-1/2–66 Mustang can be found in a variety of locations and models.

1969
    all except GT 350 and GT 500..17
    GT 350 and GT 500 18
1970
    all except GT 350 and GT 500..19
    GT 350 and GT 500 18

Emblems, Grille

Interchange

Interchange Number: 1
Part Number(s): C6OZ8213E
Design or Style: Crest
Usage: 1966 Fairlane—all models and body styles except XL and GT

Interchange Number: 2
Part Number(s): C6OZ8213D
Design or Style: "XL"
Usage: 1966 Fairlane XL models only

Interchange Number: 3
Part Number(s): C6OZ8213F
Design or Style: "GT"
Usage: 1966 Fairlane GT only

Interchange Number: 4
Part Number(s): C7OZ8213A
Design or Style: Crest
Usage: 1967 Fairlane—all models and body styles except XL and GT

Interchange Number: 5
Part Number(s): C7OZ8213C
Design or Style: "XL"
Usage: 1967 Fairlane XL models only

Interchange Number: 6
Part Number(s): C7OZ8213B
Design or Style: "GT"
Usage: 1967 Fairlane GT only

Interchange Number: 7
Part Number(s): C8OZ8213B
Design or Style: Crest
Usage: 1968 Torino (base models; not for GT)

Interchange Number: 8
Part Number(s): C8OZ8213A
Design or Style: "GT"
Usage: 1968 Torino GT and Ranchero GT—all body styles

Interchange Number: 9
Part Number(s): C9OZ8213A(G), C9OZ8213B (T)
Design or Style: "GT"
Usage: 1969 Torino GT and Ranchero GT—all body styles
Note(s): Two separate letters.

Interchange Number: 10
Part Number(s): DOOZ8213D
Design or Style: "GT"
Usage: 1970 Torino GT and Ranchero GT—all body styles

Interchange Number: 11
Part Number(s): DOOZ8213A, DOOZ8213C*
Usage: 1970 base Torino models (see notes)
Note(s): *Used after build date 12-15-61

Interchange Number: 12
Part Number(s): C5ZZ8213D
Design or Style: Running horse
Usage: 1964-1/2–65 Mustang—all body styles

Interchange Number: 13
Part Number(s): C6ZZ8213A
Design or Style: Running horse without side tabs
Usage: 1966 Mustang—all body styles without fog lamps

Interchange Number: 14
Part Number(s): C6ZZ8213B
Design or Style: Running horse with side tabs
Usage: 1966 Mustang—all body styles with fog lamps

Interchange Number: 15
Part Number(s): C7ZZ8213A
Design or Style: Running horse
Usage: 1967 Mustang—all body styles

Interchange Number: 16
Part Number(s): C8ZZ8213A
Design or Style: Running horse
Usage: 1968 Mustang—all body styles, except GT/CS
Note(s): Some Mustangs did not use the running horse emblem.

Interchange Number: 17
Part Number(s): C9ZZ8213B
Design or Style: Small running horse on tri-bar medallion
Usage: 1969 Mustang—all body styles, except GT 350 and GT 500

Interchange Number: 18
Part Number(s): C9ZZ8213C
Design or Style: 2in-high Cobra (snake)
Usage: 1969–70 GT 350 and GT 500

Interchange Number: 19
Part Number(s): DOZZ8213A
Design or Style: Running horse with tri-bar medallion
Usage: 1970 Mustang—all body styles, except GT 350 and GT 500

Interchange Number: 20
Part Number(s): S7MS8A224A
Design or Style: GT 350 badge
Usage: 1967 Mustang GT 350 (see notes for locations)
Note(s): Used on grille, instrument panel, and rear-deck panel.

Interchange Number: 21
Part Number(s): S7MS8A224B
Design or Style: GT 500 badge
Usage: 1967 Mustang GT 500 (see notes for locations)
Note(s): Used on grille, instrument panel, and rear-deck panel.

Interchange Number: 22
Part Number(s): C5GY8A223B
Design or Style: Cyclone
Usage: 1965 Cyclone models only

Interchange Number: 23
Part Number(s): C7GY8A223A (Outer) C7GY8A223B (Inner)
Usage: 1967 Comet—all models

Interchange Number: 24
Part Number(s): C9GY8A223B
Design or Style: Cyclone
Usage: 1969 Cyclone only

Interchange Number: 25
Part Number(s): C7WY8A223A
Design or Style: Medallion (center)
Usage: 1967–68 Cougar—all body styles

Interchange Number: 26
Part Number(s): C9WY8A223A
Design or Style: Medallion (center)
Usage: 1969 Cougar—all body styles

Emblems, Hood or Front Panel

Model Identification

The hood letters on a 1965–67 Fairlane can also be found on the full-size Ford.

Engine callouts on the 1967 Fairlane GT.

The Cobra Jet script for 1969–70 models.

1967–68 Cougar header script.

1970 Cougar header nameplate.

1967 fender nameplate used on Fairlane GTs with automatic transmission.

Interchange

Interchange Number: 1
Part Number(s): See notes
Design or Style: F-O-R-D
Usage: 1960 full-size Ford (except Galaxie) hood panel; also found on 1960 full-size wagon and Ranchero tailgate
Note(s): F—COAB16606A; O—COAB16606B; R—COAB16606C; D—COAB16606D.

Interchange Number: 2
Part Number(s): See notes
Design or Style: F-O-R-D
Usage: 1961 full-size Ford (except Galaxie) hood panel
Note(s): F—C1AB16606A; O—C1AB16606B; R—C1AB16606C; D—C1AB16606D.

Interchange Number: 3
Part Number(s): See notes
Design or Style: F-O-R-D
Usage: 1963 Fairlane hood panel—all models and body styles, 1962–63 Falcon hood or tail gate of Ranchero. Also, the F and O in Falcon and the R in Futura on the rear deck lid will work.
Note(s): F—C2DZ16606A; O—C2DZ16606B; R—C2DZ16606C; D—C2DZ16606D.

Interchange Number: 4
Part Number(s): See notes
Design or Style: F-O-R-D
Usage: 1964 Fairlane hood panel, deck lid, and tailgate; 1964-1/2–66 Mustang hood panel; and 1966–67 Mustang tail-end panel
Note(s): F—C4OZ16606A; O—C4OZ16606B; R—C4OZ16606C; D—C4OZ16606D.

Interchange Number: 5
Part Number(s): See notes
Design or Style: F-O-R-D
Usage: Early-1965 Fairlane and early-1965 full-size Ford hood panel, deck lid, and tailgate (see notes for build dates)
Note(s): F—C5AZ16606A; O—C5AZ16606B; R—C5AZ16606C; D—C5AZ16606D. Used only on Fairlane built before January 4, 1965, and on full-size models built before November 25, 1964.

Interchange Number: 6
Part Number(s): See notes
Design or Style: F-O-R-D
Usage: Late-1965–67 Fairlane, late-1965 full-size Ford, 1966–67 Falcon—on hood panel for all; also found on deck lid or tailgate on Fairlane and full-size models (see notes for build dates)
Note(s): F—C5AZ16606E; O—C5AZ16606F; R—C5AZ16606G; D—C5AZ16606H. Used only on Fairlane built after January 4, 1965, and on full-size models built after November 25, 1964.

Interchange Number: 7
Part Number(s): See notes
Design or Style: F-O-R-D
Usage: 1972 Torino, 1967 Mustang, 1967–68 full-size Ford, and 1971–73 Comet (compact)—on hood for all; also used on the tailgates of the 1968–69 Torino Squire station wagon, and 1969–71 full-size Country Squire station wagon, and on the rear-end panel of base 1968 Torino two-door hardtop and four-door sedan
Note(s): F—C7AZ16606A; O—C7AZ16606B; R—C7AZ16606C; D—C7AZ16606D.

Interchange Number: 8
Part Number(s): See notes
Design or Style: F-O-R-D
Usage: On the 1968–69 Torino hood panel, on the tailgate of 1968–69 Torino station wagon (except Squire series), and on the rear-end panel of all but base Torino models and GT
Note(s): F—C8OZ16606A; O—C8OZ16606B; R—C8OZ16606C; D—C8OZ16606D.

Interchange Number: 9
Part Number(s): See notes
Design or Style: F-O-R-D
Usage: On the hood panel of 1970–71 Torino base models, 1970–71 Torino Brougham, 1970 base Ranchero, and 1969–70 full-size Ford; also on tailgates and rear-end panels of 1971 full-size Ford four-door sedan and station wagon and various 1970–71 Torino sedans and station wagons
Note(s): F—C9AZ16606A; O—C9AZ16606B; R—C9AZ16606C; D—C9AZ16606D.

Interchange Number: 10
Part Number(s): See notes
Design or Style: S-H-E-L-B-Y
Usage: 1967–70 GT 350 and GT 500 hood panel and rear-end panel
Note(s): S—S8MS16A606A; H—S8MS16A606A; E—S8MS16606B; L—S8MS16606C; B—S8MS16606D; Y—S8MS16606E.

Interchange Number: 11
Part Number(s): C5GY16604A
Design or Style: Comet script
Usage: 1965 Comet—all models; used on hood panel and rear quarter panels

Interchange Number: 12
Part Number(s): C7MY16604A
Design or Style: "Mercury" script
Usage: 1968–69 Montego—all models on hood panel; also used on grille of 1967–68 full-size Mercurys, tailgate of 1968–69 Montego station wagon, and tail-end panel of 1967–68 Cougar two-door hardtop

Interchange Number: 13
Part Number(s): DOGY16604A
Design or Style: "Mercury" script
Usage: 1970–71 Montego—all models and body styles on front header panel

Interchange Number: 14
Part Number(s): C7WY16604A
Design or Style: "Mercury" script
Usage: 1967–68 Cougar—all models on front header panel

Interchange Number: 15
Part Number(s): DOOZ16720A
Design or Style: TORINO nameplate
Usage: 1970–71 Torino (true) models on the hood panel

Interchange Number: 16
Part Number(s): C6OZ16720A (right), C6OZ16721A (left)
Design or Style: Simulated air vents and "390ci" engine callout
Usage: 1966 Fairlane GT

Interchange Number: 17
Part Number(s): C7OZ16720A (right), C7OZ16721A (left)
Design or Style: Simulated hood scoops and "390ci" engine callout
Usage: 1967 Fairlane GT

Interchange Number: 18
Part Number(s): C9ZZ16720A (fits either side)
Design or Style: "Cobra Jet" script on sides of hood scoops
Usage: 1969–70 Mustang, 1969–70 Torino GT, and 1972 Torino Sport GT

Interchange Number: 19
Part Number(s): C9ZZ16637A (fits either side)
Design or Style: "427ci" engine callout on sides of scoop with Cobra Jet ID
Usage: 1969 Torino and Mustang (see Interchange Number 18)

Interchange Number: 20
Part Number(s): C9ZZ16637B (fits either side)
Design or Style: "428ci" engine callout on sides of scoop
Usage: 1969–69 Torino and Mustang

Interchange Number: 21
Part Number(s): C9ZZ16637C (fits either side)
Design or Style: "351ci" engine callout on sides of scoop
Usage: 1969–70 Torino and Mustang

Interchange Number: 22
Part Number(s): C9ZZ16637D (fits either side)
Design or Style: "390ci" engine callout on sides of scoop
Usage: 1969 Torino and Mustang

Interchange Number: 23
Part Number(s): DOWY16604A
Design or Style: Cougar nameplate on front header panel
Usage: 1970 Cougar

Emblems, Front Fenders

Model Identification

This 1967 Mustang GT emblem can be found on a variety of models.

Name is part of moldings on 1967 Ranchero.

Mustang nameplate with alternator.

198

1965–66 Mustang 2+2 badge.

1966 Cyclone GT nameplate and racing flags are separate emblems.

1965–67 MUSTANG lettering.

1964-1/2–66 horse medallion.

1969–70 Mustang fender script.

1967-68 horse medallion was combined into an engine callout badge.

The 1964-1/2–66 Mustang engine callout can be found on a variety of models.

1968–70 rear quarter nameplate.

1965–66 Fairlane engine callouts.

GT lettering on the 1970 Torino.

1967 Fairlane 289ci callout featured flags.

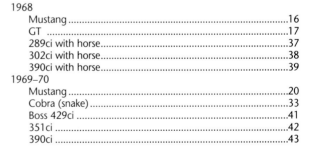

1069 Interchange

Interchange Number: 1

Part Number(s): C5OZ16098A
Design or Style: "Fairlane"
Usage: 1965–66 Fairlane—all but GT and GTA
Note(s): Postilion varies from front fender to rear quarter panel, depending on model.

1970 Boss 302 stripes.

Interchange Number: 2
Part Number(s): C6OZ16098A
Design or Style: "GTA"
Usage: 1966 Fairlane GTA 390ci with C6 automatic transmission

Interchange Number: 3
Part Number(s): C6OZ16098B
Design or Style: "GT" (plastic)
Usage: 1966 Fairlane GT 390ci with manual transmission, and late-built 1966 Mustang GT
Note(s): On Mustangs built after October 1, 1965. Before this date see Interchange Number 12.

Interchange Number: 4
Part Number(s): C7OZ16098A
Design or Style: "GTA"
Usage: 1967 Fairlane GTA and 1967 Mustang GTA 390ci with C6 automatic transmission; located on front fenders

Interchange Number: 5
Part Number(s): C7ZZ16098A (G), C7ZZ16098B (T)
Design or Style: "GT"
Usage: On the front fenders of 1967 Fairlane GT 390ci with manual transmission and 1967 Mustang GT, and on rear quarters of 1970 Torino and Ranchero GT, 1967 Cougar (after November 11, 1966), and 1970–72 Cyclone GT

Interchange Number: 6
Part Number(s): C6DZ16098C
Design or Style: "Ranchero"
Usage: 1966–67 Ranchero

Interchange Number: 7
Part Number(s): C8OZ6642558A
Design or Style: "Ranchero"
Usage: 1968–69 Ranchero front fender and 1970–71 Ranchero tailgate

Interchange Number: 8
Part Number(s): D0OZ16098H
Design or Style: "Ranchero"
Usage: 1970–71 Ranchero front fender and rear quarter panel; location varies with submodels

Interchange Number: 9
Part Number(s): C5ZZ16098A
Design or Style: "Mustang" nameplate
Usage: 1964-1/2 Mustang with a generator
Note(s): Emblem is 4-1/2in in length.

Interchange Number: 10
Part Number(s): C5ZZ16098B
Design or Style: "Mustang" nameplate
Usage: 1964-1/2–66 Mustang with an alternator (except Mustang GT and fastback)
Note(s): Emblem is 4-7/8in in length.

Interchange Number: 11
Part Number(s): C5ZZ16098C
Design or Style: "Mustang 2+2" badge
Usage: 1965–66 Mustang fastback, except GT models

Interchange Number: 12
Part Number(s): C5ZZ16098D
Design or Style: "GT" badge
Usage: 1965–66 Mustang GT with build date before October 1, 1965; after this date see model Interchange Number 3. Early badge is ceramic; late style is plastic.

Interchange Number: 13
Part Number(s): See notes
Design or Style: "M-U-S-T-A-N-G" (letters)
Usage: 1965–67 Mustangs on the front fender and rear-end panel; also used on 1968–70 Mustangs on the rear-end panel only (except GT 350 and GT 50 and GT/CS)
Note(s): M—C5ZZ16098E; U—C5ZZ16098F; S—C5ZZ16098G; T—C5ZZ16098H; A—C5ZZ16098J; N—C5ZZ16098K; G—C5ZZ16098L.

Interchange Number: 14
Part Number(s): S7MS16098A
Design or Style: "GT 350" nameplate
Usage: 1967 Mustang GT 350

Interchange Number: 15
Part Number(s): S7MS16098B
Design or Style: "GT 500" nameplate
Usage: 1967 Mustang GT 500

Interchange Number: 16
Part Number(s): C8ZZ16098A
Design or Style: "Mustang" script
Usage: All 1968 Mustang front fenders and and 1968 Mustang GT/CS front fenders and rear-end panels

Interchange Number: 17
Part Number(s): C7GY16098A
Design or Style: "GT" badge
Usage: 1968 Mustang GT, 1967 Cyclone GT, and early 1967 Cougar GT
Note(s): Used Cougar only on built before November 7, 1966.

Interchange Number: 18
Part Number(s): S8MS16098F
Design or Style: "Cobra" nameplate
Usage: 1968 GT 350 and GT 500

Interchange Number: 19
Part Number(s): S8MS16098G
Design or Style: "Cobra Jet" nameplate
Usage: 1968 GT 500 KR

Interchange Number: 20
Part Number(s): C9ZZ16098A
Design or Style: "Mustang" script
Usage: 1969–72 Mustang front fenders and on rear-end panel of 1972 Mustangs

Interchange Number: 21
Part Number(s): C3OZ16228B
Design or Style: "289ci" callout (silver in color)
Usage: 1963–64 Fairlane, 1965 Falcon, 1964-1/2–66 Mustang—all 289ci
Note(s): When equipped with 289ci 271hp engine, a backing high-performance plate (part number C5ZZ16228D) was used in 1965–66 Mustangs.

Interchange Number: 22
Part Number(s): C4OZ16228A
Design or Style: "289ci" callout (gold in color)
Usage: 1964 Fairlane two-barrel

Interchange Number: 23
Part Number(s): C5OZ16228A
Design or Style: "289ci" callout
Usage: 1965–66 Fairlane and 1966 Falcon

Interchange Number: 24
Part Number(s): C8OZ16228C
Design or Style: "289ci" callout
Usage: 1967 Fairlane, 1966 Falcon, 1967 Comet, 1968 Torino, and 1968 Montego

Interchange Number: 25
Part Number(s): C8OZ16228B
Design or Style: "302ci" callout
Usage: 1968 Torino, 1969–71 Bronco, and 1968 Montego

Interchange Number: 26
Part Number(s): C9GZ16228A
Design or Style: "351ci" callout
Usage: 1969 Torino and Montego

Interchange Number: 27
Part Number(s): C6OZ16228A
Design or Style: "390ci"·callout
Usage: 1966 Fairlane

Interchange Number: 28
Part Number(s): C8OZ16228D
Design or Style: "390ci" callout
Usage: 1967 Fairlane and Comet, 1968–69 Torino and Montego, and 1969–70 Cougar

Interchange Number: 29
Part Number(s): C6AZ16228F (right), C6AZ16229C (left)
Design or Style: "427ci" callout
Usage: 1967 Fairlane, 1966 full-size Ford, 1967 Comet, and 1967 full-size Mercury

Interchange Number: 30
Part Number(s): C8OZ16228A
Design or Style: "427ci" callout
Usage: 1968–69 Torino and Montego

Interchange Number: 31
Part Number(s): C8AZ16228B
Design or Style: "428ci" callout
Usage: 1968 Torino, Montego, and full-size Ford

Interchange Number: 32
Part Number(s): C9GY16228A
Design or Style: "428ci" callout
Usage: 1969 Torino and 1969 Montego, without Cobra Jet only

Interchange Number: 33
Part Number(s): C9OZ16228A
Design or Style: Snake logo
Usage: 1969 Torino Cobra and 1969–70 Mustang GT 350 and GT 500

Interchange Number: 34
Part Number(s): DOOZ16228B
Design or Style: "351ci" callout
Usage: 1970 Torino; no other interchange

Interchange Number: 35
Part Number(s): DOOZ16228C
Design or Style: "429ci" callout
Usage: 1970 Torino; no other interchange

Interchange Number: 36
Part Number(s): C5ZZ16228D (right), C5ZZ161229B (left)
Design or Style: Running horse medallion
Usage: 1964-1/2–66 Mustang (all applications) and 1967–68 Mustang with six-cylinder only

Interchange Number: 37
Part Number(s): C7ZZ16228C (right), C7ZZ161229C (left)
Design or Style: Running horse medallion and 289ci ID
Usage: 1967–68 Mustang 289ci only, except GT/CS models

Interchange Number: 38
Part Number(s): C8ZZ16228A (right), C7ZZ161229A (left)
Design or Style: Running horse medallion and 302ci ID
Usage: 1968 Mustang 302ci only, except GT/CS models

Interchange Number: 39
Part Number(s): C7ZZ16228D (right), C7ZZ161229D (left)
Design or Style: Running horse medallion and 390ci ID
Usage: 1967–68 Mustang 390ci only, except GT/CS models

Interchange Number: 40
Part Number(s): S1MS16229A
Design or Style: "GT 350" logo
Usage: 1965–66 Mustang GT 350

Interchange Number: 41
Part Number(s): C9ZZ16228D* or C9ZZ161229E#
Design or Style: "Boss 429ci" decal
Usage: 1969–70 Boss 429ci Mustang
Note(s): *Used on all but white cars (white logo). #Used on white cars only (black logo).

Interchange Number: 42
Part Number(s): C9ZZ16228A
Design or Style: "351ci" engine callout
Usage: 1969–70 Mustang

Interchange Number: 43
Part Number(s): C9ZZ16228B
Design or Style: "390ci" engine callout
Usage: 1969–70 Mustang

Interchange Number: 44
Part Number(s): DOGY16228B (right), DOGY16229B (left)
Design or Style: "351ci" engine callout
Usage: 1970 Montego

Interchange Number: 45
Part Number(s): DOGY16228A (right), DOGY16229A (left)
Design or Style: "429ci" engine callout
Usage: 1970 Montego

Interchange Number: 46
Part Number(s): C5GY16237A
Design or Style: "V-8" badge
Usage: 1965 Comet with V-8 engine

Interchange Number: 47
Part Number(s): C4GY16098G
Design or Style: "Cyclone" badge
Usage: 1965–66 Cyclone (on rear quarter panels) in 1965; not for 1966 Cyclone GT

Interchange Number: 48
Part Number(s): C6GY16098B
Design or Style: "Cyclone GT" badge
Usage: 1966 Cyclone GT only

Interchange Number: 49
Part Number(s): C6GY16300B (right), C6GY16301B (left)
Design or Style: Racing flag
Usage: 1966 Cyclone (all models); used with Cyclone and Cyclone GT name badges

Interchange Number: 50
Part Number(s): C3MY16300B (right), C3MY16301B (left)
Design or Style: Racing flag
Usage: 1963–64 full-size Mercury and 1964–65 Cyclone

Interchange Number: 51
Part Number(s): C7GY16098A (right), C7GY16099A (left)
Design or Style: "Cyclone" nameplate
Usage: 1967 Cyclone—all models

Interchange Number: 52
Part Number(s): C7GY16098B
Design or Style: "GT" nameplate
Usage: 1967 Cyclone GT only

Interchange Number: 53
Part Number(s): C8GY16098A
Design or Style: "GT" nameplate
Usage: 1968 Cyclone GT only

Interchange Number: 54
Part Number(s): C9GY16098D1A* or C9GY16098D1P#
Design or Style: "CJ 428ci" decal
Usage: 1968 Cyclone—all models except Spoiler
Note(s): *Black lettering. #Silver lettering.

Interchange Number: 55
Part Number(s): C9GY16098C* or C9GY16098D#
Design or Style: Decal (see notes)
Usage: 1969 Cyclone Spoiler models only
Note(s): *Cale Yarbrough decal. #Dan Gurney decal.

Interchange Number: 56
Part Number(s): DOGY16098A (right), DOGY16099A (left)
Design or Style: "CJ" nameplate
Usage: 1970 Cyclone GT

Interchange Number: 57
Part Number(s): C7WY16098A
Design or Style: "6.5 Liter" nameplate
Usage: 1967 Cougar

Interchange Number: 58

Part Number(s): C8WY16098A
Design or Style: "6.5 Liter" nameplate
Usage: 1968 Cougar

Interchange Number: 59

Part Number(s): C8WY16098B (G), C87WY16098C (T)
Design or Style: "GT" nameplate
Usage: 1968 Cougar GT and 1971–72 Cougar GT

Interchange Number: 60

Part Number(s): C8WY16098F (right), C8WY16099A (left)
Design or Style: "7.0 Liter GTE" name badge
Usage: 1968 Cougar GTE models

Interchange Number: 61

Part Number(s): C9WY16098A
Design or Style: "Cougar" script
Usage: 1969 Cougar—all models

1969 and 1970 Cougars used the same quarter panel emblem.

Emblems, Rear Quarters and Roof

Model Identification

Cougar	Interchange Number
1967	
"Cougar"	17
"XR7" (roof)	15
1968	
"Cougar"	11
"XR7" (roof)	15
"XR7G" (roof)	16
1969–70	
"Cougar"	12
"XR7"(roof)	18

Cyclone	Interchange Number
1965 "Cyclone"	19
1968 "Cyclone"	8
1969	
"Cyclone CJ"	9
"Cyclone Spoiler"	10
1970 "Cyclone"	8

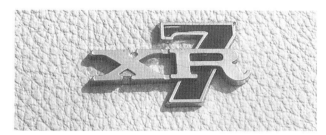

1967–68 XR7 roof quarter nameplates.

1968 limited-edition Cougar XR7G used this medallion on the roof quarters and the headlamp covers.

1968 California Special script.

1968 Cougar quarter script.

1969 Cougar XR7 roof quarter-panel medallion.

1968–69 Torinos used this quarter medallion.

1967 Fairlane 500 deck lid medallion.

1966–67 Ranchero nameplate, also found on front fenders of some models.

1964-1/2–1970 Mustang lettering is the same all seven years.

1969 Mustang Mach 1 roof quarter medallion.

1965 Comet rear panel lettering.

1970 Mercury script for higher-trim Montegos.

1959 (and possibly 1969) full-size Ford deck lid medallion.

1968 Mustang California Special deck lid script is the same as the 1968 regular Mustang script used on the front fenders.

1966 Fairlane 500 deck lid medallion.

1967–70 Mercury nameplate used on the Cougar deck lid.

1968 Cougar XR7 deck lid nameplate.

1968 Cougar XR7G deck lid nameplate.

Interchange

Interchange Number: 1
Part Number(s): C5OZ6225622A (right), C5OZ62225623A (left)
Style: "Fairlane 500" nameplate
Usage: 1965 Fairlane 500 models—all body styles

Interchange Number: 2
Part Number(s): C5OZ16098A
Style: "Fairlane " nameplate
Usage: 1965–66 Fairlane models—all body styles; also used on front fenders of some models

Interchange Number: 3
Part Number(s): C8OZ5425622A (right), C8OZ54225623A (left)
Style: "Fairlane" nameplate
Usage: 1968–70 Fairlane (base Torino models)—all body styles

Interchange Number: 4
Part Number(s): C8OZ6325622A (right), C8OZ63225623A (left)
Style: "Torino" nameplate
Usage: 1968–70 Torino models—all body styles
Note(s): Can also be found on the tailgate of 1968–69 Torino station wagon.

Interchange Number: 5
Part Number(s): C7ZZ16098A (G), C7ZZ16098B (T)
Style: "GT" nameplate
Usage: 1970 Torino GT; also used on the front fenders of 1967 Mustang, 1967 Fairlane GT, 1967 Cougar GT (built after November 7, 1966), and 1970–72 Cyclone GT

Interchange Number: 6
Part Number(s): C8ZZ6525622A (right), C8ZZ65225623A (left)
Style: "California Special" script
Usage: 1968 Mustang GT/CS only

Interchange Number: 7
Part Number(s): C9ZZ6325622B (right), C9ZZ63225623B (left)
Style: "Shelby" nameplate
Usage: 1969–70 GT 350 and GT 500 only

Interchange Number: 8
Part Number(s): C8GY6525622A
Style: "Cyclone" script
Usage: 1968 Cyclone and 1970–71 Cyclone; not for 1969 models

Interchange Number: 9
Part Number(s): C9GY6325622A* or C9GY6325622B#
Style: "Cyclone CJ" decal
Usage: 1969 Cyclone, all but Spoiler models
Note(s): Remove CJ lettering for car without 428ci Cobra Jet engine. *Black lettering. #Silver lettering.

Interchange Number: 10
Part Number(s): C9GY6525622C
Style: "Cyclone Spoiler" decal
Usage: 1969 Cyclone Spoiler models only

Interchange Number: 11
Part Number(s): C8WY6525622A
Style: "Cougar" script
Usage: 1968 Cougar

Interchange Number: 12
Part Number(s): C9WY6525622A
Style: "Cougar" script
Usage: 1969–70 Cougar

Interchange Number: 13
Part Number(s): C9ZZ6550399A
Style: "Grande" script
Usage: 1969–71 Mustang Grande (on roof quarter panels)

Interchange Number: 14
Part Number(s): C9ZZ8213A
Style: "Snake" logo
Usage: 1969–70 GT 350 and GT 500 Mustang (on roof quarter panels and grille)

Interchange Number: 15
Part Number(s): C7WY6528818B
Style: "XR7" logo
Usage: 1967–68 Cougar XR7 (on roof quarter panels)

Interchange Number: 16
Part Number(s): C8WY6528818A
Style: "XR7G" logo
Usage: 1968 Cougar XR7G (on roof quarter panels and headlamp covers)

Interchange Number: 17
Part Number(s): C7WY6528818A (right), C7WY6528819A (left)
Style: "Cougar"
Usage: 1967 Cougar
Note(s): Each side is different.

Interchange Number: 18
Part Number(s): C9WY65517A20A
Style: "XR7" with shield
Usage: 1969 Cougar XR7G and 1969–70 XR7 (on roof)

Interchange Number: 19
  Part Number(s): C4GY16098G
  Design or Style: "Cyclone" badge
  Usage: 1965 Cyclone; also 1966 Cyclone (on front fenders), except 1966 Cyclone GT

Emblems, Rear End Panel and Deck Lid

Model Identification

Interchange

Interchange Number: 1
  Part Number(s): COAB624528D
  Style: "Galaxie" script
  Usage: 1960 Ford Galaxie, all but station wagon
  Note(s): The top portion of the G in the nameplate is a separate part.

Interchange Number: 2
  Part Number(s): COAB634528B
  Style: "Starliner" script
  Usage: 1960 Starliner fastback only
  Note(s): The top portion of the S in the nameplate is a separate part. The upper portion of the S is also used in the Sunliner name.

Interchange Number: 3
  Part Number(s): COAB764528B
  Style: "Sunliner" script
  Usage: 1960 Sunliner convertible only
  Note(s): The top portion of the S in the nameplate is a separate part. The upper portion of the S is also used in the Starliner name.

Interchange Number: 4
  Part Number(s): C1AB624528A
  Style: "Galaxie" script
  Usage: 1961 Galaxie—all but station wagon

Interchange Number: 5
  Part Number(s): C1AB644528B
  Style: "Fairlane 500" script
  Usage: 1961 Fairlane (full-size Ford)

Interchange Number: 6
  Part Number(s): C2OZ624528A
  Style: "Sports Coupe" script
  Usage: 1962 Fairlane two-door sedan and 1963–65 Fairlane two-door hardtop

Interchange Number: 7
  Part Number(s): See notes
  Design or Style: F-O-R-D
  Usage: Early-1965 Fairlane and early-1965 full-size Ford—all on deck lid; also found on hood or tailgate of station wagon (see notes for build dates)
  Note(s): F—C5AZ16606A; O—C5AZ16606B; R—C5AZ16606C; D—C5AZ16606D. Used only on Fairlane built before January 4, 1965, and on full-size models built before November 25, 1964.

Interchange Number: 8
  Part Number(s): See notes
  Design or Style: F-O-R-D
  Usage: Late 1965–67 Fairlane, late 1965 full-size Ford, and 1966–67 Falcon—all on rear-end panel; also found on hood and tailgate on Fairlane and full-size models (see notes for build dates)
  Note(s): F—C5AZ16606E; O—C5AZ16606F; R—C5AZ16606G; D—C5AZ16606H. Used only on Fairlane built after January 4, 1965, and on full-sizes models built after November 25, 1964.

Interchange Number: 9
  Part Number(s): C6OZ63425A02D
  Style: "Fairlane XL" on moulding
  Usage: 1966 Fairlane XL only

Interchange Number: 10
Part Number(s): C6OZ63425A02E
Style: "Fairlane GT" on moulding
Usage: 1966 Fairlane GT only; not for cars with automatic transmission

Interchange Number: 11
Part Number(s): C6OZ63425A02F
Style: "Fairlane GTA" on moulding
Usage: 1966 Fairlane GTA models only; not for cars with manual transmission

Interchange Number: 12
Part Number(s): C7OZ6242528A
Style: "Fairlane 500" nameplate
Usage: 1967 Fairlane 500 models only—all body styles except station wagon

Interchange Number: 13
Part Number(s): C7OZ6242528B
Style: "Fairlane GT" nameplate
Usage: 1967 Fairlane GT only; not for cars with automatic transmission

Interchange Number: 14
Part Number(s): C7OZ6242528C
Style: "Fairlane GTA" nameplate
Usage: 1967 Fairlane GTA models only; not for cars with manual transmission

Interchange Number: 15
Part Number(s): C7OZ7142528B
Style: "Ford Fairlane" nameplate
Usage: 1967 base Ranchero, all 1967 Fairlane station wagons

Interchange Number: 16
Part Number(s): C8OZ5442528A
Style: "Fairlane " nameplate
Usage: 1968 Fairlane models only; not for higher-trimmed models; not used on GT.

Interchange Number: 17
Part Number(s): See notes
Design or Style: F-O-R-D
Usage: 1968 Torino rear-end panel (all models except base and fastback models), 1968–69 Torino hood, and 1968–69 Torino station wagon (except Squire) tailgates
Note(s): F—C8OZ16606A; O—C8OZ16606B; R—C8OZ16606C; D—C8OZ16606D.

Interchange Number: 18
Part Number(s): See notes
Design or Style: F-O-R-D
Usage: 1968 base Fairlane two- and four-door models on the rear-end panel; on the hood of 1972 Torino, 1967 Mustang, 1967–68 full-size Ford, and 1971–73 Comet, and on the tailgate of the 1968–69 Torino Squire station wagon and 1969–71 full-size Country Squire station wagon
Note(s): F—C7AZ16606A; O—C7AZ16606B; R—C7AZ16606C; D—C7AZ16606D.

Interchange Number: 19
Part Number(s): C9OZ6542528A
Style: "Cobra" nameplate
Usage: 1969 Torino Cobra deck lid and front fender
Note(s): See interchange 20 below for snake medallion.

Interchange Number: 20
Part Number(s): C9OZ63403A72B
Style: Cobra snake medallion
Usage: 1969 Torino Cobra deck lid only

Interchange Number: 21
Part Number(s): C89OZ66542528A
Style: "Ranchero" nameplate
Usage: 1968–71 Ranchero tailgate and front fenders

Interchange Number: 22
Part Number(s): See notes
Design or Style: "M-U-S-T-A-N-G" (letters)
Usage: 1965–70 Mustang rear-end panel (except GT 350 and GT 50 or GT/CS) and on the front fenders of 1965–67 Mustang
Note(s): M—C5ZZ16098E; U—C5ZZ16098F; S—C5ZZ16098G; T—C5ZZ16098H: A—C5ZZ16098J; N—C5ZZ16098K; G—C5ZZ16098L.

Interchange Number: 23
Part Number(s): See notes
Design or Style: "S-H-E-L-B-Y" (letters)
Usage: 1967–70 GT 350 and GT 500 on deck lid or hood
Note(s): S—S8MS16A606A, H—S8MS16606A E—S8MS16606B; L—S8MS16606C; B—S8MS16606D; Y—S8MS16606E.

Interchange Number: 24
Part Number(s): See notes
Design or Style: C-O-M-E-T
Usage: 1965 Comet (all body styles except station wagon) and 1966 Comet station wagon only
Note(s): C—C5GY6240282A; O—C5GY6240282B; M—C5GY6240282C; E—C5GY6240282D; T—C5GY6240282F.

Interchange Number: 25
Part Number(s): See notes
Design or Style: C-Y-C-L-O-N-E
Usage: 1966 Cyclone only
Note(s): C—C6GY6240282A; Y—C6GY6240282B; L—C6GY6240282C; O—C6GY6240282D; N—C6GY6240282F; E—C6GY6240282F.

Interchange Number: 26
Part Number(s): See notes
Design or Style: C-Y-C-L-O-N-E
Usage: 1967 Cyclone only
Note(s): C—C7GY6240282A; Y—C7GY6240282B; L—C7GY6240282C; O—C7GY6240282D; N—C7GY6240282F; E—C7GY6240282F.

Interchange Number: 27
Part Number(s): C8GY542528A
Design or Style: "Mercury" nameplate (on bar)
Usage: 1968–69 Montego (all body styles except fastback and station wagon) and 1970–71 Montego (except station wagon)
Note(s): Block letter design only a few higher-grade (including Cyclone) 1970–71 Montegos used a script emblem; look for only the base models in 1970–71.

Interchange Number: 28
Part Number(s): DOC8GY6542528A
Design or Style: "Mercury" script
Usage: 1970–71 Cyclone and 1970–71 Montego MX and MX Brougham models only

Interchange Number: 29
Part Number(s): C9WY6542528A
Design or Style: Cougar nameplate
Usage: 1967–70 Cougar

Interchange Number: 30
Part Number(s): C9WY6542532A (XR) C9WY6542532B (7)
Design or Style: "XR7" badge
Usage: 1969–70 Cougar

Interchange Number: 31
Part Number(s): C9GY6542532A (black), C9GY6542532B (white)
Design or Style: "Cyclone GT" decal
Usage: 1969 Cyclone GT fastback

Interchange Number: 32
Part Number(s): C7WY6543600B
Design or Style: "Mercury" logo/deck-lid lock cover
Usage: 1967 Cougar (all models) and 1968 Cougar (except XR7)

Interchange Number: 33
Part Number(s): C8WY6543600B
Design or Style: "XR7" logo/deck-lid lock cover
Usage: 1968 Cougar XR7 and XR7G (see notes)
Note(s): For XR7G models, replace emblem with part number C8WY652514A, which reads "XR7G."

Interchange Number: 34
Part Number(s): C8OZ5443504A
Design or Style: "Torino" on deck lid
Usage: 1968 Torino except base (Fairlane) and GT and Ranchero

Interchange Number: 35
Part Number(s): C8OZ5443500B
Design or Style: "GT" on deck lid
Usage: 1968 Torino, except fastback or Ranchero

Interchange Number: 36
Part Number(s): C9OZ5443504A
Design or Style: "Torino" on deck lid
Usage: 1969 Torino (except station wagon, fastback, and Ranchero) and 1969 Torino GT (except fastback and Ranchero)

Interchange Number: 37
Part Number(s): C8OZ6340316A
Design or Style: "GT" on lower panel
Usage: 1968 Torino GT fastback

Interchange Number: 38
Part Number(s): C9OZ6340316A
Design or Style: "Ford" symbol on lower panel
Usage: 1969 Torino fastback, except Talladega and GT

Interchange Number: 39
Part Number(s): C9OZ6340316B
Design or Style: "Torino GT" on lower panel
Usage: 1969 Torino GT fastback

Interchange Number: 40
Part Number(s): C9OZ6340316C
Design or Style: "T" in a circle on the lower panel
Usage: 1969 Talladega models only

Interchange Number: 41
Part Number(s): C8ZZ16098A
Design or Style: "Mustang" script
Usage: 1968 Mustang GT/CS rear-end panel; also found on front fenders of all 1968 Mustangs except T5 models

Accessories, Add-On
This section deals with bolt-on accessories that were options or part of option packages. These include hood scoops, rear spoilers, front spoilers, luggage racks.

1968–70 bolt-on Mustang hood scoop.

1969–70 bolt-on Cougar hood scoop.

Hood Scoops

Model Identification

Cougar	Interchange Number
1967–68	6
1969–70	7

Cyclone	Interchange Number
1969	5

Fairlane and Torino	Interchange Number
1969	1
1970	2

Mustang	Interchange Number
1968–70	
all except Boss 429ci	3
Boss 429ci	4

Interchange

Interchange Number: 1
Part Number(s): C9OZ16C630C
Style/Description: Cobra jet style
Usage: 1969 Torino

Interchange Number: 2
Part Number(s): DOOZ16C630A
Style/Description: Fiberglass twin nose piece
Usage: 1970 Torino

1969–70 Mustang was optional with this spoiler.

1969–70 Cougar rear wing spoiler.

Interchange Number: 3
Part Number(s): C9ZZ16C630C
Style/Description: Cobra Jet style (non-functional)
Usage: 1968–70 Mustang—all except with ram air and Boss 429ci models

Interchange Number: 4
Part Number(s): C9OZ16C630D
Style/Description: Box style (functional)
Usage: 1969–70 Mustang Boss 429ci only

Interchange Number: 5
Part Number(s): C9GY16C630B
Style/Description: Ram air style (functional)
Usage: 1969 Cyclone GT with 429ci CJ engine and with ram air option

Interchange Number: 6
Part Number(s): C8WY16C630C
Style/Description: Simulated twin snorkel (fiberglass)
Usage: 1967–68 Cougar

Interchange Number: 7
Part Number(s): C9WY16C630B
Style/Description: Ram air style
Usage: 1969–70 Cougar with or without ram air

Spoiler, Rear Deck

Model Identification

Cougar	Interchange Number
1969–70	5

Cyclone	Interchange Number
1969	2
1970	3

Fairlane and Torino	Interchange Number
1969	2
1970	3

Mustang	Interchange Number
1969–70 fastback only	1

1969 Mustang front spoiler.

Interchange

Interchange Number: 1
Part Number(s): DOZZ6344210A
Style/Description: Wing style
Usage: 1969–70 Mustang fastback only

Interchange Number: 2
Part Number(s): C9GY6344210A
Style/Description: Wing style
Usage: 1969 Cyclone and Torino GT—fastback only
Note(s): Will fit 1968 Cyclone and Torino fastbacks; will not fit convertible and hardtop.

Interchange Number: 3
Part Number(s): DOGY6544210A
Style/Description: Wing style
Usage: 1970–71 Montego and Torino two-door hardtop

Interchange Number: 4
Part Number(s): DOGY6544210A
Style/Description: Wing style
Usage: 1970–71 Montego and Torino two-door hardtop

Interchange Number: 5
Part Number(s): DOWY6544210A
Style/Description: Wing style, adjustable
Usage: 1969–70 Cougar

Spoiler, Front

Model Identification

Cougar	Interchange Number
1969	5
1970	6

Cyclone	Interchange Number
1970	4

Mustang	Interchange Number
1969	
all except GT 350	1
GT 350 and GT 500	2
1970	
all except GT 350 and GT 50	3
GT 350 and GT 500	2

Interchange

Interchange Number: 1
Part Number(s): C9ZZ63001A74A
Usage: 1969 Mustang fastback and Boss 302ci
Note(s): Will not fit GT 350 and GT 500. May fit other 1969 Mustang body styles.

Interchange Number: 2
Part Number(s): DOZZ63001A74A
Usage: 1970 GT 350 and GT 500
Note(s): Will fit 1969 GT 350 and GT 500 but was not original equipment.

1969 Cougar front spoiler.

Mustang louvers.

Interchange Number: 3
Part Number(s): DOZZ65001A6A
Usage: 1970 Mustang fastback, except GT 350 and GT 500
Note(s): Will fit other body styles of 1970 Mustangs.

Interchange Number: 4
Part Number(s): DOGY65001A74A
Usage: 1970–71 Montego two-door hardtop; will not fit Torino

Interchange Number: 5
Part Number(s): C9WY65001A74A
Usage: 1969 Cougar Eliminator
Note(s): Will fit other 1969 Cougar models.

Interchange Number: 6
Part Number(s): DOWY65001A06A
Usage: 1970 Cougar Eliminator
Note(s): Will fit other 1970 Cougar models.

Louvers, Rear Window

Model Identification

Torino	Interchange Number
1970 fastback	2

Mustang	Interchange Number
1969–70 fastback	1

Interchange

Interchange Number: 1
Part Number(s): C9ZZ6344268A
Usage: 1969–70 Mustang fastback only

Interchange Number: 2
Part Number(s): DOOZ6344270A
Usage: 1970–71 Torino fastback only

Rear deck lid luggage rack.

Rack, Luggage Rear Deck

Model Identification

Cougar	Interchange Number
1967–68	2
1969–70	1

Cyclone	Interchange Number
1966–67	2
1968–70	1

Fairlane and Torino	Interchange Number
1966–67	2
1968–70	1

Mustang	Interchange Number
1967–68	1
1969–70	2

Interchange

Interchange Number: 1
Part Number(s): C9AZ6255100A
Usage: 1969–73 full-size Ford, 1969–73 full-size Mercury, 1968–74 Torino, 1968–74 Montego, 1970–74 Maverick, 1971–74 Comet (compact), 1969–73 Mustang, 1969–73 Cougar, and 1969–73 Lincoln—permanent-mount—all body styles except fastback, Ranchero, and station wagon

Interchange Number: 2
Part Number(s): C7WY6255100A
Usage: 1967 Comet, 1968 Montego, 1967–68 Cougar, 1967–68 Lincoln, 1967–68 full-size Mercury, 1967–68 Mustang—all temporary-mount

Chapter 11

Interior

Instrument Panel

Interchange Number

Interchange

Interchange Number: 1
Part Number(s): C3OZ6204320B
Usage: 1962–63 Fairlane—all body styles

Interchange Number: 2
Part Number(s): C4OZ6204320B
Usage: 1964–65 Fairlane—all body styles
Note(s): Change occurred at build date November 18, 1963. Earlier and later styles will not interchange.

Interchange Number: 3
Part Number(s): C7OZ6204320B
Usage: 1966–67 Fairlane and Comet—all body styles except convertible

Interchange Number: 4
Part Number(s): C8OZ5401610B
Usage: 1968–69 Torino and Montego—all body styles except convertible

Interchange Number: 5
Part Number(s): DOOZ54401610A
Usage: 1970 Torino and Montego—all body styles except convertible
Note(s): 1971 dash will not interchange.

Interchange Number: 6
Part Number(s): C5ZZ6504320A
Usage: 1965–66 Mustang—all body styles
Note(s): Will not fit 1964-1/2 Mustang.

Interchange Number: 7
Part Number(s): C8ZZ6504320A
Usage: 1967–68 Mustang and Cougar—all body styles

Interchange Number: 8
Part Number(s): C9ZZ6504320C
Usage: 1969 Mustang and Cougar—all body styles

Interchange Number: 9
Part Number(s): DOZZ6504320A
Usage: 1970 Mustang and Cougar—all body styles

Interchange Number: 10
Part Number(s): C5GY6504320A
Usage: 1964–65 Comet—all body styles

Interchange Number: 11
Part Number(s): C8OZ7601610B
Usage: 1968–69 Torino and Montego, convertible only
Note(s): Other body styles will not interchange.

Interchange Number: 12
Part Number(s): DOOZ7601610A
Usage: 1970 Torino and Montego, convertible only
Note(s): Other body styles and 1971 convertible will not interchange.

Interchange Number: 13
Part Number(s): C7OZ7601610B
Usage: 1966–67 Fairlane and Comet, convertible only
Note(s): Other body styles will not interchange.

Interchange Number: 14
Part Number(s): C4DZ6204320A
Usage: 1964-1/2 Mustang and 1964 Falcon—all body styles
Note(s): Used on those produced before October 19, 1964, only.

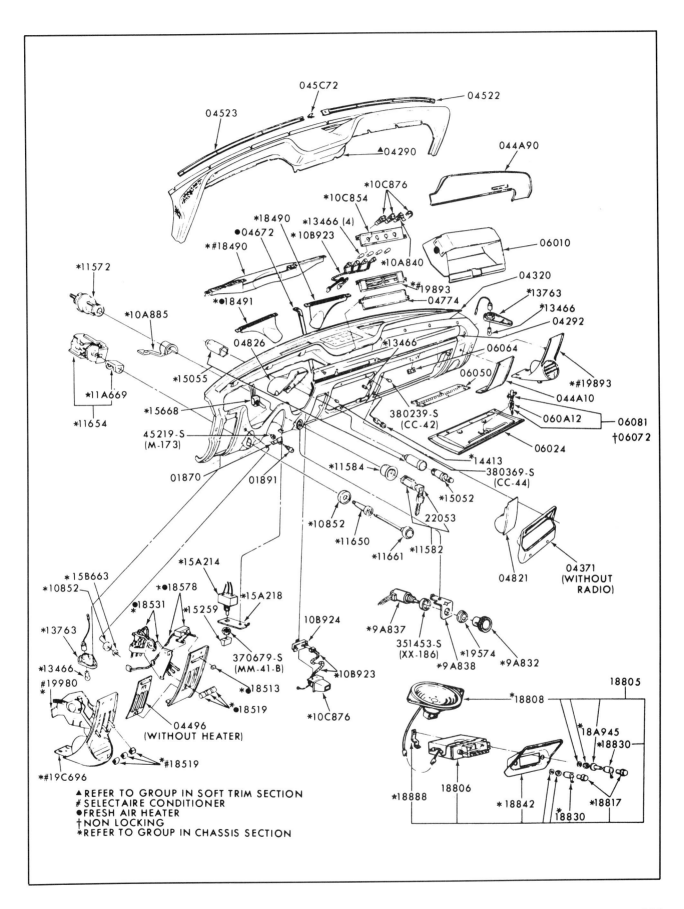

045C72

04522

04523

▲04290

044A90

*10C876

*10C854

*13466 (4)

*18490

●04672

*10B923

06010

*#18490

*10A840

04320

*#19893

*11572

04774

*13763

*●18491

*13466

04292

*10A885

04826

*13466

04292

06064

*#19893

15055

06050

044A10

*11A669

060A12

06081

380239-S

(CC-42)

†06072

*15668

06024

*11654

45219-S

(M-173)

14413

380369-S

(CC-44)

01870

*11584

01891

*15052

*10852

22053

*11650

*11661

*11582

04371

(WITHOUT

RADIO)

04821

*15B663

*15A214

*10852

*●18578

*15A218

*13763

●18531

*15259

10B924

*9A837

18805

*13466

370679-S

(MM-41-B)

*18513

*10B923

351453-S

(XX-186)

*19574

*9A838

*9A832

*18808

18A945

#19980

*

*18519

*10C876

*18830

04496

(WITHOUT HEATER)

18888

18806

18842

18830

18817

*#19C696

*#18519

▲ REFER TO GROUP IN SOFT TRIM SECTION

SELECTAIRE CONDITIONER

● FRESH AIR HEATER

† NON LOCKING

* REFER TO GROUP IN CHASSIS SECTION

211

Glovebox Compartment

Model Identification

Cougar	Interchange Number
1967–68	
without air conditioning	6
with hang-on air conditioning	2
with factory air conditioning	6
1969–70	
without air conditioning	7
with air conditioning	11

Cyclone	Interchange Number
1966–67	
without hang-on air conditioning	8
with hang-on air conditioning	2
1968–69	
without air conditioning	3
with air conditioning	9
1970	
without air conditioning	4
with air conditioning	10

Fairlane and Torino	Interchange Number
1959–61, all	12
1962–65, all	1
1966–67	
without hang-on air conditioning	8
with hang-on air conditioning	2
1968–69	
without air conditioning	3
with air conditioning	9
1970	
without air conditioning	4
with air conditioning	10

Mustang	Interchange Number
1964-1/2–66, all	5
1967–68	
without air conditioning	6
with hang-on air conditioning	2
with factory air conditioning	6
1969–70	
without air conditioning	7
with air conditioning	11

Interchange

Interchange Number: 1
Part Number(s): C2OZ620610A
Usage: 1962–65 Fairlane—all body styles

Interchange Number: 2
Part Number(s): C7OZ620610A
Usage: 1966–67 Fairlane, Comet, Falcon, and Cougar—all body styles with hang-on air conditioning

Interchange Number: 3
Part Number(s): C9DZ620610A
Usage: 1968–69 Torino, Montego, and Falcon—all body styles without air conditioning

Interchange Number: 4
Part Number(s): DOOZ620610A
Usage: 1970–71 Torino and Montego—all body style without air conditioning

Interchange Number: 5
Part Number(s): C5ZZ650610A
Usage: 1964-1/2–66 Mustang—all body styles

Interchange Number: 6
Part Number(s): C7ZZ650610A
Usage: 1967–68 Mustang and Cougar—all body styles without air conditioning
Note(s): With hang-on air conditioning, see Interchange Number 2.

Interchange Number: 7
Part Number(s): C9ZZ650610A# or C9ZZ650610B*
Usage: 1969–70 Mustang and Cougar—all body styles
Note(s): #Without air conditioning. *With air conditioning.

Interchange Number: 8
Part Number(s): C6OZ620610B
Usage: 1966–67 Fairlane, Comet, and Falcon—all body styles without hang-on air conditioning

Interchange Number: 9
Part Number(s): C8OZ620610B
Usage: 1968–69 Torino and Montego and 1970 Falcon—all body styles with air conditioning

Interchange Number: 10
Part Number(s): DOOZ5420610A
Usage: 1970–72 Torino and Montego—all body styles with air conditioning

Interchange Number: 11
Part Number(s): C9ZZ650610B
Usage: 1969–70 Mustang and Cougar—all body styles with air conditioning

Interchange Number: 12
Part Number(s): COAB640610A
Usage: 1959–62 full-size Ford—all models and body styles

Glovebox Door

Model Identification

Cougar	Interchange Number
1967–68, all	7
1969–70, all	8

Cyclone	Interchange Number
1966–67, all	3
1968–69, all	4
1970, all	5

Fairlane and Torino	Interchange Number
1962–63, all	1, 2
1964–65, all	2
1966–67, all	3
1968–69, all	4
1970, all	5

Mustang	Interchange Number
1964-1/2–66, all	6
1967–68, all	7
1969–70, all	8

Interchange

Interchange Number: 1
Part Number(s): C2DZ6406024A
Usage: 1962–63 Fairlane and 1962 Falcon
Note(s): Diecast type.

Interchange Number: 2
Part Number(s): C2AZ7606024ABD
Usage: 1963–65 Fairlane and 1962–64 full-size Ford
Note(s): Moulded-in colors. Black part number is given. Repaint as required.

Interchange Number: 3
Part Number(s): C6OZ6206024A
Usage: 1966–67 Fairlane, Falcon, and Comet

Interchange Number: 4
Part Number(s): C8OZ5406024A
Usage: 1968–69 Torino and Montego

Interchange Number: 5
Part Number(s): DOOZ6506024A
Usage: 1970–71 Torino and Montego
Note(s): Some models used a textured steel door.

Seat Adjustment Rails

Seat type, model, and position will have the greatest effects on the interchange here. Rails are matched in pairs, so a set of rails from the driver's side will fit those on the passenger's side. Bench seats and bucket seats each used a different set of rails and will not interchange. The good news is that rails are a Ford Motor Company part and can be found in a variety of Ford and Mercury models.

Model Identification

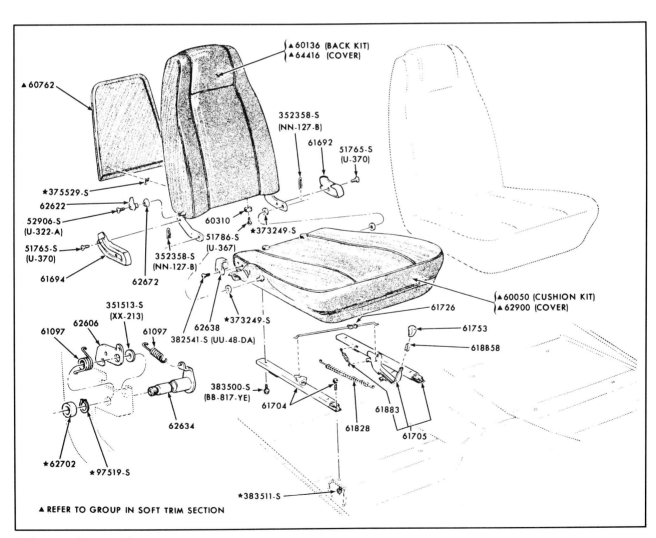

Bucket seat adjustment rails.

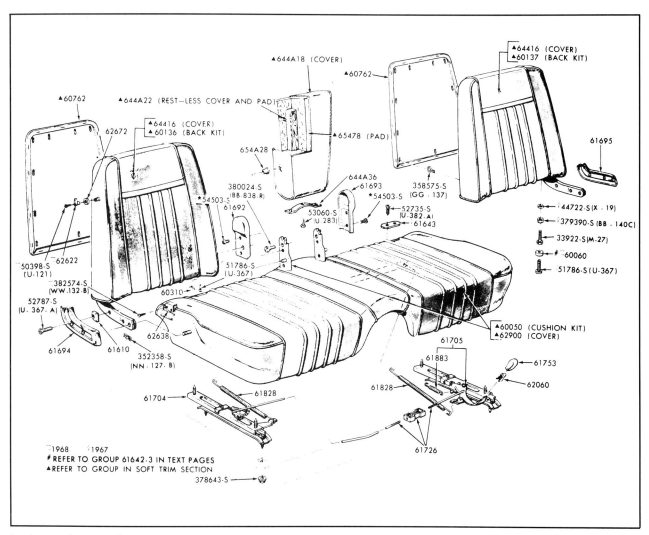

Bench seat adjustment rails.

Interchange

Interchange Number: 1
Part Number(s): COAB641704J (right), COAB641705J (left)
Seat type: Bench
Usage: 1959–63 full-size Ford and full-size Mercury

Interchange Number: 2
Part Number(s): C2OZ621704A (right), C2OZ621705A (left)
Seat type: Bench
Usage: 1962 Fairlane

Interchange Number: 3
Part Number(s): C2OZ621704B (right), C2OZ621705B (left)
Seat type: Bucket, manual control
Usage: 1962–63 Fairlane, 1960–63 Falcon, 1961–62 Meteor, and 1963 Comet

Interchange Number: 4
Part Number(s): C3OZ621704E (right), C3OZ621705C (left)
Seat type: Bench
Usage: 1963–65 Fairlane (see notes for all exceptions)
Note(s): Has 5in of travel. Used up to build date December 16, 1963, and then again after build date June 5, 1964, until the end of the 1965 model year run. Those models built from December 16, 1963, to June 5, 1964, used a rail with 4in of travel. Listed as part numbers C4OZ621704B (right), C4OZ621705B (left).

Interchange Number: 5
Part Number(s): C5OZ651704A (right), C5OZ651705A (left)
Seat type: Bucket, manual control
Usage: 1964–65 Fairlane

Interchange Number: 6
Part Number(s): C6OZ6261704C (right), C6OZ621705C (left)
Seat type: Bench
Usage: 1966–67 Fairlane, 1968–71 Torino, 1966–67 Comet, 1968–71 Montego, 1966–70 Falcon, 1971 Maverick, and 1971 Comet (compact).

Interchange Number: 7
Part Number(s): C6OZ631704A (right), C6OZ631705B (left)
Seat type: Bucket, manual
Usage: 1966–67 Fairlane and Comet, 1968–69 Torino and Montego, 1966–69 Ranchero, and 1967–69 Falcon—all except sedan and convertible

Interchange Number: 8
Part Number(s): C6OZ761704A (right), C6OZ761705B (left)
Seat type: Bucket, manual
Usage: 1966–67 Fairlane and Comet and 1968–69 Torino and Montego—all convertible only

Interchange Number: 9
Part Number(s): DOOZ651704A (right), DOOZ651705A (left)
Seat type: Bucket, manual
Usage: 1970–71 Torino and Montego

Interchange Number: 10
Part Number(s): C5ZZ651704E (right), C5ZZ651705E (left)
Seat type: Bench
Usage: 1964-1/2–66 Mustang

Interchange Number: 11
Part Number(s): C7ZZ651704A (right), C7ZZ651705A (left)
Seat type: Bench
Usage: 1967–69 Mustang and Cougar

Interchange Number: 12
Part Number(s): C5ZZ651704F (right), C5ZZ651705F (left)
Seat type: Bucket, manual control
Usage: 1965–70 Mustang and Cougar

Sun Visors

Sun visors were covered in colored vinyl trim. Color varies with color of the interior and usually matches the headliner. No interchange is given in regard to color; rather, concern here is the usage of a particular visor. The interchange here is for black or white only. Visors can always be repainted or recovered. In most cases, the visor is reversible, meaning it can fit either side of the car. Body style has little effect on their usage, with one exception—convertible. Convertibles used special visors and those from a roofed car will not fit.

Model Identification

Interchange

Interchange Number: 1
Part Number(s): COAB6404104BO9
Usage: 1960–61 full-size Ford except convertible

Interchange Number: 2
Part Number(s): C2OZ6204104BO9
Usage: 1962 Fairlane

Interchange Number: 3
Part Number(s): C3OZ6204104BO9
Usage: 1963–64 Fairlane

Interchange Number: 4
Part Number(s): C5OZ6204104AAB
Usage: 1965 Fairlane

Interchange Number: 5
Part Number(s): C6OZ6204104CAB
Usage: 1966–67 Fairlane, Comet, and Falcon—all except convertible

Interchange Number: 6
Part Number(s): C6OZ6204104AAD
Usage: 1966–67 Fairlane and Comet convertible only

Interchange Number: 7
Part Number(s): C8OZ6504104D2U
Usage: 1968–69 Torino and Montego and 1968–70 Falcon—all body styles except convertible

Interchange Number: 8
Part Number(s): C8OZ6504104C2A
Usage: 1968–69 Torino and Montego—convertible only
Note(s): Early models up to build date January 2, 1968, used the 1966–67 visors. See Interchange Number 6.

Interchange Number: 9
Part Number(s): DOOZ6504104B
Usage: 1970–71 Torino and Montego—all body styles except convertible

Interchange Number: 10
Part Number(s): DOOZ6504104C
Usage: 1970–71 Torino and Montego convertible

Interchange Number: 11
Part Number(s): C5ZZ6504104EFC
Usage: 1964-1/2–66 Mustang, 1964–65 Falcon, and 1964–65 Comet—all body styles except convertible

Interchange Number: 12
Part Number(s): C5ZZ7604104AAD
Usage: 1964-1/2–66 Mustang and 1964–65 Comet convertible

Interchange Number: 13
    Part Number(s): C7ZZ6504104B1U
    Usage: 1967–68 Mustang and Cougar—all body styles except
        convertible

Interchange Number: 14
    Part Number(s): C7ZZ7604104B1U
    Usage: 1967–68 Mustang and Cougar convertible

Interchange Number: 15
    Part Number(s): C9ZZ6504104A1A
    Usage: 1969–70 Mustang and Cougar—all body styles except
        convertible

Interchange Number: 16
    Part Number(s): C9ZZ7604104A1A
    Usage: 1969–70 Mustang and Cougar convertible

Interchange Number: 17
    Part Number(s): COAB7604104BO9
    Usage: 1960–61 full-size Ford convertible

Headrests

Headrests are greatly interchangeable. Ford and Mercury models used two different sizes of headrests. Full- and mid-size models used either the 11in headrest or a larger 13in headrest. The Mustang and Cougar used only the smaller 11in headrest. Two styles of headrests were used—the sewn type and the moulded type, and they are not interchangeable with each other. Headrests were standard and mandatory equipment only for 1969 and 1970.

Interchange is for full-size Ford and Mercury, Thunderbird, Torino, Montego, Falcon, Lincoln, Mustang, and Cougar. Just remember that there are two different lengths: 11 or 13in, and two styles: sewn or moulded—all moulded headrests are of the longer variety. But the sewn type came in both lengths. The two lengths or styles are not interchangeable. Mustang and Cougar, as previously mentioned, used only an 11in-style headrest. These are only found in two-door models of all the models above, except Lincoln.

Headrests will usually fit either the driver's or passenger's side. As for color, look for the same color as your seats or find a headrest that is in good shape and re-cover it for color match. It is usually easier to find a headrest in a non-matching color and re-cover it with a new cover than it is to find a headrest in a matching color. It is wise to order new headrest covers from the same manufacturer that made your new seat covers so that color and grain match.

Inside Door Handle

The inside door handle is a largely interchangeable item and can be found on a variety of different models. Its usage depends on the

1964-1/2–67 inner door handle for many models.

Pedal-type door handle used on 1968 Mustang.

model year and also the trim level. In some cases, two or more different sets of door handles were used. The shape or finish may be different, which will affect the interchange. Also, some handles are interchangeable from side to side and from rear door to front door; others are unique to each side or to the front doors only.

Model Identification

Cougar	Interchange Number
1967, all	4
1968, all	5
1969, all	10
1970, all	11

Cyclone	Interchange Number
1965, all	2
1966	
all except Cyclone	4
Cyclone	3
1967	
all except Cyclone	4
Cyclone	5
1968–69	7
1970	8

Fairlane and Torino	Interchange Number
1960–63, all	1
1964–65, all	2
1966	
all except GT models	4
GT models	3
1967	
all except GT models	4
GT models	5
1968–69, all	7
1970, all	8

Mustang	Interchange Number
1964-1/2–66	
without Pony interior	4
with Pony interior	6
1967	
without custom interior	4
with custom interior	12
1968, all	5
1969, all	10
1970, all	11

216

Interchange

Interchange Number: 1
Part Number(s): COAZ6422600A
Usage: 1960–62 full-size Ford, 1962–63 Fairlane, 1960–63 Falcon, 1960–63 Thunderbird, 1960–62 full-size Mercury, 1960–62 Meteor, and 1963 Comet
Note(s): Fits either side, front and rear doors.

Interchange Number: 2
Part Number(s): C3AZ6422600A
Usage: 1963–64 full-size Ford, 1964–65 Fairlane, 1963–65 Falcon, 1963–65 full-size Mercury, and 1964–65 Comet—all body styles.
Note(s): Fits either side, front doors only.

Interchange Number: 3
Part Number(s): C5MY5422600A (right), C5MY5422601A (left)
Usage: 1966 Fairlane GT and 500 XL models only, 1966 Comet Cyclone only, and 1965–66 full-size Mercury (with pedal-type handle)
Note(s): Front doors only.

Interchange Number: 4
Part Number(s): C5ZZ6522600A
Usage: 1966–67 Fairlane (except GT and 500 XL), 1966–67 Comet (except Cyclone), 1964-1/2–67 Mustang (without wood grain or 1967 with custom interior), 1966–67 Falcon, and 1967 Cougar
Note(s): Fits either side, front and rear doors.

Interchange Number: 5
Part Number(s): C7AZ5422600A (right), C7AZ5422601A (left)
Usage: 1967 Fairlane GT and 500 XL models only, 1967 Comet Cyclone only, 1967 full-size Mercury, 1967 full-size Ford (except Custom models), 1968 Mustang, and 1968 Cougar
Note(s): Front doors only. Pedal-type.

Interchange Number: 6
Part Number(s): CZZ6522600A (right), C5ZZ6522601A (left)
Usage: 1964-1/2–66 Mustang with Pony Trim interior
Note(s): Has woodgrain accents.

Interchange Number: 7
Part Number(s): C8AZ6222600B (right), C8AZ6222601B (left)
Usage: 1968–69 Torino and Montego, 1968–70 Falcon, 1968–72 Thunderbird (before build date March 1, 1972), 1968 full-size Ford, 1968 full-size Mercury, and 1969–71 Continental Mark III
Note(s): Front door only.

Interchange Number: 8
Part Number(s): DODZ6222600D (right), DODZ6222601D (left)
Usage: 1970–71 Torino and Montego, 1970 full-size Ford, 1970 Maverick (after build date September 2, 1969), and 1970 full-size Mercury
Note(s): Has brushed finish.

Interchange Number: 9
Part Number(s): D1AZ6522600A (right), D1AZ6522601A (left)
Usage: 1970–73 Torino (except 1972–73 Grand Torino fastback and 1972–73 Ranchero GT), Montego, full-size Ford, Maverick (after build date September 2, 1969), and full-size Mercury
Note(s): Has bright-finish rectangular head design. Front doors only.

Interchange Number: 10
Part Number(s): C9AZ6222600A (right), C9AZ6222601A (left)
Usage: 1969 Mustang, Cougar, full-size Ford, and full-size Mercury
Note(s): Front doors only.

Interchange Number: 11
Part Number(s): DOZZ6522600A (right), DOZZ6522601A (left)
Usage: 1970 Mustang and Cougar

Late-style 1965 Mustang window handles.

Interchange Number: 12
Part Number(s): C5ZZ6522600C
Usage: 1967 Mustang with Custom Interior group
Note(s): Fits either side.

Inside Window Regulator Handle, Front Door

Inside door window handles are greatly interchangeable and can be found in a variety of makes and models. Some models came with a knob color-keyed to the interior-trim color. There is no mention of color in this interchange, and all part numbers are for black-colored or without knobs. Knobs can be repainted or replaced.

Window handles are also interchangeable from side to side, and in most cases those used on the rear door windows will fit the front doors.

Model Identification

Cougar	Interchange Number
1967, all	7
1968, all	9
1969	
without stereo	
before build date December 2, 1968	4
after build date December 2, 1968	8
with stereo	8
1970, all	8

Cyclone	Interchange Number
1965, all	2
1966–67, all	3
1968–69, all	4
1970, all	5

Fairlane and Torino	Interchange Number
1959–63, all	1
1964–65, all	2
1966–67, all	3
1968–69	4
1970, all	5

Mustang	Interchange Number
1964-1/2–65	
before build date March 8, 1965	6
after build date March 8, 1965	7
1966–67, all	7
1968, all	9

1968-style handles for 1968 Mustang or Cougar were color-keyed to interior.

1969
    without stereo
        before build date December 2, 1968....................4
        after build date December 2, 1968.....................8
    with stereo..8
1970, all..8

Interchange

Interchange Number: 1
    Part Number(s): C2AZ6223342A
    Usage: Door, quarter, and rear door windows for 1959–62 full-size Ford, 1962–63 Fairlane, and 1960–62 full-size Mercury—all body styles

Interchange Number: 2
    Part Number(s): C4DZ6223342A
    Usage: Front and rear door window for 1964–65 Fairlane, 1964–65 Falcon, and 1964–65 Comet

Interchange Number: 3
    Part Number(s): 6OZZ6223342B
    Usage: Front and rear door and quarter windows for 1966–67 Fairlane, Comet, and Falcon

Interchange Number: 4
    Part Number(s): C8AZ6223342B1W
    Usage: Door, and rear door windows for 1968–69 Torino and Montego, 1968–70 Falcon, 1968–69 Thunderbird, 1968–71 Bronco, 1969 Mustang (without stereo), 1970 Maverick (before build date July 21, 1969), 1968–69 full-size Ford, and 1968 full-size Mercury—all body styles

Interchange Number: 5
    Part Number(s): DOAZ7630322A
    Usage: Front and rear doors or quarter windows on 1970–71 Torino (all body styles); 1970–72 full-size Ford convertible only, 1970–71 Mustang, 1971 Maverick four-door, 1970–72 Thunderbird, 1970–72 Pinto, Comet (compact), and 1971–72 Cougar (all built before October 1, 1971); 1970–71 Montego; and 1970 full-size Mercury
    Note(s): Interchange without knob.

Interchange Number: 6
    Part Number(s): C4SZ6323342A
    Usage: Front doors only on 1964-1/2–65 Mustang built before March 8, 1965, and 1965–66 Thunderbird

Interchange Number: 7
    Part Number(s): C5ZZ6523342A
    Usage: 1965–67 Mustang (after build date March 8, 1965) and 1967 Cougar

Interchange Number: 8
    Part Number(s): C9UZ8223342A
    Usage: Front door or quarter windows on 1969 Mustang after build date December 2, 1968, without stereo; 1969 Mustang with stereo; 1970 Mustang with or without stereo; and 1970–72 Maverick between build dates July 21, 1969, and October 1, 1971

Interchange Number: 9
    Part Number(s): C8ZZ653022A
    Usage: 1968 Mustang and Cougar

Console

There are many different components involved in the console swap, including the lower and upper parts, compartment door, and trim. Of these, only the upper and lower parts are given in this interchange. However, most other parts usually will interchange with them. The big consideration in interchanging is type of transmission. Some units were moulded in color, but consoles can always be repainted, so interchange by color is not given.

Model Identification

Cougar	Interchange Number
1967	
all except XR7	6
XR7	12
1968	
all except XR7 or XR7G	7
XR7	13
XR7G	14
1969, all	8
1970, all	9

Cyclone	Interchange Number
1965, all	10
1966–67, all	2
1968–69, all	3
1970, all	4

Fairlane and Torino	Interchange Number
1963–65, all	1
1966–67, all	2
1968–69, all	3
1970, all	4

Mustang	Interchange Number
1964-1/2–66, all	5
1967, all	6
1968, all	7
1969, all	8
1970, all	9

Interchange

Interchange Number: 1
    Part Number(s): C3AZ65045A36E (base), C3AZ65045A12A# or C3OZ65045A12A* (top)
    Usage: 1963–65 Fairlane and 1962–64 full-size Ford
    Note(s): Moulded-in color. #With four-speed; *without four-speed. Also, *is not found in full-size models

Interchange Number: 2
    Part Number(s): C6OZ65045A36BAB (base); C6OZ65045A12B# or C6OZ65045A12C* (top)
    Usage: 1966–67 Fairlane, 1966 Falcon, and 1966–67 Comet
    Note(s): Moulded-in color. #With four-speed; *with automatic.

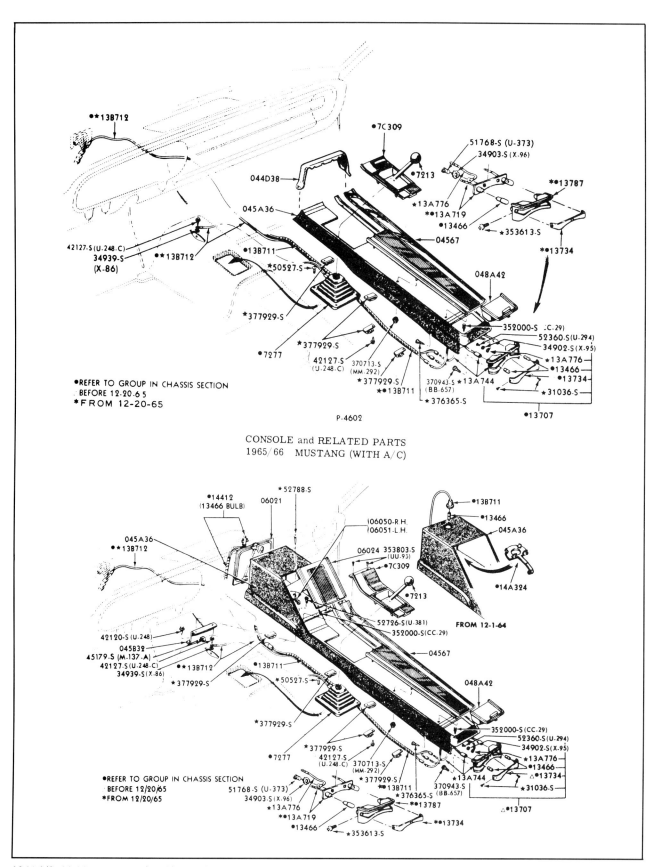

●●13B712

●7C309

51768-S (U-373)
34903-S (X-96)

●7213

044D38

★●13787

045A36
★13A776
●●13A719
●13466
★353613-S

42127-S(U-248-C)
34939-S
(X-86)
●●13B712

●13B711
★50527-S

04567

★●13734

048A42

★377929-S

352000-S :C-29)
52360-S(U-294)
34902-S(X-95)
★●13A776
●13466
★●13734
★31036-S

●7277

★377929-S

42127-S
(U-248-C)

370713-S
(MM-292)

★377929-S
●●13B711

370943-S ★13A744
(BB-657)
★376365-S

●13707

●REFER TO GROUP IN CHASSIS SECTION
 BEFORE 12-20-65
★FROM 12-20-65

P-4602

CONSOLE and RELATED PARTS
1965/66   MUSTANG (WITH A/C)

●14412
(13466 BULB)

06021

★52788-S

106050-R.H.
106051-L.H.

●13B711
●13466

045A36

045A36
●●13B712

06024 353803-S
(UU-95)

●7C309

●14A324

●7213

42120-S(U-248)

045B32
45179-S (M-137-A)
42127-S(U-248-C)
34939-S(X-86)

●●13B712

52726-S(U-381)
352000-S(CC-29)

FROM 12-1-64

04567

048A42

●13B711
★50527-S

★377929-S

★377929-S

352000-S(CC-29)
52360-S(U-294)
34902-S(X-95)
★13A776
●13466
△●13734
★31036-S

●7277

★377929-S
42127-S
(U-248-C)

370713-S
(MM-292)

★377929-S
●●13B711

★13A744
370943-S
(BB-657)

△●13707

●REFER TO GROUP IN CHASSIS SECTION
 BEFORE 12/20/65
★FROM 12/20/65

51768-S (U-373)
34903-S (X-96)
★13A776
●●13A719
●13466

★376365-S
★●13787

★●13734

★353613-S

*1964-1/2–66 Mustang console without a/c (upper) and with a/c
(lower).*

219

Interchange Number: 3

Part Number(s): C8OZ63045A36B1B (base); C8OZ6304567A#, C8OZ6304567C*, C8OZ6304567D%, or C8OZ6304567B@ (top)

Usage: 1968–69 Torino and Montego

Note(s): #Front with automatic column shift. *Rear plate with four-speed. %Rear plate with floor-shift automatic. @Rear plate with automatic column shift.

Interchange Number: 4

Part Number(s): DOOZ65045A36G (base); DOOZ6504567A#, DOOZ6604567C*, DOOZ6504567D%, DOOZ6504567B@, DOOZ6504567E^, DOOZ6504567F+, or DOOZ6504567G= (top)

Usage: 1970–71 Torino and Montego

Note(s): #Rear plate with camera-case finish (used with manual transmission). *Rear plate with wood grain (used with floor-shift automatic). %Rear plate with wood grain (used with column-shifted automatic). @Rear plate with wood grain (used with manual transmission). ^Rear plate with black trim (used with manual transmission). +Rear plate with black trim (used with floor-shift automatic transmission). =Rear plate with black trim (used with column-shifted automatic transmission).

Interchange Number: 5

Part Number(s): C5ZZ65045A36CAB (base); C5ZZ6504567A# or C5ZZ6504567C* (top)

Usage: 1964-1/2–66 Mustang

Note(s): #Camera-case finish used without air conditioning and without Pony interior. *Woodgrain finish used without air conditioning but with Pony interior.

Interchange Number: 6

Part Number(s): C7ZZ65045A36A1A (base); C7ZZ6504567A# or C7ZZ6504567B* (top)

Usage: 1967 Mustang and Cougar, except XR7 models

Note(s): #Use without warning lamps. *Use with warning lamps. Base only in Cougar. Cougar has different trim plates. Panels for shifter differ between manual and automatic.

Interchange Number: 7

Part Number(s): C8ZZ65045A36A1A (base); C8ZZ6504572A# or C5ZZ6504572B* (top)

Usage: 1968 Mustang and Cougar, except XR7 models or those with deluxe interior

Note(s): #Use with manual transmission. *Use with automatic transmission.

Interchange Number: 8

Part Number(s): C9ZZ65045A36C1A (base)

Usage: 1969 Mustang and Cougar

Note(s): Top panel differs between manual and automatic transmissions. Cougar uses different panels than those on the Mustang.

Interchange Number: 9

Part Number(s): DOZZ65045A36G (base); DOZZ6504567A#, DOZZ6504567B*, DOZZ650467C@, or DOZZ6504567D^ (top)

Usage: 1970 Mustang and Cougar

Note(s): #Use with automatic on floor shift (has teakwood finish). *Use with manual transmission (has teakwood finish). @Use with automatic on floor shift (has black finish). ^Use with manual transmission (has black finish). A change occurred in the base of all colors except red or tobacco at build date December 1, 1969. The later style will fit earlier models, but earlier base will not fit later models.

Interchange Number: 10

Part Number(s): C5DZ63045A36BFG (base)

Usage: 1965 Comet and Falcon—all except convertible

Interchange Number: 11

Part Number(s): C5DZ76045A36BFG (base)

Usage: 1965 Comet and Falcon convertible only

Interchange Number: 12

Part Number(s): C7WY65045A36B1A (base)

Usage: 1967 Cougar XR7

Interchange Number: 13

Part Number(s): C8WY65045A36A1A (base)

Usage: 1968 Cougar XR7, except XR7G

Interchange Number: 14

Part Number(s): C8WY65045A36X1A (base)

Usage: 1968 Cougar XR7G

Seatbelts

Seatbelts are a general Ford Motor Company part and can be found in a variety of makes and models. Note, however, that the convertible used special belts that differed from the cars with a roof. Seatbelts were sometimes color-keyed to the interior. No color code is given here nor is part number; this is just a guide to help you find the correct seatbelts that were used in various models. Belts are for front seats only, as they get the most wear and are more likely to have to be replaced in a restoration process. Two types of belt were used—the non-retracting type and the retracting type. Those with retractors are commonly known as custom belts. Only belts from 1966–70 are covered, as those were the years they were mandatory safety options.

Model Identification

Cougar	*Interchange Number*
1967	
all except convertible	
non-retractable	4
retractable	16
convertible	
non-retractable	5
retractable	17
1968	
all except convertible	
non-retractable	6
retractable	18
convertible	
non-retractable	7
retractable	19
1969	
all except convertible	
plastic buckle	9
chrome and plastic buckle	20
convertible	
plastic buckle	11
chrome and plastic buckle	21
1970, all	15

Cyclone	*Interchange Number*
1966–67	
all except convertible	
non-retractable	1
retractable	22
convertible	
non-retractable	2
retractable	23
1968	
all except convertible	
non-retractable	6
retractable	18
convertible	
non-retractable	7
retractable	19
1969	
all except convertible	
plastic buckle	9
chrome and plastic buckle	20
convertible	
plastic buckle	10
chrome and plastic buckle	24

1970

    all except convertible 12

    convertible..14

Fairlane and Torino   Interchange Number

1966–67

    all except convertible

        non-retractable 1

        retractable 22

    convertible

        non-retractable 2

        retractable 23

1968

    all except convertible

        non-retractable 6

        retractable 18

    convertible

        non-retractable 7

        retractable 19

1969

    all except convertible

        plastic buckle..9

        chrome and plastic buckle 20

    convertible

        plastic buckle..10

        chrome and plastic buckle 24

1970

    all except convertible or Ranchero 12

    convertible..14

    Ranchero 13

Mustang   Interchange Number

1966

    all except convertible

        non-retractable 1

        retractable 22

    convertible

        non-retractable 3

        retractable 25

1967

    all except convertible

        non-retractable 4

        retractable 16

    convertible

        non-retractable 5

        retractable 17

1968

    all except convertible

        non-retractable 6

        retractable 18

    convertible

        non-retractable 7

        retractable 19

1969

    all except convertible

        plastic buckle..9

        chrome and plastic buckle 20

    convertible

        plastic buckle..11

        chrome and plastic buckle 21

1970, all 15

Interchange

Interchange Number: 1

    Usage: 1966–67 Fairlane, 1966 Mustang, 1966–67 Falcon, 1966–67 Comet—all body styles, all except convertible

    Note(s): Standard belts were non-retractable. Retractable belts were optional (had push-button release).

Interchange Number: 2

    Usage: 1966–67 Fairlane convertible, Comet convertible, and full-size Ford and full-size Mercury (all body styles)

    Note(s): Standard belts were non-retractable, without push-button release.

Interchange Number: 3

    Usage: 1966 Mustang convertible; no other interchange

    Note(s): Non-retractable belts without push-button.

Interchange Number: 4

    Usage: 1967 Mustang and Cougar—all body styles except convertible, GT 350, and GT 500 models

    Note(s): Non-rectractable belts were standard, without push-button release

Interchange Number: 5

    Usage: 1967 Mustang and Cougar, convertible only, all except GT 350 and GT 500 models

    Note(s): Non-rectractable belts were standard, without push-button release.

Interchange Number: 6

    Usage: 1968 Torino, Montego, Mustang, Cougar, and Falcon—all body styles except convertible

    Note(s): Plastic buckle standard.

Interchange Number: 7

    Usage: 1968 Torino and Montego, convertible only

    Note(s): Plastic buckle standard.

Interchange Number: 8

    Usage: 1968 Mustang and Cougar, convertible only

    Note(s): Plastic buckle standard; chrome and plastic buckle optional.

Interchange Number: 9

    Usage: 1969 Torino, 1969 Montego, 1969 Mustang, 1969 Cougar, and 1969–70 Falcon—all body styles except convertible

    Note(s): Plastic buckle standard.

Interchange Number: 10

    Usage: 1969 Torino and Montego, convertible only

    Note(s): Plastic buckle standard.

Interchange Number: 11

    Usage: 1969 Mustang and Cougar, convertible only

    Note(s): Plastic buckle standard.

Interchange Number: 12

    Usage: 1970–71 Torino and Montego—all body styles except convertible, pickup, and four-door hardtop

Interchange Number: 13

    Usage: 1970–71 Ranchero; no other interchange

Interchange Number: 14

    Usage: 1970–71 Torino convertible only; no other interchange

Interchange Number: 15

    Usage: 1970–71 Mustang, 1970–71 Cougar, 1970–71 Maverick, and 1971 Comet (compact).

    Note(s): With three-point hitch.

Interchange Number: 16

    Usage: 1967 Mustang and Cougar—all body styles except convertible, GT 350, and GT 500 models

    Note(s): Rectractable belts with push-button release.

Interchange Number: 17

    Usage: 1967 Mustang and Cougar—all body styles except convertible, GT 350, and GT 500 models.

    Note(s): Rectractable belts with push-button release.

Interchange Number: 18

    Usage: 1968 Mustang and Cougar—all body styles except convertible, GT 350, and GT 500 models

    Note(s): Rectractable belts with chrome and plastic buckle.

Interchange Number: 19
Usage: 1967 Mustang and Cougar convertible
Note(s): Rectractable belts with chrome and plastic buckle.

Interchange Number: 20
Usage: 1969 Torino and Montego, 1969 Mustang and Cougar, and 1969–70 Falcon—all body styles except convertible
Note(s): Retractable belts with chrome and plastic buckle.

Interchange Number: 21
Usage: 1969 Torino and Montego, 1969 Mustang and Cougar, and 1969–70 Falcon, convertible only
Note(s): Chrome and plastic buckle.

Interchange Number: 22
Usage: 1966–67 Fairlane, 1966 Mustang, 1966–67 Falcon, and 1966–67 Comet—all body styles except convertible
Note(s): Retractable belts with push-button release.

Interchange Number: 23
Usage: 1966–67 Fairlane convertible, Comet convertible, full-size Ford, and full-size Mercury—all body styles
Note(s): Retractable belts with push-button release.

Interchange Number: 24
Usage: 1969 Torino and Montego convertible with chrome and plastic retractable belts.

Interchange Number: 25
Usage: 1966 Mustang convertible; no other interchange
Note(s): Retractable belts with push-button release.

Inside Rear View Mirror

Inside mirrors are largely interchangeable, regardless of the model. But in some cases a special mirror may have to be used with certain body styles. There were also different styles of mirrors, such as the breakaway-type mirror.

Model Identification

Cougar	Interchange Number
1967	
standard	6
breakaway type	7
1968–69, all	8
1970 standard	9

Cyclone	Interchange Number
1965	
standard	4
non-glare	5

1964–66-Mustang-style inside mirror.

1968–69-style inside mirror was used in a wide range of models.

1966–67	
all except convertible and two-door hardtop	
standard	6
break away	7
convertible	8
1968–69, all	8
1970, all	9

Fairlane and Torino	Interchange Number
1959–61	
all except convertible	1
convertible	2
1962–63	
all except hardtop	3
hardtop	4
1964–66	
standard	4
non-glare	5
1966–67	
all except convertible and two-door hardtop	
standard	6
break away	7
convertible	8
hardtop	8
1968–69, all	8
1970, all	9

Mustang	Interchange Number
1964-1/2–66, all	6
1967, all	7
1968–69, all	8
1970, all	9

Interchange

Interchange Number: 1
Part Number(s): COAB17700GP
Dimensions: not given
Usage: 1959–61 full-size Ford and full-size Mercury—all except convertible

Interchange Number: 2
Part Number(s): COAB17700E
Usage: 1959–61 full-size Ford and full-size Mercury, convertible only
Note(s): Chrome back.

Interchange Number: 3
Part Number(s): C2OZ17700C
Usage: 1962–63 Fairlane—all body styles except two-door hardtop in 1963

Interchange Number: 4
Part Number(s): C3DZ17700A
Usage: 1963–66 Fairlane, 1963–65 Falcon, and 1963–65 Comet, two-door hardtop and convertible models only
Note(s): Stick-on type.

Interchange Number: 5
Part Number(s): C1SZ17700D
Usage: 1963–66 Fairlane, 1963–65 Falcon, 1963–65 Comet (two-door hardtop and convertible only), and 1961–65 Thunderbird
Note(s): Non-glare type.

Interchange Number: 6
Part Number(s): C7OZ17700C
Dimensions: 2-3/8x10in long
Usage: 1964-1/2–66 Mustang (all body styles), 1966–67 Fairlane (except convertible and two-door fastback), 1966–67 Comet (except convertible and two-door fastback), 1966 Falcon, and 1967 Cougar

Interchange Number: 7
Part Number(s): C7AZ17700F1A
Dimensions: 2.42x10in long
Usage: 1967 Ranchero, 1967 Fairlane (except hardtop and convertible), 1967 Mustang, 1967 Comet (except convertible and two-door fastback), 1967 Falcon, and 1967 Cougar
Note(s): Breakaway-type mirror.

Interchange Number: 8
Part Number(s): C7AZ17700G1A
Dimensions: 2.45x10in long
Usage: 1967 Fairlane convertible and fastback, 1967 Comet convertible and fastback, 1968–69 Torino, 1968–69 Montego, 1968–69 Mustang, 1968–69 Cougar, 1968–69 full-size Ford, 1967 full-size Ford fastback and convertible, 1968–69 full-size Mercury, 1967 full-size Mercury fastback and convertible, 1967–69 Thunderbird, 1968–70 Falcon, 1968–69 Mark III, and 1968–69 Ranchero

Interchange Number: 9
Part Number(s): C9AZ17700G1A
Dimensions: 2.45x10in long
Usage: 1970–71 Torino, 1970–71 Montego, 1970–71 Mustang, 1970–71 Cougar, 1970–71 full-size Ford, 1970–71 full-size Mercury, 1970–71 Thunderbird, 1970–71 Lincoln, 1970–71 Ranchero, 1970–72 Maverick, and 1971–72 Comet (compact)
Note(s): Non-detachable arm.

Inside Door Locking Knob
A large interchange is available here, one that crosses models and sub-models.

Model Identification

Interchange

Interchange Number: 1
Part Number(s): C1DZ6421850A
Usage: 1959–62 full-size Ford and Mercury, 1962 Fairlane, 1960 Thunderbird, 1960–63 Falcon, and 1963 Comet
Note(s): This part used before build date March 11, 1963, on 1963 models. Knob is black in color.

Interchange Number: 2
Part Number(s): C3AZ6421850A
Usage: 1963 full-size Ford and Mercury, 1963 Fairlane, 1963 Falcon, and 1964-1/2–65 Mustang
Note(s): Color is moulded into the knob. The number given is for a black knob.

Interchange Number: 3
Part Number(s): C4AZ6421850A
Usage: 1964 full-size Ford and Mercury, 1964–65 Fairlane, 1964–65 Falcon, and 1964-1/2 Mustang
Note(s): Color is moulded into the knob. The number given is for a black knob.

Interchange Number: 4
Part Number(s): C5AZ6221850A
Usage: 1966–67 Fairlane, 1965–67 Thunderbird, 1965–67 full-size Ford and Mercury, 1966–67 Falcon, 1967 Mustang and Cougar, and 1966–67 Comet
Note(s): Knob is chrome.

Interchange Number: 5
Part Number(s): C8AZ6221850A
Usage: 1968–72 Torino and Montego, 1968–72 Thunderbird, 1968–72 full-size Ford and Mercury, and 1968–73 Mustang and Cougar
Note(s): Without vacuum locks only after 1972.

Interchange Number: 6
Part Number(s): C5DZ6221850A
Usage: 1964-1/2–66 Mustang, 1965 Falcon, 1965 Fairlane, 1966–67 Bronco, and 1965 Comet
Note(s): Knob is chrome.

PATENT or WARRANTY PLATE

ENGINE CODES and HORSEPOWER RATINGS

(Used in conjunction with engine identification tag codes shown in Section 60, pages 176 & 177).

CODE	ENGINE CYL.	ENGINE C.I.D.	CARB.	REMARKS	1960	1961	1962	1963	1964	CODE	ENGINE CYL.	ENGINE C.I.D.	CARB.	REMARKS	1960	1961	1962	1963	1964
B	6	223	1V	Police				138	138	R	8	427	8V	Special				425	425
B	8	406	4V	Special			385	385		S	6	144	1V		85	85	85	85	85
C	8	289	2V					195	195	T	6	200	1V					116	116
E	6	223	1V	Taxi		135	135			U	6	170	1V			101	101	101	101
F	8	260	2V				164	164	164	V	6	223	1V		135	135	135	135	138
G	8	406	6V	Special			405	405		W	8	292	2V	Standard	175	175	175		
J	8	430	4V	Auto. Trans.	375					X	8	352	2V	Special	220	220	220	220	
K	8	289	4V	Special				271	271	X	8	352	4V	Power Option					250
L	8	221	2V				145	145		Y	8	352	4V	Power Option	300				
M	8	390	6V	Special			400	400		Y	8	352	4V	Special	360				
P	8	390	4V	Police			330	330		Z	8	390	4V			300	300	300	300
Q	8	390	4V	Special			375			Z	8	390	4V	Special		375			
Q	8	427	4V	Special				410	410	Z	8	390	6V	Special		400			

BODY TYPE CODES

CODE	YEAR 19–	DESCRIPTION	CODE	YEAR 19–	DESCRIPTION
		(A) FORD 1960/ (Includes 1960/61 FAIRLANE)			
54A	60/61	Galaxie 4 Door Sedan	64F	60	Fairlane 2 Door Sedan
54A	62/	Galaxie "500" 4 Door Sedan	64G	60	Fairlane 2 Door Sedan (Business Coupe)
54B	62/63	Galaxie 4 Door Sedan	64H	60/61	Custom "300" 2 Door Sedan
54B	64/	Custom "500" 4 Door Sedan	65A	61	Galaxie 2 Door Hardtop
54E	63	Custom "300" 4 Door Sedan	65A	62/63	Galaxie "500" 2 Door Hardtop
54E	64/	Custom 4 Door Sedan	65B	62/63	Galaxie "500XL" 2 Door Hardtop
57B	64/	Galaxie "500" 4 Door Hardtop (Fastback)	71A	62/	Country Squire (9 or 10 Passenger)
57C	64	Galaxie "500XL" 4 Door Hardtop	71B	62/	Country Sedan (6 Passenger)
58A	60/61	Fairlane "500" 4 Door Sedan	71C	62/	Country Sedan (9 or 10 Passenger)
58E	60/61	Fairlane 4 Door Sedan	71D	62	4 Door Ranch Wagon (6 Passenger)
58F	60/61	Custom "300" 4 Door Sedan	71E	60/61	Country Sedan (9 Passenger)
59C	60/61	2 Door Ranch Wagon	71E	62/	Country Squire (6 Passenger)
59E	60/61	2 Door Commercial Ranch Wagon (Courier)	71F	60/61	Country Sedan (6 Passenger)
62A	60/61	Galaxie 2 Door Sedan	71G	60/61 63	Country Squire (6 or 9 Passenger)
62A	62/64	Galaxie "500" 2 Door Sedan			
62B	62/63	Galaxie 2 Door Sedan	71H	60/61	4 Door Ranch Wagon (6 Passenger)
62B	64/	Custom "500" 2 Door Sedan	71H	63	Country Squire (9 Passenger)
62E	63	Custom "300" 2 Door Sedan	71J	61	Country Squire (6 Passenger)
62E	64/	Custom 2 Door Sedan	75A	60/61	Galaxie 4 Door Hardtop
63A	60/61	Galaxie 2 Door Hardtop (Starliner)	75A	62/63	Galaxie "500" 4 Door Hardtop
63B	63/	Galaxie "500" 2 Door Hardtop	75C	63	Galaxie "500XL" 4 Door Hardtop
63C	63/64	Galaxie "500 XL" 2 Door Hardtop (Fastback)	76A	62/	Galaxie "500" Convertible
64A	60/61	Fairlane "500" 2 Door Sedan	76B	60/61	Galaxie Convertible
			76B	62/	Galaxie "500XL" Convertible
		(B) FAIRLANE 1962/			
54A	62/	4 Door Sedan	65B	63/	"500" 2 Door Sport Coupe
54B	62/	"500" 4 Door Sedan	71B	63/	Custom Ranch Wagon
62A	62/	2 Door Sedan	71D	63/	Ranch Wagon
62B	62/	"500" 2 Door Sedan	71E	63/	Squire
62C	62	"500" 2 Door Sport Coupe	71G	63	Squire
65A	63/	"500" 2 Door Hardtop			
		(S) THUNDERBIRD 1960/			
S(63A)	60/	2 Door Hardtop	S(76A)	60/	Convertible
S(63B)	62/	2 Door Hardtop (Vinyl Roof)	S(76B)	62/63	Convertible (Sports Roadster)

PATENT or WARRANTY PLATE

BODY TYPE CODES - continued

CODE	YEAR 19_	DESCRIPTION	CODE	YEAR 19_	DESCRIPTION
		(X) FALCON 1960/			
54A	63/	4 Door Sedan (Bench)	64A	60/62	2 Door Sedan (Bench)
54B	63/	Futura 4 Door Sedan	64C	62	Futura 2 Door Sedan (Bucket)
54D	64	4 Door Sedan (Deluxe)	66A	60/	Ranchero (Bench)
58A	60/62	4 Door Sedan (Bench)	66B	63/	Deluxe Ranchero (Bench)
59A	60/	2 Door Station Wagon	66H	64/	Deluxe Ranchero (Bucket)
59B	63	Deluxe 2 Door Station Wagon	71A	60/	4 Door Station Wagon
62A	63/	2 Door Sedan (Bench)	71B	62	4 Door Squire
62B	63/	Futura 2 Door Sedan (Bench)	71B	63/	Futura 4 Door Station Wagon
62C	62	Futura 2 Door Sedan (With Thunderbird Roof)	71C	63/	4 Door Squire
62C	63/	2 Door Sedan (Bucket)	71D	63	4 Door Super Deluxe Squire
62D	64/	2 Door Sedan (Deluxe-Bench)	76A	63	Convertible (Bench)
63B	63/	Futura 2 Door Hardtop (Bench)	76A	64/	Convertible (6 cyl.-Bench)
63C	63	Futura 2 Door Hardtop (Bucket)	76B	63	Convertible (Bucket)
63C	64/	2 Door Hardtop (6 cyl.-Bucket)	76B	64/	Convertible (6 cyl.-Bucket)
63D	64/	2 Door Hardtop (8 cyl.-Bucket)	76D	64	Futura Convertible (8 cyl.-Bucket)
63E	64	2 Door Hardtop (8 cyl.-Bench)	76E	64	Futura Convertible (8 cyl.-Bench)
63H	64	Futura 2 Door Hardtop (Bucket)	78A	61/	Sedan Delivery
			78B	63/	Deluxe Sedan Delivery

BODY COLOR CODE
(Refer to Paint Section)

TRIM SCHEME CODE
(Refer to Soft Trim Section)

MONTHS OF THE YEAR CODES

CODE	MONTH - FIRST YEAR	CODE	MONTH - FIRST YEAR	CODE	MONTH - SECOND YEAR	CODE	MONTH - SECOND YEAR
A	January	G	July	N	January	U	July
B	February	H	August	P	February	V	August
C	March	J	September	Q	March	W	September
D	April	K	October	R	April	X	October
E	May	L	November	S	May	Y	November
F	June	M	December	T	June	Z	December

DISTRICT CODES

CODE	DISTRICT	CODE	DISTRICT	CODE	DISTRICT	CODE	DISTRICT
11	Boston	34	Indianapolis	53	Kansas City	75	Phoenix
13	New York	35	Lansing	54	Omaha	83	Government
15	Newark	37	Buffalo	55	St. Louis	84	Home Office Reserve
16	Philadelphia	38	Pittsburgh	56	Davenport	85	American Red Cross
17	Washington	41	Chicago	61	Dallas	89	Transportation Services
21	Atlanta	42	Fargo	62	Houston	90 thru Export
22	Charlotte	43	Milwaukee	63	Memphis	99	
24	Jacksonville	44	Twin Cities	64	New Orleans		FORD OF CANADA
25	Richmond	45	Davenport	65	Oklahoma City	B1	Central
27	Cincinnati	46	Indianapolis	71	Los Angeles	B2	Eastern
28	Louisville	47	Cincinnati	72	San Jose	B3	Atlantic
32	Cleveland	51	Denver	73	Salt Lake City	B4	Midwestern
33	Detroit	52	Des Moines	74	Seattle	B6	Western
						B7	Pacific

WARRANTY PLATE or CERTIFICATION LABEL

(Refer to Pages 40 thru 44 for Bronco Warranty Plate Codes)

1965 U.S. BUILT VEHICLES
1966/ U.S. and CANADIAN BUILT VEHICLES

SERIES CODES

THE THIRD AND FOURTH DIGITS OF THE WARRANTY OR VEHICLE IDENTIFICATION NUMBER IDENTIFY THE BODY SERIES.

THE FOLLOWING CHART LISTS THESE CODES (IN CONJUNCTION WITH THE BODY TYPE CODES) AND THE SERIES OR MODEL WHICH THEY REPRESENT.

CERTIFICATION LABEL SHOWN
WARRANTY PLATE TYPICAL

```
 VEH IDENT NO
O 54 100001
 TRIM      AXLE
 5A    |    6
   NOT FOR TITLE
       MADE
```

(A) FORD 1965/

CODE SERIES	TYPE	YEAR	DESCRIPTION	CODE SERIES	TYPE	YEAR	DESCRIPTION
50	62E	67, 69	Custom 2 Door Sedan	64	54C	67/70	LTD 4 Door Sedan
51	54B	71/	Custom 4 Door Sedan	64	57B	65/66	Galaxie 500 4 Door Hardtop (Fastback)
51	54E	67/70	Custom 4 Door Sedan	64	57H	71/	LTD 4 Door Hardtop
51	62B	65/66	Custom 500 2 Door Sedan				
				65	76A	65/66	Galaxie 500 Convertible
52	54B	65/66	Custom 500 4 Door Sedan				
52	62B	67/69	Custom 500 2 Door Sedan	66	53K	71/	LTD Brougham 4 Door Pillared Hardtop
52	65D	71/	Custom 500 2 Door Hardtop	66	57F	67/70	LTD 4 Door Hardtop
				66	63B	65/66	Galaxie 500 2 Door Hardtop (Fastback)
53	54B	67/70	Custom 500 4 Door Sedan				
53	54D	71/	Custom 500 4 Door Sedan	67	57K	71/	LTD Brougham 4 Door Hardtop
53	62E	65/66	Custom 2 Door Sedan	67	63F	65/66	LTD 2 Door Fastback
54	54A	67/70	Galaxie 500 4 Door Sedan	68	63C	65/66	Galaxie 500 XL 2 Door Fastback (Bucket seats)
54	54E	65/66	Custom 4 Door Sedan	68	65K	71/	LTD Brougham 2 Door Hardtop
54	54F	71/	Galaxie 500 4 Door Sedan				
				69	76B	65/66	Galaxie 500 XL Convertible
55	63B	67	Galaxie 500 2 Door Hardtop				
55	63B	68/70	Galaxie 500 2 Door Hardtop (Fastback)	70	71B	71/	4 Door Custom Ranch Wagon
				70	71D	67/70	4 Door Ranch Wagon (6 passenger)
56	57B	67/70	Galaxie 500 4 Door Hardtop	71	71B	67	4 Door Country Sedan (6 passenger)
56	57F	71/	Galaxie 500 4 Door Hardtop	71	71D	65/66	4 Door Ranch Wagon (6 passenger)
				71	71H	68/70	4 Door Custom 500 Ranch Wagon (6 pass.)
57	76A	67/69	Galaxie 500 Convertible	72	71B	65/66	4 Door Country Sedan (6 passenger)
				72	71C	67	4 Door Country Sedan (10 passenger)
58	63C	67	Galaxie 500 XL 2 Door Hardtop (Bucket seats)	72	71D	71/	4 Door Custom 500 Ranch Wagon
58	65C	68/70	Galaxie 500 2 Door Hardtop (Formal Roof)	72	71J	68/70	4 Door Custom 500 Ranch Wagon (10 pass.)
58	65F	71/	Galaxie 500 2 Door Hardtop				
59	76B	67	Galaxie 500 XL Convertible (Bucket seats)	73	71B	68/70	4 Door Country Sedan (6 passenger)
59	65M	70	Custom 500 2 Door Hardtop	73	71E	67	4 Door Country Squire (6 passenger)
60	57F	65/66	LTD 4 Door Fastback	74	71A	67	4 Door Country Squire (10 passenger)
60	63C	68/70	XL 2 Door Hardtop (Fastback)	74	71C	65/66, 68/70	4 Door Country Sedan (10 passenger)
61	63D	66	7 Litre 2 Door Hardtop (Fastback)	74	71F	71/	4 Door Country Sedan
61	76B	68/70	XL Convertible				
61	76H	71/	LTD Convertible	75	71E	68/70	4 Door Country Squire (6 passenger)
62	54A	65/66	Galaxie 500 4 Door Sedan	76	71A	68/70	4 Door Country Squire (10 passenger)
62	63J	67	LTD 2 Door Hardtop	76	71E	65/66	4 Door Country Squire (6 passenger)
62	65A	68/70	LTD 2 Door Hardtop (Formal Roof)	76	71H	71/	4 Door Country Squire
62	65H	71/	LTD 2 Door Hardtop				
63	53H	71/	LTD 4 Door Pillared Hardtop	78	71A	65/66	4 Door Country Squire (10 passenger)
63	76D	66	7 Litre Convertible				

WARRANTY PLATE or CERTIFICATION LABEL

(Refer to Pages 40 thru 44 for Bronco Warranty Plate Codes)

SERIES CODES - continued

(B) FAIRLANE/TORINO 1965/

SERIES	TYPE	YEAR	DESCRIPTION	SERIES	TYPE	YEAR	DESCRIPTION
25	65A	71	2 Door Hardtop (Formal Roof)	41	54C	68	4 Door Sedan
25	65B	72	2 Door Hardtop (Formal Roof)	41	62B	65/66	500 2 Door Sedan
27	54A	71	Torino 4 Door Sedan	41	71B	70	500 4 Door Station Wagon
27	53B	72	4 Door Pillared Hardtop	41	76C	67	500XL Convertible
28	54B	70	500 4 Door Sedan	42	63D	68	GT 2 Door Hardtop (Fastback)
29	65B	70	500 2 Door Hardtop	42	63D	69	GT 2 Door Hardtop (Fastback-Bucket seats)
30	62A	67	2 Door Sedan	42	63F	69	GT 2 Door Hardtop (Fastback)
30	65A	68/69	2 Door Hardtop (Formal Roof)	42	54B	65/66	500 4 Door Sedan
30	65C	70	2 Door Hardtop	42	63D	67	500GT 2 Door Hardtop
30	65C	71	Torino 500 2 Door Hardtop (Formal Roof)	42	71C	70	4 Door Station Wagon
30	65C	71	500 2 Door Hardtop (Formal Roof)	42	71C	71	500 4 Door Station Wagon
30	65D	72	Gran Torino 2 Door Hardtop (Formal Roof)	42	71D	72	Gran Torino 4 Door Station Wagon
31	54A	67/69	4 Door Sedan	43	63B	66	500 2 Door Hardtop
31	54C	70	4 Door Sedan	43	65A	65	500 2 Door Hardtop
31	54C	71	500 4 Door Sedan	43	71E	70/71	Squire 4 Door Station Wagon
31	62A	65/66	2 Door Sedan	43	76D	67	500GT Convertible
31	53D	72	Gran Torino 4 Door Pillared Hardtop	43	76D	68/69	GT Convertible (Bucket seats)
				43	76F	69	GT Convertible (Bench seat)
32	54A	65/66	4 Door Sedan	43	71K	72	Gran Torino Squire 4 Door Station Wagon
32	57C	70	4 Door Hardtop	44	65D	68	GT 2 Door Hardtop (Formal Roof)
32	57C	71	500 4 Door Hardtop	44	65D	69	GT 2 Door Hardtop (Formal Roof-Bucket seats)
32	71D	67/69	4 Door Station Wagon	44	65F	69	GT 2 Door Hardtop (Formal Roof)
33	62B	67	500 2 Door Sedan	44	76D	66	500 GT Convertible
33	65B	68/69	500 2 Door Hardtop (Formal Roof)				
33	65E	68/69	500 2 Door Hardtop (Formal Roof-Bucket seats)	45	65E	69	Cobra 2 Door Hardtop (Formal Roof-Bucket seats)
33	65E	70/71	Brougham 2 Door Hardtop (Formal Roof)	45	65A	69	Cobra 2 Door Hardtop (Formal Roof-Bench seat)
34	54B	67/69	500 4 Door Sedan	45	76B	66	500 Convertible
34	63C	71	500 2 Door Hardtop (Fastback)	46	63B	69	Cobra 2 Door Hardtop (Fastback-Bench seat)
35	63B	67	500 2 Door Hardtop	46	63E	69	Cobra 2 Door Hardtop (Fastback-Bucket seats)
35	63B	68/69	500 2 Door Hardtop (Fastback)	46	66A	70/71	Ranchero
35	63E	68/69	500 2 Door Hardtop (Fastback-Bucket seats)	46	76C	66	500XL Convertible
35	63F	70/71	GT 2 Door Hardtop (Fastback)	47	63C	66	500XL 2 Door Hardtop
35	63R	72	Gran Torino 2 Door Hardtop (Fastback)	47	65B	65	2 Door Hardtop Sport Coupe
36	57E	70/71	Brougham 4 Door Hardtop	47	66A	67/69	Ranchero
36	76B	67/69	500 Convertible	47	66B	70/71	500 Ranchero
36	76E	68/69	500 Convertible (Bucket seats)	47	97D	72	500 Ranchero
37	71B	67/69	500 4 Door Station Wagon	48	66B	67/69	500 Ranchero
37	76F	70/71	GT Convertible	48	66C	70/71	GT Ranchero
38	63H	70/71	Cobra 2 Door Hardtop (Fastback)	48	71B	65	4 Door Custom Ranch Wagon
38	71D	65/66	4 Door Ranch Wagon	48	71B	66	500 4 Door Custom Ranch Wagon
38	71E	67	Squire 4 Door Station Wagon	48	97R	72	GT Ranchero
38	71E	68/69	Squire 4 Door Station Wagon	49	66C	69	GT Ranchero (Bench seat)
38	65R	72	Gran Torino Sport 2 Door Hardtop (Formal Roof)	49	66D	67	500XL Ranchero (Bucket seats)
40	63C	67	500XL 2 Door Hardtop	49	66D	68/69	GT Ranchero
40	63D	66	500GT 2 Door Hardtop	49	66E	70/71	Squire Ranchero
40	65C	68/69	2 Door Hardtop (Formal Roof)	49	71E	66	Squire 4 Door Station Wagon
40	71D	71	4 Door Station Wagon	49	97K	72	Squire Ranchero
40	71B	72	4 Door Station Wagon				

WARRANTY PLATE OR CERTIFICATION LABEL

(Refer to Pages 40 thru 44 for Bronco Warranty Plate Codes)

SERIES CODES - continued

CODE SERIES	TYPE	YEAR	DESCRIPTION	CODE SERIES	TYPE	YEAR	DESCRIPTION
			(B) FALCON 1970 - Units Built from 1/1/70				
			(For Falcon units built prior to 1/1/70 - see Catalog Symbol "X" on the next page)				
26	62A	70	Falcon 2 Door Sedan	40	71D	70	Falcon 4 Door Station Wagon
27	54A	70	Falcon 4 Door Sedan				
			(F) MUSTANG 1965/				
01	65A	67/70	2 Door Hardtop	03	76A	67/70	Convertible
01	65B	67/69	2 Door Hardtop (Luxury trim)	03	76B	68/69	Convertible (Luxury trim)
01	65B	70	Flair 2 Door Hardtop	03	76B	70	Flair Convertible
				03	76C	67	Convertible
				03	76D	67	Convertible (Luxury trim)
01	65C	67/68	2 Door Hardtop	03	76D	71/	Convertible
01	65C	69	2 Door Hardtop				
01	65D	68/69	2 Door Hardtop (Luxury trim)	04	65E	70	Grande 2 Door Hardtop
01	65D	71/	2 Door Hardtop	04	65F	71/	Grande 2 Door Hardtop
01	65E	69	Grande 2 Door Hardtop				
				05	63C	70	Mach I 2 Door Hardtop (Fastback)
				05	63R	71/	Mach I 2 Door Hardtop (Fastback)
02	63A	67, 69/70	2 Door Hardtop (Fastback)	07	65A	65/66	2 Door Hardtop
02	63B	67/69	2 Door Hardtop (Fastback-Luxury trim)	07	65B	65/66	2 Door Hardtop (Luxury trim)
02	63B	70	Flair 2 Door Hardtop (Fastback)	07	65C	65/66	2 Door Hardtop
				08	76A	65/66	Convertible
02	63C	68	2 Door Hardtop (Fastback)	08	76B	65/66	Convertible (Luxury trim)
02	63C	69	Mach I 2 Door Hardtop (Fastback)	08	76C	65/66	Convertible
02	63D	68	2 Door Hardtop (Fastback-Luxury Trim)	09	63A	65/66	2 Door Hardtop (Fastback)
02	63D	71/	2 Door Hardtop (Fastback)	09	63B	65/66	2 Door Hardtop (Fastback-Luxury trim)
			(L) PINTO 1971/				
10	62B	71/	2 Door Sedan	11	64B	71/	3 Door Sedan (Runabout)
				12	73B	72	2 Door Station Wagon

May, 1975

COPYRIGHT © 1975 — FORD MOTOR COMPANY — DEARBORN, MICHIGAN

FINAL ISSUE

WARRANTY PLATE OR CERTIFICATION LABEL

(Refer to Pages 40 thru 44 for Bronco Warranty Plate Codes)

SERIES CODES - continued

CODE SERIES	TYPE	YEAR	DESCRIPTION	CODE SERIES	TYPE	YEAR	DESCRIPTION
			(P) MAVERICK 1970/				
91	62A	70/	2 Door Sedan	93	62D	71/	Grabber 2 Door Sedan
92	54A	71/	4 Door Sedan				
			(S) THUNDERBIRD 1965/				
81	63C	66	2 Door Hardtop (Blind Quarter)	84	57B	67	4 Door Landau
81	65A	67	2 Door Hardtop	84	65B	68/71	2 Door Landau (Bucket seats)
				84	65D	68/71	2 Door Landau (Bench seat)
82	65B	67	2 Door Landau	85	76A	65/66	Convertible
				87	57B	68/69	4 Door Landau (Bucket seats)
83	63A	65/66	2 Door Hardtop	87	57B	70/71	4 Door Landau (Split Bench)
83	65A	68/71	2 Door Hardtop (Bucket seats)	87	57C	68/71	4 Door Landau (Bench seat)
83	65C	68/71	2 Door Hardtop (Bench seat)	87	63B	65	2 Door Landau
				87	65K	72	2 Door Hardtop

(X) FALCON 1965/70 - Includes Units built before 1/1/70

(For Falcon Units built from 1/1/70 - see Catalog Symbol "B" on preceding page)

CODE SERIES	TYPE	YEAR	DESCRIPTION	CODE SERIES	TYPE	YEAR	DESCRIPTION
01	62A	65	2 Door Sedan	19	62B	65	Futura 2 Door Sedan (Bench seat)
01	62A	66	2 Door Sedan				
01	62D	65	2 Door Sedan	20	62B	67	Futura 2 Door Sedan
				20	62B	68/70	Futura 2 Door Sedan (Bench seat)
02	54A	65/66	4 Door Sedan				
02	54D	65	4 Door Sedan	21	54B	67/70	Futura 4 Door Sedan
				21	59A	65	2 Door Station Wagon
06	71A	66	4 Door Station Wagon				
				22	62C	67/69	2 Door Sedan (Bucket seats)
10	62A	67/70	2 Door Sedan	22	71A	65	4 Door Station Wagon
11	54A	67/70	4 Door Sedan	23	71B	67/70	Futura 4 Door Station Wagon
11	62B	66	2 Door Sedan				
				24	71B	65	Futura 4 Door Station Wagon
12	54B	66	4 Door Sedan				
12	71A	67/68	4 Door Station Wagon	26	71C	65	4 Door Squire
12	71A	69/70	4 Door Standard Station Wagon				
13	62C	66	2 Door Sedan (Bucket seats)	27	66A	65/66	Standard Ranchero
				27	66B	65	Deluxe Ranchero
15	76A	65	Convertible (Bench seat)	27	66G	65	Standard Ranchero (Bucket seats)
15	76B	65	Convertible (Bucket seats)	27	66H	65	Deluxe Ranchero
15	76D	65	Convertible				
16	54B	65	Futura 4 Door Sedan (Bench seat)	29	66B	66	Custom Ranchero
16	71B	66	4 Door Deluxe Station Wagon	29	66D	66	Custom Ranchero
				29	78A	65	Standard Sedan Delivery
17	63B	65	Futura 2 Door Hardtop (Bench seat)				
17	63C	65	2 Door Hardtop				
17	63D	65	2 Door Hardtop (Bucket seats)				

WARRANTY PLATE OR CERTIFICATION LABEL INFORMATION

(Refer to Pages 36 thru 39 for Capri Warranty Plate Information)

1965 U.S. BUILT VEHICLES
1966/ U.S. and CANADIAN BUILT VEHICLES

SERIES CODES

CERTIFICATION LABEL SHOWN
WARRANTY PLATE TYPICAL

O : (54) 1100001

5A | 6

NOT FOR TIT

MAI

THE THIRD AND FOURTH DIGITS OF THE WARRANTY OR VEHICLE IDENTIFICATION NUMBER

IDENTIFY THE BODY SERIES.

THE FOLLOWING CHART LISTS THESE CODES (IN CONJUNCTION WITH THE BODY TYPE CODES -

EXCEPT 1965 CANADIAN BUILT VEHICLES) AND THE SERIES OR MODEL WHICH THEY REPRESENT.

(A) MERCURY

CODE SERIES	TYPE	YEAR	DESCRIPTION	CODE SERIES	TYPE	YEAR	DESCRIPTION
40	53M	69/70	Marquis 4 Door Pillared Hardtop	60	63G	69/70	Marauder 2 Door Hardtop (Tunnel Roof)
40	53X	71/	Marquis 4 Door Pillared Hardtop	61	54J	67	Brougham 4 Door Sedan
41	65M	69/70	Marquis 2 Door Hardtop	61	63H	69/70	Marauder X100 2 Door Hardtop (Tunnel Roof)
41	65X	71/	Marquis 2 Door Hardtop				
				62	50F	65/66	Parklane 4 Door Sedan (Rev. B/Lite)
42	50A	65/66	Monterey 4 Door Sedan (Rev. B/Lite)	62	53C	70	Brougham 4 Door Pillared Hardtop
42	57M	69/70	Marquis 4 Door Hardtop	62	57C	67	Brougham 4 Door Hardtop
42	57X	71/	Marquis 4 Door Hardtop	62	53K	71/	Brougham 4 Door Pillared Hardtop
43	62A	65/66	Monterey 2 Door Sedan	63	53C	69	Brougham 4 Door Pillared Hardtop
44	53B	71/	Monterey 4 Door Pillared Hardtop	63	53F	69/70	Marquis 4 Door Pillared Hardtop
44	54A	65/70	Monterey 4 Door Sedan (Fixed B/Lite)	63	53H	71/	Marquis 4 Door Pillared Hardtop
44	54B	67/68	Monterey 4 Door Sedan (Drop B/Lite)	64	54E	67/68	Parklane 4 Door Sedan (Drop B/Lite)
				64	54J	68	Parklane Brougham 4 Door Sedan
45	76A	65/70	Monterey Convertible	64	65C	70	Brougham 2 Door Hardtop (Formal Roof)
45	76G	65, 67	Monterey S-55 Convertible (Bucket Seats)	64	65K	71/	Brougham 2 Door Hardtop
46	65A	69/70	Monterey 2 Door Hardtop (Formal Roof)	65	76C	65/66	Parklane Convertible (Bucket Seats)
46	65B	71/	Monterey 2 Door Hardtop	65	76F	69/70	Marquis Convertible
46	76G	66	Monterey S-55 Convertible (Bucket Seats)	65	76F	65/68	Parklane Convertible (Bench Seat)
47	63A	65/68	Monterey 2 Door Hardtop (Fastback)	66	65C	69	Brougham 2 Door Hardtop (Formal Roof)
47	63G	65, 67	Monterey S-55 2 Door Hardtop (Bucket Seats)	66	65F	69/70	Marquis 2 Door Hardtop (Formal Roof)
				66	65H	71/	Marquis 2 Door Hardtop
48	57A	65/70	Monterey 4 Door Hardtop	67	57C	70	Brougham 4 Door Hardtop
48	57B	71/	Monterey 4 Door Hardtop	67	57K	71/	Brougham 4 Door Hardtop
49	63G	66	Monterey S-55 2 Door Hardtop (Bucket Seats)	67	63C	65/66	Parklane 2 Door Hardtop (Bucket Seats)
				67	63F	65/68	Parklane 2 Door Hardtop (Bench Seat)
52	50B	65/66	Montclair 4 Door Sedan (Rev. B/Lite)	68	57C	68/69	Parklane Brougham 4 Door Hardtop
54	53F	71/	Monterey Custom 4 Door Pillared Hardtop	68	57F	65/68	Parklane 4 Door Hardtop
54	54B	66	Montclair 4 Door Sedan	68	57F	69/70	Marquis 4 Door Hardtop
54	54C	67/68	Montclair 4 Door Sedan (Fixed B/Lite)	68	57H	71/	Marquis 4 Door Hardtop
54	54C	69/70	Monterey Custom 4 Door Sedan	69	63D	67/68	Marquis 2 Door Hardtop
54	54D	67/68	Montclair 4 Door Sedan (Drop B/Lite)	72	71B	65/68	Commuter 4 Door Station Wagon (6 Pass.)
				72	71B	69/70	Monterey 4 Door Station Wagon (10 Pass.)
56	65B	69/70	Monterey Custom 2 Door Hardtop (Formal Roof)	72	71B	71/	Monterey 4 Door Station Wagon
56	65F	71/	Monterey Custom 2 Door Hardtop	72	71C	65/68	Commuter 4 Door Station Wagon (9 or 10 Pass.)
				72	71C	69/70	Monterey 4 Door Station Wagon (10 Pass.)
57	63B	65/68	Montclair 2 Door Hardtop (Fastback)	74	71F	69	Monterey Custom 4 Door Station Wagon (6 Pass.)
57	63B	68	Montclair 2 Door Hardtop (Formal Roof)				
58	57B	65/68	Montclair 4 Door Hardtop	74	71F	70	Marquis 4 Door Station Wagon (6 Pass.)
58	57B	69/70	Monterey Custom 4 Door Hardtop	74	71G	70	Marquis 4 Door Station Wagon (10 Pass.)
58	57F	71/	Monterey Custom 4 Door Hardtop	74	71H	71/	Marquis 4 Door Station Wagon

FINAL ISSUE

LINCOLN-MERCURY CAR PARTS

WARRANTY PLATE OR CERTIFICATION LABEL INFORMATION

(Refer to Pages 36 thru 39 for Capri Warranty Plate Information)

SERIES CODES - continued

CODE SERIES	TYPE	YEAR	DESCRIPTION	CODE SERIES	TYPE	YEAR	DESCRIPTION
			(A) MERCURY - continued				
76	71A	65/68	Colony Park 4 Door Station Wagon (9 or 10) Pass.)	76	71E	65/68	Colony Park 4 Door Station Wagon (6 Pass.)
76	71A	69/70	Marquis Colony Park 4 Door Station Wagon (10 Pass.)	76	71E	69/70	Marquis Colony Park 4 Door Station Wagon (6 Pass.)
				76	71G	69	Monterey Custom 4 Door Station Wagon (10 Pass.)
				76	71K	71/	Marquis Colony Park 4 Door Station Wagon

(C) COMET (1965/67), COMET/MONTEGO (1968/70), MONTEGO (1971/)

FOR 1971/ COMET - Refer to (P) COMET Listed on Next Page

CODE SERIES	TYPE	YEAR	DESCRIPTION	CODE SERIES	TYPE	YEAR	DESCRIPTION
01	62A	65/67	202 2 Door Sedan	12	54B	65/66	404 4 Door Sedan
01	65A	68	Sports Coupe	12	57D	70/71	MX Brougham 4 Door Hardtop
01	65A	69/71	2 Door Hardtop (Formal Roof)	12	76B	68/69	MX Convertible (Bucket Seats)
				12	76D	67	Caliente Convertible
02	53B	72	4 Door Pillared Hardtop	12	76D	68/69	MX Convertible (Bench Seat)
02	54A	65/67	202 4 Door Sedan	13	63B	66	Capri 2 Door Hardtop
02	54A	70/71	4 Door Sedan				
				15	63A	68	Cyclone 2 Door Hardtop (Fastback-Bench Seat)
03	65B	72	2 Door Hardtop	15	63A	69	Cyclone 2 Door Hardtop (Fastback)
03	71A	67	Voyager 4 Door Station Wagon	15	63C	68	Cyclone 2 Door Hardtop (Fastback-Bucket Seats)
04	53D	72	MX 4 Door Pillared Hardtop	15	63E	67	Cyclone 2 Door Hardtop (Bucket Seats)
05	63D	72	MX 2 Door Hardtop (Fastback)	15	63H	67	GT 2 Door Hardtop (Bucket seats)
				15	63H	68	Cyclone GT 2 Door Hardtop (Fastback)
06	54B	67	Capri 4 Door Sedan	15	65F	70/71	Cyclone 2 Door Hardtop
06	54B	68/69	4 Door Sedan				
06	54B	70/71	MX 4 Door Sedan	16	63H	69	Cyclone CJ 2 Door Hardtop (Fastback)
06	71A	66	Voyager 4 Door Station Wagon	16	63R	72	GT 2 Door Hardtop (Fastback)
				16	65H	70/71	Cyclone GT 2 Door Hardtop
07	63B	67	Capri 2 Door Hardtop	16	71C	66	Villager 4 Door Station Wagon (Woodrail)
07	65B	68/69	2 Door Hardtop (Formal Roof)	16	76C	67	Cyclone Convertible (Bucket Seats)
07	65B	70/71	MX 2 Door Hardtop	16	76H	67	GT Convertible (Bucket Seats)
07	65D	72	MX 2 Door Hardtop (Formal Roof)				
07	65E	70	MX 2 Door Hardtop (Bucket Seats)	17	65F	68	Cyclone 2 Door Hardtop (Formal Roof-Bench Seat)
				17	65G	68	Cyclone 2 Door Hardtop (Formal Roof-Bucket Seats)
08	71A	69	MX 4 Door Station Wagon (Woodgrain)	17	65G	70/71	Cyclone Spoiler 2 Door Hardtop
08	71C	67	Villager 4 Door Station Wagon (10 Pass.)	17	65H	68	Cyclone GT 2 Door Hardtop (Bucket Seats)
08	71C	68/69	MX 4 Door Station Wagon				
08	71C	70/71	MX 4 Door Station Wagon	18	71A	70/71	MX 4 Door Station Wagon (Woodgrain)
08	71D	72	MX 4 Door Station Wagon	18	71K	72	Villager 4 Door Station Wagon
10	53K	72	Brougham 4 Door Pillared Hardtop	22	54D	65/66	Caliente 4 Door Sedan
10	54C	68	MX Brougham 4 Door Sedan	23	63C	65/66	Caliente 2 Door Hardtop (Bucket Seats)
10	54C	69	MX Brougham 4 Door Sedan	23	63D	65/66	Caliente 2 Door Hardtop
10	54D	67	Caliente 4 Door Sedan	25	76B	65/66	Caliente Convertible (Bucket Seats)
10	54D	68/69	MX 4 Door Sedan	25	76D	65/66	Caliente Convertible
10	54D	70/71	MX Brougham 4 Door Sedan				
				26	63H	66	Cyclone GT 2 Door Hardtop (Bucket Seats)
11	62B	65	404 2 Door Sedan	27	63E	65/66	Cyclone 2 Door Hardtop (Bucket Seats)
11	62C	65	404 2 Door Sedan (Bucket Seats)	27	63H	66	Cyclone GT 2 Door Hardtop (Bucket Seats)
11	63D	67	Caliente 2 Door Hardtop	28	76H	66	Cyclone GT Convertible (Bucket Seats)
11	65C	68/69	MX Brougham 2 Door Hardtop (Formal Roof)	29	76C	66	Cyclone Convertible (Bucket Seats)
11	65D	68/69	MX 2 Door Hardtop (Formal Roof-Bench Seat)	29	76H	66	Cyclone GT Convertible (Bucket Seats)
11	65D	70/71	MX Brougham 2 Door Hardtop				
11	65E	68/69	MX 2 Door Hardtop (Formal Roof-Bucket Seats)	32	71A	65	202 4 Door Station Wagon
11	65K	72	Brougham 2 Door Hardtop (Formal Roof)	34	71B	65	404 4 Door Station Wagon
				36	71C	65	404 4 Door Station Wagon (Woodrail)

WARRANTY PLATE OR CERTIFICATION LABEL INFORMATION

(Refer to Pages 36 thru 39 for Capri Warranty Plate Information)

SERIES CODES - continued

CODE SERIES	TYPE	YEAR	DESCRIPTION	CODE SERIES	TYPE	YEAR	DESCRIPTION
			(D) LINCOLN				
81	65A	68/	2 Door Hardtop	86	74A	65/67	4 Door Convertible
82	53A	65/	4 Door Sedan	89	65A	66/67	2 Door Hardtop
			(F) COUGAR				
91	65A	67/70	2 Door Hardtop (Bucket Seats)	93	65B	67/70	XR7 2 Door Hardtop (Bucket Seats)
91	65C	67/69	2 Door Hardtop (Bench Seat)	93	65F	71/	XR7 2 Door Hardtop (Bucket seats)
91	65D	71/	2 Door Hardtop (Bucket seats)				
92	76A	69/70	Convertible	94	76B	69/70	XR7 Convertible
92	76D	71/	Convertible	94	76F	71/	XR7 Convertible
			(K) MARK III, IV				
89	65A	68/71	2 Door Hardtop	89	65D	72	2 Door Hardtop

(P) COMET (1971/)
FOR 1965/70 COMET/MONTEGO - Refer to (C) Listed on Previous Page

CODE SERIES	TYPE	YEAR	DESCRIPTION	CODE SERIES	TYPE	YEAR	DESCRIPTION
30	54B	71/	4 Door Sedan	31	62B	71/	2 Door Sedan

(Y) METEOR
SERIES CODES NOT USED IN 1965

CODE SERIES	TYPE	YEAR	DESCRIPTION	CODE SERIES	TYPE	YEAR	DESCRIPTION
20	53B	71/	Rideau 4 Door Pillared Hardtop	28	71B	68/69	Rideau 500 4 Door Station Wagon (6 Pass.)
20	54A	68/70	Rideau 4 Door Sedan	28	71J	67	Rideau 500 4 Door Station Wagon (6 Pass.)
20	54F	67	Rideau 4 Door Sedan	28	76C	70	Montcalm Convertible
				28	76E	70	Montcalm S-33 Convertible
21	54B	68/69	Rideau 500 4 Door Sedan				
21	54G	67	Rideau 500 4 Door Sedan	29	71C	68/69	Rideau 500 4 Door Station Wagon (10 Pass.)
				29	71M	67	Rideau 500 4 Door Station Wagon (10 Pass.)
22	53D	71/	Rideau 500 4 Door Pillared Hardtop				
22	54B	70	Rideau 500 4 Door Sedan	30	54C	68/69	Montcalm 4 Door Sedan
22	63B	68	Rideau 500 2 Door Hardtop (Fastback)	30	54H	67	Montcalm 4 Door Sedan
22	63L	67	Rideau 500 2 Door Hardtop	30	71X	66	Rideau 500 4 Door Station Wagon (6 Pass.)
23	65B	69/70	Rideau 500 2 Door Hardtop	31	62X	66	Rideau 2 Door Sedan
23	65D	71/	Rideau 500 2 Door Hardtop	31	63D	68	Montcalm 2 Door Hardtop (Fastback)
				31	63E	68	Montcalm S-33 2 Door Hardtop (Fastback)
24	65F	69	LeMoyne 2 Door Hardtop	31	63J	67	Montcalm 2 Door Hardtop
				31	63M	67	Montcalm S-33 2 Door Hardtop
25	53F	71/	Montcalm 4 Door Pillared Hardtop	32	54X	66	Rideau 4 Door Sedan
25	54C	70	Montcalm 4 Door Sedan	32	57G	67	Montcalm 4 Door Hardtop
25	63F	68	LeMoyne 2 Door Hardtop (Formal Roof)	32	63C	68	Montcalm 2 Door Hardtop (Formal Roof)
25	63K	67	Montego 2 Door Hardtop				
				33	57C	68	Montcalm 4 Door Hardtop (Fastback)
26	65B	69	Rideau 2 Door Hardtop	33	57C	69	Montcalm 4 Door Hardtop
26	65C	70	Montcalm 2 Door Hardtop	33	62T	66	Rideau 500 2 Door Sedan
26	65E	70	Montcalm S-33 2 Door Hardtop	33	76J	67	Montcalm Convertible
26	65F	71/	Montcalm 2 Door Hardtop	33	76L	67	Montcalm S-33 Convertible
26	76F	68	LeMoyne Convertible				
26	76K	67	Montego Convertible	34	54T	66	Rideau 500 4 Door Sedan
				34	65F	70	LeMoyne 2 Door Hardtop
27	57C	70	Montcalm 4 Door Hardtop	34	76C	68	Montcalm Convertible
27	57F	68	LeMoyne 4 Door Hardtop	34	76C	69	Montcalm Convertible
27	57F	69	LeMoyne 4 Door Hardtop	34	76E	68	Montcalm S-33 Convertible
27	57F	71/	Montcalm 4 Door Hardtop	34	76E	69	Montcalm S-33 Convertible

LINCOLN-MERCURY CAR PARTS

WARRANTY PLATE OR CERTIFICATION LABEL INFORMATION

(Refer to Pages 36 thru 39 for Capri Warranty Plate Information)

SERIES CODES - continued

(Y) METEOR - continued
SERIES CODES NOT USED IN 1965

CODE SERIES	TYPE	YEAR	DESCRIPTION	CODE SERIES	TYPE	YEAR	DESCRIPTION
35	57F	70	LeMoyne 4 Door Hardtop	38	57A	66	Montcalm 4 Door Hardtop
35	65C	69	Montcalm 2 Door Hardtop	38	71E	68/70	Montcalm 4 Door Station Wagon (6 Pass.)
35	65E	69	Montcalm S-33 2 Door Hardtop	38	71F	71/	Montcalm 4 Door Station Wagon
35	76A	66	Montcalm Convertible	38	71K	67	Montcalm 4 Door Station Wagon (6 Pass.)
				39	71A	68/70	Montcalm 4 Door Station Wagon (10 Pass.)
36	54A	66	Montcalm 4 Door Sedan	39	71B	66	Montcalm 4 Door Station Wagon (6 Pass.)
36	71B	70	Rideau 500 4 Door Station Wagon (6 Pass.)	39	71L	67	Montcalm 4 Door Station Wagon (10 Pass.)
36	71D	71/	Rideau 500 4 Door Station Wagon				
				90	71T	66	Rideau 500 4 Door Station Wagon (10 Pass.)
37	63A	66	Montcalm 2 Door Hardtop	95	76G	66	Montcalm S-33 Convertible
37	71C	70	Rideau 500 4 Door Station Wagon (10 Pass.)	97	63G	66	Montcalm S-33 2 Door Hardtop
				99	71C	66	Montcalm 4 Door Station Wagon (10 Pass.)

1965 U.S. BUILT VEHICLES
1966/ U.S. and CANADIAN BUILT VEHICLES

CERTIFICATION LABEL SHOWN
WARRANTY PLATE TYPICAL

```
┌──────────────────────┐
│              │        │
│   OS5 (H) 30001       │
├──────────────┬───────┤
│    5A        │   6    │
├──────────────┴───────┤
│   NOT FOR T'          │
│                       │
│              MA       │
└──────────────────────┘
```

ENGINE CODES

THE FIFTH DIGIT OF THE WARRANTY OR VEHICLE IDENTIFICATION NUMBER INDICATES BASIC ENGINE IDENTIFICATION.

THE FOLLOWING CHART LISTS THESE CODES AS WELL AS NUMBER OF CYLINDERS, CUBIC INCH DISPLACEMENT AND NUMBER OF CARBURETOR VENTURI.

FOR FURTHER ENGINE IDENTIFICATION REFER TO SECTION 60 IN THIS CATALOG.

CODE	YEAR	ENGINE CYL.	ENGINE C.I.D.	CARB.	REMARKS	CODE	YEAR	ENGINE CYL.	ENGINE C.I.D.	CARB.	REMARKS
A	65	8	289	4V	P.F.	P	65	8	390	4V	P/C
	67/68	8	289	4V	P.F.		66/70	8	428	4V	P/C
	68/	8	460	4V			71/	8	429	4V	P/C
C	65/67	8	289	2V		Q	66/68	8	428	4V	
	70/71	8	429	4V	CJ-w hyd.lifters		69/70	8	428	4V	CJ-w/hyd.lifters
D	65	8	289	4V	Special		71/	8	351	4V	GT
	69	8	302	4V	Taxi	R	65/67	8	427	8V	Special
	71/	8	302	2V	Taxi		69/70	8	428	4V	CJ-Ram air
F	68/	8	302	2V		S	66/69	8	390	4V	GT
G	66/68	8	462	4V			71/	8	400	2V	
	69/70	8	302	4V	Special	T	65/68	6	200	1V	
H	65/67	8	390	2V	C6 auto.		71/	6	200	1V	
	69/	8	351	2V		U	71/	6	170	1V	
J	68	8	302	4V		W	66/68	8	427	4V	Hi Perf.
	69	8	428	4V	CJ-w mech.lifters	X	67/69	8	390	2V	P.F.
	71	8	429	4V	CJ-Ram air						
K	69/	8	429	2V		Y	65/67	8	390	2V	M/T
L	69/	6	250	1V			68/70	8	390	2V	R.F.
M	66/67	8	410	4V		Z	65/66	8	390	4V	
	69/71	8	351	4V			68	8	390	4V	
N	65	8	430	4V			69/70	8	429	4V	Special
	69/	8	429	4V							

WARRANTY PLATE OR CERTIFICATION LABEL INFORMATION

(Refer to Pages 36 thru 39 for Capri Warranty Plate Information)

ENGINE CODES - continued

ENGINE CODES

THE FIRST DIGIT OF THE "ENGINE" CODE INDICATES BASIC ENGINE IDENTIFICATION. THE FOLLOWING CHART LISTS THESE CODES AS WELL AS NUMBER OF CYLINDERS, CUBIC INCH DISPLACEMENT AND NUMBER OF CARBURETOR VENTURI.

FOR FURTHER ENGINE IDENTIFICATION REFER TO SECTION 60 IN THIS CATALOG.

1965 CANADIAN BUILT VEHICLES

CODE	CYL.	C.I.D.	REMARKS	CODE	CYL.	C.I.D.	REMARKS
B	6	170		F	8	289	
C	6	240		G	8	352	
D	6	200		J	8	390	
				M	8	260	

NUMERICAL SEQUENCE OF ASSEMBLY

THE LAST SIX DIGITS OF THE SERIAL NUMBER CORRESPOND TO SERIAL NUMBERS SHOWN IN THE CATALOG. THESE ASSIST IN DETERMINING THE CORRECT PART NUMBER IN THE CASE OF "BEFORE. . ." AND "FROM. . ." DATES.

1965 CANADIAN BUILT VEHICLES

BODY TYPE CODES

THIS CODE APPEARS ABOVE OR BELOW "BODY" AND IDENTIFIES THE BODY TYPE OF THE UNIT. THE FOLLOWING CHART LISTS THESE CODES (IN CONJUNCTION WITH THE SERIES CODES) AND THE BODY TYPE WHICH THEY REPRESENT.

1965   U.S. BUILT VEHICLES
1966/ U.S. and CANADIAN BUILT VEHICLES

CERTIFICATION LABEL SHOWN WARRANTY PLATE TYPICAL

(54A)	B
X	33

OR REGISTRATION

IN U.S.A.

BODY TYPE CODES

THE SECOND, THIRD AND FOURTH DIGITS OF THE SERIAL NUMBER IDENTIFY THE BODY TYPE OF THE UNIT.

1965 CANADIAN BUILT VEHICLES

ENGINE SERIAL NO. IS LOCATED O

PAINT | TRIM | ENGINE | SPEC
2HH | 342 | JB3 |
SERIAL NUMBER
1(54A) 65L 700001

FINAL ISSUE

WARRANTY PLATE OR CERTIFICATION LABEL INFORMATION

(Refer to Pages 36 thru 39 for Capri Warranty Plate Information)

BODY TYPE CODES - continued

(A) MERCURY

CODE TYPE	SERIES	YEAR	DESCRIPTION	CODE TYPE	SERIES	YEAR	DESCRIPTION
50A	42	65/66	Monterey 4 Door Sedan (Rev. B/Lite)	63G	47	65, 67	Monterey S-55 2 Door Hardtop (Bucket Seats)
50B	52	65/66	Montclair 4 Door Sedan (Rev. B/Lite)	63G	49	66	Monterey S-55 2 Door Hardtop (Bucket Seats)
50F	62	65/66	Parklane 4 Door Sedan (Rev. B/Lite)	63G	60	69/70	Marauder 2 Door Hardtop (Tunnel Roof)
53B	44	71/	Monterey 4 Door Pillared Hardtop				
53C	62	70	Brougham 4 Door Pillared Hardtop	63H	61	69/70	Marauder X100 2 Door Hardtop (Tunnel Roof)
53C	63	69	Brougham 4 Door Pillared Hardtop				
53F	54	71/	Monterey Custom 4 Door Pillarded Hardtop	65A	46	69/70	Monterey 2 Door Hardtop (Formal Roof)
53F	63	69/70	Marquis 4 Door Pillared Hardtop	65B	46	71/	Monterey 2 Door Hardtop
53H	63	71/	Marquis 4 Door Pillared Hardtop	65B	56	69/70	Monterey Custom 2 Door Hardtop (Formal Roof)
53K	62	71/	Brougham 4 Door Pillared Hardtop	65C	64	70	Brougham 2 Door Hardtop (Formal Roof)
53M	40	69/70	Marquis 4 Door Pillared Hardtop	65C	66	69	Brougham 2 Door Hardtop (Formal Roof)
53X	40	71/	Marquis 4 Door Pillared Hardtop				
54A	44	65/70	Monterey 4 Door Sedan (Fixed B/Lite)	65F	56	71/	Monterey Custom 2 Door Hardtop
54B	44	67/68	Monterey 4 Door Sedan (Drop B/Lite)	65F	66	69/70	Marquis 2 Door Hardtop (Formal Roof)
54B	54	66	Montclair 4 Door Sedan	65H	66	71/	Marquis 2 Door Hardtop
54C	54	67/68	Montclair 4 Door Sedan (Fixed B/Lite)	65K	64	71/	Brougham 2 Door Hardtop
54C	54	69/70	Monterey Custom 4 Door Sedan				
54D	54	67/68	Montclair 4 Door Sedan (Drop B/Lite)	65M	41	69/70	Marquis 2 Door Hardtop (Formal Roof)
54E	64	67/68	Parklane 4 Door Sedan (Drop B/Lite)	65X	42	71/	Marquis 2 Door Hardtop (Formal Roof)
54J	61	67	Brougham 4 Door Sedan	71A	76	65/68	Colony Park 4 Door Station Wagon (9 or 10 Pass.)
54J	64	68	Parklane Brougham 4 Door Sedan	71A	76	69/70	Marquis Colony Park 4 Door Station Wagon (10 Pass.)
57A	48	65/70	Monterey 4 Door Hardtop	71B	72	65/68	Commuter 4 Door Station Wagon (6 Pass.)
57B	48	71/	Monterey 4 Door Hardtop	71B	72	69/70	Monterey 4 Door Station Wagon (10 Pass.)
57B	58	65/68	Montclair 4 Door Hardtop	71B	72	71/	Monterey 4 Door Station Wagon
57B	58	69/70	Monterey Custom 4 Door Hardtop	71C	72	65/68	Commuter 4 Door Station Wagon (9 or 10 Pass.)
57C	62	67	Brougham 4 Door Hardtop	71C	72	69/70	Monterey 4 Door Station Wagon (10 Pass.)
57C	67	70	Brougham 4 Door Hardtop				
57C	68	68/69	Parklane Brougham 4 Door Hardtop	71E	76	65/68	Colony Park 4 Door Station Wagon (6 Pass.)
57F	58	71/	Monterey Custom 4 Door Hardtop	71E	76	69/70	Marquis Colony Park 4 Door Station Wagon (6 Pass.)
57F	68	65/68	Parklane 4 Door Hardtop	71F	74	69	Monterey Custom 4 Door Station Wagon (6 Pass.)
57F	68	69/70	Marquis 4 Door Hardtop				
57H	68	71/	Marquis 4 Door Hardtop	71F	74	70	Marquis 4 Door Station Wagon (6 Pass.)
57K	67	71/	Brougham 4 Door Hardtop	71G	74	70	Marquis 4 Door Station Wagon (10 Pass.)
57M	42	69/70	Marquis 4 Door Hardtop	71G	76	69	Monterey 4 Door Station Wagon (10 Pass.)
57X	42	71/	Marquis 4 Door Hardtop	71H	74	71/	Marquis 4 Door Station Wagon
62A	43	65/66	Monterey 2 Door Sedan	71K	76	71/	Marquis Colony Park 4 Door Station Wagon
63A	47	65/68	Monterey 2 Door Hardtop (Fastback)	76A	45	65/70	Monterey Convertible
63B	57	65/67	Montclair 2 Door Hardtop (Fastback)	76C	65	65/66	Parklane Convertible (Bucket Seats)
63B	57	68	Montclair 2 Door Hardtop (Fastback or Formal Roof)	76F	65	65/68	Parklane Convertible (Bench Seat)
63C	67	65/66	Parklane 2 Door Hardtop (Bucket Seats)	76F	65	69/70	Marquis Convertible (Bench Seat)
63D	69	67/68	Marquis 2 Door Hardtop	76G	45	65, 67	Monterey S-55 Convertible (Bucket Seats)
63F	67	65/68	Parklane 2 Door Hardtop (Bench Seat)	76G	46	66	Monterey S-55 Convertible (Bucket Seats)

WARRANTY PLATE OR CERTIFICATION LABEL INFORMATION

(Refer to Pages 36 thru 39 for Capri Warranty Plate Information)

BODY TYPE CODES - continued

CODE TYPE	SERIES	YEAR	DESCRIPTION	CODE TYPE	SERIES	YEAR	DESCRIPTION
(C) COMET (1965/67), COMET/MONTEGO (1970), MONTEGO (1971/)							
FOR 1971/ COMET - Refer to (P) COMET Listed on Next Page							
53B	02	72	4 Door Pillared Hardtop	65B	07	68/69	2 Door Hardtop (Formal Roof)
53D	04	72	MX 4 Door Pillared Hardtop	65B	07	70/71	MX 2 Door Hardtop
53K	10	72	Brougham 4 Door Pillared Hardtop	65B	03	72	2 Door Hardtop
				65C	11	68/69	MX Brougham 2 Door Hardtop(Formal Roof)
54A	02	65/67	202 4 Door Sedan	65D	11	68/69	MX 2 Door Hardtop (Formal Roof-Bench Seat)
54A	02	70/71	4 Door Sedan	65D	11	70/71	MX Brougham 2 Door Hardtop
54B	06	67	Capri 4 Door Sedan	65D	07	72	MX 2 Door Hardtop
54B	06	68/69	4 Door Sedan	65E	07	70	MX 2 Door Hardtop (Bucket Seats)
54B	06	70/71	MX 4 Door Sedan	65E	11	68/69	MX 2 Door Hardtop (Formal Roof-Bucket Seats)
54B	12	65/66	404 4 Door Sedan				
54C	10	68	MX Brougham 4 Door Sedan	65F	15	70/71	Cyclone 2 Door Hardtop
54C	10	69	MX Brougham 4 Door Sedan	65F	17	68	Cyclone 2 Door Hardtop (Formal Roof-Bench Seat)
54D	10	67	Caliente 4 Door Sedan	65G	17	68	Cyclone 2 Door Hardtop (Formal Roof-Bucket Seats)
54D	10	68/69	MX 4 Door Sedan	65G	17	70/71	Cyclone Spoiler 2 Door Hardtop
54D	10	70/71	MX Brougham 4 Door Sedan				
54D	22	65/66	Caliente 4 Door Sedan	65H	16	70/71	Cyclone GT 2 Door Hardtop
57D	12	70/71	MX Brougham 4 Door Hardtop	65H	17	68	Cyclone GT 2 Door Hardtop (Bucket Seats)
62A	01	65/67	202 2 Door Sedan	65K	11	72	Brougham 2 Door Hardtop
62B	11	65	404 2 Door Sedan				
62C	11	65	404 2 Door Sedan (Bucket Seats)	71A	03	67	Voyager 4 Door Station Wagon
				71A	06	66	Voyager 4 Door Station Wagon
63A	15	68	Cyclone 2 Door Hardtop (Fastback-Bench Seat)	71A	08	69	MX 4 Door Station Wagon (Woodgrain)
63A	15	69	Cyclone 2 Door Hardtop (Fastback)	71A	18	70/71	MX 4 Door Station Wagon (Woodgrain)
63B	07	67	Capri 2 Door Hardtop	71A	32	65	202 4 Door Station Wagon
63B	13	66	Capri 2 Door Hardtop	71B	34	65	404 4 Door Station Wagon
63C	15	68	Cyclone 2 Door Hardtop (Fastback-Bucket Seats)	71C	08	67	Villager 4 Door Station Wagon (10 Pass.)
63C	23	65/66	Caliente 2 Door Hardtop (Bucket Seats)	71C	08	68/69	MX 4 Door Station Wagon (Bench Seat)
				71C	08	70/71	MX 4 Door Station Wagon (Metal)
63D	11	67	Caliente 2 Door Hardtop	71C	16	66	Villager 4 Door Station Wagon (Woodrail)
63D	23	65/66	Caliente 2 Door Hardtop	71C	36	65	404 4 Door Station Wagon (Woodrail)
63D	05	72	MX 2 Door Hardtop				
63E	15	67	Cyclone 2 Door Hardtop (Bucket Seats)	71D	08	72	MX 4 Door Station Wagon
63E	27	65/66	Cyclone 2 Door Hardtop (Bucket Seats)	71K	18	72	Villager 4 Door Station Wagon
63H	15	67	GT 2 Door Hardtop (Bucket Seats)	76B	12	68/69	MX Convertible (Bucket Seats)
63H	15	68	Cyclone GT 2 Door Hardtop (Fastback-Bucket Seats)	76B	25	65/66	Caliente Convertible (Bucket Seats)
63H	16	69	Cyclone CJ 2 Door Hardtop (Fastback)	76C	16	67	Cyclone Convertible (Bucket Seats)
63H	26	66	Cyclone GT 2 Door Hardtop (Bucket Seats)	76C	29	66	Cyclone Convertible (Bucket Seats)
63H	27	66	Cyclone GT 2 Door Hardtop (Bucket Seats)	76D	12	67	Caliente Convertible
63R	16	72	GT 2 Door Hardtop (Fastback)	76D	12	68/69	MX Convertible (Bench Seat)
				76D	25	65/66	Caliente Convertible
65A	01	68	Sports Coupe	76H	16	67	GT Convertible (Bucket Seats)
65A	01	69	2 Door Hardtop (Formal Roof-Sports Coupe)	76H	28	66	Cyclone GT Convertible (Bucket Seats)
65A	01	70/71	2 Door Hardtop	76H	29	66	Cyclone GT Convertible (Bucket Seats)

November, 1975   COPYRIGHT © 1975— FORD MOTOR COMPANY   —DEARBORN, MICHIGAN   **FINAL ISSUE**

WARRANTY PLATE OR CERTIFICATION LABEL INFORMATION

(Refer to Pages 36 thru 39 for Capri Warranty Plate Information)

BODY TYPE CODES - continued

CODE TYPE	SERIES	YEAR	REMARKS	CODE TYPE	SERIES	YEAR	REMARKS
			(D) LINCOLN				
53A	82	65/	4 Door Sedan	65A	81	68/	2 Door Hardtop
65A	89	66/67	2 Door Hardtop	74A	86	65/67	4 Door Convertible
			(F) COUGAR				
65A	91	67/70	2 Door Hardtop (Bucket Seats)	76A	92	69/70	Convertible
65B	93	67/70	XR7 2 Door Hardtop (Bucket Seats)	76B	94	69/70	XR7 Convertible
65C	91	67/69	2 Door Hardtop (Bench Seats)				
65D	91	71/	2 Door Hardtop (Bucket seats)	76D	92	71/	Convertible
65F	93	71/	XR7 2 Door Hardtop (Bucket seats)	76F	94	71/	XR7 Convertible
			(K) MARK III, IV				
65A	89	68/71	2 Door Hardtop	65D	89	72	2 Door Hardtop
			(P) COMET (1971/)				
			FOR 1965/70 COMET/MONTEGO - Refer to (C) Listed on Previous Page				
54B	30	71	4 Door Sedan	62B	31	71	2 Door Sedan
			(Y) METEOR				
			SERIES CODES NOT USED IN 1965				
53B	20	71/	Rideau 4 Door Pillared Hardtop	57F	27	68/69	LeMoyne 4 Door Hardtop
53D	22	71/	Rideau 500 4 Door Pillared Hardtop	57F	27	71/	Montcalm 4 Door Hardtop
53F	25	71/	Montcalm 4 Door Pillared Hardtop	57F	35	70	LeMoyne 4 Door Hardtop
54A		65	Montcalm 4 Door Sedan	57G	32	67	Montcalm 4 Door Hardtop
54A	20	68/70	Rideau 4 Door Sedan				
54A	36	66	Montcalm 4 Door Sedan	62T		65	Rideau 500 2 Door Sedan
				62T	33	66	Rideau 500 2 Door Sedan
54B	21	68/69	Rideau 500 4 Door Sedan	62X		65	Rideau 2 Door Sedan
54B	22	70	Rideau 500 4 Door Sedan	62X	31	66	Rideau 2 Door Sedan
54C	25	70	Montcalm 4 Door Sedan				
54C	30	68/69	Montcalm 4 Door Sedan	63A		65	Montcalm 2 Door Hardtop (Bench Seat)
				63A	37	66	Montcalm 2 Door Hardtop
54F	20	67	Rideau 4 Door Sedan	63B	22	68	Rideau 500 2 Door Hardtop
54G	21	67	Rideau 500 4 Door Sedan	63C	32	68	Montcalm 2 Door Hardtop (Formal Roof)
54H	30	67	Montcalm 4 Door Sedan				
				63D	31	68	Montcalm 2 Door Hardtop (Fastback)
54T		65	Rideau 500 4 Door Sedan	63E	31	68	Montcalm S-33 2 Door Hardtop
54T	34	66	Rideau 500 4 Door Sedan	63F	25	68	LeMoyne 2 Door Hardtop
54X		65	Rideau 4 Door Sedan				
54X	32	66	Rideau 4 Door Sedan	63G		65	Montcalm 2 Door Hardtop (Bucket Seats)
				63G	97	66	Montcalm S-33 2 Door Hardtop
57A		65	Montcalm 4 Door Hardtop	63J	31	67	Montcalm 2 Door Hardtop
57A	38	66	Montcalm 4 Door Hardtop				
57C	27	70	Montcalm 4 Door Hardtop	63K	25	67	Montego 2 Door Hardtop
57C	33	68/69	Montcalm 4 Door Hardtop	63L	22	67	Rideau 500 2 Door Hardtop
				63M	31	67	Montcalm S-33 2 Door Hardtop

WARRANTY PLATE OR CERTIFICATION LABEL INFORMATION

(Refer to Pages 36 thru 39 for Capri Warranty Plate Information)

BODY TYPE CODES - continued

(Y) METEOR - continued
SERIES CODES NOT USED IN 1965

CODE TYPE	SERIES	YEAR	REMARKS	CODE TYPE	SERIES	YEAR	REMARKS
65B	23	69/70	Rideau 500 2 Door Hardtop	71J	28	67	Rideau 500 4 Door Station Wagon (6 Pass.)
65B	26	69	Rideau 2 Door Hardtop	71K	38	67	Montcalm 4 Door Station Wagon (6 Pass.)
65C	26	70	Montcalm 2 Door Hardtop	71L	39	67	Montcalm 4 Door Station Wagon (10 Pass.)
65C	35	69	Montcalm 2 Door Hardtop	71M	29	67	Rideau 500 4 Door Station Wagon (10 Pass.)
65D	23	71/	Rideau 500 2 Door Hardtop	71T	90	66	Rideau 500 4 Door Station Wagon (10 Pass.)
65E	26	70	Montcalm S-33 2 Door Hardtop	71X		65	Rideau 4 Door Station Wagon (6 Pass.)
65E	35	69	Montcalm S-33 2 Door Hardtop	71X	30	66	Rideau 500 4 Door Station Wagon (6 Pass.)
65F	24	69	LeMoyne 2 Door Hardtop	76A		65	Montcalm Convertible (Bench Seat)
65F	26	71/	Montcalm 2 Door Hardtop	76A	35	66	Montcalm Convertible
65F	34	70	LeMoyne 2 Door Hardtop	76C	28	70	Montcalm Convertible
71A	39	68/70	Montcalm 4 Door Station Wagon (10 Pass.)	76C	34	68/69	Montcalm Convertible
71B		65	Montcalm 4 Door Station Wagon (6 Pass.)	76E	28	70	Montcalm S-33 Convertible
71B	28	68/69	Rideau 500 4 Door Station Wagon (6 Pass.)	76E	34	68/69	Montcalm S-33 Convertible
71B	36	70	Rideau 500 4 Door Station Wagon (6 Pass.)	76F	26	68	LeMoyne Convertible
71B	39	66	Montcalm 4 Door Station Wagon (6 Pass.)	76G		65	Montcalm Convertible (Bucket Seats)
71C		65	Montcalm 4 Door Station Wagon (10 Pass.)	76G	95	66	Montcalm S-33 Convertible
71C	29	68/69	Rideau 500 4 Door Station Wagon (10 Pass.)	76J	33	67	Montcalm Convertible
71C	37	70	Rideau 500 4 Door Station Wagon (10 Pass.)	76K	26	67	Montego Convertible
71C	99	66	Montcalm 4 Door Station Wagon (10 Pass.)	76L	33	67	Montcalm S-33 Convertible
71D	36	71/	Rideau 500 4 Door Station Wagon				
71E	38	68/70	Montcalm 4 Door Station Wagon (6 Pass.)				
71F	38	71/	Montcalm 4 Door Station Wagon				

COLOR CODES (EXTERIOR PAINT)

THE CODE ABOVE OR BELOW "COLOR" INDICATES THE EXTERIOR PAINT COLOR OF THE VEHICLE. REFER TO THE PAINT SECTION FOR A LISTING OF THESE CODES AND THE PART NUMBER OF THE REQUIRED PAINT.

1965 U.S. BUILT VEHICLES
1966/ U.S. and CANADIAN BUILT VEHICLES

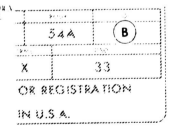

COLOR CODES (EXTERIOR PAINT)

THE SECOND AND THIRD DIGITS OF THE "PAINT" CODE IDENTIFY THE EXTERIOR PAINT COLOR OF THE VEHICLE. REFER TO THE PAINT SECTION FOR A LISTING OF THESE CODES AND THE PART NUMBER OF THE REQUIRED PAINT.

1965 CANADIAN BUILT VEHICLES

WARRANTY PLATE OR CERTIFICATION LABEL INFORMATION

(Refer to Pages 36 thru 39 for Capri Warranty Plate Information)

COLOR CODES - continued

COLOR CODES (INTERIOR PAINT)

THE FIRST DIGIT OF THE "PAINT" CODE IDENTIFIES THE INTERIOR PAINT COLOR OF THE VEHICLE.

REFER TO THE PAINT SECTION FOR A LISTING OF THESE CODES AND THE PART NUMBER OF THE REQUIRED PAINT.

1965 CANADIAN BUILT VEHICLES

TRIM CODES

THE CODE SHOWN ABOVE OR BELOW "TRIM" INDICATES THE COLOR AND TYPE OF MATERIALS USED IN THE INTERIOR UPHOLSTERY AS WELL AS THE COLOR OF THE INTERIOR PAINT.

REFER TO THE APPROPRIATE SOFT TRIM SECTION FOR A LISTING OF THESE CODES AND THE COLOR AND TYPE OF MATERIALS USED IN THE INTERIOR UPHOLSTERY.

REFER TO THE PAINT SECTION FOR A LISTING OF THESE CODES AND THE PART NUMBER FOR THE REQUIRED PAINT.

1965 U.S. BUILT VEHICLES
1966/ U.S. and CANADIAN BUILT VEHICLES

CERTIFICATION LABEL SHOWN
WARRANTY PLATE TYPICAL

TRIM CODES

THE CODE UNDER "TRIM" IDENTIFIES THE COLOR AND TYPE OF MATERIALS USED IN THE INTERIOR UPHOLSTERY.

REFER TO THE 1965 SOFT TRIM SECTION FOR A LISTING OF THESE CODES AND THE COLOR AND TYPE OF MATERIALS USED IN THE INTERIOR UPHOLSTERY.

1965 CANADIAN BUILT VEHICLES

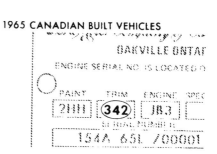

Index